Rick Riolo, Terence Soule and Bill Worzel (Eds.)

Genetic Programming Theory and Practice IV

T0135108

Genetic and Evolutionary Computation Series

Series Editors

David E. Goldberg
Consulting Editor
IlliGAL, Dept. of General Engineering
University of Illinois at Urbana-Champaign
Urbana, IL 61801 USA
Email: deg@uiuc.edu

John R. Koza
Consulting Editor
Medical Informatics
Stanford University
Stanford, CA 94305-5479 USA
Email: john@johnkoza.com

Selected titles from this series:

Markus Brameier, Wolfgang Banzhaf
Linear Genetic Programming, 2007
ISBN 978-0-387-31029-9

Nikolay Y. Nikolaev, Hitoshi Iba
Adaptive Learning of Polynomial Networks, 2006
ISBN 978-0-387-31239-2

Tetsuya Higuchi, Yong Liu, Xin Yao
Evolvable Hardware, 2006
ISBN 978-0-387-24386-3

David E. Goldberg
The Design of Innovation: Lessons from and for Competent Genetic Algorithms, 2002
ISBN 978-1-4020-7098-3

John R. Koza, Martin A. Keane, Matthew J. Streeter, William Mydlowec, Jessen Yu, Guido Lanza
Genetic Programming IV: Routine Human-Computer Machine Intelligence
ISBN: 978-1-4020-7446-2 (hardcover), 2003; ISBN: 978-0-387-25067-0 (softcover), 2005

Carlos A. Coello Coello, David A. Van Veldhuizen, Gary B. Lamont
Evolutionary Algorithms for Solving Multi-Objective Problems, 2002
ISBN: 978-0-306-46762-2

Lee Spector
Automatic Quantum Computer Programming: A Genetic Programming Approach
ISBN: 978-1-4020-7894-1 (hardcover), 2004; ISBN 978-0-387-36496-4 (softcover), 2007

William B. Langdon
Genetic Programming and Data Structures: Genetic Programming + Data Structures = Automatic Programming! 1998
ISBN: 978-0-7923-8135-8

For a complete listing of books in this series, go to http://www.springer.com

Rick Riolo
Terence Soule
Bill Worzel
(Eds.)

Genetic Programming
Theory and Practice IV

 Springer

Rick Riolo
Center for the Study of Complex Systems
University of Michigan

Terence Soule
University of Idaho

Bill Worzel
Genetics Squared, Inc.

e-ISBN-10: 0-387-49650-5
ISBN 978-1-4419-4123-7   e-ISBN-13: 978-0-387-49650-4

9 8 7 6 5 4 3 2 1

springer.com

Contents

Contributing Authors

Varun Aggarwal is a PhD student at Massachusetts Institute of Technology in the Computer Science and Artificial Intelligence Laboratory. (varun_ag@mit.edu).

Arpit Arvindkumar Almal is an evolutionary engineer at Genetics Squared, Inc., a computational discovery company (aalmal@umich.edu).

Sameer H. Al-Sakran is a researcher at Genetic Programming, Inc. in Mountain View, CA (al-sakran@genetic-programming.com).

R. Muhammad Atif Azad is a Post Doctoral Researcher at the Biocomputing and Developmental Systems Group in the Department of Computer Science and Information Systems at University of Limerick, Ireland (atif.azad@ul.ie).

Ying Becker is Vice President, Advanced Research Center, State Street Global Advisors, Boston, MA USA (Ying_Becker@ssga.com).

Olaf René Birkeland is Chief Technology Officer at Interagon AS (olaf.birkeland@interagon.com).

Alexandre Castellini is a petroleum engineer in the Reservoir Simulation Consulting Team at Chevron Energy Technology Company, San Ramon, CA, USA (ACastellini@chevron.com).

Flor A. Castillo is a Research Specialist in the Modeling Group within the Engineering and Process Sciences R&D Organization of the Dow Chemical Company (facastillo@dow.com).

Jason M. Daida is an Associate Research Scientist in the Space Physics Research Laboratory, Department of Atmospheric, Oceanic and Space Sciences, and is affiliated with the Center for the Study of Complex Systems at the University of Michigan, Ann Arbor (daida@umich.edu).

Peng Fei is a quantitative research analyst for the advanced research center at State Street Global Advisors (SSgA), the investment management arm of State Street Corporation, Boston, MA (peng_fei@ssga.com).

Erik D. Goodman is Professor of Electrical and Computer Engineering and of Mechanical Engineering at Michigan State University (goodman@egr.msu.edu).

Hitoshi Iba is Professor in the Department of Frontier Informatics at the University of Tokyo, Japan (iba@iba.k.u-tokyo.ac.jp).

Lee W. Jones is a researcher at Genetic Programming, Inc. in Mountain View, CA (lee@genetic-programming.com).

Jon Klein is a Senior Research Fellow in the School of Cognitive Science at Hampshire College in Amherst, Massachusetts, and a doctoral candidate in Physical Resource Theory at Chalmers University of Technology and Göteborg University in Göteborg, Sweden (jk@artificial.com).

Pavan Komireddy is a Software Engineer for Yahoo!, working in Burbank, CA (pavan@yahoo-inc.com)

Arthur K. Kordon is a Research and Development Leader in the Modelling Group within the Engineering and Process Sciences R&D Organization of the Dow Chemical Company (akordon@dow.com).

Michael F. Korns is Chief Technology Officer at Investment Science Corporation (mkorns@korns.com).

Mark E. Kotanchek is Chief Technology Officer of Evolved Analytics, a data modeling consulting and systems company (mark@evolved-analytics.com).

John R. Koza is Consulting Professor at Stanford University in the Department of Electrical Engineering (koza@stanford.edu).

William B. Langdon is Principal Research Officer in the Department of Computer Science of the University of Essex, UK (wlangdon@essex.ac.uk).

Anna Lester is a Vice President of the US Active Equity Group, State Street Global Advisors, Boston, MA (Anna_Lester@ssga.com).

Hod Lipson is an Assistant Professor at the School of Mechanical & Aerospace Engineering and at the Faculty of Computing & Information Science at Cornell University, Ithaca NY, USA (hod.lipson@cornell.edu).

Duncan MacLean is co-founder of Genetics Squared, Inc., a computational discovery company working in the pharmaceutical industry (dmaclean@acm.org).

Hammad Majeed is PhD Student in the Department of Computer Science and Information Systems at University of Limerick, Ireland where he is a member of Biocomputing and Developmental Systems Group (hammad.majeed@ul.ie).

Jason H. Moore is the Frank Lane Research Scholar in Computational Genetics and Associate Professor of Genetics at Dartmouth Medical School (Jason.H.Moore@Dartmouth.edu).

Una-May O'Reilly is a Principal Research Scientist and leader of the EVO-DesignOpt group at the Computer Science and Artificial Intelligence Laboratory at the Massachusetts Institute of Technology (unamay@csail.mit.edu).

Topon Kumar Paul is a PhD student at the University of Tokyo in the Department of Frontier Informatics. His research includes applications of evolutionary computation methods to computational biology and bioinformatics (topon@iba.k.u-tokyo.ac.jp).

Riccardo Poli is Professor of Computer Science at the University of Essex (rpoli@essex.ac.uk).

Rick Riolo is Director of the Computer Lab and Associate Research Scientist in the Center for the Study of Complex Systems at the University of Michigan (rlriolo@umich.edu).

Ronald C. Rosenberg is Professor of Mechanical Engineering at Michigan State University (roserber@egr.msu.edu).

Conor Ryan is Senior Lecturer in the Department of Computer Science and Information Systems at University of Limerick, Ireland where he leads the Biocomputing and Developmental Systems Group (conor.ryan@ul.ie).

Pål Sætrom is a Postdoctoral Fellow in the Department of Computer and Information Science at the Norwegian University of Science and Technology, and a Research Scientist at Interagon AS (paal.saetrom@interagon.com).

Michael D. Schmidt is a Ph.D. student in the field of Computational Biology at Cornell University, Ithaca NY, USA (mds47@cornell.edu).

Guido F. Smits is a Research and Development Leader in the Modelling Group within the Engineering and Process Sciences R&D Organization of the Dow Chemical Company (gfsmits@dow.com).

Terence Soule is an Associate Professor of Computer Science at the University of Idaho, Moscow, ID (tsoule@cs.uidaho.edu).

Ola Snøve Jr. is a Postdoctoral Fellow in the Department of Cancer Research and Molecular Medicine at the Norwegian University of Science and Technology, and a Research Scientist at Interagon AS (ola.snove@interagon.com).

Lee Spector is a Professor of Computer Science in the School of Cognitive Science at Hampshire College in Amherst, Massachusetts (lspector@hampshire.edu).

Ekaterina Vladislavleva is in the Modelling Group within the Engineering and Process Sciences R&D Organization of the Dow Benelux B.V., and a Ph.D student in the Department of Operations Research, Faculty of Economics and Business Administration, Tilburg University, Netherlands (CVladislavleva@dow.com).

Bill C. White is a Senior Programmer in the Computational Genetics Laboratory at Dartmouth Medical School (Bill C. White <Bill.C.White@Dartmouth.edu>).

Dave Wilkinson is a geophysicist in the Seismic Analysis and Reservoir Property Estimation Team at Chevron Energy Technology Company, San Ramon, CA, USA (DavidAWilkinson@chevron.com).

Bill Worzel is the Chief Technology Officer and co–founder of Genetics Squared, Inc., a computational discovery company working in the pharmaceutical industry (billw@genetics2.com).

Tina Yu is Associate Professor of Computer Science at Memorial University of Newfoundland, St. John's, Canada (tinayu@cs.mun.ca).

Preface

The work described in this book was first presented at the Fourth Workshop on Genetic Programming, Theory and Practice, organized by the Center for the Study of Complex Systems at the University of Michigan, Ann Arbor, 11-13 May 2006. The goal of this workshop series is to promote the exchange of research results and ideas between those who focus on Genetic Programming (GP) theory and those who focus on the application of GP to various real-world problems. In order to facilitate these interactions, the number of talks and participants was small and the time for discussion was large. Further, participants were asked to review each other's chapters *before* the workshop. Those reviewer comments, as well as discussion at the workshop, are reflected in the chapters presented in this book. Additional information about the workshop, addendums to chapters, and a site for continuing discussions by participants and by others can be found at http://cscs.umich.edu/gptp2006.

We thank all the workshop participants for making the workshop an exciting and productive three days. In particular we thank all the authors, without whose hard work and creative talents, neither the workshop nor the book would be possible. We also thank our keynote speaker Dario Floreano, Professor of Intelligent Systems at the Swiss Federal Institute of Technology in Lausanne (EPFL) where he is director of the Laboratory of Intelligent Systems and of the Institute of Systems Engineering. Prof. Floreano delivered a thought-provoking talk, as well as some amazing and amusing videos, all of which inspired a great deal of discussion among the participants.

The workshop received support from these sources:

- The Center for the Study of Complex Systems (CSCS);

- Third Millennium Venture Capital Limited;

- State Street Global Advisors, Boston, MA;

- Biocomputing and Developmental Systems Group, Computer Science and Information Systems, University of Limerick;

- Christopher T. May, RedQueen Capital Management; and

- Michael Korns, Investment Science Corporation.

We thank all of our sponsors for their kind and generous support for the workshop and GP research in general.

A number of people made key contributions to running the workshop and assisting the attendees while they were in Ann Arbor. Foremost among them was Howard Oishi, assisted by Sarah Cherng and Mike Bommarito. After the workshop, many people provided invaluable assistance in producing this book. Special thanks go to Sarah Cherng, who did a wonderful job working with the authors, editors and publishers to get the book completed very quickly. Valerie Schofield and Melissa Fearon's editorial efforts were invaluable from the initial plans for the book through its final publication. Thanks also to Deborah Doherty of Springer for helping with various technical publishing issues. Finally, we thank Carl Simon, Director of CSCS, for his support for this endeavor from its very inception.

RICK RIOLO, TERENCE SOULE AND BILL WORZEL

Foreword

Genetic programming (GP) has reached a level of maturity that invites not only continuing to expand the reaches of its applications, but also reflecting on its underlying principles. In a very short time, genetic programming has gone from a purely theoretical concept to real-life applications in a growing set of scientific and industrial areas. However, the drive to apply genetic programming to a wider set of fields should not blind us to the constant need to examine current theory and make improvements. The interaction between theoretical and applied researchers in genetic programming is critical to maintaining this balance of theory and practice.

Genetic programming experts have distinguished themselves in facilitating the transformation of academic theory into practical applications. The Genetic Programming Theory and Practice workshop, organized by the University of Michigan's Center for the Complex Systems, is the forum that has helped make this possible. As documented in this book and in the workshop presentations, genetic programming has provided insights that have enabled many technical advances across a wide swath of industries. For example, within financial asset management, GP has overcome the limitation of traditional/empirical approaches to factoring combinations that are linear. This evolutionary computational approach has enabled the creation of models that evaluate nonlinear relationships in order to reflect the complexity of a changing set of new factors in financial markets.

It is the creative and symbiotic collaboration between theorists and practitioners at the workshop that makes this field so exciting. The speed with which new genetic programming insights are translated into targeted, practical applications makes this a remarkable field. It also bodes well for the future as a growing body of solid theory offers itself for applications not yet thought possible. What an exciting future.

It has been my good fortune to be invited back to contribute to this year's workshop. I look forward to the atmosphere of intellectual enthusiasm and creative spirit inherent in each presentation, whether on the possibilities of genetic programming for improving productivity and advancing the frontiers of innovation in target applications or the development of new lines of theoretical investigation.

Most importantly, it is the working relationships and intellectual exchange fostered during the workshops that contribute so much to my own research and the general advancement of the field. This fertile human dimension is often cited by other attendees. I already look forward to next year's event where we can share our latest findings and inspire future endeavors.

Ying L. Becker, Ph.D.
Vice President, Advanced Research Center
State Street Global Advisors
Boston, MA USA

Chapter 1

GENETIC PROGRAMMING: THEORY AND PRACTICE

An Introduction to Volume IV

Terence Soule[1], Rick L. Riolo[2] and Bill Worzel[3]

[1]*Department of Computer Science, University of Idaho, Moscow, ID;* [2]*Center for the Study of Complex Systems, Univeristy of Michigan;* [3]*Genetics, Squared, Ann Arbor MI.*

1. Theory and Practice: Crossing a Watershed

The talks and discussion during the fourth annual Genetic Programming Theory and Practice workshop (GPTP IV), held in Ann Arbor, Michigan, from May 11 to May 13 2006, suggest that the development of GP has crossed a watershed, from an emphasis on exploratory research to focusing on tackling large, real-world applications. Organized by the Center for the Study of Complex Systems (CSCS) of the University of Michigan and supported by Third Millenium, State Street Global Advisors (SSgA), Christopher T. May of Red Queen Capital Management, Michael Korn, and the Biocomputing and Developmental Systems Group of the University of Limerick, the goal of the workshop is to bridge the gap between theory and practice. Paraphrasing the introduction to the first workshop, the goal is "to allow theory to inform practice and practice to test theory." To that end, the GPTP workshop again assembled a group of leading theoreticians and practitioners to present and discuss their recent work.

In previous workshops the research generally focused on using a combination of theory and practice to support the hypothesis that genetic programming (GP) can be an effective and efficient technique to solve practical problems. In this workshop it was clear that GP's ability to solve real world problems was broadly accepted, but that often this success was not, and could not be, accomplished by a "pure" GP system. Participants repeatedly showed that real world problems have hurdles that could not be solved by a blind application of pure GP.

The combination of broad acceptance of GP as a technique for solving real world problems and acknowledgement that pure GP is often not sufficient represents a significant shift in the field. It led researchers at the workshop to focus on a different set of fundamental questions than in previous workshops. Instead of asking "How does GP work?" or "How can we optimize GP?," one recurring question was "What can we add to vanilla GP to overcome the hurdles introduced by specific classes of real world problems?" In many cases these hurdles were common to a broad class of problems and led to theoretical questions regarding the most effective and efficient approaches to overcoming them.

In this chapter we present a brief summary of the work presented at the workshop and described in the chapters of this book. We first discuss common themes, application areas and hurdles that emerged in the course of the workshop, then discuss ideas that arose for improving GP to overcome those hurdles, and conclude with suggestions for next steps.

2.   Common Themes

Three broad themes emerged from the presentations at the GPTP IV workshop. First, as noted above, GP has developed a track record of successes on real world applications that demonstrates empirically that GP is an effective technique. This record is leading to growing support for its use even by people outside of the evolutionary algorithm community. Second, each application area has hurdles that must be overcome. In some cases these hurdles are common across application domains and in other cases they are unique. Third, the solutions to these hurdles are often common across multiple application domains, but also often fall outside of 'pure' GP.

Most promising of these themes is the growing support for GP techniques. Some of the most telling examples came from State Street Global Advisors (Becker, Fei, and Lester, Chapter 18). Based on previous successes with GP they have expanded its use to address additional financial problems, such as the development of models for stock selection. They also noted that their clients are now both interested and enthusiastic that GP is being used as a financial modeling tool. Similarly, representatives from other companies with experience applying GP to practical problems, including DOW, Investment Science Corporation, and Chevron reported that repeated success with GP is leading to a more general acceptance of GP as a practical technique for solving real world problems.

The second theme to emerge from the "practice" portions of the workshop is that each application area has specific hurdles that have to be overcome. However, as the workshop proceeded, it became clear that many of these hurdles are common across a range of applications and thus represent important areas for future research, as solutions to these problems will be applicable to a range of problems. We describe both the hurdles and the favored approaches to overcome them later in this chapter.

The third common theme was that plain vanilla GP is often not sufficient to overcome these hurdles. A range of techniques, taken from both within and outside of the evolutionary community, were combined with GP to achieve acceptable results. The use of other techniques to boost GP performance was marked by two important and promising trends. First, in many cases the same or similar techniques were independently adopted by different groups, often for solving very different problems. This implies that there is a largely unspoken consensus regarding what techniques are most likely to contribute to GP's success. Second, to a surprising extent the theoretical papers mirrored the applied papers; the majority of the theory papers focused on understanding how techniques can be optimally combined with GP and in many cases these techniques were the same techniques that the practitioners had independently adopted to overcome their hurdles. Thus, there was a distinct convergence between the techniques that the practitioners chose to apply and that the theoreticians chose to study.

3. Common Applications

In addition to the common themes that emerged during the workshop there was a clear convergence in the real world problems to which GP was being applied. In particular, the 12 papers focused on applications that fit into four areas: inxrobotics, bioinformatics, symbolic regression, and design, marking these as the areas in which GP is currently being applied with the most success. Dario Floreano in his keynote presentation and Paul and Iba (Chapter 4) presented work on evolving robot controllers. Moore and White (Chapter 2), Worzel (Chapter 3), Paul and Iba (Chapter 4), and Sætrom, Birkeland, and Snøve (Chapter 5) all address problems from bioinformatics. The general problem of symbolic regression was addressed by Castillo, Kordon and Smits (Chapter 10), Kotanchek, Smits, and Vladislavleva (Chapter 11), and specifically as it applies to investment by Becker, Fei, and Lester (Chapter 18), and Korns (Chapter 19). Design, including the design of electrical and quantum circuits, optics, and controllers is addressed by Koza, Al-Sakran, and Jones (Chapter 9), by Goodman, Peng, and Rosenberg (Chapter 13), and by Aggarwal and O'Reilly (Chapter 14).

The paper by Koza et al. (Chapter 9) presents a summary of results from using GP to design circuits and optics, in order to address the broader question of what leads to successful applications of GP in these areas, and in other areas as well. The chapter describes the general problem of evolutionary design and discusses the common domain characteristics and features of solutions that make evolutionary design such a successful application domain for GP. The paper also addresses techniques that can be used to improve results in this domain. The authors find several features that are commonly observed in the design domain: native representations are sufficient for evolutionary techniques; evolved solutions tend to be both simulatable and 'reasonable'; GP starts by focusing on solutions with few operative parts; and GP often creates novel designs. More broadly, the authors note several important domain characteristics that indicate whether GP is likely to be useful in any given application domain: the ability to efficiently evaluate the fitness of many individuals; the need to evolve structure, not just size parameters; a domain where obtaining solutions is considered an art, not a science; and the existence of problems in the domain that are not adequately addressed by existing methods.

4.   Common Hurdles

Participants described a number of common hurdles to the application of GP to real world problems. Many of these hurdles are already well recognized within the GP community, but their scale often far exceeds what is normally considered in GP research. Thus, one important lesson to be learned from this workshop is that the research community needs to reconsider what a 'typical' GP problem looks like. It is clear that common benchmark problems, problems like symbolic regression with only a few variables, inter-twined spirals, and multiplexer, fall several orders of magnitude short of the scale of real world problems.

For many of the applications the dimensionality of the search space remains a significant hurdle. Investment Science Cooperation deals with symbolic regression problems of twenty variables and a million or more data points (Chapter 19); State Street Global Advisors may consider 65 variables for each of 350 companies (Chapter 18); in the area of bioinformatics Genetics Squared analyzes microarray data with over 4000 variables (Chapter 3). These are values that are far beyond the scale of typical benchmark GP problems.

Another common hurdle was the time required to evaluate individuals' fitness, often complicated by hard limits on the allowable computation time. A typical example comes from Investment Science Cooperation (Chapter 19) where evaluating an individual solution to a symbolic regression problem involves calculating the error at a million independent points, but to be considered successful GP must come up with successful answers in under fifty hours. Similarly, representatives from Chevron (Chapter 12) and Dow (Chapters 10 and 11) discussed practical problems where evaluation time is a significant hurdle to successful application of GP. It has been commonly accepted that the time required to evaluate fitness is a limiting factor in GP, but, as with the dimensionality of the problems being addressed, the applications presented at the workshop increase the scale of the problem several orders of magnitude beyond what is generally considered in GP research.

Design problems are another example of a class of problems that are often limited by evaluation times. Reasonable evaluation time was included by Koza et al. as one of the characteristics of successful design domains (Chapter 9). Aggarwal and O'Reilly discussed the difficulties with evaluation times faced when using simulations of systems as fitness evaluators in design problems (Chapter 14).

The last common hurdle discussed by many of the participants was the need for robust solutions. Participants discussed the need for robust solutions in mathematical models (Chapter 10, and Chapter 11), circuits (Chapter 13), and classifiers (Chapter 5). For example, Peng et al. in particular focused on the need to evolve filters that are robust with respect to the components' parameters (Chapter 13). Allowing GP to freely evolve specific parameters values for components introduced two significant problems. First, the evolved parameter values often defined components that didn't exist or weren't commercially available. Second, the filters were often very sensitive to changes in the component values. Thus, substituting commercially available components with slightly different or noisy values into an evolved filter could cause a significant degradation of performance. They tested two alternative approaches, evaluation with perturbation and evaluation with perturbation combined with restricting evolution to using components whose parameter values were predefined ('evolution with nominal value set'). Both approaches significantly improved robustness, but evolution with the nominal value set was the more successful of the two.

Generally, practitioners reported that the dimensionality of the search space, long evaluation times, and the need for robust solutions were the most common and most serious hurdles to successfully applying GP. Much of the research presented by both the practitioners and the theoreticians focused on techniques for improving GP to overcome these hurdles.

5. Improving GP: convergence of practice and theory

Over the years an enormous number of techniques have been combined with GP in order to improve its performance when faced with specific hurdles. Thus, one of the most interesting features of the workshop was the commonality between the techniques that were independently applied by the practitioners and studied by the theoreticians. Out of all of the possible techniques to improve GP a relatively small number were repeatedly, and independently, chosen by the workshop participants. Few of these techniques are completely novel, but these are the techniques that the contributors independently selected as the most promising and/or successful. This strongly suggests that they are techniques that should interest the general GP community.

Fitness approximation

With evaluation times a major hurdle for many applications there is considerable interest in methods to reduce evaluation times. One promising approach explored by several researchers in the workshop is using fast, approximate evaluation functions in the place of exhaustive fitness evaluations. The general technique adopted by the workshop participants was to use evolutionary techniques to evolve the approximate evaluation functions.

In order to reduce evaluation times Schmidt and Lipson co-evolved fitness predictors, i.e., light weight functions that heuristically predict the fitness of individuals without requiring full evaluations (Chapter 8). They applied the technique to symbolic regression problems where the fitness predictors identified important features of the dataset and significantly improved evolution times, despite the increased overhead of the co-evolutionary process. They also applied the technique to a drawing problem that required human interaction in the evaluation stage - a user defined fitness function. The co-evolved fitness predictors effectively modeled the users preferences, significantly reducing the amount of user time required for the evaluation process.

Yu et al. used GP to evolve a proxy fitness function that can differentiate between good and poor oil reservoir models (Chapter 12). The reservoir history matching problem requires building fluid flow models of underground oil reservoirs that agree with historical oil production levels for the reservoir and can be used to predict future production. The history matching problem is difficult because each fluid flow simulation typically takes 2 to 10 hours to run and multiple models may accurately model historic flows. Using GP they evolved a proxy for the fluid flow simulation that quickly distinguished between good and bad models. This allowed them to build up a large set of good models that could be used to collectively predict future production flows.

Solution caching

Solution caching, storing trees or subtrees within and between runs, was another approach adopted to reduce the load imposed by long evaluation times and to maximize GP efficiency. To address the problem of symbolic regression with millions of test points, Korns used a system that cached every well formed function (Chapter 19). Referring to this library of previously evaluated functions significantly reduced the number of evaluations that needed to be computed and the overall computation time.

Kotanchek, Smits, and Vladislavleva introduced cascades, sets of parallel GP runs, that used a common archive of solutions (Chapter 11). Individuals in these archives could participate in the evolutionary process between cascades. This both reduced evaluation times, because archived individuals did not require reevaluation, and improved overall results by increasing diversity through exchanging individuals between runs.

Efficient experiment control and parameter optimization

In addition to increasing the efficiency of individual GP runs, e.g. by fast approximate fitness evaluations, researchers also looked for ways to optimize the general GP process across multiple runs.

Daida et al.'s research focused on determining whether GP search goes through phase shifts, which requires hundreds of thousands of individual runs (Chapter 15). Thus, they introduced Commander, run control software that easily and efficiently controls large sets of experiments. In addition to being a general experiment control tool Commander makes it considerably easier to make parameter sweeps for finding optimal parameters sets.

Castillo, Kordan, and Smits used design of experiments (DOE) methodologies to minimize the number of trials required to identify and optimize the most significant run parameters for a Pareto Front GP (Chapter 10). Their goal was to find parsimonious mathematical models to fit a variety of industrial data sets. Thus, an additional complication was the need to find robust parameters, parameters that were appropriate for a variety of data sets. By using design of experiment methodologies to find optimal parameters they reduced the total computation time required to find parsimonious models by 50%.

Cooperation

Several forms of cooperation were explored to improve performance and to reduce fitness variances between runs.

In his keynote address Floreano discussed how selection at the individual vs. colony level, and degrees of relatedness in homogenous vs. heterogeneous colonies, influenced the evolution of cooperative strategies and communication in colonies of autonomous robots. His research uses colonies of ant inspired robots, with robot sizes ranging from sugar cubes to soccer balls. The results clearly demonstrated that cooperation and communication assisted cooperation evolve comparatively easily, particularly among genetically related individuals.

Spector and Klein reexamined previous results on the evolution of cooperative altruism and showed that it could be stable under a much wider range of conditions than previously believed (Chapter 7). As with Florenao's results, they found that increased genetic similarity, in their experiments created by limiting the breeding radius, lead to higher levels of cooperation. In addition, multi-dimensional tags, which make invasion by selfish mimics more difficult, also increased the levels of altruistic cooperation.

Paul and Iba applied majority voting algorithms to cancer classification problems (Chapter 4). A major limitation for this problem is the very limited number of cases for training and testing. They found that single rules or rule sets tended to perform very poorly compared to large ensembles of independently evolved rules that used majority voting to reach consensus.

In similar research, Sætrom, Birkeland, and Snøve used boosting algorithms to generate cooperative ensembles of classifiers as a means of reducing the variation in best-of-run results and improving overall performance. The classifiers were used to identify microRNA target sites, a significant problem from bioinformatics. They clearly showed that for this problem using GP to find the best classifier on the training set produced significantly poorer results than combining weak classifiers into a single ensemble.

Soule and Komireddy use illustrative and benchmark problems to expose weaknesses in current approaches to evolving ensembles based on majority voting (Chapter 6). They use the expected failure rate model to measure correlation of errors between ensemble members. Their results show that team approaches produce relatively successful ensembles built from relatively poor members. In contrast island approaches, approaches based on independent populations, produce highly fit members, but correlated errors, and thus relatively poor ensemble performance. They introduce a new approach, orthogonal evolution of teams, that appears to combine the strengths of the two other approaches.

Pareto optimization

Castillo, Kordon, and Smits (Chapter 10) and Kotanchek, Smits, and Vladislavleva (Chapter 11) use Pareto optimization to search for high fitness, low complexity, solutions. They were studying symbolic regression problems—finding robust, parsimonious mathematical models to fit industrial data to aid in chemical process control. They treated the problem as a multiobjective optimization problem with fitness and parsimony the two goals. It was assumed that more parsimonious solutions, e.g. smaller solutions, would be less likely to overfit the training data. Kotanchek, Smits, and Vladislavleva explored several variations of Pareto optimization and found that they could significantly affect the ability of GP to successfully solve both problems simultaneously.

Pre- and post- processing

There was wide acceptance of the idea that successful application of GP to most real-world problems requires both pre- and post-processing. Almost every one of the real-world applications required some degree of data preprocessing to achieve reasonable results from GP. Pre-processing was commonly used to make the underlying data representations more amenable to GP, to reduce the number of erroneous data points and to reduce the dimensionality of the search space. Post-processing often involved something as simple as a human expert examining the evolved solution for "reasonablness," but this is an important sanity check in real world applications where millions or billions of dollars are at stake.

In a slightly different approach, Aggarwal and O'Reilly used evolutionary computation as the pre-processing step of another optimization method named Geometric Programming. They trained posynomial models of mosfets with a genetic algorithm. The evolved posynomial models are statistically much more accurate than those generated using conventional methods. This insertion of an evolutionary algorithm into an existing circuit design flow contrasts with how the predominant GP approach which attempts to span an entire flow. The insertion approach significantly reduces the typical expensive part of an evolutionary algorithm –simulation time. The authors also pointed out that this technique, evolving models to be optimized with Geometric Programming, can be applied to problems beyond mosfets.

Theory

Only a few of the papers focused on GP in general, rather than looking at a particular technique, or subtype, of GP.

Daida et al. used the Lid problem to look for phase transitions in GP (Chapter 15). If phase transitions do occur during GP search it would imply that well defined statistical techniques used to characterize thermodynamic systems could be applied to GP, which would introduce a broad new approach to understanding the dynamics of GP search. The lid problem is to find trees with a specific maximum depth and number of nodes (size). Daida et al. show that as the target depth and size are changed there are sudden, abrupt shifts in the difficulty of the problem. When mapped onto the space of tree structures these shifts define distinct regions of varying difficulty similar to traditional thermodynamic phase diagrams. This research strongly suggests that if a problem only has solutions whose tree structure falls in the regions of high difficultly GP will perform very poorly and is likely to fail to find any solutions.

Poli and Langdon examined the probability that programs evolved using a linear, assembly-like representation would halt (Chapter 16). Their representation was a Turing complete system that included jump, add, branch if overflow and copy instructions. They used a Markov chain model to determine the probability that programs would halt or enter infinite loops. Comparisons of the Markov model to actual programs confirmed that it accurately predicted halting probabilities for programs whose lengths extended over 5 orders of magnitude (from 10 to 1,000,000 instructions). The Markov model showed that for their representation the probability of a program halting approaches 1 as the program size increases. More importantly their approach can be used to test other representations, allowing GP practitioners to determine in advance whether a particular code representation is likely to be plagued with non-halting solutions.

Majeed and Ryan proposed an improved version of crossover, which they call "context-aware crossover," that finds the optimal insertion point for the subtree selected for crossover (Chapter 17). In context-aware crossover a subtree is selected from the first parent and then it is tested in *every* legal insertion point in the second parent. The insertion point creating the offspring with the highest fitness is then used. Applied to symbolic regression, 11-bit multiplexer, lawnmower and blood flow modeling problems, this approach significantly reduced the destructiveness of crossover and increased GP efficiency, despite the large number of evaluations required per crossover.

6.   Next Steps

There was a clear consensus among the participants that GP can be successful at solving extremely large scale real-world problems, even problems that are several orders of magnitude more difficult than typical GP benchmark problems. But there also was a clear consensus that these large scale real world problems pose hurdles that in many cases can't be solved efficiently by 'pure' GP.

One telling discussion addressed how GP could best be packaged for the non-expert. The majority of participants felt that a simple GP engine, one that someone relatively unfamiliar with GP could simply plug their problem into, would be counter-productive. It was argued that for large scale, real world problems a basic GP engine would give relatively poor results and discourage, rather than encourage, interest in GP. The favored alternative was to build GP into domain specific software. For example, a GP engine within SPICE specifically for evolutionary circuit design. This approach allows the specialized knowledge about successful evolutionary circuit design (the use of developmental GP, ADFs, limiting evolution to using nominal component values, etc.) to be built directly into the system.

This workshop makes it clear that GP practitioners are making significant progress by adapting GP or combining it with other techniques in order to meet the demands imposed by real-world problems. Theoretician can contribute to this process by expanding our understanding of how those adaptations work in conjunction with GP. For example, if practitioners are going to use GP to evolve cooperative swarms, then we need to predict, as Spector and Klein did here (Chapter 7), under what conditions cooperation is likely to evolve. If practitioners are going to use fast, approximate fitness functions to overcome long evaluation times then we need to know the best ways to create appropriate fitness function models. We believe this symbiotic relationship between practice and theory, with each generating and exchanging new ideas and new avenues to explore, will have a great impact on the field.

Chapter 2

GENOME-WIDE GENETIC ANALYSIS USING GENETIC PROGRAMMING: THE CRITICAL NEED FOR EXPERT KNOWLEDGE

Jason H. Moore[1] and Bill C. White[1]

[1] *Computational Genetics Laboratory, Department of Genetics, Dartmouth Medical School*

Abstract　　Human genetics is undergoing an information explosion. The availability of chip-based technology facilitates the measurement of thousands of DNA sequence variation from across the human genome. The challenge is to sift through these high-dimensional datasets to identify combinations of interacting DNA sequence variations that are predictive of common diseases. The goal of this study is to develop and evaluate a genetic programming (GP) approach to attribute selection and classification in this domain. We simulated genetic datasets of varying size in which the disease model consists of two interacting DNA sequence variations that exhibit no independent effects on class (i.e. epistasis). We show that GP is no better than a simple random search when classification accuracy is used as the fitness function. We then show that including pre-processed estimates of attribute quality using Tuned ReliefF (TuRF) in a multi-objective fitness function that also includes accuracy significantly improves the performance of GP over that of random search. This study demonstrates that GP may be a useful computational discovery tool in this domain. This study raises important questions about the general utility of GP for these types of problems, the importance of data pre-processing, the ideal functional form of the fitness function, and the importance of expert knowledge. We anticipate this study will provide an important baseline for future studies investigating the usefulness of GP as a general computational discovery tool for large-scale genetic studies.

Keywords:　genetic programming, human genetics, expert knowledge, epistasis, multifactor dimensionality reduction

1.   Introduction

Genetic programming (GP) is an automated computational discovery tool that is inspired by Darwinian evolution and natural selection (Koza, 1992; Koza, 1994; Koza et al., 1999; Koza et al., 2003; Banzhaf et al., 1998; Langdon, 1998; Haynes et al., 1999). The goal of GP is to evolve computer programs to solve problems. This is accomplished by first generating random computer programs that are composed of the building blocks needed to solve or approximate a solution to a problem. Each randomly generated program is evaluated and the good programs are selected and recombined to form new computer programs. This process of selection based on fitness and recombination to generate variability is repeated until a best program or set of programs is identified. Genetic programming and its many variations have been applied successfully to a wide range of different problems including data mining and knowledge discovery e.g. (Freitas, 2002). Despite the many successes, there are a large number of challenges that GP practitioners and theorists must address before this general computational discovery tool becomes a standard in the modern problem solver's toolbox. (Yu et al., 2005) list 22 such challenges. Several of these are addressed by the present study. First, is GP useful for the analysis of large and high-dimensional datasets? Second, what is the best way to use pre-processing? Third, what is the best way to construct more complicated fitness functions? Finally, what is the best way to incorporate domain-specific knowledge? The goal of this paper is to explore the feasibility of using GP for genome-wide genetic analysis in the domain of human genetics.

The Problem Domain: Human Genetics

Biological and biomedical sciences are undergoing an information explosion and an understanding implosion. That is, our ability to generate data is far outpacing our ability to interpret it. This is especially true in the domain of human genetics where it is now technically and economically feasible to measure thousands of DNA sequence variations from across the human genome. For the purposes of this paper we will focus exclusively on the single nucleotide polymorphism or SNP which is a single nucleotide or point in the DNA sequence that differs among people. It is anticipated that at least one SNP occurs approximately every 100 nucleotides across the $3 * 10^9$ nucleotide human genome. An important goal in human genetics is to determine which of the many thousands of SNPs are useful for predicting who is at risk for common diseases such as prostate cancer, cardiovascular disease, or bipolar depression. This genome-wide approach is expected to revolutionize the genetic analysis of common human diseases (Hirschhorn and Daly, 2005; Wang et al., 2005).

The charge for computer science and bioinformatics is to develop algorithms for the detection and characterization of those SNPs that are predictive of human health and disease. Success in this genome-wide endeavor will be difficult due to nonlinearity in the genotype-to-phenotype mapping relationship that is due, in part, to epistasis or nonadditive gene-gene interactions. Epistasis was recognized by (Bateson, 1909) nearly 100 years ago as playing an important role in the mapping between genotype and phenotype. Today, this idea prevails and epistasis is believed to be a ubiquitous component of the genetic architecture of common human diseases (Moore, 2003). As a result, the identification of genes with genotypes that confer an increased susceptibility to a common disease will require a research strategy that embraces, rather than ignores, this complexity (Moore, 2003; Moore and Williams, 2005; Thornton-Wells et al., 2004). The implication of epistasis from a data mining point of view is that SNPs need to be considered jointly in learning algorithms rather than individually. Because the mapping between the attributes and class is nonlinear, the concept difficulty is high. The challenge of modeling attribute interactions has been previously described (Freitas, 2001). Due to the combinatorial magnitude of this problem, intelligent feature selection strategies are needed.

A Simple Example of the Concept Difficulty

Epistasis can be defined as biological or statistical (Moore and Williams, 2005). Biological epistasis occurs at the cellular level when two or more biomolecules physically interact. In contrast, statistical epistasis occurs at the population level and is characterized by deviation from additivity in a linear mathematical model. Consider the following simple example of statistical epistasis in the form of a penetrance function. Penetrance is simply the probability (P) of disease (D) given a particular combination of genotypes (G) that was inherited (i.e. $P[D|G]$). A single genotype is determined by one allele (i.e. a specific DNA sequence state) inherited from the mother and one allele inherited from the father. For most single nucleotide polymorphisms or SNPs, only two alleles (encoded by A or a) exist in the biological population. Therefore, because the order of the alleles is unimportant, a genotype can have one of three values: AA, Aa or aa. The model illustrated in Table 2-1 is an extreme example of epistasis. Let's assume that genotypes AA, aa, BB, and bb have population frequencies of 0.25 while genotypes Aa and Bb have frequencies of 0.5 (values in parentheses in Table 2-1). What makes this model interesting is that disease risk is dependent on the particular combination of genotypes inherited. Individuals have a very high risk of disease if they inherit Aa or Bb but not both (i.e. the exclusive OR function). The penetrance for each individual genotype in this model is 0.5 and is computed by summing the products of the genotype frequencies and penetrance values. Thus, in this model there is no difference in disease risk for each single genotype as specified by the single-genotype penetrance values. This genetic model was first described by (Li and

Table 2-1. Penetrance values for genotypes from two SNPs.

	AA (0.25)	Aa (0.50)	aa (0.25)
BB (0.25)	0	1	0
Bb (0.50)	1	0	1
bb (0.25)	0	1	0

Reich, 2000). Heritability or the size of the genetic effect is a function of these penetrance values. In this model, the heritability is maximal at 1.0 because the probability of disease is completely determined by the genotypes at these two DNA sequence variations. This is a special case where all of the heritability is due to epistasis. As (Freitas, 2001) reviews this general class of problems has high concept difficulty.

Genome-Wide Genetic Analysis: A Needle-in-a-Haystack Problem

(Moore and Ritchie, 2004) have outlined three significant challenges that must be overcome if we are to successfully identify genetic predictors of health and disease. First, powerful data mining and machine learning methods will need to be developed to statistically model the relationship between combinations of DNA sequence variations and disease susceptibility. Traditional methods such as logistic regression have limited power for modeling high-order nonlinear interactions (Moore and Williams, 2002). A second challenge is the selection of genetic variables or attributes that should be included for analysis. If interactions between genes explain most of the heritability of common diseases, then combinations of DNA sequence variations will need to be evaluated from a list of thousands of candidates. Filter and wrapper methods will play an important role here because there are more combinations than can be exhaustively evaluated. A third challenge is the interpretation of gene-gene interaction models. Although a statistical model can be used to identify DNA sequence variations that confer risk for disease, this approach cannot be translated into specific prevention and treatment strategies without interpreting the results in the context of human biology. Making etiological inferences from computational models may be the most important and the most difficult challenge of all (Moore and Williams, 2005).

Combining the concept difficulty described in Section 1.3 with the challenge of attribute selection yields what (Goldberg, 2002) calls a needle-in-a-haystack problem. That is, there may be a particular combination of SNPs that together with the right nonlinear function are a significant predictor of disease susceptibility. However, individually they may not look any different than thousands of other SNPs that are not involved in the disease process and are thus noisy.

Under these models, the learning algorithm is truly looking for a genetic needle in a genomic haystack. A recent report from the International HapMap Consortium (Altshuler et al., 2005) suggests that approximately 300,000 carefully selected SNPs may be necessary to capture all of the relevant variation across the Caucasian human genome. Assuming this is true (it is probably a lower bound), we would need to scan $4.5*10^{10}$ pairwise combinations of SNPs to find a genetic needle. The number of higher order combinations is astronomical. Is GP suitable for a problem like this? At face value the answer is no. There is no reason to expect that a GP or any other wrapper method would perform better than a random attribute selector because there are no building blocks for this problem when accuracy is used as the fitness measure. The fitness of any given classifier would look no better than any other with just one of the two correct SNPs in the model. Indeed, we have observed this in our preliminary work (White et al., 2005).

Research Questions Addressed

The goal of the present study was to develop and evaluate a GP approach to genetic analysis in the context of genome-wide data. How does GP perform in this problem domain? Is GP a good approach for attribute selection? Is GP better than a random search when there are no building blocks? Is expert knowledge useful for defining building blocks that can be used by the GP?

The rest of this paper is organized in the following manner. Section 2 describes the GP algorithm we used. Section 3 describes the multifactor dimensionality reduction (MDR) method used as a function in the GP trees. Section 4 describes the attribute quality measure that is used as expert knowledge. Section 5 summarizes the data simulation and data analysis methods used to evaluate the GP approaches.

2. Genetic Programming Methods

There are two general approaches to selecting attributes for predictive models. The filter approach pre-processes the data by algorithmically assessing the quality of each attribute and then using that information to select a subset for classification. The wrapper approach iteratively selects subsets of attributes for classification using either a deterministic or stochastic algorithm. The key difference between the two approaches is that the classifier plays no role in selecting which attributes to consider in the filter approach. As (Freitas, 2002) reviews, the advantage of the filter is speed while the wrapper approach has the potential to do a better job classifying. For the problem domain considered here, there is an additional concern that the filter approach may eliminate important attributes from the dataset since no estimator of attribute quality will be perfect across all datasets. Thus, a stochastic wrapper or search method such as GP

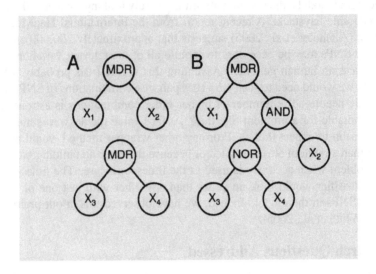

Figure 2-1. Example GP trees for solutions (A). Example of a more complex tree that will be considered in future studies (B).

always maintains some probability of including any attribute in the dataset. The goal of the present study is to develop and evaluate a GP approach to genome-wide genetic analysis. In this initial study, the GP is functioning exclusively as an attribute selector. We have intentionally kept the solution representation simple as a baseline to demonstrate whether the learning algorithm is performing better than random search. Future studies will expand the function set to more than one function.

Tree Representation of Solutions

Figure 2-1A illustrates an example GP tree for this problem. As stated, we have kept the initial solution representation simple with one function in the root node and two children. We have selected the multifactor dimensionality reduction or MDR approach as an attribute constructor for the function set because it is able to capture interaction information (see Section 3). Each tree has two leaves or terminals consisting of attributes. The terminal set consists of 1000 attributes. Although we have started with a simple tree representation, Figure 2-1B illustrates what a more complex tree structure for a higher-order model derived from a larger function set might look like. Expanding the size and complexity of GP trees will be the focus of future studies.

Table 2-2. Summary of GP Parameters.

Population Size	5,000
Generations	10
Crossover	Single-point subtree
Crossover frequency	0.9
Mutation frequency	0.0
Fitness Function	$\alpha * A + \beta * Q$
Selection	Binary tournament
Function Set	MDR
Terminal Set	Attributes 1-1000
Maximum Tree Depth	1.0

Fitness Function

We used a multiobjective fitness function in this study that consisted of two pieces in a simple linear combination of the form $\alpha * A + \beta * Q$. Here, A is our measure of accuracy obtained from the analysis of the single constructed attribute from the GP tree using a naive Bayes classifier. The parameter α is used to weight the accuracy measures. Q in this function represents the attribute quality estimate obtained from pre-processing the attributes using the TuRF algorithm (see Section 4). The parameter β is used to weight the quality measures. We explored parameter settings of $\alpha = 1$ and $\beta = 0$, $\alpha = 1$ and $\beta = 1$, and $\alpha = 1$ and $\beta = 2$. When $\beta = 0$ the fitness is solely determined by accuracy. Both A and Q were scaled using a Z transformation.

Parameter Settings and Implementation

Table 2-2 summarizes the parameter settings for the GP in a Koza-style tableau (Koza, 1992). Since each tree has exactly two attributes, an initial population size of 5,000 trees will include 10,000 total attributes. Since there are only 1,000 attributes in the terminal set we are confident that each attribute will be represented as a building block in the initial population. However, the probability of any one tree receiving both functional attributes (i.e. the solution) is $0.001 * 0.001$ or 10^{-6}. Thus, it is unlikely that any one tree in the initial population will be the correct solution. For the random search, we generated an initial population of $5,000 * 10$ or 50,000 trees and selected the best. The GP was implemented in C++ using GAlib (http://lancet.mit.edu/ga/). The crossover operator was modified to ensure binary trees of depth one.

3.   Multifactor Dimensionality Reduction (MDR) for Attribute Construction

Multifactor dimensionality reduction (MDR) was developed as a nonpara-metric and genetic model-free data mining strategy for identifying combina-tion of SNPs that are predictive of a discrete clinical endpoint (Ritchie et al., 2001; Hahn et al., 2003; Ritchie et al., 2003; Hahn and Moore, 2004; Moore, 2004; Moore et al., 2006). The MDR method has been successfully applied to detecting gene-gene interactions for a variety of common human diseases including, for example, sporadic breast cancer (Ritchie et al., 2001), essential hypertension (Moore and Williams, 2002; Williams et al., 2004), atrial fibril-lation (Tsai et al., 2004), myocardial infarction (Coffey et al., 2004), type II diabetes (Cho et al., 2004), prostate cancer (Xu et al., 2005), bladder cancer (Andrew et al., 2006), schizophrenia (Qin et al., 2005), and familial amyloid polyneuropathy (Soares et al., 2005). The MDR method has also been suc-cessfully applied in the context of pharmacogenetics and toxicogenetics e.g. (Wilke et al., 2005). At the heart of the MDR approach is an attribute construc-tion algorithm that creates a new attribute by pooling genotypes from multiple SNPs. Constructive induction using the MDR kernel is accomplished in the following way. Given a threshold T, a multilocus genotype combination is considered high-risk if the ratio of cases (subjects with disease) to controls (healthy subjects) exceeds T, else it is considered low-risk. Genotype combina-tions considered to be high-risk are labeled G1 while those considered low-risk are labeled G0. This process constructs a new one-dimensional attribute with levels G0 and G1. It is this new single variable that is returned by the MDR function in the GP function set. Open-source software in Java and C are freely available from http://www.epistasis.org/mdr.html.

4.   Expert Knowledge from Tuned ReliefF

Our goal was to provide an external measure of attribute quality that could be used as expert knowledge by the GP. Here, this external measure used was statistical but could just as easily be biological, for example. There are many different statistical and computational methods for determining the quality of attributes. Our goal was to identify a method that is capable of identifying attributes that predict class primarily through dependencies or interactions with other attributes. (Kira and Rendell, 1992) developed an algorithm called Relief that is capable of detecting attribute dependencies. Relief estimates the quality of attributes through a type of nearest neighbor algorithm that selects neighbors (instances) from the same class and from the different class based on the vector of values across attributes. Weights (W) or quality estimates for each attribute (A) are estimated based on whether the nearest neighbor (nearest hit, H) of a ran-domly selected instance (R) from the same class and the nearest neighbor from the other class (nearest miss, M) have the same or different values. This process of adjusting weights is repeated for m instances. The algorithm produces weights for each attribute ranging from -1 (worst) to +1 (best). (Kononenko, 1994) improved upon Relief by choosing n nearest neighbors instead of just one. This new ReliefF algorithm has been shown to be more robust to noisy attributes (Robnik-Sikonja and Kononenko, 2003) and is widely used in data mining applications.

We have previously developed our own extension, Tuned ReliefF (TuRF), that is significantly better than ReliefF in this domain (Moore et al., 2006). ReliefF is able to capture attribute interactions because it selects nearest neighbors using the entire vector of values across all attributes. However, this advantage can also be problematic because the presence of many noisy attributes can reduce the signal the algorithm is trying to capture. The TuRF algorithm systematically removes attributes that have low quality estimates so that the ReliefF values in the remaining attributes can be re-estimated. The motivation behind this algorithm is that the ReliefF estimates of the true functional attributes will improve as the noisy attributes are removed from the dataset. We applied TuRF as described by (Moore et al., 2006) to each dataset.

5. Data Simulation and Analysis

The goal of the simulation study is to generate artificial datasets with high concept difficulty to evaluate the power of GP in the domain of human genetics. We first developed 30 different penetrance functions (see Section 1.3) that define a probabilistic relationship between genotype and phenotype where susceptibility to disease is dependent on genotypes from two SNPs in the absence of any independent effects. The 30 penetrance functions include groups of five with heritabilities of 0.025, 0.05, 0.1, 0.2, 0.3, or 0.4. These heritabilities range from a very small to a large genetic effect size. Each functional SNP had two alleles with frequencies of 0.4 and 0.6. Table 2-3 summarizes the penetrance values to three significant digits for one of the 30 models. The values in parentheses are the genotype frequencies. All 30 models with full precision are available upon request. Each of the 30 models was used to generate 100 replicate datasets with a sample size of 1600. This is a medium sample size for a typical genetic study. Each dataset consisted of an equal number of case (disease) and control (no disease) subjects. Each pair of functional SNPs was combined within a genome-wide set of 998 randomly generated SNPs for a total of 1000 attributes. A total of 3,000 datasets were generated and analyzed. For each set of 100 datasets we count the number of times the correct two functional attributes are selected as the best model by the GP. This count expressed as a percentage is an estimate of the power of the method. That is, how often does GP find the right answer that we know is there? We statistically compared these

Table 2-3. Penetrance values for an example epistasis model.

	AA (0.25)	Aa (0.50)	aa (0.25)
BB (0.25)	0.137	0.484	0.187
Bb (0.50)	0.482	0.166	0.365
bb (0.25)	0.193	0.361	0.430

power estimates between the methods (e.g. random search vs. GP) using a chi-square test of independence. Results were considered statistically significant when the p-value for the chi-square test statistic was ≤ 0.05.

6.   Experimental Results

Figure 2-2 summarizes the average power for each method and each heritability level. Each bar in the barplots represents the power averaged over the five different models for each of the heritabilities. Here, power represents the number of times out of 100 replicates the GP found the right two attributes (SNPs). Results are shown for random search (R), GP using classification accuracy (A) as the fitness function ($\alpha = 1$ and $\beta = 0$), GP with accuracy and attribute quality (Q1) with a weight of one as the fitness function ($\alpha = 1$ and $\beta = 1$), and GP with accuracy and attribute quality (Q2) with a weight of two as the fitness function ($\alpha = 1$ and $\beta = 2$).

We find that GP with accuracy (A) as the fitness function does no better than random search (R) across all genetic models and all genetic effect sizes. In a few select cases random search was significantly better ($P < 0.05$) than GP using just accuracy for fitness. One might expect random search to outperform GP in this case because random search consists of one population of 50,000 solutions. The GP only works with an initial population of 5,000 that is then processed for 10 generations. Thus, random search starts with a greater diversity of trees than GP. If GP is truly learning then this difference shouldn't matter.

At a heritability of 0.05 and greater there is clear difference between the GP that uses attribute quality in the fitness function (Q1 and Q2) versus the GP that just uses accuracy (A). This difference was statistically significant ($P < 0.05$) across most models and most heritabilities. Here, GP is also outperforming random search ($P < 0.05$). This is clear evidence that learning is occurring. It is interesting to note that increasing the weight of the attribute quality to twice that of accuracy ($\alpha = 1$ and $\beta = 2$) performed no better than equal weighting ($\alpha = 1$ and $\beta = 1$) ($P > 0.05$).

7.   Discussion and Conclusion

There are several important conclusions from this study. First, a GP that uses classifier accuracy as the fitness function does not perform better than random

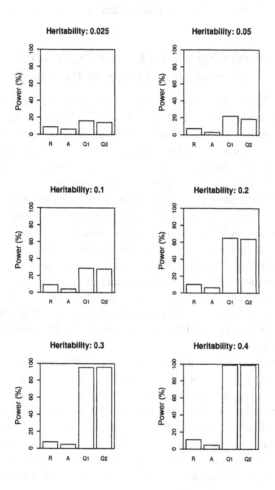

Figure 2-2. Barplots summarizing the power of random search (R), GP using classification accuracy (A) as the fitness function ($\alpha = 1$ and $\beta = 0$), GP with accuracy and attribute quality (Q1) with a weight of one as the fitness function ($\alpha = 1$ and $\beta = 1$), and GP with accuracy and attribute quality (Q2) with a weight of two as the fitness function ($\alpha = 1$ and $\beta = 2$).

search in this specific domain. Second, a multi-objective fitness function that uses expert knowledge in addition to classifier accuracy improves the ability of GP to exploit building blocks and thus learn in a manner that is significantly better than a random search. The discussion of these findings is organized according to the four questions presented in Section 1.1 that are also listed by (Yu et al., 2005).

Is Genetic Programming Useful for the Analysis of Genome-Wide Datasets in the Domain of Human Genetics?

(Langdon, 1998) reviews three general classes of search methods that can be employed for solving large-scale problems. The first and simplest is the enumerative approach. The goal of this search method is to explore all possible solutions. This is clearly the first choice because it is guaranteed to find the best solution. However, it is often the case that the enumerative approach exceeds available computer time. The next class of search methods includes calculus based algorithms. Calculus-based search methods are often looking for maxima or minima using derivatives or gradients. These approaches are also called hill-climbers because they inch towards a global best solution at the top of a smooth hill. The third general class of search algorithms is referred to as stochastic. Stochastic algorithms are based on random number generators and probabilities rather than deterministic rules. The simplest and most naive stochastic search simply generates random solutions that are independently evaluated. Genetic programming is an example of a stochastic search algorithm that usually starts out random and then uses probability functions to select and recombine solutions based on their fitness or value.

Stochastic search algorithms such as GP are more appealing for the genome-wide genetic analysis problem because the search space is astronomical and the fitness landscape is rugged, perhaps even resembling a needle in a haystack. Enumerative approaches aren't computationally feasible and hill-climbers will get lost in the local structure of the fitness landscape. Is a stochastic approach like GP useful for this type of problem? Is it better than a simple random search? Based on the results of the present study we would argue that GP is useful for the analysis of complex genetic datasets only when building blocks are present. When building blocks are not present or are poorly defined a GP may not perform any better than a random search. This is consistent with our previous experiments in this domain (White et al., 2005). This is also consistent with the idea of a competent genetic algorithm (cGA) reviewed by (Goldberg, 2002). Goldberg argues that understanding and exploiting building blocks (schemata) is essential to the success of GAs and by extension to GP (Sastry et al., 2004). There are two important issues here. The first issue is to make sure the building blocks needed to construct good solutions are present.

The second is to make sure the good building blocks are used and exploited during evolution. The present paper uses pre-processing the quality of the attributes to establish building blocks that otherwise don't exist. It was noted by (Yu et al., 2005) that providing rewards for building blocks is necessary for complex adaptation. This idea came from the artificial life work of (Lenski et al., 2003).

How Important is Pre-Processing to the Success of Genetic Programming for Genome-Wide Genetic Analysis?

As described above, the problem as we have defined it lacks building blocks that are critical to GP success. We have approached this problem by first estimating the quality of each genetic attribute or SNP using the TuRF algorithm that is based on ReliefF (see Section 4). Here, we used the attribute quality information as expert knowledge in a multi-objective fitness function. This use of the pre-processing information is described below in Sections 7.3 and 7.4. Although not implemented here, the attribute quality information could also be used to seed an initial GP population as a form of sensible initialization (Ryan and Azad, 2003). This is consistent with Goldberg's ideas for a competent GA (Goldberg, 2002). The idea behind sensible initialization is to fill the initial population with valid solutions.

Do More Complicated Fitness Functions Improve the Success of Genetic Programming for Genome-Wide Genetic Analysis?

We explored two fitness functions in the present study. First, we used a fitness function based exclusively on the estimate of accuracy obtained from a naive Bayes classifier. Second, we used a multi-objective fitness function that included the TuRF score in addition to accuracy in a linear function. We showed that including the expert knowledge in the fitness function significantly improved the performance of the GP. In fact, the GP approaches that measured fitness only as a function of accuracy did not perform better than a simple random search. Both pieces of this fitness function are important. The TuRF scores "help" the fitness by exploiting good building blocks. The accuracy piece comes into play when the right building blocks come together to form a predictive statistical model. One piece of the fitness measure cannot succeed without the other. The use of multi-objective fitness functions has been explored extensively (Coello et al., 2002; Deb, 2001; Zhang and Rockett, 2006). For example, (Koza et al., 2005) used a GP with a multi-objective fitness function that had 16 different pieces to design analog circuits. As (Freitas, 2002) reviews, others have included pre-computed attribute quality estimates in the fitness function for attribute selection e.g. (Bala et al., 1996). Exploring the use of Pareto fronts will also be important.

What is the Best Way to Include Expert Knowledge in Genetic Programming for Genome-Wide Genetic Analysis?

There are multiple different sources of information that could be used as expert knowledge in a GP. In this study, we used a statistical measure of attribute quality. However, future work needs to explore ways to include domain specific knowledge in the GP. There are a number of different public databases available to geneticists that could be mined for expert knowledge. For example, the PubMed database (http://www.ncbi.nlm.nih.gov/entrez/query.fcgi?db=PubMed) from the U.S. National Library of Medicine holds over 16 million citations from life science journal articles. There are a number of computational algorithms and tools available now for extracting information such as the co-occurrence of keywords from abstracts from the PubMed database (Jensen et al., 2006). If two genes co-occur frequently in journal abstracts then one could infer that there is a functional relationship. This type of information could be used to guide a GP search for combinations of SNPs that predict disease.

The availability of domain-specific expert knowledge raises the question of the best way to use it in a GP. This is a topic that has received some attention in recent years. (Jin, 2005) covers the use of expert knowledge in population initialization, recombination, mutation, selection, reproduction, multi-objective fitness functions, and human-computer interaction, for example. We focused in this study exclusively on the fitness function. It would be interesting to see if expert knowledge might play an important role in selection, for example. Using TuRF scores for selection might make sense in this domain given accuracy doesn't provide any useful information until the right model is found. Similar arguments could be made for reproduction, recombination and mutation, for example.

Future Studies

This study presents preliminary evidence suggesting that GP might be useful for the genome-wide genetic analysis of common human diseases that have a complex genetic architecture. These results raise numerous questions, some of which have been discussed here. It will be important to extend this study to higher-order genetic models. How well does GP do when faced with finding three, four, or more SNPs that interact in a nonlinear manner to predict disease susceptibility? How does extending the function set to additional attribute construction functions impact performance? How does extending the attribute set impact performance? Is using GP better than available or similar filter approaches? To what extent can GP theory help formulate an optimal GP approach to this problem? Does GP outperform other evolutionary or non-evolutionary search methods? This paper provides a starting point to begin addressing some of these questions.

8. Acknowledgment

This work was supported by National Institutes of Health (USA) grants LM009012, AI59694, HD047447, RR018787, and HL65234. We also thank the anonymous reviewers for their time and effort to help make this manuscript better.

References

Altshuler, D., Brooks, L.D., Chakravarti, A., Collins, F.S., Daly, M.J., and Donnelly, P. (2005). International hapmap consortium: A haplotype map of the human genome. *Nature*, 437:1299–1320.

Andrew, A.S., Nelson, H.H., Kelsey, K.T., Moore, J.H., Meng, A.C., Casella, D.P., Tosteson, T.D., Schned, A.R., and Karagas, M.R. (2006). Concordance of multiple analytical approaches demonstrates a complex relationship between dna repair gene snps, smoking and bladder cancer susceptibility. *Carcinogenesis*.

Bala, J., Jong, K. De, Huang, J., Vafaie, H., and Wechsler, H. (1996). Using learning to facilitate the evolution of features for recognizing visual concepts. *Evolutionary Computation*, 4:297–312.

Banzhaf, W., Nordin, P., Keller, R.E., and Francone, F.D. (1998). *Genetic Programming: An Introduction: On the Automatic Evolution of Computer Programs and Its Applications*. Morgan Kaufmann Publishers.

Bateson, W. (1909). *Mendel's Principles of Heredity*. Cambridge University Press, Cambridge.

Cho, Y.M., Ritchie, M.D., Moore, J.H., Park, J.Y., Lee, K.U., Shin, H.D., Lee, H.K., and Park, K.S. (2004). Multifactor-dimensionality reduction shows a two-locus interaction associated with type 2 diabetes mellitus. *Diabetologia*, 47:549–554.

Coello, C.A., Veldhuizen, D.A. Van, and Lamont, G.B. (2002). *Evolutionary Algorithms for Solving Multi-Objective Problems*. Kluwer.

Coffey, C.S., Hebert, P.R., Ritchie, M.D., Krumholz, H.M., Morgan, T.M., Gaziano, J.M., Ridker, P.M., and Moore, J.H. (2004). An application of conditional logistic regression and multifactor dimensionality reduction for detecting gene-gene interactions on risk of myocardial infarction: The importance of model validation. *BMC Bioinformatics*, 4:49.

Deb, K. (2001). *Multi-Objective Optimization Using Evolutionary Algorithms*. Wiley.

Freitas, A. (2001). Understanding the crucial role of attribute interactions. *Artificial Intelligence Review*, 16:177–199.

Freitas, A. (2002). *Data Mining and KNowledge Discovery with Evolutionary Algorithms*. Springer.

Goldberg, D.E. (2002). *The Design of Innovation*. Kluwer.

Hahn, L.W. and Moore, J.H. (2004). Ideal discrimination of discrete clinical endpoints using multilocus genotypes. *Silico Biology*, 4:183–194.

Hahn, L.W., Ritchie, M.D., and Moore, J.H. (2003). Multifactor dimensionality reduction software for detecting gene-gene and gene-environment interactions. *Bioinformatics*, 19:376–382.

Haynes, Thomas, Langdon, William B., O'Reilly, Una-May, Poli, Riccardo, and Rosca, Justinian, editors (1999). *Foundations of Genetic Programming*, Orlando, Florida, USA.

Hirschhorn, J.N. and Daly, M.J. (2005). Genome-wide association studies for common diseases and complex traits. *Nature Reviews Genetics*, 6(95):108–118.

Jensen, L.J., Saric, J., and Bork, P. (2006). Literature mining for the biologist: from information retrieval to biological discovery. *Nature Review Genetics*, 7:119–129.

Jin, Y. (2005). *Knowledge Incorporation in Evolutionary Computation*. Springer.

Kira, K. and Rendell, L.A. (1992). A practical approach to feature selection. In *Machine Learning: Proceedings of the AAAI'92*.

Kononenko, I. (1994). Estimating attributes: analysis and extension of relief. *Machine Learning: ECML*, 94:171–182.

Koza, John R. (1992). *Genetic Programming: On the Programming of Computers by Means of Natural Selection*. MIT Press, Cambridge, MA, USA.

Koza, John R. (1994). *Genetic Programming II: Automatic Discovery of Reusable Programs*. MIT Press, Cambridge Massachusetts.

Koza, John R., Andre, David, Bennett III, Forrest H, and Keane, Martin (1999). *Genetic Programming 3: Darwinian Invention and Problem Solving*. Morgan Kaufman.

Koza, John R., Keane, Martin A., Streeter, Matthew J., Mydlowec, William, Yu, Jessen, and Lanza, Guido (2003). *Genetic Programming IV: Routine Human-Competitive Machine Intelligence*. Kluwer Academic Publishers.

Koza, J.R., Jones, L.W., Keane, M.A., Streeter, M.J., and Al-Sakran, S.H. (2005). Toward automated design of industrial-strength analog circuits by means of genetic programming. In O'Reilly, U.M., Yu, T., Riolo, R., and Worzel, B., editors, *Genetic Programming Theory and practice*. Springer.

Langdon, William B. (1998). *Genetic Programming and Data Structures: Genetic Programming + Data Structures = Automatic Programming!*, volume 1 of *Genetic Programming*. Kluwer, Boston.

Lenski, R.E., Ofria, C., Pennock, R.T., and Adami, C. (2003). The evolutionary origin of complex features. 423:139–144.

Li, W. and Reich, J. (2000). A complete enumeration and classification of two-locus disease models. *Human Heredity*, 50:334–349.

Moore, J.H. (2003). The ubiquitous nature of epistasis in determining susceptibility to common human diseases. *Human Heredity*, 56:73–82.

Moore, J.H. (2004). Computational analysis of gene-gene interactions in common human diseases using multifactor dimensionality reduction. *Expert Rev. Mol Diagn*, 4:795–803.

Moore, J.H., Gilbert, J.C., Tsai, C.T., Chiang, F.T., Holden, W., Barney, N., and White, B.C. (2006). A flexible computational framework for detecting, characterizing, and interpreting statistical patterns of epistasis in genetic studies of human disease susceptibility. *Journal of Theoretical Biology*.

Moore, J.H. and Ritchie, M.D. (2004). The challenges of whole-genome approaches to common diseases. *JAMA*, 291:1642–1643.

Moore, J.H. and Williams, S.W. (2002). New strategies for identifying gene-gene interactions in hypertension. *Annals of Medicine*, 34:88–95.

Moore, J.H. and Williams, S.W. (2005). Traversing the conceptual divide between biological and statistical epistasis: Systems biology and a more mordern synthesis. *BioEssays*, 27:637–646.

Qin, S., Zhao, X., Pan, Y., Liu, J., Feng, G., Fu, J., Bao, J., Zhang, Z., and He, L. (2005). An association study of the n-methyl-d-aspartate receptor nr1 subunit gene (grin1) and nr2b subunit gene (grin2b) in schizophrenia with universal dna microarray. *European Journal of Human Genetics*, 13:807–814.

Ritchie, M.D., Hahn, L.W., and Moore, J.H. (2003). Power of multifactor dimensionality reduction for detecting gene-gene interactions in the presence of genotyping error, phenocopy and genetic heterogeneity. *Genetic Epidemiology*, 24:150–157.

Ritchie, M.D., Hahn, L.W., Roodi, N., Bailey, L.R., Dupont, W.D., Parl, F.F, and Moore, J.H. (2001). Multifactor dimensionality reduction reveals high-order interactions among estrogen metabolism genes in sporadic breast cancer. *American Journal of Human Genetics*, 69:138–147.

Robnik-Sikonja, M. and Kononenko, I. (2003). Theoretical and empirical analysis of relieff and rrelieff. *Machine Learning*, 53:23–69.

Ryan, C. and Azad, R.M. (2003). Sensible initialization in chorus. *EuroGP 2003*, pages 394–403.

Sastry, Kumara, O'Reilly, Una-May, and Goldberg, David E. (2004). Population sizing for genetic programming based on decision making. In O'Reilly, Una-May, Yu, Tina, Riolo, Rick L., and Worzel, Bill, editors, *Genetic Programming Theory and Practice II*, chapter 4, pages 49–65. Springer, Ann Arbor.

Soares, M.L., Coelho, T., Sousa, A., Batalov, S., Conceicao, I., Sales-Luis, M.L., Ritchie, M.D., Williams, S.M., Nievergelt, C.M., Schork, N.J., Saraiva, M.J., and Buxbaum, J.N. (2005). Susceptibility and modifier genes in portuguese transthyretin v30m amyloid polygeuropathy: complexity in a single-gene disease. *Human Molecular Genetics*, 14:543–553.

Thornton-Wells, T.A., Moore, J.H., and Haines, J.L. (2004). Genetics, statistics and human disease: analytical retooling for complexity. *Trends in Genetics*, 20:640–647.

Tsai, C.T., Lai, L.P., Lin, J.L., Chiang, F.T., Hwang, J.J., Ritchie, M.D., Moore, J.H., Hsu, K.L., Tseng, C.D., Liau, C.S., and Tseng, Y.Z. (2004). Renin-angiotensin system gene polymorphisms and atrial fibrillation. *Circulation*, 109:1640–1646.

Wang, W.Y., Barratt, B.J., Clayton, D.G., and Todd, J.A. (2005). Genome-wide association studies: theoretical and practical concerns. *Nature Reviews Genetics*, 6:109–118.

White, B.C., Gilbert, J.C., Reif, D.M., and Moore, J.H. (2005). A statistical comparison of grammatical evolution strategies in the domain of human genetics. *Proceedings of the IEEE Congress on Evolutionary Computing*, pages 676–682.

Wilke, R.A., Reif, D.M., and Moore, J.H. (2005). Combinatorial pharmacogenetics. *Nature Reviews Drug Discovery*, 4:911–918.

Williams, S.M., Ritchie, M.D., 3rd, J.A. Phillips, Dawson, E., Prince, M., Dzhura, E., Willis, A., Semenya, A., Summar, M., White, B.C., Addy, J.H., Kpodonu, J., Wong, L.J., Felder, R.A., Jose, P.A., and Moore, J.H. (2004). Multilocus analysis of hypertension: a hierarchical approach. *Human Heredity*, 57:28–38.

Xu, J., Lowery, J., Wiklund, F., Sun, J., Lindmark, F., Hsu, F.C., Dimitrov, L., Chang, B., Turner, A.R., Adami, H.O., Suh, E., Moore, J.H., Zheng, S.L., Isaacs, W.B., Trent, J.M., and Gronberg, H. (2005). The interaction of four inflammatory genes significantly predicts prostate cancer risk. *Cancer Epidemiology Biomarkers and Prevention*, 14:2563–2568.

Yu, Tina, Riolo, Rick L., and Worzel, Bill (2005). Genetic programming: Theory and practice. In Yu, Tina, Riolo, Rick L., and Worzel, Bill, editors, *Genetic Programming Theory and Practice III*, volume 9 of *Genetic Programming*, chapter 1, pages 1–14. Springer, Ann Arbor.

Zhang, Yang and Rockett, Peter I. (2006). Feature extraction using multi-objective genetic programming. In Jin, Yaochu, editor, *Multi-Objective Machine Learning*, volume 16 of *Studies in Computational Intelligence*, chapter 4, pages 79–106. Springer. Invited chapter.

Chapter 3

LIFTING THE CURSE OF DIMENSIONALITY

W.P. Worzel,[1] A. Almal[1] and C.D. MacLean[1]

[1] *Genetics Squared Inc., Ann Arbor.*

Abstract   In certain problem domains, "The Curse of Dimensionality" (Hastie et al., 2001) is well known. Also known as the problem of "High P and Low N" where the number of parameters far exceeds the number of samples to learn from, we describe our methods for making the most of limited samples in producing reasonably general classification rules from data with a larger number of parameters. We discuss the application of this approach in classifying mesothelioma samples from baseline data according to their time to recurrence. In this case there are 12,625 inputs for each sample but only 19 samples to learn from. We reflect on the theoretical implications of the behavior of GP in these extreme cases and speculate on the nature of generality.

Keywords: microarray, mesothelioma, cancer, curse of dimensionality, classifier, genetic programming, correlation analysis, diagnostic rule, ensemble, N-fold cross-validation

1.   Introduction

Genetic programming is often used to develop classification programs that identify the signature of a sub-class of elements in a data set. Recently this has been used to identify sub-groups of patients using molecular data such as gene expression profiles (Driscoll et al., 2003; MacLean et al., 2004; Moore et al., 2002; Langdon and Buxton, 2004) with a view toward using such signatures as diagnostics that inform clinicians about the nature of the disease in order to guide their treatment decisions. However, particularly with microarray data, there are often far more inputs than there are patients to learn from so the problem of overfitting the data becomes quite severe. This is known as "The Curse of Dimensionality" (Hastie et al., 2001) and in the case of modern oligonucleotide arrays, this can lead to cases where there are tens of thousands of inputs for a patient population of less than 50.

In this chapter we outline some of the methods we have developed to reduce the risk of overfitting while still identifying effective diagnostic rules and to test the likelihood of overfitting in the result achieved. We demonstrate these techniques using a set of data from a study done by researchers at New York University on outcome prediction using microarray data from mesothelioma tissue (Pass et al., 2004). We then discuss the results of our analysis and suggest likely reasons for GP behavior in this study.

2.   Statement of Problem

Mesothelioma is a cancer of the lining of the chest and is usually (though not always) associated with exposure to asbestos. It is often malignant and recurs frequently even after radical surgery and chemotherapy. In the cited study, diseased tissue removed during surgery on a patient was profiled using the Affymetrix U95A Gene $Chip^{TM}$. The U95A chip has 12,625 gene probes and produces a continuous value that is associated with the total mRNA of the gene sequence produced during transcription (Affymetrix, 2006). Clinical follow-up of the patients showed that there were two fairly distinct groups of patients: those with a recurrence of mesothelioma within six months (n=10) and those with a recurrence at more than 12 months (n=8). One patient had a recurrence in 8 months and was excluded from the analysis since the goal was to produce a simple diagnostic rule that differentiated between "early recurrence" and "later recurrence."

Because of the large number of inputs and the extremely small patient set, we were very aware of the danger of producing rules that were overfit to the limited sample set available to us. Contrary to our usual methodology (Almal et al., 2006), we felt that we could not realistically reserve a number of samples for external validation of the rule on unseen samples because we felt that if we reserved such a validation set, it would increase the likelihood of overfitting the remaining samples and also risked having a validation set with too great a bias. If we reserved, say, 6 samples for validation out of the 18 available to us, then even a single sample in the validation set that was different from the other samples would reduce the accuracy of the rule derived from the training set by almost 17%. For this reason we developed a specialized form of cross-validation that we feel strikes a reasonable balance between variance and bias from a small sample set.

3.   Methods

One approach to developing a classifier is to use correlation analysis or a similar approach to select a subset of inputs that is likely to be predictive of the two subgroups defined in the study. In the past we have found that GP can not only find many of the same genes that PCA or correlation analysis will find but it can also find other useful genes that are not found by single-input analyses. For example, in (Almal et al., 2006), three genes are identified in a signature associated with metastasis. None of the genes by themselves are good predictors but, taken together, they create a useful classifier combination. It is the ability of GP to find combinations of inputs that are useful when working with large set of inputs such as microarray data.

However, using all the genes available has its own perils. In particular, our collaborators have found that there is a certain "background noise" in terms of expression levels. Expression values that fall below this threshold cannot be relied on. We therefore were provided with a set of inputs that were at, or above, this threshold on the assumption that rules developed using these inputs would more reliably find a true signal rather than a "ghost signal" buried in the noise. In this study we used both sets in order to compare the results.

We use a relatively common GP setup with a list of simple arithmetic operators (+, *, - and /), Boolean operators (&, |, not) and simple structural elements (if-then-else), tournament selection with a tournament size of 4 in a multi-deme setting where 5% of the population migrates to a the next deme in order after 10 generations. As described in (Driscoll et al., 2003), each function in the population produces a value for each sample and a "slice-point" is chosen from the training set that best separates the samples into classes. The fitness of these functions is based on how well it segregates the samples into these classes using the Area-Under-The-Curve (AUC) of the Receiver-Operator-Characteristic curve (ROC) based on the values produced by the evolved function.

Starting with the full set of inputs, we selected a population size of 40,000 individuals, less than (Sastry et al., 2004) recommends, as a compromise between computational resources available and the number of inputs. In order to compensate for the comparatively small population size, we used a high mutation rate (0.4) and a relatively low crossover rate (0.6) in order to increase the global search and decrease the tendency toward premature convergence. Next we used N-fold cross-validation (Hastie et al., 2001) with N=8 because there were 8 samples in the late recurrence patient set. As a general rule, with small sample sets, we select N to be the smaller of the number of target class members so each fold has at least one sample from each set in the test fold.

We then ran the system through 30 runs of 8 folds, producing 240 rules that were the best on the training set. For each run of 8-folds, we looked at the sum of the test fitnesses and found that even limiting the genes selected to two genes per rule, it was still quite possible to get perfect or nearly perfect results on the training set while doing comparatively poorly on the test set (e.g., accuracy of about 50% or less) suggesting that it was very easy to overfit the data.

We also forced the system to use a single gene and found that no single gene was perfect on the training set although it was still very easy to get in the 90%-95% accuracy range with a single gene. Similarly, varying the number of genes used upwards did not get improved generality (unsurprisingly) but neither did it reduce the fitness on the test folds. This suggested that it would be very difficult, if not impossible to find general rules from the limited number of samples. However, we have had success in using GP to select sets of genes that are the most successful in producing classifiers, essentially using GPs global search capability to find combinations of inputs that work well together. By looking at the relative frequency of gene usage across all rules, we can find a pattern that indicates which genes carry the most weight in producing a successful classifier.

Table 3-1 shows the list of 36 genes that were used more frequently than chance would allow (assuming a uniform random selection of genes as limited by the depth of the tree permitted). As a footnote, in composing this list, we combined rules that targeted the patients that had an early recurrence and those that targeted the patients who had a late recurrence. Curiously, there was not a lot of overlap in the genes selected by the two sets of rules: only the two genes that are shown in bold face in Table 3-1 occur with a high degree of frequency in both sets of rules. We speculate this may be because there are more contributing factors that can delay recurrence than produce an early recurrence, i.e., late recurrence is a more complex story than early recurrence.

Table 3-2 shows the list of most frequently chosen genes from the list of genes whose values are above the noise threshold.

4.   Concentrating the Data

The next step was to use only the genes shown in Table 1 and then try the same approach . The rationale for this is that as Daida has suggested (Daida, 2004) there are two phases in the GP process: identifying the key elements and then finding the best combination of these factors. Because of the high dimensionality of the inputs, if the full data set is used, the other variables become a distraction to the process of finding the best combination of the inputs. The results seem to justify the approach as the fitness on the test folds increased noticeably. The average fitness before selecting the most frequently used genes was 0.61 where 1.0 is perfect while the fitness using only the highly selected genes was 0.9225 although there were no classifiers that were perfect on all of the test folds. The best result, with 1 false positive is shown in the set of eight rules (one for each fold) shown below.

This set of rules could be used as a single ensemble voting together using a simple majority voting scheme where each rule casts one vote for an unknown sample and if the majority (at least 4) agree on whether it is an aggressive class member, then it is so classed. A variation of this is to give a rating of certainty by dividing the credit by giving each rule a 12.5% value so that the entire ensemble gives a confidence of prediction based on the value calculated. A

Table 3-1. Most frequently used genes from full gene chip GP analyses for Early Recurrence and Late Recurrence.

Early Name	Recurrence Rules	Late Name	Recurrence Rules
40810_at	104	34194_at	30
41175_at	15	39837_s_at	14
1213_at	14	32089_at	13
33845_at	12	39721_at	12
31744_at	7	32137_at	12
35612_at	7	33750_at	10
35773_i_at	7	34798_at	10
40881_at	6	754_s_at	8
39839_at	6	36923_at	7
39886_at	5	33659_at	7
38349_at	4	**33845_at**	6
40195_at	4	1825_at	6
33893_r_at	4	35176_at	6
39600_at	4	32073_at	5
34736_at	4	36194_at	4
36254_at	4	39532_at	4
		41689_at	4
		38730_at	4
		40810_at	4
		35444_at	4

0% value gives a high certainty that a sample does not belong in the aggressive class and a value of 100% gives it a high certainty that it does.

While an argument can be made for creating an ensemble by selecting the set of rules from all of the folds that are most different from one another based on their content and the way features are mathematically combined (Hong and Cho, 2004), we have found that this is a dangerous idea because the rules are so dependent on which samples are in the test fold. Just because rules are very different in their construction and content does not necessarily mean they are more general in their application, particularly if they were developed from using the same, or nearly the same, sample set for training. In other words, rules often differ more because of which samples are not in the training set than because of which samples are in the training set. We therefore take the approach that an ensemble must be taken together based on the samples presented to it: you cannot "cherry pick" rules that work well without looking at the samples used to derive them. However, if instead of picking only the best but most different rules, you look for the ensemble that performs best and has the most diversity

Table 3-2. Most frequently Used Genes From Filtered Data.

Early Name	Recurrence Rules	Late Name	Recurrence Rules
40810_at	38	38721_at	23
33659_at	17	39839_at	21
33845_at	14	41266_at	17
38721_at	12	**40810_at**	14
1213_at	9	34798_at	11
39839_at	9	1825_at	10
34798_at	8	35626_at	9
40881_at	6	36194_at	9
41175_at	6	41715_at	8
31991_at	6	34305_at	8
38744_at	5	32137_at	8
32607_at	5	1308_g_at	7
38824_at	5	32523_at	7
38763_at	5	**33845_at**	7
1599_at	5	36079_at	7
33893_r_at	5	37762_at	7
35159_at	5	33659_at	6
39231_at	5	37964_at	6
38188_s_at	4	32073_at	6
831_at	4	35645_at	5
35978_at	4	35159_at	5
35645_at	4	39750_at	5
37640_at	4	39685_at	5
41266_at	4	32792_at	5
1307_at	4	35709_at	5
38571_at	4	41175_at	5
35626_at	4	36554_at	4
34736_at	4	39097_at	4
40407_at	4	1599_at	4
36070_at	4	35773_i_at	4
40271_at	4	38592_s_at	4
1516_g_at	4	35170_at	4
36702_at	4	40962_s_at	4
40864_at	4	39348_at	4
33354_at	4		

Table 3-3. Best rules using genes in Table 3-2.

IF $[(34736\_at - 34798\_at)] >= -106.150002$ THEN Agr
IF $[(39532\_at/32089\_at)] >= 9.538611$ THEN Agr
IF $[(40195\_at * 41175\_at)] >= 654024.125000$ THEN Agr
IF $[(41175\_at * 35612\_at)] >= 121017.914062$ THEN Agr
IF $[(40810\_at + 39600\_at)] >= 763.850037$ THEN Agr
IF $[(31744\_at/36254\_at)] >= 4.257979$ THEN Agr
IF $[(40810\_at * 35612\_at)] >= 63739.949219$ THEN Agr
IF $[(37847\_at - 32137\_at)] >= -423.600006$ THEN Agr

(i.e., review the rule diversity in the ensemble as a whole), it is possible that you may get a more general solution. However, in this case, many of the ensembles that performed perfectly were dominated by a single rule that is repeated within the ensemble.

5. Testing for Generality

Given the very small size of the training set, the lack of an external validation set and the questions raised about the lack of similarity between the genes selected using GP and the genes identified by correlation analysis, we were concerned about the generality of the solution described above. Without further samples to test the generality of the rule selected, it was necessary to test the generality of the process used to arrive at the solution. A simple way of testing this is to take the same steps of concentrating the data and reviewing the ensemble rules produced in the final step with the same randomly labeled samples. In other words, if we randomly re-label the samples as being either belonging to the early recurrence or the late recurrence sets, and follow the same steps, will the result be as good? If so, it makes the results produced suspect as it suggests that the method can fit any arrangement of the samples available.

Table 3-4. Best ensemble on randomly labeled samples.

IF $[(32388\_at + 33445\_at)] >= 58.299999$ THEN Agr
IF $[(31407\_at/1266\_s\_at)] >= 0.266798$ THEN Agr
IF $[(36356\_at - 41002\_at)] >= -202.500000$ THEN Agr
IF $[(1614\_s\_at - 39190\_s\_at)] >= -47.050003$ THEN Agr
IF $[(40975\_s\_at/40196\_at)] >= 0.220629$ THEN Agr
IF $[(38516\_at/34633\_s\_at)] >= 58.412941$ THEN Agr
IF $[(40975\_s\_at/34131\_at)] >= 0.733498$ THEN Agr
IF $[(31407\_at/33073\_at)] >= 0.355404$ THEN Agr

Indeed, when we randomized the labels, and applied the same technique, the results were fairly good as those reported above with an average fitness of 0.85 but with a completely different set of rules using a very different set of genes. Table 3-4 shows an ensemble of 8 rules that had only 1 false positive on the randomly labeled samples. We therefore conclude that while the rules produced in Table 3-3 may be of interest, they cannot be relied on in a clinical setting. We would not use these prospectively to identify patients who are likely to have an early recurrence of mesothelioma.

We then applied the same approach to the set of genes in Table 3-2 that had a signal-to-noise ratio above the background noise of the chip as we did to the Table 3-1 genes. The full set of genes with a high signal-to-noise ration were reduced the input set to 4,360 probes from the original 16,625 probes. However, despite having only a quarter of the inputs, it still required a round of gene reduction to find two genes that were the best and an ensemble (shown in Table 3-5) that was accurate at predicting an early recurrence of disease. This ensemble also had one false positive across all test folds.

This naturally leads to the question of whether the problem resides more in the limited number of samples than in the high dimensionality of the inputs, but when we applied the same test of the process by randomly re-labeling the samples, even with a round of data concentration, the system was unable even to classify all of the training samples correctly and had an accuracy of scarcely more than 50% on the test folds. This result suggests that these rules may be more general in predicting the recurrence of mesothelioma and that the process of data concentration does not necessarily result in overfitting.

Table 3-5. Best Ensemble Rules From Filtered Data.

IF $[(1516\_g\_at - 39839\_at)] >= -350.649902$ THEN Agr
IF $[(32607\_at * 38763\_at)] >= 1227593.625000$ THEN Agr
IF $[(31991\_at/41266\_at)] >= 0.376580$ THEN Agr
IF $[(33893\_r\_at - 32073\_at)] >= -229.150009$ THEN Agr
IF $[(40864\_at/38721\_at)] >= 7.020071$ THEN Agr
IF $[(33659\_at/38592\_s\_at)] >= 8.819026$ THEN Agr
IF $[(33845\_at + 33659\_at)] >= 10856.700195$ THEN Agr
IF $[(35978\_at/38721\_at)] >= 0.662271$ THEN Agr

6.   Discussion

An extreme case such as the one described here, where the number of samples available is at the very edge of being large enough to be useful and the number of inputs is very high, is a difficult test for GP and confirms some of the theoretical work done on the mechanisms of GP. The inherently noisy data provided by this technique adds to the complexity of the problem as does the uncertainty of the endpoint under study: while tumors clearly have a point at which they recur, the causes of recurrence may be outside of the scope of the data available even with the broad nature of the inputs. Though the problem of high dimensionality exists regardless of the approach taken to discover general classifiers, the approach described here of using GP's population based and stochastic nature to concentrate the data allows us to reduce the danger of overfitting and to test when we might have overfit the data despite our best efforts.

Despite the results presented on this data set, the process of data concentration seems to have the potential to discover key combinations of genes. Almal, et al (Almal et al., 2006) shows the importance of using GP to discover combinations of inputs rather than single inputs identified using statistical methods. In Almal, et al (Almal et al., 2006), the three genes identified as being key to predicting metastasis are not predictive on their own but are only significant after being mathematically combined to produce a biomarker function. This fits well with the established GP theory of building block assembly (Poli, 2000). At the same time, data concentration reduces the "noise" that other inputs produce where, either through mutation or crossover, building blocks are broken apart by inclusion with other inputs lowering the overall fitness of the solution. This matches Daida's conclusion that continuing diversity is not always useful in producing successful results (Daida, 2004). It also tends to support his idea that once key inputs are identified, GP shifts its focus to finding the best combinations of key inputs.

Another approach that might achieve similar results with less danger of overfitting would be to use a simulated annealing approach where early in the study of high dimensional data sets higher crossover and mutation rates are used that later are reduced (Poli and Langdon, 1997) as the key building blocks are discovered, thus reducing the risk of breaking apart these building blocks. However, the question of when and by how much to reduce these GP parameters is difficult and we suspect that, done at the wrong time, this would actually reduce the efficiency of GP and produce the worst of all possible worlds by reducing the global search capabilities of GP before finding the key building blocks. We have done some preliminary work that suggests population diversity (where diversity is not just a matter of content but also of structure) can change rapidly and unexpectedly in a seemingly stable population. The data concentration approach makes the assumption that key building block pieces are present, if not perfectly ordered, in a run that has a high degree of "mixing" due to the mutation rate and by selecting the most frequently used inputs that resist dispersion, it is possible to create a clearer path for GP to assemble the building blocks in the right manner.

However, this study also shows the importance of assessing overfitting in such extreme cases and offers a way to test for it by using randomized labels as a control against which the results can be compared. To tame the problem of overfitting, you must be able to know when it occurs.

What other conclusions can be drawn about GP and overfitting extreme data sets? As Holland has pointed out in his collaboration with the poet Alice Fulton, constraints are the source of creativity (Holland, 2003). This is as true in machine learning as in poetry. By adding additional constraints to a problem, you can force GP to find only those solutions that fit the entire set of constraints. We look at this somewhat as an enrichment of the environment in which evolution is taking place. An ecological niche is a niche because it has a unique set of constraints.

In the case of the mesothelioma study, developing simple, early recurrence/late recurrence classifiers is a simplification of a complex problem. What is truly desired is a prediction of when a tumor will recur. However, after some trials we decided that even with the large set of inputs and the relatively coarse-grained time increments of months as the unit of measure until recurrence, it was unlikely that we would be able to make precise predictions of the number of months until there was a recurrence, probably in part because there may be many factors in recurrence that is not captured by the input data. We are experimenting with the idea of relaxing the constraint slightly by using GP to evolve a function that produces a "score" that can be correlated with the actual time-to-recurrence without actually predicting the exact time-to-recurrence value but have not yet produced any conclusive results with this approach.

7.   Summary

"The Curse of Dimensionality" is a problem that appears frequently in the life sciences where there are many more inputs than samples to work with. This creates a situation where it is very easy to overfit the data and produce results that are not reliable in a larger population. By using a carefully constructed N-fold cross validation to produce an ensemble of classification rules, it is possible to produce results that are likely to be general across a larger population. However, there are limits to this approach and in hard classification problems it is often difficult to reach the kind of accuracy required for clinical use of such rules.

In this study we used what we call "data concentration" to select smaller subsets of inputs that produce better material for building block construction using GP. We then proposed a method of testing the generality of the results, even when there are no external validation samples available, through an indirect method of creating a control set by randomizing the labels of the samples and comparing the results of a GP analysis of this randomly labeled set with the results produced on the correctly labeled samples. Using this approach we demonstrated that our initial analysis of recurrence of mesothelioma was uncertain at best, while a second analysis on a selected subset of genes using the same approach produced results that seem to be more reliable pending the generation of further data to validate the results.

Finally, we discussed the relationship of constraints to generality and introduced the idea that, by increasing the constraints such that the GP analysis not only needs to classify the samples correctly, but also needs to rank the results according to a more difficult measure of success, we maybe be able to improve the results and produce a solution that is more robust.

References

Affymetrix (2006). Human genome u95 set.

Almal, A., Mitra, A., Datar, R., Lenehan, P., Fry, D., Cote, R., and Worzel, W. (2006). Using genetic programming to classify node positive patients in bladder cancer. In *Proceedings of the Genetic and Evolutionary Computation Conference (GECCO-2006)*.

Daida, Jason (2004). Considering the roles of structure in problem solving by a computer. In O'Reilly, Una-May, Yu, Tina, Riolo, Rick L., and Worzel, Bill, editors, *Genetic Programming Theory and Practice II*, chapter 5, pages 67–86. Springer, Ann Arbor.

Driscoll, Joseph A., Worzel, Bill, and MacLean, Duncan (2003). Classification of gene expression data with genetic programming. In Riolo, Rick L. and Worzel, Bill, editors, *Genetic Programming Theory and Practice*, chapter 3, pages 25–42. Kluwer.

Hastie, T., Tibshirani, R., and Friedman, J. (2001). The elements of statistical learning: Data mining, inference, and prediction. In *Springer series in statistics*. Springer, Berlin.

Holland, J.H. (2003). Personal communication.

Hong, Jin-Hyuk and Cho, Sung Bae (2004). Lymphoma cancer classification using genetic programming with SNR features. In Keijzer, Maarten, O'Reilly, Una-May, Lucas, Simon M., Costa, Ernesto, and Soule, Terence, editors, *Genetic Programming 7th European Conference, EuroGP 2004, Proceedings*, volume 3003 of *LNCS*, pages 78–88, Coimbra, Portugal. Springer-Verlag.

Langdon, W. and Buxton, B. (2004). Genetic programming for mining dna chip data from cancer patients. *Genetic Programming and Evolvable Machines*, 5(3):251–257.

MacLean, Duncan, Wollesen, Eric A., and Worzel, Bill (2004). Listening to data: Tuning a genetic programming system. In O'Reilly, Una-May, Yu, Tina, Riolo, Rick L., and Worzel, Bill, editors, *Genetic Programming Theory and Practice II*, chapter 15, pages 245–262. Springer, Ann Arbor.

Moore, Jason H., Parker, Joel S., Olsen, Nancy J., and Aune, Thomas M. (2002). Symbolic discriminant analysis of microarray data in automimmune disease. *Genetic Epidemiology*, 23:57–69.

Pass, H.I., Liu, Z., Wali, A., Bueno, R., Land, S., Lott, D., Siddiq, F., Lonardo, F., Carbone, M., and Draghid, S. (2004). Gene expression profiles predict survival and progression of pleural mesothelioma. *Clinical Cancer Research*, 10(3):849–859.

Poli, R. (2000). Hyperschema theory for gp with one-point crossover, building blocks, and some new results in ga theory. In *Proceedings of Euro GP'2000, LNCS*, pages 163–180. Springer-Verlag.

Poli, Riccardo and Langdon, W. B. (1997). Genetic programming with one-point crossover and point mutation. Technical Report CSRP-97-13, University of Birmingham, School of Computer Science, Birmingham, B15 2TT, UK.

Sastry, Kumara, O'Reilly, Una-May, and Goldberg, David E. (2004). Population sizing for genetic programming based on decision making. In O'Reilly, Una-May, Yu, Tina, Riolo, Rick L., and Worzel, Bill, editors, *Genetic Programming Theory and Practice II*, chapter 4, pages 49–65. Springer, Ann Arbor.

Chapter 4

GENETIC PROGRAMMING FOR CLASSIFYING CANCER DATA AND CONTROLLING HUMANOID ROBOTS

Topon Kumar Paul[1] and Hitoshi Iba[1]

[1]*Department of Frontier Informatics, The University of Tokyo, 5-1-5 Kashiwanoha, Kashiwa-shi, Chiba 277-8561, Japan.*

Abstract   In this chapter, we show the real-world applications of genetic programming (GP) to bioinformatics and robotics. In the bioinformatics application, we propose majority voting technique for the prediction of the class of a test sample. In the application to robotics, we use GP to generate the motion sequences of humanoid robots. We introduce an integrated approach, i.e., the combination of GP and reinforcement learning, to design the desirable motions. The effectiveness of our proposed approaches is demonstrated by performing experiments with real data, i.e., classifying real micro-array gene expression profiles and controlling real humanoid robots.

Keywords: Data mining, bioinformatics, classification, gene expression data, majority voting, humanoid robots, cooperative transportation, genetic programming

1.   Introduction

In this chapter, we show the real-world applications of GP to two different domains, i.e., bioinformatics and robotics.

Recently, many researchers are trying to correlate the clinical behavior of cancers with the differential gene expression levels in cancerous and normal tissues (Paul and Iba, 2005b). In this context, different machine learning classifiers like k-nearest neighbor (kNN) classifier and support vector machine (SVM) are used with different gene selection methods like signal-to-noise ratio (Golub et al., 1999), genetic algorithm (GA) (Ando and Iba, 2004), RPMBGA (Paul and Iba, 2005a; Paul and Iba, 2005b), and PMBGA (Paul and Iba, 2004a; Paul and Iba, 2004b). See (Paul and Iba, 2005b) for a good review on gene expression based classification of patient samples. However, the main disadvantage of these approaches of gene selection is that it is very difficult to find an optimal ensemble of gene selection algorithms and classifiers. Genetic programming (Koza, 1992), an evolutionary computation method, has recently been applied to the classification of gene expression data (Driscoll et al., 2003; Hong and Cho, 2004; Langdon and Buxton, 2004; Moore et al., 2002). The main advantage of GP is that it acts as a classifier as well as a gene selection algorithm. In its typical implementation, a training set of gene expression data of patient-samples are presented to GP to evolve a Boolean or an arithmetic expression of genes describing whether a given sample belongs to a given class or not. Then the evolved best rule (s) is (are) applied to the test samples to get the generalized accuracy on unknown samples. However, the potential challenge for genetic programming is that it has to search two large spaces of functions and genes simultaneously to find an optimal solution. In most cases, the evolved single rules or sets of rules produce very poor classification accuracy on the test samples. To overcome this limitation of genetic programming, we propose a majority voting technique for prediction of the class of a test sample. We call this method *majority voting genetic programming classifier* (MVGPC). The motivation behind this is that a group of rules can be more accurate than the best member of the group (Kuncheva and Whitaker, 2003). However, the success of MVGPC is very much dependent on the number of members in a voting group. In this chapter, we investigate the optimal size of the voting group for MVGPC.

The second application domain is robotics, more precisely, humanoid robotics. Machine learning techniques can be applied to a robot in order to achieve a task for it if the appropriate actions are not predetermined. In such a situation, the robot can learn the appropriate actions by using trial-and-error in a real environment. GP can generate programs to control a robot directly, and many studies have been done showing this. Genetic algorithm (GA) in combination with neural networks (NN) can also be used to control robots. Regardless of the method used, the evaluation of real robots requires a significant amount of time partly due to their complex mechanical actions. Moreover, evaluations have to be repeated over several generations for many individuals in both GP and GA. Therefore, in most studies, the learning is conducted in simulation, and the acquired results are applied to real robots. To solve these difficulties, we propose an integrated technique of genetic programming and reinforcement learning (RL) to enable a real robot to adapt its actions in a real environment. Our technique does not require a precise simulator because actual learning is done by using the real robots. In addition, our technique makes it possible for real robots to learn effective actions. Based on this proposed technique, common programs are evolved using GP, which are applicable to various types of robots. Using this evolved program, we execute reinforcement learning in a real robot.

With our method, the robot can adapt to its own operational characteristics and thus learn effective actions.

2.   Classification of Gene Expression Data

GP-based classification

Creation of GP rules.   Each S-expression of a rule in a GP population consists of randomly chosen functions and genes. Each gene in the expression is represented by an 'X' followed by the gene number. For example, $X1314$ represents gene 1314 of a data set. A generic example of a GP rule might look as follows:

IF (2*X2474-X1265/X1223)$\geq$ 0 THEN 'Cancerous' ELSE 'Normal'

where $X2474$, $X1265$ and $X1223$ correspond to the expression levels of genes 2474, 1265 and 1223, respectively. As functions, arithmetic and/or Boolean functions can used for evolution of classification rules. For a binary classification problem, the class of a sample is determined as follows:

Boolean output: IF (rule) THEN 'Class A' ELSE 'Class B';
Real-valued output: IF $(rule \geq 0)$ THEN 'Class A' ELSE 'Class B'.

During writing of a computer program for genetic programming, we have to choose a function set depending on our targeted output of the S-expression of a rule. If we want Boolean outputs, we can consider a set of functions consisting of either arithmetic and Boolean functions like $\{+, -, *, /, sqr, sqrt, exp, and, or, not, >, >=, <, <=, =\}$ or only Boolean functions like $\{and, or, not, xor, >, >=, <, <=, =\}$. If our targeted output is a real-valued number, we consider only arithmetic functions like $\{+, -, *, /, sqr, sqrt, ln, exp, power, sin, cos, tan\}$.

Fitness calculation.   The success of an evolutionary computation method is very much dependent on the fitness function used to measure the goodness of an individual. For classification problems, the accuracy or the error rate of a predicting program can be used as a fitness measure; however, these methods may not get the optimum fitness. (Matthews, 1975) proposed the correlation between the prediction and the observed reality as the measure of raw fitness of a predicting method. For a binary classification problem, the correlation (C) is calculated as follows:

$$C = \frac{N_{tp}N_{tn} - N_{fp}N_{fn}}{\sqrt{(N_{tn} + N_{fn})(N_{tn} + N_{fp})(N_{tp} + N_{fn})(N_{tp} + N_{fp})}} \tag{4.1}$$

where N_{tp}, N_{tn}, N_{fp} and N_{fn} are the number of true positives, true negatives, false positives and false negatives, respectively. When the denominator of equation (4.1) is 0, C is set to 0. The standardized fitness of a rule is calculated as follows:

$$fitness(rule) = \frac{1 + C}{2}. \tag{4.2}$$

Since C ranges between -1.0 and +1.0, the standardized fitness ranges between 0.0 and +1.0, the higher values being the better and 1.0 being the best. The ultimate objective of GP is to find a rule that can classify all the samples correctly and thus has fitness=1.0. During execution of a rule on a sample, we take precautions so that the two functions 'sqrt' and '/' do not produce undefined results. In the case of undefined results, we treat them as follows: $\frac{x}{0} = 1$, and $\sqrt{x} = 0$ if $x < 0$. Note that after adjustment, $\sqrt{(x)^2} \neq (\sqrt{x})^2 \neq x$. For example, if $x = -3$, then $\sqrt{(x)^2} = 3$ while $(\sqrt{x})^2 = 0$. Similarly, $z * (x/y) \neq (z * x)/y$; if $y = 0$, then $z * (x/y) = z$ while $(z * x)/y = 1$.

Majority voting genetic programming classifier

In each GP run, one rule is evolved—it does not matter whether it is a binary or multi-class classification problem. For a binary classification problem, if the output of a rule for a class on a test sample is positive, the vote in favor of that class is increased by one; otherwise, the vote in favor of the other class is increased by one. The test sample gets the label of the class that has the higher number of votes. For a multiclass problem having c types of samples, if the output of a rule for class i on a test sample is positive, the positive vote in favor of class i is increased by one; otherwise, the negative vote against class i is increased by one. Then the class of a test sample Y is predicted as follows:

$$Class(Y) = \max_i\{r_1, r_2, \ldots, r_c\} \qquad (4.3)$$

where r_i is the ratio of positive and negative votes. The test sample gets the label of the the class that has the highest ratio of positive and negative votes. If two or more ratios are the same, the class corresponding to the lower index ratio is assigned as the label of the test sample. If all ratios are zero, the test sample is treated as misclassified. Let us give an example. Suppose that there are four types (A, B, C, D) of samples in a microarray data set, and the number of rules (v) per class in a voting group is 7. If the number of positive and negative votes for the classes are $\{0, 5, 6, 6\}$ and $\{7, 2, 1, 1\}$, respectively, the label of the test sample will be C.

Experiments and results

Microarray datasets.   For our experiments, we chose two bench-mark microarray data sets: breast cancer (Hedenfalk et al., 2001) and lung carcinoma (Bhattacharjee et al., 2001) data sets.

The breast cancer data set contains 22 cDNA microarrays, each representing 5361 genes based on biopsy specimens of primary breast tumors of 7 patients with germ-line mutations of BRCA1, 8 patients with germ-line mutations of BRCA2, and 7 with sporadic cases. After preprocessing, only 3226 genes were left. The preprocessed data set is available at http://research.nhgri.nih. gov/microarray/NEJM_Supplement/. We divide this data set into two mutually exclusive training and test subsets containing 17 and 5 samples, respectively. Note here that one sample which is labeled as 'Sporadic/Meth.BRCA1' in the original data set is treated as 'BRAC1' type in our experiments. The numbers of BRAC1, BRAC2 and sporadic samples into the training and test subsets are (6,6,5) and (2,2,1), respectively.

The lung carcinoma data set contains mRNA expression levels corresponding to 12,600 transcript sequences in 203 lung tumor and normal samples. The 203 samples consist of 139 lung adenocarcinomas (AD), 21 squamous (SQ) cell carcinoma cases, 20 pulmonary carcinoid (COID) tumors and 6 small cell lung cancers (SCLC), as well as 17 normal lung (NL) samples. Negative gene expression values were replaced by setting a lower threshold of 0. Using a standard deviation threshold of 50 expression units, only 3312 genes were selected out of 12600. The complete sets of data are available at http://research.dfci.harvard.edu/meyersonlab/lungca.html. Since this data set is not divided into training and test subsets, we divided it into mutually exclusive training subset containing 103 samples (AD:70, SQ:11, COID:10, SCLC:3 and NL:9), and test subset containing 100 samples (AD:69, SQ:10, COID:10, SCLC:3 and NL:8). We treated this data set as a five-class (AD, SQ, COID, SCLC, and NL) classification problem.

Settings of parameters.   The values of different genetic programming parameters were: population size=4000; maximum size of a rule=100; maximum number of generations in a run=100; maximum crossover depth=7; maximum initial depth=6; crossover, reproduction, and mutation probabilities were 0.9, 0.1 and 0.1, respectively. The initial population of each run was generated using the ramped half-and-half method (Koza, 1992). We used Koza's greedy over selection for choosing mating pairs for crossing over and elitism so that the best found rule of a population survived for the next generation. In each run, the algorithm terminated when either all the training samples were correctly classified or the maximum number of generations had passed. As a set of functions, we used only arithmetic functions: $\{+, -, *, /, sqr, sqrt\}$. However, if more functions (especially complementary functions like ln and exp) are used or the depth of a rule is increased, the evolved rules may be more complex with little or no improvement in accuracy.

Results.   First we performed different experiments on the breast cancer data with different number of rules (v) per class in a voting group. For a particular v, we performed 20 experiments. In Figure 4-1, we present our experimental results on the breast cancer data. In each experiment, the majority voting accuracy is much better than the average accuracy. However, the best test accuracy was obtained when the number of rules per class in a voting group was equal to the number of samples in the training data (when v=17). In this

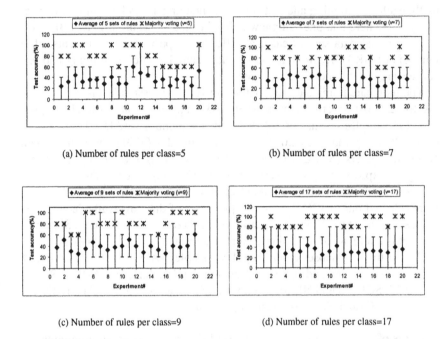

(a) Number of rules per class=5   (b) Number of rules per class=7

(c) Number of rules per class=9   (d) Number of rules per class=17

Figure 4-1. Test accuracies on the breast cancer data under different conditions. For each experiment, in addition to the average accuracy of v sets of rules, the maximum and the minimum accuracies are plotted on the graphs through error bars.

type of 20 experiments, we got 100% accuracy in 11 cases and in the remaining 9 cases, the accuracy was 80%. Note here that the total number of voting rules in each experiment was 51 (=17*3).

The lung carcinoma data set contains five-category of samples, and has 103 training and 100 test samples, making it a more difficult problem than the breast cancer data set. Since the minimum number of rule per class in a voting group should be 3, we performed experiments with $v = 3$. We also performed experiments with $v = 15$, which is the equal to the product of the number of types of samples in the data set and the minimum number of required voting members per class; the number of rules in each of this type of experiments was 75 (=15*5), and we needed 75 GP runs to get those 75 rules. In Figure 4-2, we have presented the experimental results on the lung carcinoma data. In each experiment, the majority voting accuracy was much better than the average accuracy; it was even better than the maximum accuracy of v sets of rules. Of the two types of experiments, the better results were obtained with $v = 15$. In this case, the average, the maximum and the minimum accuracies of the majority voting technique were 95.55%, 98% and 92%, respectively.

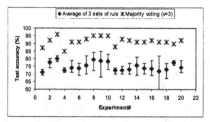 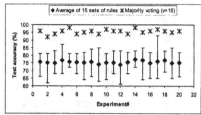

(a) Number of rules per class=3   (b) Number of rules per class=15

Figure 4-2. Test accuracies on the lung carcinoma data under different conditions. For each experiment, in addition to the average accuracy of v sets of rules, the maximum and the minimum accuracies are plotted on the graphs through error bars.

Table 4-1. Some of the more frequently selected genes in GP rules.

Serial	Accession#	Symbol	Gene name	Frequency
Breast cancer data				
X860	NM_002658	PLAU	plasminogen activator, urokinase	25
X1479	NM_053056	CCND1	cyclin D1	20
X2152			ESTs	20
X2804	NM_002709	PPP1CB	protein phosphatase 1, catalytic subunit, beta isoform	20
X336	NM_005749	TOB1	transducer of ERBB2, 1	20
Lung carcinoma data				
X1888	NM_001005862	ERBB2	neuroblastoma/glioblastoma derived oncogene homolog	125
X198	NM_003786	ABCC3	ATP-binding cassette, sub-family C (CFTR/MRP), member 3	106
X105	NM_006907	PYCR1	pyrroline-5-carboxylate reductase 1	102
X808	NM_003665	FCN3	ficolin (collagen/fibrinogen domain-containing) 3 (Hakata antigen)	101

The more frequently occurring genes in the 1020 (=17*3*20) and 1500 (=15*5*20) GP rules of the breast cancer and the lung carcinoma data are shown in Table 4-1. Among these genes, X860 (PLAU) [NM_002658] and X1479 (CCND1) [NM_053056] of the breast cancer data, and X1888 (ERBB2) [NM_001005862] of the lung carcinoma data are of biological interest because they are known to be associated with the type of cancers being studied in this chapter. PLAU and PAI-1 have roles in progression and recurrence of breast cancer (Harbeck et al., 2004); CCND1 is overexpressed in human breast cancers and is required for oncogene-induced tumorigenesis (Wang et al., 2003). Overexpression of ERBB2 is associated with recurrent non-small cell lung cancer (Onn et al., 2004).

Discussions

The task of classification of gene expression data faces many challenges due to smaller number of available training samples compared to huge number of genes. In traditional approaches employing a gene selection algorithm and a classifier, the training accuracy of a gene subset is calculated through leave-one-out-cross-validation (LOOCV) technique. However in genetic programming classification system, the training accuracy of a rule cannot be calculated through LOOCV technique because different rules may evolve in different GP runs, and we cannot choose one particular rule as a representative one. In most cases, the training accuracy of a rule is calculated in one pass by executing it on the test samples and counting the correct predictions. These single rules or sets of rules produce poor test accuracy. Majority voting technique can be a possible remedy for this problem. However, the success of majority voting depends on the number of rules per class in a voting group. From our experiments presented in this chapter and other preliminary results on other microarray data sets, we have found that increasing the number of voting rules improves the prediction accuracy. When the number of training samples is very small, the best accuracy can be obtained when the number of voting rules per class is equal to the number of training samples. However, for a data set containing many training samples, generation of all the rules may not be feasible; smaller number of rules may be sufficient. For a larger multi-category data set like lung carcinoma, our hypothesis is that the total number of rules per experiment should be approximately equal to the number of training samples; in that case, the number of rules per class will be $2 * \lfloor \frac{\#\text{training samples}}{2*(\#categories)} \rfloor + 1$. We need further experiments to verify this hypothesis.

3.   Evolutionary Humanoid Robots

In this section, we show how GP and its extension can successfully be applied to generate motion sequences of humanoid robots. The obtained results demonstrate that our proposed technique performs better than the traditional method in the box-moving task. We also provide results of other applications for more complicated tasks, e.g., multi-agent cooperation and interactive evolutionary computation (IEC) based motion design.

Box moving by humanoid robots

Proposed technique.   We propose a technique that integrates GP and RL. As seen in Figure 4.3(a), individual learning by RL, is outside the GP loop in the proposed technique. This enables us to (1) speed up learning in a real robot and (2) adapt to a real robot using the programs acquired from simulation.

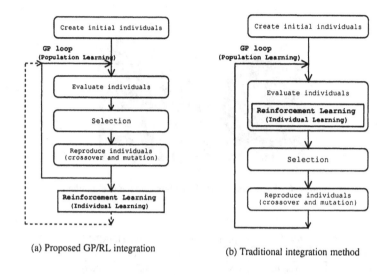

(a) Proposed GP/RL integration

(b) Traditional integration method

Figure 4-3. Flow charts of our proposed algorithm and the traditional method.

The proposed technique consists of the following two stages, the GP part and the RL part:

Step 1 Run GP on a simplified simulator and formulate programs that control the robot for achieving a task.

Step 2 Conduct RL after loading the best program obtained in **Step 1**.

In the first stage, the programs for the standard actions required for a real robot to execute a task are created through the GP process. The learning process of RL can be sped up in the second stage because the state space is divided into partial spaces according to the judgment standards established in the first stage. Moreover, preliminary learning from the simulator allows us to anticipate that a robot will perform target-oriented actions from the beginning of the second stage.

Experimental environment. The robot used in this experiment is "HOAP-1", manufactured by Fujitsu Automation Limited. It is a humanoid robot with 20 degrees of freedom (Figure 4-4). The specifications of the robot are shown in Table 4-2. This robot acts on commands given by a host computer (RT-Linux operating system). It is equipped with a CCD camera in its head, which provides image data for the purpose of environmental understanding.

The target of the robot is to move a box from an initial position to a goal position. The target object, i.e., a box, has wheels on the bottom so that it can

Figure 4-4. The robot HOAP-1, the box, and the goal marker.

Table 4-2. The specifications of the robot HOAP-1.

Height	about 48cm
Weight	about 6kg, including 0.7kg of battery
Joint Mobility	6DOF/foot ×2, 4DOF/arm ×2
Sensors	Joint angle sensor
	3-axis acceleration sensor
	3-axis gyro sensor
	Foot load sensor

easily be pushed. Note that the strength of a humanoid robot's arm is so weak that it has difficulty in carrying something heavy. Thus, we have chosen to fix the arm position and use a push action for the sake of simplicity. The goal position is marked with a red marker. When the humanoid robot has pushed the box in front of the red marker, we regard the task as successfully completed.

Moving the box to an arbitrary position is generally difficult. The moving behavior is achieved when the robot pushes the box with its knees while walking. If the box is in front of one leg, the box may be pushed forward or sometimes moved outside of the leg area. It is unpredictable because of these physical interactions and friction. It is very difficult to construct a precise simulator which expresses this movement. Therefore, the robot must learn these actions in the real environment.

Reinforcement learning of real robot.   Q-learning is conducted in the real robot. Each action node of the GP is assigned Q-tables for Q-learning. The real action is selected from the Q-tables of the action nodes according to the state of the real robot. Figure 4-5 illustrates this situation.

The robot can choose one of the following seven actions (Table 4-3): "Forward" (6 steps), "Left-turn", "Right-turn", "Left-sidestep" (one step to the

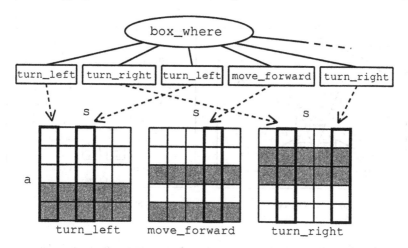

Figure 4-5. Action nodes determine the real action according to the Q-value of a real robot's state.

Table 4-3. Action nodes and their selectable real actions for HOAP-1.

action node	real actions that Q-table can select
move-forward	"Forward" , "Left-sidestep", "Right-sidestep"
turn-left	"Left-turn" , "Left-turn + sidestep", "Left-sidestep"
turn-right	"Right-turn" , "Right-turn + sidestep", "Right-sidestep"

left), "Right-sidestep" (one step to the right), the combination of "Left-turn" and "Right-sidestep", and the combination of "Right-turn" and "Left-sidestep". However, these actions are far from ideal. For instance, the robot tends to move slightly backwards during the "Right-turn" or "Left-turn". Thus, it is necessary to adapt to the motion's characteristics. As mentioned above, although the robot has an arm, its strength is so weak that we cannot rely on it to move a box.

As is often the case with a real robot, any action gives rise to some errors. For example, it is inevitably affected by the slightest roughness of the floor or the friction change due to a balance shift. Thus, even though the robot starts from the same position under the same conditions, it does not necessarily follow the same path. In addition, every action takes approximately ten seconds. Therefore, it is desirable to keep the learning time as short as possible.

The state space structure is based on positions from which the box and the goal marker can be seen in the CCD image. This recognition is performed after every action. Figures 4.6(a) and 4.6(b) are the projections of the box state and the goal marker state on the ground surface. These state spaces are constructed from rough directions and qualitative distances of objects. We used four levels

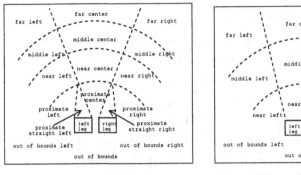

(a) States of the box

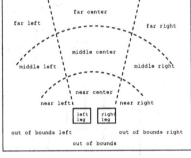

(b) States of the goal marker

Figure 4-6. Defined states in HOAP-1. The front of the robot faces up in the figures.

of distance for the box ("proximate", "near", "middle", "far") and three levels for the goal marker ("near", "middle", "far"). Additionally, we have defined "proximate straight left" and "proximate straight right" states at the frontal positions of the robot's legs.

The state is defined to be "out of bounds" when the robot misses the box or the goal position. Remember that the CCD camera of our robot is fixed in a forward direction and is not movable. As a result of this, the robot often misses the box or goal marker. To recover from the misses, we use the following strategy. The robot records the missing direction, i.e., left or right, when it has missed the box or goal marker. The robot can use this information for a certain number of action steps in order to generate the "out of bounds left" or "out of bounds right" states, which means that the target had disappeared in either the left or right direction within the last few action steps.

As shown in Figures 4.6(a) and 4.6(b), there are 17 states for the box and 14 states for the goal marker. The number of states over the whole environment is represented by their cross product. Hence, there are 238 states in total. When the goal marker is "near center" and the box is near the front of the robot, i.e., one of the states in "box proximate center", "box proximate straight left", "box proximate straight right", and "box near center", the robot recognizes that it has completed the task.

We applied the $Q(\lambda)$−learning method to a real robot in this experiment. $Q(\lambda)$−learning is a variant of Q-learning and is more efficient than normal Q-learning. The reward is set to 1.0 when the task is achieved and to 0.0 for all other states. As for other $Q(\lambda)$-learning parameters, we chose the learning rate

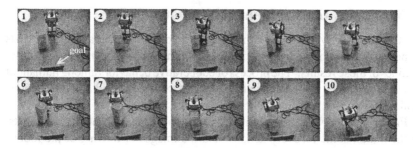

Figure 4-7. Series of actions for a successful task. The goal is at the bottom center of each figure.

$\alpha = 0.3$, the discount factor $\gamma = 0.8$ and the trace-decay parameter $\lambda = 0.5$. These parameters were determined from preliminary experiments.

Experimental results with humanoid robot HOAP-1. In this experiment using the humanoid robot, the starting state was limited to an arrangement in which both the box and the goal marker were visible. This was justified for one reason; even if learning is performed from an arrangement in which either the box or the goal is "out of bounds", it cannot be predicted that the box or goal position will subsequently become visible. Thus, there will be substantial variations in state transitions, and a long period of time will be required for learning.

For a single trial, learning was performed until the robot moved out of bounds or the predetermined number of action steps, i.e., 30 action steps, was exceeded. Learning in the real robot was performed for six hours.

In many situations, the robot succeeded in completing the task just after the initial learning. This is because the robot acted relatively well using the program evolved with the simulator. However, the robot took a long time in some situations. This proves that the actions acquired from the simulator are not always effective in a real environment because of the differences between the simulator and the real robot. These differences necessitate two added box states for the real robot, i.e., "proximate straight left" and "proximate straight right". The operational characteristics in these states are unknown to the robot before on-line learning.

After six-hour learning (about 1800 actions), much improved actions were observed—the robot selected very appropriate actions. Figure 4-7 shows the sequences of actions for one successful task. It completed the task much faster than it did before the on-line learning.

Other applications of humanoid robots

We are currently working on the application of GP to generate various kinds of humanoid motions. Because of the page limitation, we can only give brief outlines of those results. The process of cooperative behaviors among humanoid robots is described in detailed in (Iba et al., 2004; Kamio and Iba, 2005; Inoue et al., 2004).

Figure 4-8 shows the cooperative transportation by two humanoid robots. In the figure, some recovery actions, and the images of moving of the robots, captured by the active camera, are also shown. As can be seen, three recovery actions were performed in the case of side motions. By GP-based learning, the robots achieved the task successfully. However, sometimes a positional shift occurred during transportation of an object, which caused the recalculation of the path to the goal. To correct the positional shift, the two robots needed to revise their positions simultaneously. Therefore, learning is necessary to solve these sorts of difficulties.

Figure 4-9 shows another application of the cooperative task, which is called the piano movers' problem; here two robots have to transport an object through a narrow L-shaped path. By performing experiments, we have found evidences that GP successfully evolved effective motion sequences to reach the goal while avoiding the collision with the walls.

In another application, we have used interactive evolutionary computation method to design humanoid motions. The motion sequences are encoded as GP programs. The optimization is carried out for the sake of maintaining stability or satisfying other criteria, e.g., ball distance for kicking motions. Figure 4-10 gives an overview of the experiment. Figure 4-11 shows an example of the cooperation dance among multiple robots. The dance of each robot was created with the above-mentioned method. Although the robot moved slowly, the dance, which included the elements of a shift in the center of mass and a tilting of the upper body, was carried out by the actual robots. With the simulator, the generated motion was stable without adding any particular changes. However, when the dance was executed by the three HOAP-1 robots, one of the robots was unstable during lifting of its feet. When the motions were modified so that the feet were not lifted very high, all three robots demonstrated the stable motion shown in Figure 4-11.

4.   Conclusion

In this chapter, we have shown the applications of GP to bioinformatics and robotics. In bioinformatics domain, we have investigated the effectiveness of genetic programming in classification of gene expression data. In this problem, we have found that the single rules of GP are not capable of producing high

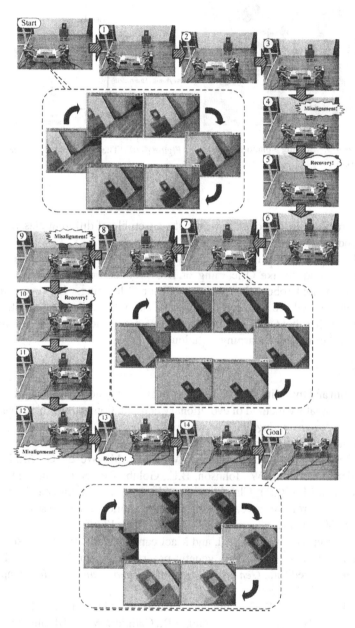

Figure 4-8. Cooperative transportation by two humanoid robots.

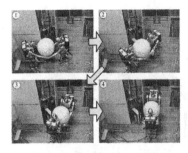
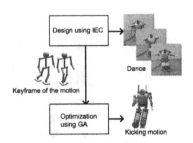

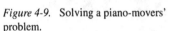

Figure 4-9. Solving a piano-movers'   *Figure 4-10.* The flow of the experiment.
problem.

test accuracy on unseen data; however, the ensemble of different classification rules produce very higher test accuracy.

In the application to robotics, the hybridization of GP and other machine learning techniques like Q-learning or IEC produce better action sequences for the humanoid robots than the core GP or Q-learning. However, further improvements will be required for the sake of higher robustness or stability. We believe that these real-world domains are a good test-bed for developing GP with other machine learning techniques.

References

Ando, Shin and Iba, Hitoshi (2004). Classification of gene expression profile using combinatory method of evolutionary computation and machine learning. *Genetic Programming and Evolvable Machines*, 5(2):145–156.

Bhattacharjee, A., Richards, W.G., Stauton, J., Li, C., Monti, S., Vasa, P., Ladd, C., Behesti, J., Buneo, R., Gillete, M., Loda, M., Weber, G., Mark, E.J., Lander, E.S., Wong, W., Johnson, B.E., Golub, T.R., Sugarbaker, D.J., and Meyerson, M. (2001). Classification of human lung carcinomas by mRNA expression profiling reveals distinct adenocarcinoma subclasses. *Proceedings of National Academy of Science*, 98:13790–13795.

Driscoll, Joseph A., Worzel, Bill, and MacLean, Duncan (2003). Classification of gene expression data with genetic programming. In Riolo, Rick L. and Worzel, Bill, editors, *Genetic Programming Theory and Practice*, chapter 3, pages 25–42. Kluwer.

Golub, T.R., Slonim, D.K., Tamayo, P., Huard, C., Gaasenbeek, M., Mesirov, J.P., Coller, H., Loh, M.L., Downing, J.R., Caligiuri, M.A., Bloomfield, C.D., and Lander, E.S. (1999). Molecular classification of cancer: class discovery and class prediction by gene expression monitoring. *Science*, 286(15):531–537.

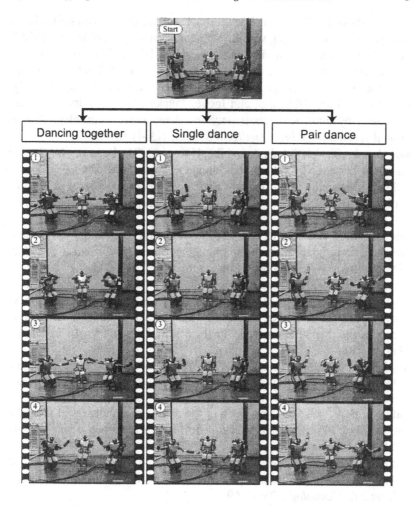

Figure 4-11. Example of motion design: cooperation dance.

Harbeck, N., Kates, R.E., Gauger, K., Willems, A., Kiechle, M., Magdolen, V., and Schmitt, M. (2004). Urokinase-type plasminogen activator (upa) and its inhibitor pai-i: novel tumor-derived factors with a high prognostic and predictive impact in breast cancer. *Thromb Haemost.*, 91(3):450–456.

Hedenfalk, I., Duggan, D., Chen, Y., Radmacher, M., Bittner, M., Simon, R., Meltzer, P., Gusterson, B., Esteller, M., Kallioniemi, O.P., Wilfond, B., Borg, A., and Trent, J. (2001). Gene-expression profiles in hereditary breast cancer. *The New England Journal of Medicine*, 344(8):539–548.

Hong, Jin-Hyuk and Cho, Sung Bae (2004). Lymphoma cancer classification using genetic programming with SNR features. In Keijzer, Maarten, O'Reilly, Una-May, Lucas, Simon M., Costa, Ernesto, and Soule, Terence, editors, *Genetic Programming 7th European Conference, EuroGP 2004, Proceedings*, volume 3003 of *LNCS*, pages 78–88, Coimbra, Portugal. Springer-Verlag.

Iba, Hitoshi, Tohge, Takahiro, and Inoue, Yutaka (2004). Cooperative transportation by humanoid robots—solving piano movers' problem. *International Journal of Hybrid Intelligent System*, 1(3–4):189–201.

Inoue, Yutaka, Tohge, Takahiro, and Iba, Hitoshi (2004). Learning for cooperative transportation by autonomous humanoid robots. In Nedjah, Nadia and de Macedo Mourelle, Luiza, editors, *Evolvable Machines: Theory & Practice*, volume 161 of *Studies in Fuzziness and Soft Computing*, chapter 1, pages 3–20. Springer, Berlin.

Kamio, Shotaro and Iba, Hitoshi (2005). Adaptation technique for integrating genetic programming and reinforcement learning for real robots. *IEEE Transactions on Evolutionary Computation*, 9(3):318–333.

Koza, John R. (1992). *Genetic Programming: On the Programming of Computers by Means of Natural Selection*. MIT Press, Cambridge, MA, USA.

Kuncheva, L.I. and Whitaker, C.J. (2003). Measures of diversity in classifier ensembles and their relationships with the ensemble accuracy. *Machine Learning*, 51:181–207.

Langdon, W. B. and Buxton, B. F. (2004). Genetic programming for mining DNA chip data from cancer patients. *Genetic Programming and Evolvable Machines*, 5(3):251–257.

Matthews, B.W. (1975). Comparison of the predicted and observed secondary structure of T4 phage lysozyme. *Biochemica et Biophysica Acta.*, 405:442–451.

Moore, Jason H., Parker, Joel S., Olsen, Nancy J., and Aune, Thomas M. (2002). Symbolic discriminant analysis of microarray data in automimmune disease. *Genetic Epidemiology*, 23:57–69.

Onn, Amir, Correa, Arlene M., Gilcrease, Michael, Isobe, Takeshi, Massarelli, Erminia, Bucana, Corazon D., O'Reilly, Michael S., Hong, Waun K., Fidler, Isaiah J., Putnam, Joe B., and Herbst, Roy S. (2004). Synchronous overexpression of epidermal growth factor receptor and her2-neu protein is a predictor of poor outcome in patients with stage i non-small cell lung cancer. *Clinical Cancer Research*, 10:136–143.

Paul, Topon Kumar and Iba, Hitoshi (2004a). Identification of informative genes for molecular classification using probabilistic model building genetic algorithm. In *Proceedings of Genetic and Evolutionary Computation Conference 2004*, number 3102 in Lecture Notes in Computer Science, LNCS, pages 414–425. Springer-Verlag.

Paul, Topon Kumar and Iba, Hitoshi (2004b). Selection of the most useful subset of genes for gene expression-based classification. In *Proceedings of the 2004 Congress on Evolutionary Computation (CEC2004)*, pages 2076–2083, Portland, Oregon, USA.

Paul, Topon Kumar and Iba, Hitoshi (2005a). Extraction of informative genes from microarray data. In *Proceedings of the Genetic and Evolutionary Computation Conference (GECCO) 2005*, pages 453–460, Washington DC, USA. ACM Press.

Paul, Topon Kumar and Iba, Hitoshi (2005b). Gene selection for classification of cancers using probabilistic model building genetic algorithm. *BioSystems*, 82(3):208–225.

Wang, C., Pattabiraman, N., Zhou, J.N., Fu, M., Sakamaki, T., Albanese, C., Li, Z., Wu, K., Hulit, J., Neumeister, P., Novikoff, P.M., Brownlee, M., Scherer, P.E., Jones, J.G., Whitney, K.D., Donehower, L.A., Harris, E.L., Rohan, T., Johns, D.C., and Pestell, R.G. (2003). Cyclin d1 repression of peroxisome proliferator-activated receptor gamma expression and transactivation. *Molecular and Cellular Biology*, 23(17):6159–6173.

Chapter 5

BOOSTING IMPROVES STABILITY AND ACCURACY OF GENETIC PROGRAMMING IN BIOLOGICAL SEQUENCE CLASSIFICATION

Pål Sætrom[1,2], Olaf René Birkeland[1] and Ola Snøve Jr.[1,3]

[1]*Interagon AS, Laboratoriesenteret, Trondheim, Norway;* [2]*Department of Computer and Information Science, Norwegian University of Science and Technology, Trondheim, Norway;* [3]*Department of Cancer Research and Molecular Medicine, Faculty of Medicine, Norwegian University of Science and Technology, Trondheim, Norway*

Abstract   Biological sequence analysis presents interesting challenges for machine learning. With an important problem – the recognition of functional target sites for microRNA molecules – as an example, we show how multiple genetic programming classifiers improve accuracy and stability. Moving from single classifiers to bagging and boosting with crossvalidation and parameter optimization requires more computing power. A special-purpose search processor for fitness evaluation renders boosted genetic programming practical for our purposes.

Keywords: Bioinformatics, microRNA, gene prediction, RNAi

1.   Introduction

In a typical conversation between a biologist and a computer scientist, the former will often refer to the enormous amount of biological sequence information and slip in a sentence about exponential growth of available data. In reality, however, the current fifty odd billion characters of sequence data will not scare off many programmers, and the relative growth is likely to slow down or be upheld only due to redundant information (Benson et al., 2005). Add to that the fact that any real application that you would work on is likely a much smaller problem that allows you to slash most of the data volume and you may start to think that computational biology is a piece of cake.

Unfortunately, biology is so incredibly complex that almost any problem turns out to be challenging. Famous Professor Emeritus of Stanford University,

Donald Knuth, once said that he was confident that biology will easily keep scientists busy for 500 years (Knuth, 2002). He is probably not far off.

In this paper, we will focus on the need for robust learning methods in bioinformatics in general, and the applicability of boosted genetic programming in particular. In addition, we will show how we use special-purpose pattern matching hardware to speed up the learning process, which despite limited data volumes becomes necessary when you have to make millions of passes over the same data.

Molecular biology is in many ways digital. DNA codes for RNA that codes for protein, which is a simplistic version of the central dogma for genetic information transfer (Crick, 1958). Digitalized, we may view this as a two-step process where DNA's letters A,C,G, and T can be translated to U,G,C, and A in RNA's alphabet. From a sequence of RNA letters, protein factories called ribosomes translate triplets of RNA characters to the amino acids that constitute proteins (Brenner et al., 1961). DNA is a double-stranded helix where the strands base-pair according to Watson-Crick rules, which means A to T and C to G. RNA is preferentially single-stranded, but RNA may also base-pair in an A to U and C to G configuration. Characters that preferentially base-pair to each other are complementary, which means that A is complementary to T in DNA and U in RNA, whereas G is complementary to C. Strands are said to be antiparallel, which refers to the internal configuration of the nucleotides that we view as characters. Sometimes, we need to specify the end we are talking about, and DNA and RNA strands are therefore said to run in 5' to 3' direction (see chapter 1 in (Lewin, 2000) for a detailed discussion of nucleic acids and their properties).

Sequence analysis in computational biology usually means to find sequences that are similar to a given template or to find complex patterns that are functionally significant. Our machine learning examples will describe methods for identification of functionally significant patterns in RNA sequences, but the methods are applicable to DNA and amino acid sequence mining as well.

2.   Methods

Genetic programming with string queries

The inspiration for our genetic programming (GP) system came from our ability to quickly evaluate an expression's fitness with the special-purpose search processor (Halaas et al., 2004) that will be described at the end of this section.

Our algorithm is designed to solve two-class classification problems and operate directly on positive and negative string samples without additional encoding steps. The population of solutions consist of syntax trees that represent queries in a formal query language (Koza, 1992); we use strong typing to ensure that all individuals are legal expressions in the language (Montana, 1995). Although we base our solution language on a query language that can be evaluated on our search hardware (http://www.interagon.com/pub/whitepapers/ IQL.reference-latest.pdf), we may restrict expressions to a subset of the full functionality, depending on the application (see Figure 5-2 for an example).

In all our experiments, we use strongly typed crossover and mutation (Montana, 1995), and standard reproduction as genetic operators (89%, 1%, and 10%); ramped half-n-half with a maximum tree depth of 7 to initialize populations; and a modified tournament selection (Ø. Grotmol, unpublished) that treats individuals with identical phenotypes as a single individual for the purpose of selecting individuals to a tournament (tournament size 5). The fitness function is (Sætrom, 2004)

$$\varepsilon(h, S, D) = \sum_{i=1}^{|S|} d_i \cdot |h(x_i) - y_i|, \qquad (5.1)$$

where h is the individual, S is the training set consisting of sequences x and binary labels y, and D is a weight vector that gives the relative importance d of each sequence in the training set. The weights are initialized to $1/(2 \cdot p)$ and $1/(2 \cdot n)$ for the positive and negative sequences, where p and n are the number of positive and negative sequences. This ensures that the naive solutions that predict all positives or all negatives have a fitness of 0.5.

Boosted genetic programming

Our classifiers are queries that are either present or not in an input string. In our experience, a single binary classifier can not satisfactorily capture the complexity of the applications we have addressed. A way of mending this problem is to build a soft classifier $f = \sum_{t=1}^{T} \alpha_t h_t$, by assigning weights α_t to our so-called hard classifiers h_t. There are several ways to assign the weights to each classifier. In the simplest case, each weight is set to $1/T$, which means that the model corresponds to the average of the hard classifiers. Boosting algorithms attempt to assign the weights iteratively. Our implementation is based on AdaBoost, which puts more effort into learning the difficult parts of the dataset (Freund and Schapire, 1997). Since GP is stochastic, two independent runs will generally not produce identical results. To reduce the variance, we construct a model that corresponds to the average of several boosted classifiers, which in addition to the reduced variance can also give higher accuracy (Hansen and Salamon, 1990). In this work, averaged classifiers consist of ten single classifiers.

Note that AdaBoost works similar to maximum margin classifiers known from statistical machine learning (Meir and Rätsch, 2003). One example of a maximum margin classifier is the popular support vector machine, which attempts to construct a classifier that maximizes the distance to any example in the training set (Burges, 1998). As a result, however, our algorithm would be expected to have problems with noise and outliers. We therefore implemented a regularized boosted genetic programming algorithm along the lines of Rätsch (Rätsch et al., 2001) and have successfully used it in genetic sequence classifications (Sætrom, 2004; Sætrom et al., 2005b). As the regularized algorithm has an extra parameter that should be optimized, estimating the regularized algorithm's performance on a particular problem is more complex and time-consuming than estimating the performance of the standard or averaged AdaBoost. In addition, simple averaging of boosted classifiers often has performance similar to the regularized algorithm (Sætrom, 2004). We therefore do not use the regularized algorithm in this work.

The pattern matching chip

Interagon's pattern matching chip (PMC) is a custom processor for finding patterns in data (Halaas et al., 2004). Instead of building data structures, the PMC makes a pass through the entire data set on every search. Each chip has a dedicated local memory bank, with a 100 MB/s search bandwidth. Multiple patterns can be evaluated towards the data in parallel due to the MISD architecture.

Each chip has 1024 parallel processing elements (PEs). Sixteen chips are integrated into a PCI accelerator card along with 2 GB of DRAM. One PC can typically hold up to 6 of these cards, rendering a total of $6 \cdot 16 \cdot 1024 \approx 100000$ parallel PEs in one PC. Operating at 100 MHz, this corresponds to 10^{13} symbol comparisons per second. The aggregated processing bandwidth of one such system is 9.6 GB/s.

The individual symbol comparisons are combined in a programmable binary tree, allowing for any Boolean operators, counting, ordering or adjacency between symbols or subexpressions. The throughput of the PMC is thus not limited by the complexity of the operators within the query, but rather the number of symbols used.

This capability is important when screening short nucleotide patterns built from a grammar rich in operators. As a bonus, the tree structure of PMC query processing is easily manipulated during mutation and crossover steps in GP.

Other sequence similarity screening methods exists, most notably the BLAST (Altschul et al., 1990) and Smith-Waterman (Smith and Waterman, 1981) algorithms. The Smith-Waterman algorithm is considered the gold standard for such searches. It uses dynamic programming to build a cost table for the potential alignments of a query versus the reference data. The different types of individual nucleotide alignments – that is, match, mismatch, insertion or deletion – have different costs. Smith-Waterman requires extensive updating

Table 5-1. Run time of sequence similarity searches on different algorithms and platforms. Run time is measured for screening 3519 individual 25 nucleotide sequences versus a 3 billion nucleotide data base.

Algorithm	Platform	Run time
Proprietary	PMC system with 6 cards	15 minutes
Smith-Waterman	PC	44 days
Smith-Waterman	GeneMatcher2 (Paracel)	255 minutes
BLAST	BlastMachine2 (Paracel)	15 hours
Smith-Waterman	DeCypher (TimeLogic)	14 hours
BLAST	Tera-BLAST ($n = 7$, TimeLogic)	3 hours

Table 5-2. Capability comparison for short sequence similarity searches using the pattern matching chip (PMC), BLAST and Smith-Waterman. Entries marked with a dash indicates a search not feasible with the specified algorithm.

Query	PMC	BLAST ($n = 11$)	BLAST ($n = 7$)	Smith-Waterman
GGGAAACCCTTTGGGAAACCCT	•	•	•	•
GGGAAACCC...GGGAAACCCT	•	–	•	•
GGGAAA...TTTGGG...CCCT	•	–	–	•
{GGGAAACCCTTTGGGAAACCCT : p ≥ 21}	•	–	•	•
{GGGAAACCC...GGGAAACCCT : p ≥ 20}	•	–	–	•

of the cost table for each query symbol processed, and is thus inherently slow (see Table 5-1). In our experience, insertions and deletions are less relevant when working with short nucleotides, rendering a considerable fraction of the processing in the Smith-Waterman algorithm as unnecessary.

BLAST uses heuristics to speed up the search, by indexing all consecutive n nucleotides in the reference data, with n typically being 11. This index is used as seed points, from which longer alignments are found through similar cost functions as in Smith-Waterman. Consequently, BLAST can not search for patterns unless there are n consecutive exact matches in the query. For queries in the same order of magnitude as n, this implies that BLAST can only find exact matches, without any operators on the character level (see Table 5-2). BLAST becomes more sensitive for smaller values of n, but also slows down a factor of 4 for each reduction in n. $BLAST_{n=7}$ is thus 256 times slower than $BLAST_{n=11}$, and is considered to be the practical lower limit.

(a) The near-perfect complementarity between the human mir-196a miRNA and Hoxb8 mRNA results in mRNA degradation (Yekta et al., 2004).

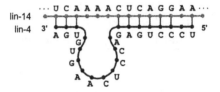

(b) The imperfect complementarity between the C. elegans lin-4 miRNA and lin-14 mRNA results in translational repression (Wightman et al., 1993).

Figure 5-1. Two ways miRNAs can decrease the expression of their targets.

3.   Results

Predicting microRNA targets

Most genes – that is, functionally important stretches of DNA – code for proteins. But during the last decade, biologists have become aware that some genes encode RNA that is not translated into a protein. MicroRNAs (miRNAs) – so named because they are only about 22 nucleotides long – constitute one such class of non-protein-coding RNAs. MicroRNAs base-pair with the RNA intermediate of genes before protein translation occurs, and thereby marks them for destruction by designated protein complexes. This provides a way for miRNAs to decrease the protein output from regular genes.

There are two ways that miRNAs can decrease the expression of their targets. First, their sequence may be an almost perfect complement of their target's RNA intermediate, as shown in Figure 5.1(a). Second, the complementarity may be more fuzzy, but still prevalent in one end of the miRNA, as shown in Figure 5.1(b). Near-perfect complementarity results in target cleavage (Martinez and Tuschl, 2004), whereas partial complementarity prevents the ribosomes from completing protein translation (Petersen et al., 2006). The latter binding form is more challenging from a computational point of view, as we only have a few examples of valid target sites and have to deduct the rules from these.

Currently, several hundred human miRNAs are known (Griffiths-Jones, 2004) (332 in Release 8.0), but only a limited number of mRNA targets have been verified (Sethupathy et al., 2006). Several tools for predicting miRNA target sites have been published (see Sethupathy et al., 2006, for an overview), but these tools were developed based on the current imperfect understanding of miRNA target site recognition. Many of the tools may therefore be overly biased towards the authors' preconceptions of an ideal miRNA target site; especially, the importance of overall binding energy between the miRNA and mRNA target site.

Our approach is to use machine learning to create a miRNA target site predictor (Sætrom et al., 2005a). Although this approach is not without its biases – especially regarding the data set used to train the predictor – the approach should at least create a predictor that is consistent with currently available data. In addition, we can easily create new predictors as new data becomes available.

We have previously shown that our boosted GP solution creates miRNA target site predictors that are at least as good and better than human created predictors (Sætrom et al., 2005a). In the following sections we will study the robustness of our algorithm in terms of the impact of the choice of GP parameters and of the boosting step. We start, however, by defining the query language we will use to predict miRNA target sites. The genetic programming step will search for candidate solutions in this language.

A query language for recognizing microRNA target sites

A microRNA target site is characterized by the base-pair interactions between the miRNA and the mRNA; that is, certain nucleotides in the miRNA binds to nucleotides in the mRNA target site. These base-pairing characteristics can be used to search for other similar target sites, by using search queries that match the base-pair interactions of the target site. To illustrate, the query CCCAACAACAUGAAACUGC will find target sites identical to the mir-196a site in Hoxb8 (Figure 5.1(a)) and the query UCA...CUCAGG.A, where the dot (.) matches any character, will find target sites similar to the lin-4 site in lin-14 (Figure 5.1(b)).

To make this basic idea applicable for general miRNA target site prediction, we extend the query language as follows. First, as we want our queries to represent the characteristics of miRNA target sites in general and be independent of the particular miRNAs, we use the positions of the miRNA nucleotides instead of the nucleotides themselves. Thus, we write the general query for the lin-4 site in Figure 5.1(b) as $p_{21}p_{20}p_{19}\ldots p_8p_7p_6p_5p_4p_3 \cdot p_1$, where p_i represents the complement of the miRNA nucleotide at position i counted from the miRNA's 5' end. We can then search for the target sites of a particular miRNA by replacing the p_i's with the miRNA's corresponding nucleotide.

Production	Semantic Rule
(1) $Q \rightarrow \{C : p \geq x\}$	$C.in := -1$
	$x := C.cut$
	$Q.hit := C.count \geq x$
(2) $C \rightarrow C_1 C_2$	$C_1.in := C.in$
	$C_2.in := C_1.index$
	$C.index := C_2.index$
	$C.count := C_1.count + C_2.count$
	$C.cut := C_1.cut + C_2.cut$
(3) $C \rightarrow A$	$A.in := C.in$
	$C.index := A.index$
	$C.count := A.count$
	$C.cut := A.cut$
(4) $C \rightarrow N$	$N.in := C.in$
	$C.index := N.index$
	$C.count := N.count$
	$C.cut := N.cut$
(5) $A \rightarrow p_i, i \in \{1, \ldots, 21\}$	$k := A.in = -1\,?\,i : A.in - 1$
	$A.cut := 1$
	$A.count := match(p_k)$
	$A.index := k$
(6) $N \rightarrow p_i, i \in \{1, \ldots, 21\}$	$k := N.in = -1\,?\,i : N.in - 1$
	$N.cut := 0$
	$N.count := match(p_k)$
	$N.index := k$

Figure 5-2. The grammar and semantics of the pattern language used in our microRNA target prediction experiments. The grammar and semantics are explained in the main text.

Second, to introduce more flexibility when searching for potential sites, we allow a certain number of mismatches between our query Q and potential target sites. We write this as $\{Q : p \geq x\}$, where x is the number of nucleotides that have to match in the original query. Note that this is identical to requiring a Hamming distance of at most $|Q| - x$ between the query and target sequences, where $|Q|$ is the number of nucleotides in the query.

Third, we require that the positions in the query are continual and in sequence. Thus, $p_6 p_5 p_4 p_3$ is a valid query, but $p_6 p_4 p_2$ is not. Figure 5-2 formally defines our query language. The grammar shows the legal production rules in the language with alternatives represented as separate productions and nonterminals represented by uppercase letters.

The terminal p_i represents a position in the miRNA sequence, and, as the semantic productions in Figure 5-2 show, the exact position depends on the terminal's position in the parse tree. More specifically, the first terminal encountered in a walk of the parse tree defines the query's start position in the miRNA sequence; the rest of the terminals have their positions derived from the initial terminal to ensure that the final query defines a continual sequence of miRNA positions. The *in* and *index* node attributes in the semantic rules handle this.

A query matches a sequence if $Q.hit$ is true. $match(p_k)$ returns 1 if the character in the position indicated by p_k is identical to the character it is compared with. Note that we use two sets of terminals A and N to define the cutoff value on the number of mismatches. The cutoff is initially zero and each terminal from A increases the cutoff by one. Consequently, queries where all terminals are from N have a cutoff of zero, and queries where all terminals are from A have a cutoff equal to the number of terminals. This ensures that the cutoff always has a meaningful value.

Genetic programming produces good but unstable classifiers

The choice of parameters in a GP run often has a major impact on the quality of the results (Eiben et al., 1999; Feldt and Nordin, 2000). We therefore wanted to study how different input parameters affected the performance of the target site queries created by the GP step in our machine learning system. To do this, we ran several experiments where we varied the population size and the number of generations in the GP run. We used the same dataset as in (Sætrom et al., 2005a), which consisted of 36 experimentally verified miRNA target sites for 4 miRNAs and 3000 random negative sites, and used leave-one-miRNA-out cross-validation, as defined in (Sætrom et al., 2005a), to train and test classifiers.

As Figure5.3(a) shows, increasing the number of generations and the population size resulted in GP finding queries that had an increasingly higher performance in the training set. This was expected, as increasing the population size and the number of generations increases GP's ability to find better candidate solutions (Koza, 1992; Feldt and Nordin, 2000). Good performance in the training set does, however, not guarantee good performance on unseen data (Vapnik, 1998); this is especially the case when the training set is small or contains noise. In this case it is both, as the positive set only consists of 36 experimentally verified target sites and the random negatives likely contain sites that closely resemble the verified sites. Nevertheless, the target site queries produced by GP show no sign of overfitting, as their performance in the test set closely resemble their performance in the training set.

What is more, the graph indicates that the solutions produced with the largest population size run for more than five generations are the best possible with

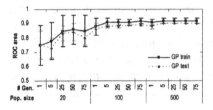
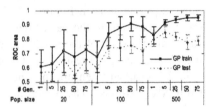

(a) The ROC-score of the best-of-run individual increases with increasing population size and number of generations in both the training and test sets. The graph shows the ROC-score average and standard deviation of 10 independent GP runs on the query language in Figure 5-2

(b) GP overfits a more complex query language. The graph shows the ROC-score average and standard deviation of 10 independent GP runs on the query language used in (Sætrom et al., 2005a)

Figure 5-3. Effect of varying GP Parameters on test and training performance, for a simple (a) and more complex (b) query language.

our solution language. This is because neither the performance in the training set nor in the test set improves with increasing number of generations, and because there is no variance in the test scores. Manual inspection of the results confirmed the convergence: all the 30 runs on the 3 largest training sets produced the query $\{p_8p_7p_6p_5p_4p_3p_2 : p \geq 6\}$; the 10 runs on the smallest training set with the let-7 sites excluded produced the query $\{p_8p_7p_6p_5p_4p_3p_2p_1 : p \geq 6\}$ or equivalents. These results indicate that base-pairs between nucleotides 2-8 are most important for miRNA target site recognition, but also that some mismatches are tolerated.

Sætrom et al. defined a query language that used variable length wildcards to join the sequence motif of Figure 5-2 and an unordered motif (Sætrom et al., 2005a). This is a query language that can model more complex relationships in the data, and we wanted to determine if GP could evolve even better solutions than the ones based on our initial query language. As Figure 5.3(b) shows, however, genetic programming could not. Even though the best solutions have a higher performance in the training set, their performance in the test set is much worse. Thus, even though GP now finds solutions that better describe the training data, these solutions are overfitted and do not generalize to unseen data.

From statistical learning theory, we know that overfitting is closely related to the capacity of the set of functions from which we draw our solutions (Vapnik, 1998). The above results illustrate this relationship. The above analysis also illustrates the impact that parameter choices have on the results produced

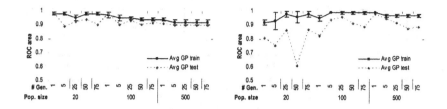

Figure 5-4. Averaging GP classifiers improves performance and reduces parameter variance. The graphs show the ROC-scores in the training and test sets for the classifiers created by averaging the expressions from Figure 5.3(a) (left) and Figure 5.3(b) (right).

by genetic programming. First, the average ROC-score on the test set varies greatly depending on the parameter choice (standard deviations of 0.055 and 0.099 for the ROC-score averages in Figures 5.3(a) and 5.3(b)). Second, even though genetic programming can in some cases produce optimal results simply by choosing a large population size and running for many generations, this is a sure recipe for overfitting in the general case. Consequently, finding good solutions requires parameter optimization, but on problems where slight changes in parameters give large changes in results, this is inherently difficult (Prechelt, 1998). Furthermore, parameter optimization is an extra training step that risks overfitting, which means that the parameter optimization must be kept completely independent of the test set. Otherwise one will get biased estimates of the classifier's performance in unseen data (Salzberg, 1997).

Averaging significantly improves predictor accuracy and stability

The previous section illustrated a major problem with using genetic programming for pattern mining: the solutions produced by genetic programming are brittle, as slight changes in input parameters can give large changes in solution quality. This is illustrated by the large variances in the average ROC-scores for the different parameter settings and in the ROC-scores for some of the individual parameter settings. This latter observation does, however, hint at a possible way to improve the GP results, as diverse and accurate classifiers can be combined to produce more accurate and less variable classifiers (Hansen and Salamon, 1990).

Figure 5-4 shows the result of averaging the solutions from the GP runs in Section 3.0. A comparison with Figures 5.3(a) and 5.3(b) shows the improved performance of the average classifiers compared to the individual classifiers. For all parameter settings where GP produce varying solutions, the average classifiers have a higher performance than the individual classifiers. The increased performance was significant ($p = 4 \cdot 10^{-3}$ and $p = 3 \cdot 10^{-8}$ with paired Student's

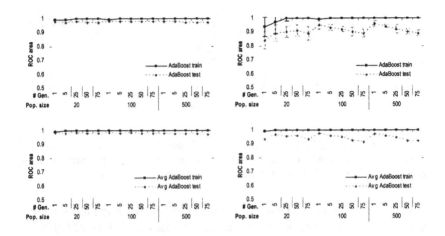

Figure 5-5. Boosting further improves performance and reduces parameter variance. The graphs show the ROC-scores in the training and test sets for the classifiers created by boosting the expressions from Figure 5.3(a) (top left) and Figure 5.3(b) (top right) for 25 iterations, and by averaging the boosted classifiers (bottom left) and (bottom right).

t-tests on the simple and complex grammar) and the ROC-scores also varied less across the different parameter settings for the simple grammar ($p = 0.04$ with an F-test), which indicates that the average classifiers are more robust than the single classifiers. In fact, the average classifiers use the stochastic nature of GP to improve the classifier performance.

Boosting further improves predictor accuracy and stability

To try to improve our classifiers further, we combined our genetic programming system with the AdaBoost algorithm (Freund and Schapire, 1997). Figure 5-5 shows the performance of the resulting weighted sequence motif classifiers for different parameter settings of GP.

Comparing with the single and averaged GP results (Figures 5.3(a) and 5-4), the boosted expressions from Figure 5-2 have both increased performance and parameter stability ($p = 7 \cdot 10^{-7}$ and $p = 9 \cdot 10^{-7}$ with paired Student's t-tests and $p = 9 \cdot 10^{-12}$ and $p = 6 \cdot 10^{-8}$ with F-tests). The boosted versions of the more complex expressions from (Sætrom et al., 2005a) also had increased performance and parameter stability, but the differences were not as large as for the simpler grammar ($p = 6 \cdot 10^{-7}$ and $p = 0.1$ with paired Student's t-tests and $p = 6 \cdot 10^{-5}$ and $p = 1 \cdot 10^{-4}$ with F-tests). Averaging the boosted classifiers further improved the performance and parameter stability for both grammars (Figures 5-5 bottom left and right; $p = 0.004$ and $p = 1 \cdot 10^{-5}$ with paired Student's t-tests and $p = 0.1$ and $p = 0.1$ with F-tests).

Running the boosting algorithm for additional iterations had a minor impact on the classifiers' performance. We repeated the above experiment with both classifier languages for the different GP parameters, but increased the number of boosting iterations to 75. The only difference between these results and the results from the 25 iteration boosting was a small, but significant decrease in the average performance across the different parameter settings for the averaged boosted classifiers based on the complex expressions (from 0.947 to 0.924; p-value $= 6 \cdot 10^{-6}$ with a paired Student's t-test).

The AdaBoost algorithm creates a classifier that maximizes the minimum margin in the training set (Bartlett et al., 1998), and theoretically, AdaBoost converges exponentially towards this maximum margin classifier with the number of boosting iterations (Meir and Rätsch, 2003). Thus, the first boosting steps have the highest impact on the final boosted classifier's performance, and increasing the number of boosting iterations have less and less impact on the performance of the final classifier.

In summary, boosting the classifiers created by GP significantly improved the classifiers' performance and significantly improved the stability of the algorithm with respect to the choice of GP parameters. In particular, the average performance of the boosted classifiers was, for all the parameter settings, higher than the best performance of any of the single classifiers created by GP. Thus, we do not get the best performance by ensuring that GP finds the optimal solution in the training set; we get better results by running many GP runs on small populations for few generations and combining the suboptimal solutions found in these runs into a single robust classifier.

The solution language has a major impact on classifier performance

As the previous sections showed, both the solution languages we investigated could accurately separate real miRNA target sites from random sequences. These solution languages were based on the hamming distance filtering function, which our special purpose hardware evaluates fast and efficiently. We used this hardware in our experiments to accelerate the fitness evaluation of the candidate expressions and thereby reduced the total runtime of the experiments. Simpler solution languages that use exact matching can, however, be evaluated much faster in software than can the approximate Hamming distance-based expressions. We therefore wanted to determine whether we could create accurate miRNA target predictors based on a solution language that only allowed exact matches between miRNAs and potential target sites.

To create a solution language that only allowed exact matches, we removed productions (4) and (6) from the grammar in Figure 5-2. Consequently, a query now only returns a hit when all the positions in the query report a match. Using

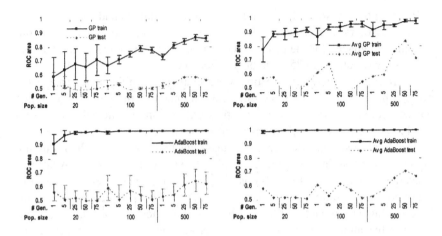

Figure 5-6. Classifiers that only allow exact matches between miRNAs and target sites have a much lower accuracy than the classifiers based on approximate matches (Figures 5.3(a), 5.3(b), 5-4, and 5-5). The graphs show the ROC-scores in the training and test sets for single GP (top left), averaged GP (top right), GP boosted 25 iterations (bottom left), and averaged boosted GP (bottom right) classifiers based on a solution language that only allowed exact matches.

this solution language, we repeated the analyses of the miRNA target site data. Figure 5-6 summarizes the results.

A comparison with the previous results showed that all the "approximate match" classifiers were significantly more accurate than the "exact match" classifiers (all p-values $< 1 \cdot 10^{-6}$ with paired Student's t-tests). The "exact match" classifiers did, however, have relatively high accuracies in their training sets; in other words, these classifiers were severely overfitted to their training sets. And even though some of the classifiers had a relatively high performance in the test set – especially, the averaged GP classifiers – this best accuracy is still much lower than the best accuracy for the "approximate match" classifiers. This high accuracy may also be an artefact of our multiple testing.

These results show that the solution language that only allows exact matches is inappropriate for predicting miRNA target sites. This was expected as miRNA binding is inexact in itself. The results also illustrate the impact the solution language has on the classifier performance.

The superior performance of ensemble classifiers generalize to other sequence classification problems

The previous sections have shown that when predicting microRNA target sites, combining several single GP classifiers into an ensemble classifier gives classifiers that are significantly more accurate than the single GP classifiers. To

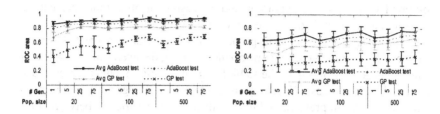

Figure 5-7. Ensemble classifiers are more accurate than single genetic programming classifiers. The graphs show the test set ROC-scores for the non-coding RNA gene prediction (left) and short interfering RNA efficacy prediction (right) problems.

show that this property also generalizes to other problems, we compared the performance of the single, averaged, boosted, and averaged boosted GP classifiers on two other sequence classification problems. These were (i) predicting whether 50 nucleotide long sequences are parts of non-protein-coding RNA genes (Sætrom et al., 2005b), and (ii) predicting the knockdown efficacy of 19 nucleotide-long short interfering RNAs (Sætrom, 2004).

We used the same test setup as in the previous experiments, except that we excluded 50 generations from the set of parameters tested. We used the solution language from (Sætrom, 2004) in both experiments. This language resembles the one in Figure 5-2, except that the terminals are the four nucleotides and not a template position in the sequence. The language also allows alternatives at each position; see (Sætrom, 2004) for complete details.

As Figure 5-7 shows, the ensemble classifiers are better than the single classifiers for all parameter settings, and the averaged boosted classifiers have the highest overall performance. The differences are significant for both problems. More specifically, all p-values in the paired Student's t-tests that compare the performance of the single GP classifiers to the ensemble classifiers are $< 3 \cdot 10^{-8}$. Similarly, all p-values for the averaged boosted classifiers are $< 4 \cdot 10^{-8}$.

4.   Discussion

We have presented our boosted genetic programming (GP) system, and shown how we can use a special-purpose search processor for fitness evaluation by operating on parse trees that represent search queries. Using a motivating example from molecular biology – recognition of viable target sites for small RNA molecules called microRNAs – we have demonstrated how the system's performance varies with different setups.

Importantly, GP can produce classifiers with satisfactory performance for target recognition. Populations with more than 100 individuals that are run for 50 or more generations seem to be adequate for good performance. The solution language is very important, and increasing the algorithm's capacity by allowing more complex queries is a recipe for overfitting.

Unfortunately, the stochastic property of GP results in a great difference between best-of-run classifier performances. Using the average of several classifiers significantly improves the stability of our algorithm, but accuracy is also improved in the process. When we used a boosted GP algorithm on our problem, we saw an impressive stability with negligible variance between runs. Also, the boosted classifiers have higher accuracy and increased generalization performance, as shown by their high and stable performance on the test set.

References

Altschul, S. F., Gish, W., Miller, W., Myers, E. W., and Lipman, D. J. (1990). Basic local alignment search tool. *Journal of molecular biology*, 215(3):403–410.

Bartlett, P., Freund, Y., Lee, W. S., and Schapire, R. E. (1998). Boosting the margin: a new explanation for the effectiveness of voting methods. *Annals of Statistics*, 26(5):1651–1686.

Benson, D. A., Karsch-Mizrachi, I., Lipman, D. J., Ostell, J., and Wheeler, D. L. (2005). GenBank. *Nucleic Acids Research*, 33(DB):D34–D38.

Brenner, S., Jacob, F., and Meselson, M. (1961). An unstable intermediate carrying information from genes to ribosomes for protein synthesis. *Nature*, 190:576–581.

Burges, C. J. C. (1998). A tutorial on support vector machines for pattern recognition. *Knowledge Discovery and Data Mining*, 2(2):121–167.

Crick, F. H. C. (1958). The biological replication of macromolecules. *Symposia of the Society for Experimental Biology*, 12:138–163.

Eiben, Agoston Endre, Hinterding, Robert, and Michalewicz, Zbigniew (1999). Parameter control in evolutionary algorithms. *IEEE Transations on Evolutionary Computation*, 3(2):124–141.

Feldt, Robert and Nordin, Peter (2000). Using factorial experiments to evaluate the effect of genetic programming parameters. In Poli, Riccardo, Banzhaf, Wolfgang, Langdon, William B., Miller, Julian F., Nordin, Peter, and Fogarty, Terence C., editors, *Genetic Programming, Proceedings of EuroGP'2000*, volume 1802 of *LNCS*, pages 271–282, Edinburgh. Springer-Verlag.

Freund, Y. and Schapire, R. E. (1997). A decision-theoretic generalization of on-line learning and an application to boosting. *Journal of Computer and System Sciences*, 55(1):119–139.

Griffiths-Jones, S. (2004). The microRNA registry. *Nucleic Acids Research*, 32(90001):D109–111.

Halaas, A., Svingen, B., Nedland, M., Sætrom, P., Snøve Jr., O., and Birkeland, O. R. (2004). A recursive MISD architecture for pattern matching. *IEEE*

Transactions on Very Large Scale Integration (VLSI) Systems, 12(7):727–734.

Hansen, L. K. and Salamon, P. (1990). Neural network ensembles. *IEEE Transactions on Pattern Analysis and Machine Intelligence*, 12(10):993–1001.

Knuth, D. E. (2002). All questions answered. *Notices of the AMS*, 49(3):318–324.

Koza, John R. (1992). *Genetic Programming: On the Programming of Computers by Means of Natural Selection*. MIT Press, Cambridge, MA, USA.

Lewin, B. (2000). *Genes VII*. Oxford University Press, Oxford, UK.

Martinez, J. and Tuschl, T. (2004). RISC is a 5' phosphomonoester-producing RNA endonuclease. *Genes & development*, 18(9):975–980.

Meir, R. and Rätsch, G. (2003). An introduction to boosting and leveraging. In Mendelson, S. and Smola, A., editors, *Advanced Lectures on Machine Learning*, volume 2600, pages 118–183. Springer-Verlag.

Montana, David J. (1995). Strongly typed genetic programming. *Evolutionary Computation*, 3(2):199–230.

Petersen, C. P., Bordeleau, M.-E., Pelletier, J., and Sharp, P. A. (2006). Short RNAs repress translation after initiation in mammalian cells. *Molecular cell*, 21(4):533–542.

Prechelt, L. (1998). Automatic early stopping using cross validation: quantifying the criteria. *Neural Networks*, 11(4):761–767.

Rätsch, G., Onoda, T., and Müller, K.-R. (2001). Soft margins for AdaBoost. *Machine Learning*, 42(3):287–320.

Sætrom, O., Snøve Jr., O., and Sætrom, P. (2005a). Weighted sequence motifs as an improved seeding step in microRNA target prediction algorithms. *RNA*, 11(7):995–1003.

Sætrom, P. (2004). Predicting the efficacy of short oligonucleotides in antisense and RNAi experiments with boosted genetic programming. *Bioinformatics*, 20(17):3055–3063.

Sætrom, P., Sneve, R., Kristiansen, K. I., Snøve Jr., O., Grünfeld, T., Rognes, T., and Seeberg, E. (2005b). Predicting non-coding RNA genes in *Escherichia coli* with boosted genetic programming. *Nucleic Acids Research*, 33(10):3263–3270.

Salzberg, S. (1997). On comparing classifiers: Pitfalls to avoid and a recommended approach. *Data Mining and Knowledge Discovery*, 1(3):317–328.

Sethupathy, P., Corda, B., and Hatzigeorgiou, A. G. (2006). TarBase: a comprehensive database of experimentally supported anima l microRNA targets. *RNA*, 12(2):192–197.

Smith, T. F. and Waterman, M. S. (1981). Identification of common molecular subsequences. *Journal of molecular biology*, 147(1):403–410.

Vapnik, V. N. (1998). *Statistical Learning Theory*. Wiley-Interscience, New York, NY, USA.

Wightman, B., Ha, I., and Ruvkun, G. (1993). Posttranscriptional regulation of the heterochronic gene *lin-14* by *lin-4* mediates temporal pattern formation in *C. elegans*. *Cell*, 75(5):855–862.

Yekta, S., Shih, I., and Bartel, D. P. (2004). MicroRNA-directed cleavage of *HOXB8* mRNA. *Science*, 304(5670):594–596.

Chapter 6

ORTHOGONAL EVOLUTION OF TEAMS: A CLASS OF ALGORITHMS FOR EVOLVING TEAMS WITH INVERSELY CORRELATED ERRORS

Terence Soule[1] and Pavankumarreddy Komireddy[1]

[1]*Department of Computer Science, University of Idaho, Moscow, ID.*

Abstract   Several general evolutionary approaches have proven quite successful at evolving teams (or ensembles) consisting of cooperating team members. However, in this paper we demonstrate that the existing approaches have subtle, but significant, weaknesses. We then present a novel class of evolutionary algorithms (orthogonal evolution of teams (OET)) for evolving teams that overcomes these weaknesses. Specifically it is shown that a typical algorithm from the OET class of algorithms successfully generates team members that have fitnesses comparable to those evolved independently and that have inversely correlated errors, which maximizes the teams' overall performance. Finally it is shown that the OET approach performs significantly better than the standard evolutionary approaches.

Keywords: Teams, ensembles, expected failure rate, island models, team models, orthogonal evolution of teams

1.   Introduction

Many real-world problems are too large and too complex to expect a single, monolithic intelligent agent to solve them successfully. Monolithic agents, because they are monolithic, tend to overlook specialized sub-domains within a larger problem space and thus to make errors on those sub-domains. As programs are expected to solve progressively larger and more complex problems this weakness will become increasingly critical. Thus, considerable research has been devoted to developing problem solvers consisting of integrated sub-systems *specialized* to find solutions within sub-domains of the total problem space. These structured solutions are robust and can solve problems defined over huge domains with no (or very few) gaps or errors. Much of this research has focused on team, or ensemble, learning in which each member of the team receives the same inputs and solutions are determined via a cooperation mechanism, such as a vote. Such cooperative teams have been successful at solving complex problems ranging from predicting disordered regions in proteins (Peng et al., 2004) to learning musical models (Widmer, 2003) to weather prediction (Maqsood et al., 2004).

There are two fundamental requirements to creating successful teams. The individual team members must be relatively successful and the team members must cooperate in a way that improves the performance of the team as a whole. Typically this means that the members *specialize* on distinct, but potentially overlapping, sub-domains of the problem space. To be deemed successful any technique should be shown to meet both of these requirements.

Recently evolutionary techniques, including both genetic algorithms (GAs) and genetic programming (GP), have proven to be extremely effective at automatically *evolving* teams. Evolutionary approaches for creating teams have been applied to a wide range of knowledge representations including teams of: neural networks(Liu et al., 2000), oblique decision trees (Cantu-Paz and Kamath, 2003), stack based predictors (Platel et al., 2005), and teams of induced functions (Soule, 1999) and to a wide range of problem domains including robot navigation (Iba, 1997), sporting strategies (Raik and Durnota, 1994), predator strategies (Haynes et al., 1995; Luke and Spector, 1996), hazard assessment (Obitz et al., 1999), and cancer and diabetes diagnosis (Cantu-Paz and Kamath, 2003; Liu et al., 2000). These results demonstrate the effectiveness and broad applicability of evolutionary techniques to the problem of automatically generating teams.

However research suggests that the two general approaches, *island* and *team*, each have significant, if subtle, weaknesses. Island approaches produce highly fit team members, but there is a high probability that those members have *correlated* errors resulting in less than optimal team performance (Imamura et al., 2002; Imamura et al., 2003). In contrast team approaches can produce team members with *inversely correlated* errors leading to relatively good team performance, but the members themselves are relatively poor, which limits the teams' performance (Soule, 2003).

In this paper we use a simple illustrative problem and the standard benchmark problem inter-twined spirals to confirm the weaknesses of the island and team approaches and introduce a novel evolutionary algorithm design: Orthogonal Evolution of Teams (OET) that overcomes these weaknesses. OET defines a new class of cooperative, co-evolutionary algorithms that evolves team members with distinct areas of specialization. Our results show that OET algorithms combine the advantages of both the island and team approaches.

OET algorithms generate highly successful individual solutions, whose members specialize on distinct sub-domains of the problem space, leading to robust solutions that cover an entire problem domain with no (or few) gaps or errors.

2. Background

In this work specialization within a team is directly measured using the idea of error correlation between team members. If members have evolved to specialize on distinct (but over-lapping) sub-domains of the problem space then their errors will be *inversely* correlated. Correlation is measured using the expected failure rate model that was initially derived for the investigation fault tolerant systems.

Fault tolerance is the ability of a system to perform despite faults or deficiencies within components of the system. It is fundamental to ensuring the reliability, availability and accuracy of a system and is a requirement for critical systems. Commonly software systems with redundant components achieve fault tolerance via a majority vote. For example, if five redundant components are used ($n = 5$) then three of the components ($m = 3$) must fail concurrently to produce a failure.

For fault masking to successfully mask errors (at least in software) the redundant members must be different. If one member has an error that causes the member to exhibit a fault on a particular input then making n copies of the member and having them all vote will not solve the problem. Thus, for fault masking to be successful the redundant components, e.g. team members, must be significantly different from each other. The degree of difference is measured by calculating the correlation of errors between team members. If errors are highly correlated the team members will tend to return errors for the same input cases and there is little advantage to forming a team. If the errors are independent, or better, are inversely correlated, then the members will rarely return errors for the same input cases and the performance of the team will be dramatically better than the members' performance. This can be viewed as a measure of cooperation - the team performs much better than the individual members. Or as a measure of specialization - inversely correlated errors imply that the members have specialized to cover distinct sub-domains of the problem space.

To determine whether the errors between voting team members are correlated, independent or inversely correlated we use the expected failure rate model (Avizienis and Kelly, 1984). Let n be the number of team members, let p be the probability of each member producing an error for a given input and let m be the minimum number of concurrent errors required for a system to fail. The expected failure rate (f) for the whole system, assuming independent errors between the team members, is

$$f = \sum_{k=m}^{n} \binom{n}{k} (1-p)^{(n-k)} p^k \qquad (6.1)$$

If the failure rate of a system with redundant components is greater than f then the errors are correlated. If the failure rate is equal to f then the errors are uncorrelated. This is generally assumed to be the best achievable condition for fault tolerance. However, if the failure rate of the system is less than f then the errors are inversely correlated. This can only occur if the team members are specifically designed to have this property. Any approach that produces the members independently can, at best, be expected to produce independent faults.

In N-version programming, which is commonly used to produce fault tolerant software for critical computing systems, independent programming teams, often from independent companies, produce software from the same set of requirements (Avizienis and Kelly, 1984; Hilford et al., 1997). The software produced by each programming team is used as one of the redundant components. N-version programming produces software components that individually have very few faults, as few as can be achieved via hand coding. However, studies of N-version programming by Knight and Levenson (Knight and Leveson, 1986) and by Hatton (Hatton, 1997) have shown that N-version programming still produces software components with correlated faults, even when independent design and coding methodologies are used. They hypothesized that this occurs for several reasons: human programmers tend to make the same (incorrect) assumptions and the same logic errors, and most programmers learned similar design and coding strategies.

To avoid the problems introduced by human programmers a number of researchers have examined using evolutionary computation (EC) to evolve teams. Because EC is a highly randomized process it is assumed that any errors will be randomly distributed. In fact, this assumption is suspect. EC generally takes the path of least resistance; the pressure to survive encourages EC to find the easiest solutions first. Thus, it seems likely that even independent populations will tend to favor the same general solutions and may produce correlated errors.

N-Version Genetic Programming (NVGP) developed by Imamura et al. evolves n independent populations (islands), when evolution halts the NVGP algorithm draws a random individual from each population to create a team of n individuals (Imamura et al., 2002; Imamura et al., 2003). Although NVGP produces some teams with independent errors for a range problems, the majority of teams are *not* qualified. In general, it takes a large number of random draws to find a qualified team. This appears to invalidate the assumption that independent evolutionary runs will consistently generate solutions with independent errors.

Several other researchers have experimented with algorithms using independent populations, although without directly measuring predicted failure rates (Feldt, 1998; Zang and Joung, 1997). In general, it seems likely that any approach that uses independent populations (island approaches) will have a similar flaw.

An alternative to the island approach is the team approach: in team approaches a single population evolves; each individual in the population represents a team of n components (Haynes et al., 1995; Luke and Spector, 1996; Soule, 1999; Brameier and Banzhaf, 2001). The fitness of an 'individual' (which represents a team) is based on the performance of the entire team. Studies of the team approach strongly suggest that it avoids correlated errors, each team member evolves to have few errors on a particular domain of the problem and the domain for each member is different (Soule, 1999; Brameier and Banzhaf, 2001). Thus, the whole team has very few unmasked errors. Although none of the studies directly measured expected failure rates the results strongly suggest that the member errors are inversely correlated. This is a reasonable result as all of the selective pressure is on the team - there is direct pressure on the individuals to evolve teams consisting of members that mask each others' errors.

Unfortunately, team based evolution has its own drawbacks. When the team members are tested as isolated solutions they perform significantly worse than evolved individuals, even though the team performs better than those same individuals (Soule, 2000; Brameier and Banzhaf, 2001). Thus, the team approach produces highly fit teams consisting of relatively poor individuals; whereas the island approach creates a reasonable team from highly fit individuals.

Bagging and boosting are two closely related techniques that have been combined with evolutionary techniques to create voting teams. Bagging uses a different set of training instances for each training round of the learning algorithm (Breiman, 1994). The training sets are created by randomly sampling, with replacement, from the set of all training instances. The team is created by combining the best individuals from each of the training iterations weighted according to how well the individual performs.

Boosting uses the entire set of training instances at each iteration of the learning algorithm. However, each training instance has a weight associated with it and the weight of the instances change with each iteration. Typically, training instances that were handled correctly in previous iterations have their weight reduced and training instances that were handled incorrectly have their weight increased (Schapire and Freund, 1999).

In combination algorithms an individual from each training round is kept to create the team, as in the bagging algorithm, and the instances used in each iteration have different weights, as in the boosting algorithm. Typically, the instances chosen for a given training round are those with the highest current weights (i.e. the instances that have proven hardest to solve). In 1999, Iba used boosting and bagging with evolutionary computation (Iba, 1999). His experiment validated that these techniques produce teams that perform better than individuals. There is evidence that boosting can introduce a large bias in the evolved teams, particularly when the training set is noisy or includes a few very difficult instances which will tend to dominate the training (Schapire and Freund, 1999; Maclin and Optiz, 1999; Kohavi, 1995; Obitz et al., 1999). This seems likely to produce members that are highly correlated because they have all evolved to focus on the same, heavily weighted, instances.

The algorithm proposed in this paper combines the island approach with the team approach to produce teams with highly fit components and with inversely correlated faults (or inversely correlated misclassifications for classification problems). We refer to our approach as orthogonal evolution of teams (OET).

3.   Orthogonal Evolution of Teams

OET defines a class of algorithms designed to put evolutionary pressure on both the evolving teams as a whole (as in existing team approaches) and on the team members (as in existing island approaches) by alternately treating the evolving population as a series of N independent populations/islands and as a single population of teams of M members.

The basic OET algorithm follows the steady-state evolutionary model: two offspring are generated each iteration and replace two existing individuals in the population. The specific algorithm tested here is:

```
Generate a population of teams
Repeat for X iterations{
    Repeat for each of the N islands{
        Select two highly fit team members
        // This produces two new team of highly fit
        // members to act as parents.
    }
    Apply crossover and mutation
    // This generates two offspring teams
    Select two low fitness teams to delete
    Insert the two offspring teams
    }
}
```

Here team members must have high fitness to be selected to act as parents and teams must have a high fitness to avoid being selected for replacement. Several similar algorithms could be employed. For example, teams could be selected for crossover and members for replacement or whole teams and individual members could be selected on alternate iterations.

To test the effectiveness of OET we test the following hypotheses:

1 OET produces team members whose fitness is significantly better than members produced with the team approach.

2 OET produces teams whose errors are inversely correlated. This shows that OET produces members that cooperate better than members evolved using island approaches.

3 OET produces teams whose performance is significantly better than evolved individuals.

4 OET produces teams whose performance is significantly better than teams evolved using either island or team approaches.

4. Experiments

Two problems are used to test these hypotheses: a simple, illustrative problem and a standard benchmark problem, the inter-twined spirals problem (Koza, 1992). Two versions of the illustrative problem are used, an unbiased version and a biased version, described in detail below.

Illustrative test problem

The illustrative test problem was specifically developed so that it would be easy to analyze the performance of the algorithms, particularly with respect to their error rates. In this problem there are 100 abstract 'errors', numbered 1 through 100, that can occur. The evolved members are integer vectors consisting of 70 integers in the range 1 to 100. Each integer represents a successfully detected or avoided error. For example, the individual member represented by the vector:

$$5|15|3|5|2|12|15$$

avoids errors 2, 3, 5, 12, and 15 and would have a fitness of 5 (a success rate of 5%) because it 'avoided' five of 100 the potential errors. Because individual members are only 70 integers long they can at best avoid 70 of the 100 errors. Having the same integer repeated (e.g. 5 and 15 in the above example) confers no additional benefit.

This simplified problem has several significant advantages for analyzing team behavior. First, the number of errors is known. Second, we can determine which errors are avoided by each individual. Third, the difficulty of avoiding a particular error is the same for every error, but can be changed (see the biased problem below). Finally, a perfect solution requires a team; any single member must have at least a 30% failure rate.

Voting.   For teams fitness is measured via majority vote in which each agent gets only one vote per fault. For example, given the three members:

5|15|3|5|2|12|15
2|11|9|7|2|15|21
1|17|3|9|1|17|17

errors 2, 3, 9, and 15 are avoided. Note that the errors do not have to have the same position in two team members to be masked by the vote. E.g. in the above example error 9 is avoided because members 2 and 3 both list it, at positions 3 and 4 respectively. However, the errors are only counted once per member. E.g. error 17 is not masked because it only appears in member 3, albeit 3 times. Other approaches are clearly possible, but this one most closely resembles the voting process commonly used in real world problems.

A simple and a biased version of this problem is used in these experiments. In the simple version every integer is equally likely in the initial, random population. None of the errors are easier or more likely to be found.

In the biased version of the problem the initial random individuals consists of integers in the range 1 to 80 only. The values 81 through 100 can only be obtained through mutation. This is analogous to a problem where some cases are relatively easy to solve (here cases 1 through 80) and some cases require additional searching (here 81 through 100).

We hypothesize that the island approach will produce correlated faults with the biased problem because in the island model there is no interaction between the islands to encourage independence. We further hypothesize that both the team approach and OET will generate independent or better members even with the biased problem.

Test algorithms.   Three algorithms, each based on a steady-state algorithm, are compared. The first algorithm is an island approach: n islands are allowed to evolve and the best individual from each island is used to form a team. The second algorithm uses the team approach: one population is evolved and each individual in the population is a team. The final algorithm is the OET algorithm described previously. Note that the results of single individual from a single in the island approach is equal to what would be achieved using a (steady-state) non-team approach.

Crossover is performed by randomly choosing one member of the first parent team and performing two point crossover with the equivalent member from the second parent team. Thus, member X of parent one is always crossed with member X of the second parent. This method has been show to improve the evolution of specialization and overall team performance (Haynes et al., 1995). The parameters for the steady-state algorithm are given in Table 6-1. Mutation changes an integer to a randomly selected integer in the range 1 to 100. Each of the three algorithms is tested with teams of size 3, 5 and 7 on both the biased and unbiased problems. Each test is run 100 times.

Table 6-1. Summary of the evolutionary algorithm parameters for the illustrative problem (middle column) and inter-twined spirals problem (rightmost column).

Fitness	Number of unique integers	error rate
Integer values	1 through 100	NA
Function Set	NA	+, -, *, /, sin, cos, iflt
Terminal Set	NA	X, Y, Constants
Population Size	500	400
Mutation Prob.	0.014	0.01
Selection	3 member tournament	
Run Time	500 Generations	200,000 iterations 600,000 for non-teams
Init. Population	Random individuals (len 70)	ramped half and half
Num. of trials	100	40

Computational complexity. A non-team, steady-state algorithm is used as the baseline for measuring the computational complexity of these algorithms. It requires two evaluations per iteration, one evaluation for each of the offspring. So, n iterations requires $2n$ evaluations.

The island approach evolves m independent populations, each of which uses a non-team, steady-state algorithm. Thus, the island approach requires $2nm$ evaluations. The team approach uses a single population so it requires $2n$ evaluations, but evaluating an 'individual' requires evaluating m team members. Thus, the total number of evaluations is also $2nm$. The OET algorithm also requires a total of $2nm$ evaluations, because it generates two teams for evaluation per iteration. We are assuming that the computational complexity of the voting process itself is negligible.

Expected Failure Rates. For each team the error rate of the members is measured using the expected error rate given by Equation 6.1. The expected error rates for teams of 3, 5, and 7 members whose individual failure rates are 30% are given in Table 6-2. A 30% failure rate is used because it represents the best possible performance by a single team member.

Results - illustrative problem. Figure 6-1 shows histograms for the six test cases (island, team, and OET approaches on the biased and unbiased problem). The histograms show the distribution of the members of the best teams and of the best teams as a function of fitness in the final generation. The data is plotted for the teams with three members so there are three sets of data for the team members totaling 300 members (100 trials * 3 members per best team per trial).

Table 6-2. Expected failure rates for majority vote teams with 3, 5, and 7 members each of which has a 0.3 failure rate and independent faults.

Team Size	Expected Failure Rate	Expected Success Rate
3	21.60	78.4
5	16.31	83.69
7	12.60	87.4

The bars for the team members tend to overlap because the members all have similar fitnesses. The bars for the best team total 100 (the best team from each of 100 trials) and show that the teams consistently perform better than the team members.

The upper-left histogram shows the distribution of fitnesses for the island approach on the unbiased problem. As expected the individual members are clustered very closely to the 70% success rate, with 222 members out of 300 having the optimal success rate. The success of the teams created by combining these members are distributed around the 78% success rate with an average success rate of 78.31%. This is not significantly different from the success rate predicted by the expected failure rate model (78.4%) (Student's t-test, $t = 0.28$, $P > 0.01$). (The results for the final generation for all of the algorithms and all three team sizes are summarized in Table 6-3.) Thus, the island approach produces members with independently correlated faults.

The upper-right histogram shows the distribution of fitnesses for the island approach on the biased problem. Again all three of the islands produce individuals with optimal or very close to optimal fitness. However, the average fitness of the best teams is now 77.13%. This is significantly below the 78.4% success rate predicted by the expected failure rate model (Student's t-teast, $P < 0.05$) and significantly below the results of the island approach on the unbiased problem. Thus, for problems in which some of the cases are easier to find solutions to the island approach does not produce members with independently correlated faults. If the bias were sufficiently extreme it is possible that the island model would produce individuals with perfectly correlated faults (each island would find the same solution) and there would be no benefit from producing teams.

The middle two histograms show the distribution of fitnesses for the team approach. For both the biased and unbiased problem the team members are distributed around a success rate that is lower than the optimal. E.g. for the biased problem the average member fitness is 67%, which is slightly, but significantly, poorer than those produced with the island approach (Student's two-tailed t-test, $t = 16.2$, $P < 0.01$). However, the average team success rates are quite good 98.08% and 97.39%; these significantly exceed the performance of the island approach (t = 82.9, P < 0.01 for the unbiased problem) and the predicted failure rate. Thus, confirming that the team approach does produce members with inversely correlated errors. The results also confirm that the team approach produces poorer members than the island approach. For this problem the difference is relatively small (see Table 6-3), but for more difficult problem the difference is more significant (see the inter-twined spirals problem below).

The last two histograms show the distribution of fitnesses for the OET approach. These histograms make it clear that the OET approach does combine the advantages of the island and team approaches. The team members are near optimal (average success rates of 69.89% and 69.84%). Further, the performance of the teams generated with the OET approach clearly exceeds the 78.4% success rate predicted by the failure rate model. This is significantly better than the team approach (e.g. t = 22.3, P < 0.01 for the unbiased problem). Thus, the OET approach clearly produces highly fit members whose errors are inversely correlated.

Table 6-3 summarizes the results in the final generation for all three team sizes on both the biased and unbiased problems. The results for teams of size 5 and 7 are similar to those observed for teams of size 3. The island approach produces optimal or near optimal individuals and teams whose fitnesses match the prediction of the expected failure rate model for the unbiased problem, but not for the biased problem. Confirming that the island approach is likely to fail to produce members with uncorrelated errors if some instances are easier to solve. Interestingly as the team size increases this becomes less of a problem.

For all team sizes the team approach produces sub-optimal individuals, but teams whose fitness significantly exceeds the fitness predicted by the expected failure rate model. Importantly, Table 6-3 shows that for the team approach, as the team size increases the average fitness of the team members declines significantly, resulting in poorer overall performance. This is a significant weakness of the team approach. We believe that the decline in member performance occurs because in the team approach selection is based on the team's fitness; the individual team members are only indirectly subjected to selection pressure and poor members may 'hitchhike' along with better members. As the teams become larger the importance of each member is decreased and the hitchhiking effect may be emphasized.

In all cases the OET approach produces highly fit members and highly fit teams. Unlike with the team approach member performance does not decline as team size increases. Demonstrating that the selective pressure applied directly to the team members in the OET approach is sufficient to maintain the members' fitness.

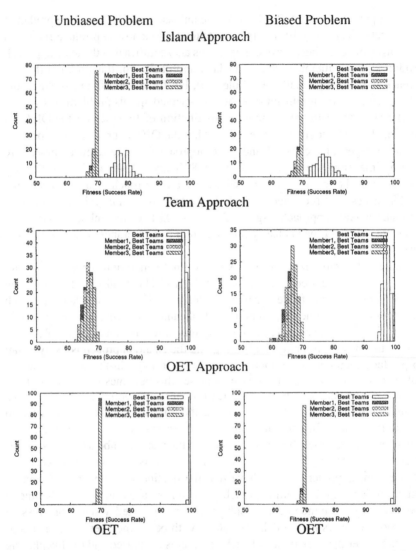

Figure 6-1. Distribution of fitnesses for each of the three algorithms (island, team, and OET top-to-bottom) on the unbiased (left column) and biased (right column) problems. Bars for the team members overlap significantly.

Inter-twined Spirals

The next set of results is based on the inter-twined spirals problem. For the inter-twined spirals problem two spirals coil around the origin of the x-y plane. Each spiral is defined by 97 points along its length. The goal is to find a function

Table 6-3. Average results for the best teams and members of the best teams for the biased and unbiased problems. Values in parentheses are standard deviations.

algorithm		Unbiased		Biased	
		Best Teams	Members Best	Best Teams	Members Best
Size 3	Island	78.31(2.24)	69.64(0.69)	77.13(2.58)	69.53(0.81)
	Team	98.08(0.82)	67.01(1.47)	97.39(1.07)	66.79(1.64)
	OET	99.96(0.20)	69.89(0.32)	99.95(0.22)	69.84(0.43)
Size 5	Island	83.51(2.35)	69.68(0.66)	77.54(1.67)	69.76(0.48)
	Team	97.57(1.18)	64.50(1.97)	92.85(1.31)	63.11(2.16)
	OET	100(0.00)	69.56(0.65)	100(0.00)	69.48(0.77)
Size 7	Island	86.93(2.61)	69.56(0.80)	85.47(2.75)	69.62(0.73)
	Team	93.45(1.66)	62.59(2.25)	87.35(1.74)	60.35(2.35)
	OET	100(0.00)	69.25(0.85)	99.97(0.17)	69.24(0.81)

that classifies the points as belonging to spiral 1 or spiral 2 based on the x,y value of the point. An evolved program return a real value. Values less than zero are mapped to spiral 1, values larger than or equal to zero are mapped to spiral 2.

The function set is {+, -, *, /, iflte, sine, cosine}. Division is protected as in the symbolic regression problem. The function iflte ("if less than else") takes four arguments, if the first is less than the second then the third argument is returned, otherwise the fourth argument is returned. The terminal set is {x, y, constant}; x and y are the x,y values of the point to be classified. Constants are real values, randomly generated in the range (-1.0,1.0). For constants, mutation adds a random value in the range (-1.0,1.0) to the constant's current value. Fitness is the percent of points misclassified. 0 is best, no points misclassified; 1.0 is worst, all points misclassified. On average a random classification will receive a fitness of 0.5. Parameter details are givien in Table 6-1.

Four algorithms are tested for the inter-twined spirals problem: evolved individuals (normal GP), the island model (with 3 islands), the teams model (teams of size 3), and OET (teams of size 3). The island, team, and OET approaches require three times as many evaluations as evolved individuals for the same number of iterations. Thus, to fairly compare the algorithms the evolving individuals are allowed to evolve for three times as many steady state iterations (600,000 iterations versus 200,000).

Table 6-4 presents the results, including expected team fitnesses, where appropriate. The performance of the members generated using the team approach is very poor, however, the teams' performance exceeds the expected performance confirming that the team approach produces teams members with inversely correlated errors.

Table 6-4. Results for the inter-twined spirals problem. Values in parentheses are standard deviations. The final column (predicted) is the predicted error rate of the average teams for the team and OET approaches and for the best teams (the only ones generated) with the island approach. For both the team and OET approach the actual failure rate is better (lower) than the predicted rate, showing that the members' errors are inversely correlated. For the island model the predicted error rate and actual error rate are similar showing that the errors are independent.

	Best Teams	Average Teams	Average Member	Predicted
Individuals	0.0960(0.0770)	0.1158(0.0780)	–	–
Team	0.0813(0.0555)	0.1160(0.0517)	0.3242(0.0609)	0.2472
OET	0.0439(0.0357)	0.0654(0.0377)	0.1806(0.0576)	0.0861
Island	0.0492(0.0293)	–	0.1375(0.0717)	0.0515

In contrast the performance of the members evolved with OET are fairly good, although they are not as fit as the evolved individuals. The performance of the best teams evolved with the OET approach is significantly better than either the evolved individuals (Student's t-test, $t = 4.74$, $P < 0.01$) or the evolved teams (Student's t-test, $t = 4.65$, $P < 0.01$). Comparison of the predicted and actual average team fitnesses confirms that OET also generates members with inversely correlated errors.

The members evolved with the island approach are also very fit (they are not as fit as the evolved individuals because the individuals evolved for 3 times as many iterations). The average fitness of the best teams evolved with the island approach is equivalent to the prediction of the expected failure rate model, confirming that the island approach produced members with independent failures.

5.   Conclusions

The results confirm that island approaches do produce members with independent errors, but only if all possible solutions are equivalent. For problems where some solutions are easier to find (e.g. the biased problem) all of the islands are likely to find the same, easier solutions, leading to correlated errors and decreasing the advantage of using teams.

Second, the results confirm that team approaches do produce members with inversely correlated errors, but with relatively poor members. This agrees with previous results that suggested that team approaches produce relatively poor members, but teams with high degrees of specialization and cooperation. The results also suggest that the drawbacks of having poor members will increase as the team size increases (Table 6-3) a serious limitation on the ability of team approaches to scale.

Third, OET clearly combines the advantages of the island and team approaches. OET generated both highly fit members and generated teams with inversely correlated faults.

Most importantly the results show the importance of considering both the fitness of the members and of the resulting teams. In particular, how the teams' fitness compares to the expected fitness as predicted by the expected failure rate model. The goal of any team or ensemble algorithm should be to optimize both member performance and the degree of correlation between members' errors. An algorithm that generates either substandard members or members with correlated errors has room for significant improvement.

References

Avizienis, A. and Kelly, J. B. J. (1984). Fault tolerance by design diversity: Concepts and experiments. In *IEEE Computer*, volume 17(8), pages 67–80.

Brameier, Markus and Banzhaf, Wolfgang (2001). Evolving teams of predictors with linear genetic programming. *Genetic Programming and Evolvable Machines*, 2(4):381–408.

Breiman, L. (1994). Bagging predictor, technical report 421. Technical report, University of California Berkley.

Cantu-Paz, Erick and Kamath, Chandrika (2003). Inducing oblique decision trees with evolutionary algorithms. *IEEE Transactions on Evolutionary Computation*, 7(1):54–68.

Feldt, R. (1998). Generating multiple diverse software versions with genetic programming. In *Proceedings of the 24th EUROMICRO Conference, Workshop on Dpendable Computing Systems*, pages 387–396.

Hatton, L. (1997). N-version vs. one good program. In *IEEE Software*, volume 14(6), pages 71–76.

Haynes, Thomas, Sen, Sandip, Schoenefeld, Dale, and Wainwright, Roger (1995). Evolving a team. In Siegel, E. V. and Koza, J. R., editors, *Working Notes for the AAAI Symposium on Genetic Programming*, pages 23–30, MIT, Cambridge, MA, USA. AAAI.

Hilford, V., Lyu, M. R., Cukie, B., Jamoussi, A., and Bastani, F. B. (1997). Diversity in the software development process. In *Proceedings of WORDS'97*.

Iba, Hitoshi (1997). Multiple-agent learning for a robot navigation task by genetic programming. In Koza, John R., Deb, Kalyanmoy, Dorigo, Marco, Fogel, David B., Garzon, Max, Iba, Hitoshi, and Riolo, Rick L., editors, *Genetic Programming 1997: Proceedings of the Second Annual Conference*, pages 195–200, Stanford University, CA, USA. Morgan Kaufmann.

Iba, Hitoshi (1999). Bagging, boosting, and bloating in genetic programming. In *Proceedings of the Genetic and Evolutionary Computation Conference: GECCO-1999*, pages 1053–1060. Morgan Kaufmann.

Imamura, Kosuke, Heckendorn, Robert B., Soule, Terence, and Foster, James A. (2002). N-version genetic programming via fault masking. In Foster, James A., Lutton, Evelyne, Miller, Julian, Ryan, Conor, and Tettamanzi, Andrea G. B., editors, *Genetic Programming, Proceedings of the 5th European Conference, EuroGP 2002*, volume 2278 of *LNCS*, pages 172–181, Kinsale, Ireland. Springer-Verlag.

Imamura, Kosuke, Soule, Terence, Heckendorn, Robert B., and Foster, James A. (2003). Behavioral diversity and a probabilistically optimal GP ensemble. *Genetic Programming and Evolvable Machines*, 4(3):235–253.

Knight, J. C. and Leveson, N. B. (1986). An experimental evaluation of the assumption of independence in multiversion programming. In *IEEE Transactions on Software Engineering*, volume 12.

Kohavi, R. (1995). A study of cross-validation and bootstrap for accuracy estimation and model selection. In *Proceedings of the 14th International Joint Conference on Artificial Intelligence (ICJA)*, pages 1137–1145. Morgan Kaufmann.

Koza, John (1992). A genetic approach to the truck backer upper problem and the inter-twined spiral problem. In *Proceedings of IJCNN International Joint Conference on Neural Networks*, pages 310–318. IEEE Press.

Liu, Yong, Yao, Xin, and Higuchi, Tetsuya (2000). Evolutionary ensembles with negative correlation learning. *IEEE Transactions on Evolutionary Computation*, 4(4):380–387.

Luke, Sean and Spector, Lee (1996). Evolving teamwork and coordination with genetic programming. In Koza, John R., Goldberg, David E., Fogel, David B., and Riolo, Rick L., editors, *Genetic Programming 1996: Proceedings of the First Annual Conference*, pages 150–156, Stanford University, CA, USA. MIT Press.

Maclin, R. and Optiz, D. (1999). An empirical evaluation of bagging and boosting. In *Proceedings of the 14th International Conference on Artificial Intelligence*, pages 546–551. AAAI Press/MIT Press.

Maqsood, Imran, Khan, Muhammad Raiz, and Abraham, Ajith (2004). An ensemble of neural networks for weather prediction. *Neural Computing and Applications*, 13(2):112–123.

Obitz, D. W., Basak, S. C., and Gute, B. D. (1999). Hazard assessment modeling: An evolutionary ensemble approach. In *Proceedings of the Genetic and Evolutionary Computation Conference: GECCO-1999*, pages 1543–1650. Morgan Kaufmann.

Peng, K., Vucetic, S., Radivojac, P., Brown, C.J., Dunker, A.K., and Obradovic, Z. (2004). Optimizing long intrinsic disorder predictors with protein evolutionary information. *Journal of Bioinformatics and Computational Biology*, 3(1):1–26.

Platel, Michael Defoin, Chami, Malik, Clergue, Manuel, and Collard, Philippe (2005). Teams of genetic predictors for inverse problem solving. In *Proceeding of the 8th European Conference on Genetic Programming - EuroGP 2005*.

Raik, Simon and Durnota, Bohdan (1994). The evolution of sporting strategies. In Stonier, Russel J. and Yu, Xing Huo, editors, *Complex Systems: Mechanisms of Adaption*, pages 85–92. IOS Press.

Schapire, R. E. and Freund, Y. (1999). A short introduction to boosting. In *Journal of the Japanese Society for Artificial Intelligence*, volume 14(5), pages 771–780.

Soule, Terence (1999). Voting teams: A cooperative approach to non-typical problems. In Banzhaf, Wolfgang, Daida, Jason, Eiben, Agoston E., Garzon, Max H., Honavar, Vasant, Jakiela, Mark, and Smith, Robert E., editors, *Proceedings of the Genetic and Evolutionary Computation Conference*, pages 916–922, Orlando, Florida, USA. Morgan Kaufmann.

Soule, Terence (2000). Heterogeneity and specialization in evolving teams. In *Proceedings of the Genetic and Evolutionary Computation Conference (GECCO-2000)*, pages 778–785, Las Vegas, Nevada, USA. Morgan Kaufmann.

Soule, Terence (2003). Cooperative evolution on the intertwined spirals problem. In *Genetic Programming: Proceedings of the 6th European Conference on Genetic Programming, EuroGP 2003*, pages 434–442. Springer-Verlag.

Widmer, Gerhard (2003). Discovering simple rules in complex data: a meta-learning algorithm and some surprising musical discoveries. *Artificial Intelligence*, 146:129–148.

Zang, B. T. and Joung, J. G. (1997). Enhancing robustness of genetic programming at the species level. In *Proceedings of the 2nd Annual Conference on Genetic Programming*, pages 336–342. Morgan Kaufmann.

Chapter 7

MULTIDIMENSIONAL TAGS, COOPERATIVE POPULATIONS, AND GENETIC PROGRAMMING

Lee Spector[1] and Jon Klein[2]

[1] *Cognitive Science, Hampshire College, Amherst, MA, 01002-3359 USA.;* [2] *Physical Resource Theory, Chalmers University of Technology & Göteborg University, Göteborg, Sweden.*

Abstract   We present new results on the evolution of tag-mediated cooperation, demonstrating that the use of multidimensional tags can enhance the emergence of high levels of cooperation. We discuss these results in the context of prior cases in which work on the evolution of cooperation has led to practical techniques for improving the problem-solving performance of genetic programming systems.

Keywords: genetic programming, cooperation, tags, diversity, multi agent systems, population structure

1.   Cooperation and adaptive complexity

In this chapter we explore the conditions under which altruistic cooperation is produced by natural selection, and we do so as part of an effort to improve the problem-solving performance of genetic programming systems. But why would anyone think that the evolution of cooperation would provide clues for the improvement of problem solving systems? What does cooperation have to do with the kinds of adaptive complexity that we seek from our genetic programming systems?

One answer is that this connection—between the study of the evolution of cooperation and the improvement of problem-solving performance—has been fruitful in the past, so it might be worth exploring further (see Section 6 below). But a deeper answer might also draw on the observation that many biological systems appear to make use of cooperative interactions at several levels of organization, and that these interactions may be important for the evolution of adaptive complexity.

Adaptive complexity in nature is usually produced not by isolated individuals but rather by ecosystems that are structured by both genetic and economic relationships. Typically many of these relationships involve cooperation or other forms of mutualism. Indeed, some theorists have credited cooperation with an essential role in the evolutionary transitions that produced successive levels of adaptive complexity in the history of life. For example, in discussing the origin of multicellularity Michod writes:

> We see the formation of cooperative interactions among lower-level individuals
> as a necessary step in evolutionary transitions; only cooperation transfers fitness
> from lower levels (costs to group members) to higher levels (benefits to the group).
> —(Michod, 2003, p. 292)

So there are reasons to think that cooperation can be important in adaptive evolutionary systems. It is therefore reasonable to expect useful insights, even for practical applications, to emerge from the study of the evolution of cooperation.

In the remainder of this chapter we discuss these issues in more concrete terms, focusing on a particular model of cooperation and on ways in which a new development within this model might be applied to genetic programming practice. In the next two sections we describe the model (tag-mediated cooperation) and then the new development (the use of multidimensional tags). We then provide quantitative results, a discussion of the meaning of those results, and several suggestions for incorporation of related mechanisms into genetic programming systems. These suggestions are speculative but we argue that they merit further exploration.

2.   Tag-mediated cooperation

Altruism and cooperation are behavioral traits that have long drawn the attention of evolutionary theorists. From a naive reading of Darwinian theory one might expect that natural selection would produce only selfish agents, and that cooperation would be maladaptive and therefore rare. Early theorists recognized, however, that while natural selection may favor selfish *genes* it does not necessarily favor selfish *agents*. Beginning with Hamilton in the 1960s biologists have built and tested quantitative theories of the evolution of cooperative behavior among kin, grounded in the understanding that degree of kinship and degree of genetic similarity are closely related (Hamilton, 1963; Hamilton, 1964). More recent work has expanded the class of conditions under which cooperation can be expected to evolve; such conditions now include the presence of reciprocating partners (Axelrod and Hamilton, 1981; Trivers, 1972) and the presence of partners with good reputations (Nowak and Sigmund, 1998).

Models of "tag-mediated" cooperation have the potential to explain the evolution of cooperation in an even wider range of cases. A tag is a simple marker, represented in most of the prior models as a floating point number, that is attached to each agent and is visible to other agents (Holland, 1995). Tags can be used to model a variety of identity-based interactions in biological systems, some of which have physical implementations that are far simpler than those that underly judgments of kinship, reciprocation, or reputation.

In the models of tag-mediated cooperation first presented by Riolo et al. (Riolo et al., 2001) each agent has both a floating point tag and a floating point "tolerance," and one agent will make an altruistic donation to another if the tags of the two agents differ by no more than the donor's tolerance. The simulation proceeds through rounds of donation attempts followed by reproductive tournaments, the winners of which become, after possible mutation, the agents for the next generation of donations and reproductive tournaments.

Roberts and Sherratt raised concerns about the original model and noted that cooperation failed to emerge if tolerances were allowed to drop below zero, thereby permitting truly selfish agents (Roberts and Sherratt, 2002). While Roberts and Sherratt were correct in the context of the particular values that they chose for system parameters, subsequent work has shown that tag-mediated cooperation does indeed arise robustly under a variety of equally reasonable parameter settings (Riolo et al., 2002; Axelrod et al., 2004; Spector and Klein, 2006). Some of our previous work, in particular, showed that cooperation readily emerges, even when tolerances are allowed to drop below zero, if mutation rates are low and/or if agent interactions are geographically limited (Spector and Klein, 2006). These results inspired a practical technique for improving the performance of genetic programming systems, which we discuss briefly in Section 6. The new work presented in Sections 3, 12-3 and 5 extends our previous results and may have additional implications for genetic programming practice (also discussed in Section 6).

3.   Multidimensional tags

Our observations of the previous models and their dynamics revealed that a group of cooperators can be destabilized in a number of ways. Downward tolerance drift is dangerous for a group of cooperators because a mutation resulting in low or even negative tolerance produces a selfish agent situated to exploit its generous neighbors with similar or identical tags. Upward tolerance drift is also dangerous because it may lead to overly generous agents that begin to donate to agents outside of the group. Finally, even agents with well-balanced tolerance values may be invaded by selfish agents that are able to mimic their tags. Because agents are not able to explicitly manipulate their own tags, this can occur only as a result of random mutation.

This last possibility is the focus of our current work. Invasions by selfish mimics can occur only when the invaders successfully "guess," by means of mutation, the tags of nearby cooperators. One can think of each cooperator's tag as a password and a successful invader as a hacker who has discovered that password, although the hacker's only means for discovery is random mutation. On the other hand, the hacker need not get the password exactly right; it will succeed if it falls within the cooperator's tolerance of the cooperator's tag.

This analogy leads naturally to a hypothesis that cooperation may be more easily maintained if tag values are made more difficult to mimic. To improve the security of a password-secured system we can increase the length of the password; by analogy we can increase the "security" of tag-mediated cooperation by adding additional dimensions to the tags.

In this chapter we explore how the introduction of multidimensional real-valued tags can lead to improved cooperation in evolving populations. Earlier work on this theme has been conducted by Hales and Edmonds, who have experimented with multidimensional tags in the form of bit strings (Hales, D., 2005; Edmonds, 2006). Some of these models allow only exact tag matching, while others use the Hamming distance between bit strings as a measure of tag difference. By contrast, we have retained the real-valued tag and tolerance scheme from the models of Riolo et al. (Riolo et al., 2001) but we have extended it to use tags consisting of sequences of real values.[1]

We begin with a model similar to those used in prior work deriving from Riolo et al., (Riolo et al., 2001) in which a population of 100 agents is run through a series of generations (30,000 in previous work; 400,000 here). At each generation, agents begin with a score of 0 and are given the opportunity to make donations to $P = 3$ randomly chosen agents. An agent makes a donation to a recipient if and only if the difference between their tag values is less than or equal to the potential donor's tolerance value. If a donation event occurs then a cost C is deducted from the donor's score (which is allowed to go negative) and a benefit B is added to the recipient's score. In the original model, the values $C = 0.1$ and $B = 1.0$ were used; in this chapter and in our previous work we investigate a variety of cost to benefit ratios with $C = \{0.1, 0.5, 1.0\}$ and $B = 1.0$.

After all donation interactions have been completed, agents are selected for reproduction based on their scores. Each agent at position N is paired randomly with another agent; the agent with a higher score (or the agent at N in the event of a tie) is selected for reproduction at position N. The child inherits its tag and tolerance from the parent, but each is mutated with probability $m = \{0.001, 0.01, 0.1\}$. When a tag is mutated it is replaced by a new value, sampled uniformly from $[0, 1]$. Tolerance values are mutated by summation with random Gaussian noise with standard deviation 0.01. As in the work

---

[1] Edmonds refers to systems with "multi-dimensional binary and continuous vectors" but we are not aware of published details (Edmonds, 2006).

of Roberts and Sherratt (Roberts and Sherratt, 2002), the tolerance value is clamped to a lower bound of -10^{-6}.

As in our previous work on this model we introduce a simple form of spatial structure, or geography, that changes the way that agents interact. We model the population as a one dimensional ring in which agents consider only others in a local radius R when selecting recipients for donations or competitors for reproduction. We examine a variety of values for R from 1 up to 50. Note that the special case of $R = 50$ is equivalent to the non-spatial populations used in previous models.

In our multidimensional tag model the single floating point tag value is replaced by a vector of floating point values. The definition of the distance between two tags, t_1 and t_2, is generalized for n dimensions as:

$$\sqrt{\sum_{i=1}^{n} (t_1[i] - t_2[i])^2} \tag{7.1}$$

As in previous models, tag mutation produces completely new tag values; each value in the tag vector is replaced by a new random value, uniformly sampled from $[0, 1]$.

Tolerance values remain as single floating point values and are interpreted as they were in previous models: an agent shares with another agent if and only if the difference in their tags is less than or equal to the donor's tolerance. We note that while the maximum multidimensional tag distance, given by $\sqrt{n}$, exceeds the 1.0 limit found in the previous tag models, there is no upper bound on the tolerance value so that the model allows for cooperation between any pair of agents, even those with large tag differences. In practice, tolerance values tend to be far smaller than the maximum distance value.

4. Results

We performed 92 runs for each condition and collected average donation rates and tolerance values. The results are presented here as averages over all runs in each condition.

We first discuss the results in the conditions in which the cost (C) charged to a cooperating agent for a successful donation was 0.1. This is the cost structure that has received the greatest attention in the literature. As in the prior work we characterize the amount of cooperation in a condition by reporting the percentage of donation attempts that are successful across the entire population and across the entire simulation; we call this measure the "donation rate."

Figure 7-1 shows the average donation rates under all $C = 0.1$ conditions. The vertical bars show the average donation rates for standard, one-dimensional tags for each combination of mutation rate and interaction radius. This data

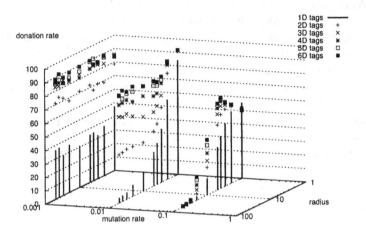

Figure 7-1. Average donation rates as a function of mutation rate, interaction radius, and number of tag dimensions. For the data in this graph the cost (C) charged to a cooperating agent for each donation was 0.1, as in most of the prior research. Each plotted point represents the average of 92 independent runs.

replicates that from our previous studies, although the data plotted here is from new, independent runs. In line with and generally above each vertical bar in Figure 7-1 are symbols plotting the average donation rates for runs with higher-dimensional tags.

The one-dimensional data demonstrates that cooperation readily emerges except in a few conditions with high mutation rates and large interaction radii (the very conditions that formed basis of the critique by Roberts and Sherratt (Roberts and Sherratt, 2002)). In all but the most recalcitrant of these conditions the levels of cooperation are further boosted by increasing the dimensions of the tags. Substantial improvements result from the first augmentation to two-dimensional tags, and significant improvements result from the next several augmentations as well. In most cases the payoff for additional dimensions eventually tapers off, presumably because the advantages that can be gained by making one's tag hard to mimic have a natural limit; as the probability of randomly generating a particular tag approaches zero, little is to be gained by decreasing the probability further.

Figure 7-2 shows the average donation rates under all $C = 0.5$ conditions. In this higher cost regime cooperation is slightly harder to achieve, but significant cooperation nonetheless results from most of the parameter sets that we tested. Note that the levels of cooperation for higher numbers of dimensions are more

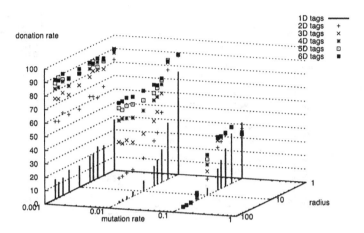

Figure 7-2. Average donation rates as a function of mutation rate, interaction radius, and number of tag dimensions. For the data in this graph the cost (C) charged to a cooperating agent for each donation was 0.5, which is five times the cost used in most of the prior research. Each plotted point represents the average of 92 independent runs.

spread out, and that in many cases a significant improvement can be achieved when increasing the number of dimensions from 5 to 6. This may reflect the fact that invasions by selfish agents, while rare in a simulation with five-dimensional tags, are highly disruptive when they do occur.

Figure 7-3 shows the average donation rates under all of the $C = 1.0$ conditions. In these "zero sum" conditions the cost to a donor is equivalent to the benefit gained by a recipient, and cooperation is significantly harder to achieve. As was reported previously, significant levels of cooperation can nonetheless be achieved even with one-dimensional tags, with donation rates exceeding 12% in one of our tested configurations. As can be seen in Figure 7-3, however, one can achieve significantly higher levels of cooperation with higher-dimensional tags. Indeed, with a mutation rate of $m = 0.01$, an interaction radius of $R = 1$, and six-dimensional tags we observe a donation rate of 75.7%.

Figures 7-4, 7-5, and 7-6 show the average observed tolerances in the conditions with donation cost $C = 0.1$, $C = 0.5$, and $C = 1.0$ respectively. Note that cooperation is possible even with a tolerance of zero, although a zero-tolerance agent will cooperate only with others that have identical tags. The presence of larger tolerances indicates agents that will donate to a wider range of recipients. Note also that while negative tolerances are possible, all of the

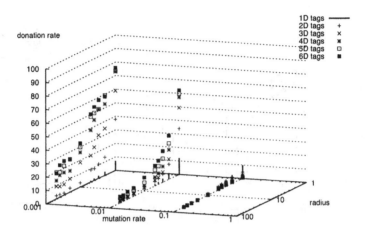

Figure 7-3. Average donation rates as a function of mutation rate, interaction radius, and number of tag dimensions. For the data in this graph the cost (C) charged to a cooperating agent for each donation was 1.0, the same as the benefit to the recipient. Each plotted point represents the average of 92 independent runs.

average tolerance values that we observed were non-negative; this is why no negative tolerances appear in our graphs.

In nearly all cases the observed tolerance is higher with higher-dimensional tags. This can be explained as resulting from the fact that multidimensional tags increase the size of the "tag space" and thereby reduce the risk of outside invasion. By doing this they allow groups of cooperating agents to safely raise their tolerance values and thus protect themselves from the secondary threat of self-destruction due to a crash in tolerance values.

5.   Discussion

In our previous analysis of the one-dimensional case we suggested that the mechanism behind tag-mediated cooperation can be thought of as a kind of "probabalistic kin selection" (Spector and Klein, 2006). While the agents in the model have no access to explicit kinship information, and therefore cannot be certain that they are donating to kin, successful tag-mediated cooperation can nonetheless arise because kin are more likely to have similar tags.

Our findings here bolster this notion by clarifying the evolutionary dynamic behind the perpetuation of cooperating subpopulations. The tag mutation scheme in our model, which was taken from the previous work in the literature (Riolo et al., 2001), does not generally produce new tag values that are close to

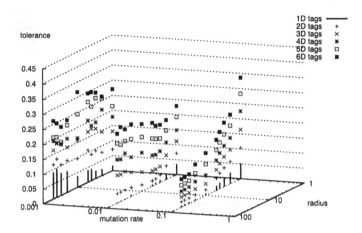

Figure 7-4. Average tolerances as a function of mutation rate, interaction radius, and number of tag dimensions. For the data in this graph the cost (C) charged to a cooperating agent for each donation was 0.1, as in most of the prior research. Each plotted point represents the average of 92 independent runs.

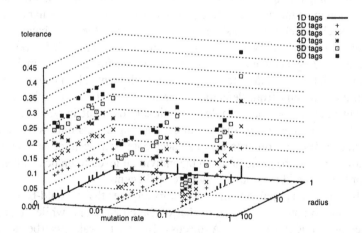

Figure 7-5. Average tolerances as a function of mutation rate, interaction radius, and number of tag dimensions. For the data in this graph the cost (C) charged to a cooperating agent for each donation was 0.5, which is five times the cost used in most of the prior research. Each plotted point represents the average of 92 independent runs.

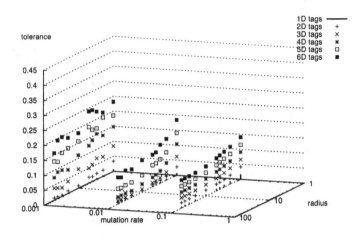

Figure 7-6. Average tolerances as a function of mutation rate, interaction radius, and number of tag dimensions. For the data in this graph the cost (C) charged to a cooperating agent for each donation was 1.0, the same as the benefit to the recipient. Each plotted point represents the average of 92 independent runs.

those of their ancestors. Instead, tags mutate spontaneously to entirely new values, meaning that agents with a common ancestor have either identical tag values or, following a mutation event, tag values that are no more similar than those of completely unrelated agents. Tolerance values, on the other hand, are subject to incremental drift. Were it not for incremental tolerance drift a population of cooperating agents would probably settle on an infinitesimally small "optimal" value which would allow for cooperation with identically tagged agents while avoiding invasion from defectors. The incremental drift of tolerance values, however, creates a more complex evolutionary dynamic in which, on the group level, a subpopulation of successful cooperating agents must strive for *higher* tolerance values in order to avoid an accidental self-destructive tolerance drop below zero. At the same time, on the individual level, tolerance values must be kept low to avoid exploitation by unrelated agents.

Invasion of a population of cooperators requires that a would-be freeloader's tag value mutates to be close to that of the cooperators, while maintaining a tolerance value close to zero. As discussed above, tag values can be thought of as passwords shared among kin, albeit passwords with "fuzzy" interpretations due to the effects of tolerance values. With multidimensional tags, the passwords become exponentially more difficult to guess. Note that the exponential nature of the "password guessing problem" means that multidimensional tags cannot be exploited simply by increasing the mutation rate: the complexity of the passwords grows too quickly for mutation to keep up. Note also that there is a tradeoff between the advantages of multidimensional tags and the need for more sophisticated mechanisms (cognitive, chemical or otherwise) to maintain and recognize them.

Although we feel that our findings support the notion of "probabalistic kin selection" in this model and similar models, our findings do not preclude the possibility that other mechanisms can also support tag-mediated cooperation. For example, Hales has shown that tag-based models can lead to cooperation among groups of unrelated agents with diverse skills (Hales, 2002). Our probabalistic kin selection interpretation is also compatible with other recent analyses of tag mediated cooperation (e.g. (Jansen and van Baalen, 2006)).

6.   Cooperation and genetic programming

Researchers have previously drawn several connections between work on the evolution of cooperation and work on evolutionary computation. One example comes from our own prior work on tag-mediated cooperation , in which we highlighted the ways in which a particularly simple form of spatial structure can enhance the evolvability of cooperative behavior (Spector and Klein, 2006). Spatial structure has also long been applied to evolutionary computation, often as a mechanism to preserve population diversity (Collins and Jefferson, 1991; Pettey, 1997; Fernandez et al., 2003; Folino et al., 2003). But the models of spatial structure previously employed in evolutionary computation have generally been more complex than the simple one-dimensional geographic scheme we used in our study of cooperation, and we were curious about whether the our scheme, which we called "trivial geography," would provide benefits for GP. In our contribution to last year's meeting of the *Genetic Programming Theory and Practice* workshop we presented results showing that, indeed, trivial geography can enhance the problem-solving power of GP systems, at least on the symbolic regression problems that we studied (Spector and Klein, 2005).

In the context of the new results presented above we are also curious about ways in which tags themselves might contribute to advances in genetic programming practice. Our comments about such possibilities here are speculative, but we believe there are several avenues worth pursuing.

One possibility is that tags, like trivial geography, might be used to better control the diversity of an evolving population. We have seen that tags can be used as surrogates for kin identifiers, and therefore as easily computed probabilistic indicators of genetic similarity or diversity. A great deal of recent work in genetic programming has focused on diversity metrics that may form the basis of mechanisms for diversity management (Burke et al., 2002). A number of specific mechanisms for diversity management have also been developed, for example mechanisms based on mate selection (Fry and Tyrrell, 2003; Fry et al., 2005). We speculate that multidimensional tags, which we have shown to facilitate the formation of clusters of cooperatively interacting agents, might also be used as the basis of mate selection schemes that combine in-breeding and out-breeding to balance exploration and exploitation.

Another way that these results might be exploited in genetic programming concerns work on the evolution of cooperative multiagent systems. Several researchers have previously used genetic programming to produce teams of cooperating agents, using a variety of mechanisms for team-member recognition and coordination (Luke and Spector, 1996; Soule, 2000; Brameier and Banzhaf, 2001). The prospect raised by new theoretical work on tag-mediated cooperation is that the very simple mechanisms used for team-member recognition and coordination in these models might also serve as a solid foundation for cooperation in much more complex systems. We have previously shown that tag-mediated cooperation readily emerges in evolving multiagent swarms (Spector et al., 2005), and more recently we have seen tag-mediated cooperation emerge in evolving populations of blocks that can grow and divide. To the extent that any such multiagent systems can benefit from tag-based cooperation we might expect multidimensional tags to provide even greater advantages.

Finally, there is a sense in which GP systems are themselves multiagent systems within which the "agents" — in this case the individual programs in an evolving population — might benefit from cooperation with one another. For example, in some of our prior work we allowed all of the individuals in a population and across evolutionary time to access a shared indexed memory, or "culture" (Spector and Luke, 1996). Several researchers have experimented with shared code in the form of automatically defined library functions (Racine et al., 1998; Ryan et al., 2004; Keijzer et al., 2005). And several fitness sharing, niching, and crowding schemes involve the sharing or distribution of positions in fitness space (McKay, 2000; Gustafson, 2004). Where there are common resources there are probably also opportunities for cooperation and coordination, for example to arbitrate the retention of commonly useful data or code fragments. Tags might provide a simple yet effective mechanism for achieving the requisite cooperation and coordination, and if they do so then again one would expect multidimensional tags to have even greater utility.

More generally the study of the evolution of cooperation, insofar as it challenges naive perspectives on Darwinian mechanisms, has helped to lay bare some of the fundamental dynamical properties of interdependent populations under natural selection. It would not be surprising, therefore, for such studies produce models with features that are applicable to evolutionary computation in general, and to genetic programming in particular. We note also that this research strategy, of borrowing specific pieces of theory from recent work in evolutionary biology and using them to enhance genetic programming systems, follows our general methodological suggestion from the first *Genetic Programming Theory and Practice* workshop (Spector, 2003).

7. Conclusions

We have presented the results of new experiments on computational models of tag-mediated cooperation . Our results demonstrate that the evolution of tag-mediated cooperation can be facilitated by the use of multidimensional tags. We analyzed these results as a form of "probabilistic kin selection" and used the analogy of password-guessing to explain the observed patterns of cooperation and tolerance.

We discussed possible applications of these results to GP. While our suggestions for application were speculative we noted that similar efforts have already borne fruit and that there are good reasons to be optimistic about future results. More generally, we argued that cooperative exchanges build networks of interaction that can support the evolution of adaptive complexity. For this reason we expect that the study of the evolution of cooperation will continue to produce important insights that can be applied to genetic programming.

Acknowledgments

This material is based upon work supported by the United States National Science Foundation under Grant No. 0308540 and Grant No. 0216344. Any opinions, findings, and conclusions or recommendations expressed in this publication are those of the authors and do not necessarily reflect the views of the National Science Foundation. The authors also thank Jason Daida, Michael Korns, and the other participants in the Genetic Programming Theory and Practice IV Workshop for many helpful suggestions.

References

Axelrod, R. and Hamilton, W. D. (1981). The evolution of cooperation. *Science*, 211:1390–1396.

Axelrod, R., Hammond, R. A., and Grafen, A. (2004). Altruism via kin-selection strategies that rely on arbitrary tags with which they coevolve. *Evolution*, 58:1833–1838.

Brameier, Markus and Banzhaf, Wolfgang (2001). Evolving teams of predictors with linear genetic programming. *Genetic Programming and Evolvable Machines*, 2(4):381–407.

Burke, Edmund, Gustafson, Steven, and Kendall, Graham (2002). A survey and analysis of diversity measures in genetic programming. In Langdon, W. B., Cantú-Paz, E., Mathias, K., Roy, R., Davis, D., Poli, R., Balakrishnan, K., Honavar, V., Rudolph, G., Wegener, J., Bull, L., Potter, M. A., Schultz, A. C., Miller, J. F., Burke, E., and Jonoska, N., editors, *GECCO 2002: Proceedings of the Genetic and Evolutionary Computation Conference*, pages 716–723, New York. Morgan Kaufmann Publishers.

Collins, Robert J. and Jefferson, David R. (1991). Selection in massively parallel genetic algorithms. In Belew, Rick and Booker, Lashon, editors, *Proceedings of the Fourth International Conference on Genetic Algorithms*, pages 249–256, San Mateo, CA. Morgan Kaufman.

Edmonds, Bruce (2006). The emergence of symbiotic groups resulting from skill-differentiation and tags. *Journal of Artificial Societies and Social Simulation*, 9(1).

Fernandez, Francisco, Tomassini, Marco, and Vanneschi, Leonardo (2003). An empirical study of multipopulation genetic programming. *Genetic Programming and Evolvable Machines*, 4(1):21–51.

Folino, G., Pizzuti, C., Spezzano, G., Vanneschi, L., and Tomassini, M. (2003). Diversity analysis in cellular and multipopulation genetic programming. In Sarker, Ruhul, Reynolds, Robert, Abbass, Hussein, Tan, Kay Chen, McKay, Bob, Essam, Daryl, and Gedeon, Tom, editors, *Proceedings of the 2003 Congress on Evolutionary Computation CEC2003*, pages 305–311, Canberra. IEEE Press.

Fry, Rodney, Smith, Stephen L., and Tyrrell, Andy M. (2005). A self-adaptive mate selection model for genetic programming. In Corne, David, Michalewicz, Zbigniew, Dorigo, Marco, Eiben, Gusz, Fogel, David, Fonseca, Carlos, Greenwood, Garrison, Chen, Tan Kay, Raidl, Guenther, Zalzala, Ali, Lucas, Simon, Paechter, Ben, Willies, Jennifer, Guervos, Juan J. Merelo, Eberbach, Eugene, McKay, Bob, Channon, Alastair, Tiwari, Ashutosh, Volkert, L. Gwenn, Ashlock, Dan, and Schoenauer, Marc, editors, *Proceedings of the 2005 IEEE Congress on Evolutionary Computation*, volume 3, pages 2707–2714, Edinburgh, UK. IEEE Press.

Fry, Rodney and Tyrrell, Andy (2003). Enhancing the performance of GP using an ancestry-based mate selection scheme. In Cantú-Paz, E., Foster, J. A., Deb, K., Davis, D., Roy, R., O'Reilly, U.-M., Beyer, H.-G., Standish, R., Kendall, G., Wilson, S., Harman, M., Wegener, J., Dasgupta, D., Potter, M. A., Schultz, A. C., Dowsland, K., Jonoska, N., and Miller, J., editors, *Genetic and Evolutionary Computation – GECCO-2003*, volume 2724 of *LNCS*, pages 1804–1805, Chicago. Springer-Verlag.

Gustafson, Steven (2004). *An Analysis of Diversity in Genetic Programming*. PhD thesis, School of Computer Science and Information Technology, University of Nottingham, Nottingham, England.

Hales, David (2002). Smart agents don't need kin - evolving specialisation and cooperation with tags. Technical Report CPM Working Paper 02-89 (version 1), Centre for Policy Modelling.

Hales, D. (2005). Altruism ÒFor FreeÓ using Tags. In *Paris ECCS'05 Conference, Nov. 2005*.

Hamilton, W. D. (1963). The evolution of altruistic behavior. *American Naturalist*, 97:354–356.

Hamilton, W. D. (1964). The genetical evolution of social behaviour. i. *Journal of Theoretical Biology*, 7:1–16.

Holland, J. H. (1995). *Hidden Order: How Adaptation Builds Complexity*. Perseus Books.

Jansen, V. A. A. and van Baalen, M (2006). Altruism through beard chromodynamics. *Nature*, 440:663–666.

Keijzer, Maarten, Ryan, Conor, Murphy, Gearoid, and Cattolico, Mike (2005). Undirected training of run transferable libraries. In Keijzer, Maarten, Tettamanzi, Andrea, Collet, Pierre, van Hemert, Jano I., and Tomassini, Marco, editors, *Proceedings of the 8th European Conference on Genetic Programming*, volume 3447 of *Lecture Notes in Computer Science*, pages 361–370, Lausanne, Switzerland. Springer.

Luke, Sean and Spector, Lee (1996). Evolving teamwork and coordination with genetic programming. In Koza, John R., Goldberg, David E., Fogel, David B., and Riolo, Rick L., editors, *Genetic Programming 1996: Proceedings of the First Annual Conference*, pages 150–156, Stanford University, CA, USA. MIT Press.

McKay, R I (Bob) (2000). Fitness sharing in genetic programming. In Whitley, Darrell, Goldberg, David, Cantu-Paz, Erick, Spector, Lee, Parmee, Ian, and Beyer, Hans-Georg, editors, *Proceedings of the Genetic and Evolutionary Computation Conference (GECCO-2000)*, pages 435–442, Las Vegas, Nevada, USA. Morgan Kaufmann.

Michod, R. E. (2003). Cooperation and conflict mediation during the origin of multicellularity. In Hammerstein, Peter, editor, *Genetic and Cultural Evolution of Cooperation*, pages 291–307. The MIT Press, Cambridge, MA.

Nowak, M. A. and Sigmund, K. (1998). Evolution of indirect reciprocity by image scoring. *Nature*, 393:573–577.

Pettey, Chrisila C. (1997). Diffusion (cellular) models. In Bäck, Thomas, Fogel, David B., and Michalewicz, Zbigniew, editors, *Handbook of Evolutionary Computation*, pages C6.4:1–6. Institute of Physics Publishing and Oxford University Press, Bristol, New York.

Racine, Alain, Schoenauer, Marc, and Dague, Philippe (1998). A dynamic lattice to evolve hierarchically shared subroutines: DL'GP. In Banzhaf, Wolfgang, Poli, Riccardo, Schoenauer, Marc, and Fogarty, Terence C., editors, *Proceedings of the First European Workshop on Genetic Programming*, volume 1391 of *LNCS*, pages 220–232, Paris. Springer-Verlag.

Riolo, R. L., Cohen, M. D., and Axelrod, R. (2001). Evolution of cooperation without reciprocity. *Nature*, 414:441–443.

Riolo, R. L., Cohen, M. D., and Axelrod, R. (2002). Riolo et al. reply. *Nature*, 418:500.

Roberts, G. and Sherratt, T. N. (2002). Does similarity breed cooperation? *Nature*, 418:499–500.

Ryan, Conor, Keijzer, Maarten, and Cattolico, Mike (2004). Favorable biasing of function sets using run transferable libraries. In O'Reilly, Una-May, Yu, Tina, Riolo, Rick L., and Worzel, Bill, editors, *Genetic Programming Theory and Practice II*, chapter 7, pages 103–120. Springer, Ann Arbor.

Soule, Terence (2000). Heterogeneity and specialization in evolving teams. In Whitley, Darrell, Goldberg, David, Cantu-Paz, Erick, Spector, Lee, Parmee, Ian, and Beyer, Hans-Georg, editors, *Proceedings of the Genetic and Evolutionary Computation Conference (GECCO-2000)*, pages 778–785, Las Vegas, Nevada, USA. Morgan Kaufmann.

Spector, L. and Klein, J. (2006). Genetic stability and territorial structure facilitate the evolution of tag-mediated altruism. *Artificial Life*, 12(4):1–8.

Spector, Lee (2003). An essay concerning human understanding of genetic programming. In Riolo, Rick L. and Worzel, Bill, editors, *Genetic Programming Theory and Practice*, chapter 2, pages 11–24. Kluwer.

Spector, Lee and Klein, Jon (2005). Trivial geography in genetic programming. In Yu, Tina, Riolo, Rick L., and Worzel, Bill, editors, *Genetic Programming Theory and Practice III*, volume 9 of *Genetic Programming*, chapter 8, pages 109–123. Springer, Ann Arbor.

Spector, Lee, Klein, Jon, Perry, Chris, and Feinstein, Mark (2005). Emergence of collective behavior in evolving populations of flying agents. *Genetic Programming and Evolvable Machines*, 6(1):111–125.

Spector, Lee and Luke, Sean (1996). Cultural transmission of information in genetic programming. In Koza, John R., Goldberg, David E., Fogel, David B., and Riolo, Rick L., editors, *Genetic Programming 1996: Proceedings of the First Annual Conference*, pages 209–214, Stanford University, CA, USA. MIT Press.

Trivers, R. (1972). The evolution of reciprocal altruism. *Quarterly Review of Biology*, 46:35–57.

Chapter 8

COEVOLVING FITNESS MODELS FOR ACCELERATING EVOLUTION AND REDUCING EVALUATIONS

Michael D. Schmidt[1] and Hod Lipson[2]

[1] *Computer Science, Cornell University.*
[2] *Mechanical & Aerospace Engineering, Cornell University.*

Abstract   Fitness models are used to reduce evaluation frequency and cost. There are three fundamental challenges faced when using fitness models: (1) the model learning investment, (2) the model level of approximation, and (3) the lack of convergence to optima. We propose a coevolutionary algorithm to resolve these problems automatically during evolution. We discuss applications of this approach and measure its impact in symbolic regression. Results show coevolution yields significant improvement in performance over other algorithms and different fitness modeling approaches. Finally we apply coevolution to interactive evolution of pen stroke drawings where no true fitness function is known. These results demonstrate coevolution's ability to infer a fitness landscape of a user's preference while minimizing user interaction.

Keywords: Coevolution, fitness modeling, symbolic regression

1.   Introduction

Fitness modeling is the technique of replacing the fitness evaluation in evolutionary algorithms with an approximate calculation. A fitness model is often used to reduce the computational cost of evolution e.g. (Jin et al., 2001; Luke and Wiegand, 2002) where the exact fitness must be measured by an expensive physical simulation or experimentation. Fitness modeling has other advantages: The approximation can smooth rugged fitness landscapes, map discrete fitness values to continuous values, and diversify populations through ambiguity.

Recent work in fitness modeling has focused on approximation methods, model incorporation, and the management/control of model evaluation (Jin,

2005). This research has made significant strides in accelerating evolution and applying evolutionary computation to domains that were formerly infeasible.

There are three fundamental difficulties that remain to be addressed when utilizing fitness modeling:

1 **Model Training:** Often great computational effort is required ahead of time to train the desired fitness model.

2 **Level of approximation:** It is often unclear what (possibly adaptive) level of approximation to use for efficiency while still maintaining evolutionary progress.

3 **Convergence to optima:** Due to different levels of approximation, the global maximum of the fitness model may not correspond to the global maximum of the exact fitness.

The goal of this paper is to address these issues through coevolution. In the general framework, there are three populations: (1) solutions to the original problem, (2) fitness models of the problem, and (3) trainers, used to improve the models. Solutions are evolved to maximize their modeled fitness using a model from the model population. Fitness models are evolved to minimize predicted fitness error of select individuals from of the solution population. Both populations start with random solutions and random fitness models which evolve in parallel, using trainers.

We introduce a coevolutionary algorithm based on this general framework and discuss its application in example domains. We then apply it to a benchmark problem in genetic programming, symbolic regression, to measure its impact. We compare performance with three other symbolic regression fitness model algorithms on various problem difficulties. We duplicate experiments in recent symbolic regression publications and compare results. Finally, we apply coevolution of fitness models to human interactive evolution of pen-stroke drawings where no fitness function exists to show how models can be coevolved to infer a fitness landscape.

2.   Preliminaries

Coevolution

Coevolution holds the potential of perpetually refining solutions without the need to manually restate the problem. As one individual improves, newer fitness objectives are imposed on another, and vice versa. Ideally, the separate individuals or populations continually encourage each other to improve. In general, coevolution occurs when the fitness of an individual is defined by another individual. More formally, in a coevolutionary process, one individual can determine the relative ranking between two other individuals (in the same or in a separate population) (Hillis, 1992; Ong et al., 2003).

Much research has been done on the use and application of coevolution to enhance problem solving (Jong and Pollack, 2004; Ficici, 2004; Ficici and Pollack, 2001; Potter and De Jong, 2000; Rosin and Belew, 1996; Stanley and Miikkulainen, 2004; Zykov et al., 2005), with the main goal of controlling coevolutionary dynamics that often result in lack of progress or progress in unanticipated directions (Cliff and Miller, 1995; Luke and Wiegand, 2002; Watson and Pollack, 2001). Here we use a specific form of coevolution which addresses many of these challenges (Bongard and Lipson, 2004; Bongard and Lipson, 2005).

Fitness Modeling

Fitness modeling has become an active area in evolutionary computation with many varying approaches and results (Jin, 2005). Here we discuss the motivations, methods, and challenges tied to fitness modeling.

Methods

The technique of fitness modeling falls most naturally in the field of machine learning. Depending on the structure of solution encodings, many different machine learning approaches such as neural nets, support vector machines, decision trees, Bayesian networks, k-nearest-neighbor, and polynomial regression can be learned to map individuals to approximate fitnesses very efficiently. Modern approaches utilize boosting, bagging, and ensembles learning to produce very accurate models. A major drawback however is it is often unclear which machine learning approach will work best (Jin, 2005).

Sub-sampling of training data is also a very common way to reduce the cost of fitness evaluation (Albert and Goldberg, 2002). In many problems, fitness is calculated by evaluating individuals on random training cases and combining the total error. With a sub-sample, only a fraction of the training data is evaluated.

Evolutionary specific fitness modeling methods include fitness inheritance and fitness imitation. In fitness inheritance (Chen et al., 2002), fitness values are transferred from parents to child during crossover (similar to parent passing on a legacy or education). In fitness imitation (Jin and Sendhoff, 2004), individuals are clustered into groups based on a distance metric. The fitness of the central individual of each cluster is then evaluated in full and assigned to all individuals in that cluster.

Once a fitness model has been learned, there are many ways to incorporate it into evolution. It can be used simply to initialize the population, guide crossover and mutation, or replace (some) fitness evaluations (Jin, 2005). For this paper however, we focus only on replacing actual fitness evaluations with the fitness model.

Challenges

The use of an approximate fitness model comes at a cost and potentially unacceptable consequences.

Training the model: Fitness models like neural nets, SVMs, and Gaussian processes require significant overhead to train. When advanced methods like bagging, boosting, and ensemble methods are used, this investment becomes significantly larger. In addition, a significant amount of exact fitnesses must be calculated for training and validation data to effectively learn any type of model ahead of time.

By using coevolution, we can learn these models in parallel with the problem solutions. As seen in (Yang and Flockton, 1995), early stages of evolution only require coarse fitness models. As the solution population progresses, so do the fitness models. In this fashion, coevolution encompasses automatic coarseness adjustment without the need to train several different approximations before hand.

Level of approximation: How powerful must the fitness model be to facilitate progress throughout evolution? If a single fitness model is used, it likely must be very complex in order to model all possible solutions in the fitness landscape.

When fitness models are coevolved, the models can be optimized for only the individuals in the current population. The models do not need to encapsulate the entire landscape, only a subset, so the method chosen can be significantly less complex.

Convergence to optima: Often the global maximum of the fitness model is not the same as that of the exact fitness function. In this case, the model was either too coarse or the training data given was insufficient to identify the true maxima. The consequence is convergence to local maxima and suboptimal solutions.

By using coevolution, we can intelligently select individuals for training data (active learning). As the solution population evolves, training data for the fitness models can focus heavily on recent solutions which have high predicted fitness. Therefore, optimizing fitness models to the current population can also optimize the models to promising areas of the fitness landscape refining true fitness maxima.

Symbolic Regression

Symbolic Regression (SR) is the challenging problem of identifying the exact mathematical description of a hidden system from experimental data (Augusto and Barbosa, 2000; Duffy and Engle-Warnick, 2002). Unlike polynomial regression or machine learning methods which minimize error, SR is a system identification method. SR typically has strong advantages in resisting overfitting, extrapolating future points, and providing descriptive models at the cost of greater complexity.

For experiments in this paper, we represent functional expressions as a binary tree of primitive operations (Duffy and Engle-Warnick, 2002; Ferreira, 2003; Keijzer, 2003; Soule and Heckendorn, 2001). The operations can be unary operations such as abs, exp, and log, or binary operations such as add, mult, and div. If some a priori knowledge of the problem is known, the types of operations available can be chosen ahead of time (Augusto and Barbosa, 2000; Dolin et al., 2002; Duffy and Engle-Warnick, 2002; Eggermont and van Hemert, 2001; Hoai et al., 2002; Koza, 1992). The terminal values available consist of the function's input variables and the function's evolved constant values (Ferreira, 2003).

The fitness objective of a SR solution is to minimize error on the training set (Augusto and Barbosa, 2000; Koza, 1992). There are many ways to measure the error such as squared error, absolute error, log error, etc. Though the choice is not critical to the optimal solution, different metrics work better on different problems. For experiments in this paper, we simply use the mean absolute error for fitness measurement.

We generate training data by randomly sampling from the hidden function. The training set is used for fitness evaluation and convergence testing. A large randomly sampled test set is held out for final solution performance evaluation.

3. Coevolved Fitness Models

In this section we give a simple framework before presenting our implementation. A conventional evolutionary algorithm can be viewed as an optimization function with objective:

$$s^* = arg\ max\ fitness(s) \qquad s \varepsilon S \qquad (8.1)$$

where $s \varepsilon S$ is an individual solution to the problem and *fitness*(s) is the exact computed fitness of solution s. Here we are interested in replacing all fitness evaluations with a fitness model. In this instance, the objective becomes:

$$s^* = arg\ max\ m(s) \qquad s \varepsilon S \qquad (8.2)$$

where $m \varepsilon M$ is the fitness model used. For coevolution, both solutions and models are being evolved. There are thus two objectives:

$$s_t^* = arg\ max\ m_t(s) \qquad s \varepsilon S \qquad (8.3)$$

$$m_t^* = arg\ min|fitness(S_t) - m(S_t)| \qquad m \varepsilon M \qquad (8.4)$$

where the t subscripts denote time dependence. The solution population evolves to maximize the fitness of the current fitness model. The fitness model population evolves minimize the difference between exact and modeled fitnesses of the current population.

Algorithm
Overview

The algorithm presented in this paper evolves two populations simultaneously: the individuals and their fitness models. This section outlines the basics needed to implement this coevolutionary approach. A high-level algorithm overview is given in Figure 8-1.

At the start, both solutions and fitness models are randomly initialized. The algorithm then chooses an individual from the solution population to measure its exact fitness for use in training the fitness models (more on this in next section). The algorithm then evolves the solution population using the most fit fitness model of the model population, and evolves the models using the known exact fitnesses. Finally, the highest modeled fitness individual is tested for convergence, and the algorithm completes if successful.

Evaluating an Exact Fitnesses

The objective of this step is to select an individual from the solution population that will improve the fitness models' ability to model the current solutions the most. Therefore, we want to choose the individual with the least certainty in modeled fitness. To do this efficiently, we select the individual that has the highest variance in modeled fitness among models in the model population such as done in (Bongard and Lipson, 2004).

A key goal of the fitness models is to optimize to the current population. In many model types, it is often beneficial to "forget" past solution fitness information to do this. For our SR experiments, we discard the exact fitness calculations that are older than 1000 generations.

Evolving the Populations

In the framework, we evolve both populations until a new exact fitness calculation can be done. Alternatively, the populations could be evolved until they plateau. For our experiments however, we simply evolve at regular intervals of 100 generations.

Although the two populations can be evolved in parallel, we manage the effort spent in each for performance measurement. To do this, we throttle back evolution on either population based on the total number of training example evaluations to maintain some ratio. Figure 8-2 (left) and 8-2 (right) show the

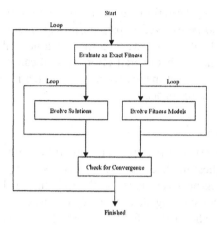

Figure 8-1. The high-level overview of the coevolution of solutions and fitness models algorithm

impact this ratio has on performance on the function $f_2(x)$ experimented on later in the paper.

The choice of the ratio is surprisingly tolerant as seen in Figure 8-2 (left). Ratios in the range 5% to 30% of effort spent training the fitness model population all yield approximately optimal convergence time. If extremely little effort is given to fitness models, performance suffers greatly since the models never adapt.

If an extremely high amount of effort is spent the fitness model population plateaus and makes no further improvement even with the extra effort. The ratio also has a generally weak impact on the number of generations before convergence as seen in Figure 8-2 (right). Over-training the fitness models does not reduce the number of generations required to find the hidden function.

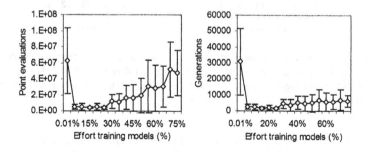

Figure 8-2. Left: The expected number of point evaluations before convergence versus the effort (percent of point evaluations) while training the fitness models. Right: The expected number of generations before convergence versus the effort (percent of point evaluations) while training the fitness models

Note that in practice, the ratio is not vital to the algorithm's performance. Each population could be evolved in parallel provided appropriate hardware. For experimentation however, we want to show that not only can we parallel out some computation, but that overall effort as well can be reduced through coevolution. In our SR experiments, we use 5% which is near the minimum while still enhancing performance.

Convergence Test

The convergence test determines when the algorithm terminates based on the solution with the highest modeled fitness. For symbolic regression, we define convergence as having near zero error on the training set (less than epsilon). If the solution has not converged, a new exact fitness is calculated and the algorithm continues. The final performance test however measures the fitness using a held out test set.

4. Training Data Sample Fitness Model

In our SR experimentation, we use a general fitness model which is simply a small subset of the training data. So the total error is measured by evaluating functions on only a few training examples. First we examine the importance of the number of samples in the training subset fitness model.

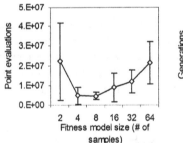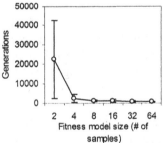

Figure 8-3. Left: The expected point evaluations before convergence versus the number of samples in the fitness model. Error bars show the standard deviation. Right: The expected generations before convergence versus the number of samples in the fitness model. Error bars show the standard deviation.

The sample size choice is fairly tolerant in as seen in Figure 8-3 (left). Sample sizes of four through eight have very similar performance. Even when using only two samples in the subset performance is acceptable.

When the fitness model only has two samples, fitness evaluations are extremely light-weight but the evolution requires many more generations as evident in Figure 8-3 (right). The larger subsets are sufficiently large for accurate modeling and do not reduce the number of generations greatly.

In our SR experiments, we use an 8-sample subset for all experiments. Although it may not be the optimal choice for all target functions, these results suggest it will not have a dramatic impact on final performance unless the target function is extremely simple or extremely complex.

5. Experiments in Symbolic Regression

Here we use symbolic regression (SR) as an example genetic programming problem for experimentation. For each run, all parameters are held constant. We use a solution population size of 128, a fitness model population size of 8. For both populations we use deterministic crowding selection, 0.1 mutation probability, and 0.5 crossover probability. The operator set is $+, -*, /, exp, log, sin, cos$ and the terminal set consists of the input variable and one evolved constant.

Fitness Model Experiments

We compare four fitness model algorithms in symbolic regression (SR). All fitness models are 8-sample subsets of the training set except for the exact fitness algorithm which evaluates fitness on the full training set. The differences in these algorithms are summarized in Table 8-1.

Table 8-1. Summary of the Compared Algorithms

Fitness model	Sample Size	Sample Selection
Coevolved Fitness Model	8	Evolved Subset
Static Fitness Model	8	Random subset chosen at runtime
Dynamic Fitness Model	8	Changing random subset
Exact Fitness	200	Use all training data

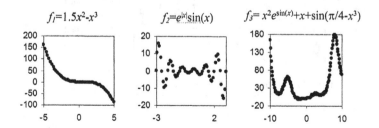

Figure 8-4. The training data of the three target functions experimented on.

We test on three different target functions of varying difficulty shown in Figure 8-4. Each test is repeated 50 times, and the average fitness for each

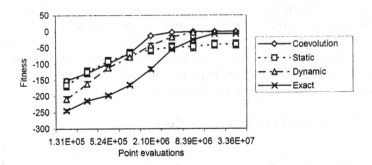

Figure 8-5. The test set fitness during evolution for target function $f_1(x)$. Results are averaged over 50 test runs. Error bars show the standard error.

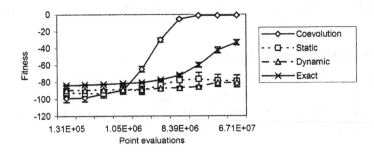

Figure 8-6. The test set fitness during evolution for target function $f_2(x)$. Results are averaged over 50 test runs. Error bars show the standard error.

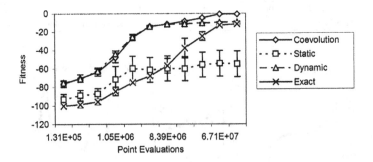

Figure 8-7. The test set fitness during evolution for target function $f_3(x)$. Results are averaged over 50 test runs. Error bars show the standard error.

run is recorded over time. The training and test data are generated by random sampling each target function uniformly.

The performances on these three functions for each algorithm are shown versus the number of point evaluations in Figures 8-5 – 8-7.

In these experiments, we see the coevolution algorithm converges first and maintains higher fitness throughout evolution. On the simple function $f_1(x)$ the difference in performance is small. On the non-linear functions $f_2(x)$ and $f_3(x)$, the difference is more pronounced.

The fitness curves of the coevolution and exact fitness algorithms are very similar in shape. The exact fitness algorithm is delayed and elongated by extra point evaluations but endures similar average evolutionary paths.

The static and dynamic random training subset fitness model algorithms are less predictable in performance as is shown by their higher standard errors and ranks on the differing functions. The static model algorithm appears to suffer if the sample is not very informative by chance or if the target function is too complex to adequately represent with eight samples. The dynamic model appears to perform well on finding simple features but poorly on detail and high-frequency terms.

Comparison to Previously Published Methods

In this section, we compare the coevolution algorithm with four recently published symbolic regression techniques: Stepwise Adaptive Weights (SAW), Grammar Guided Genetic Programming (GGGP), Tree-Adjunct Grammar Guided Genetic Programming (TAG3P), and Coevoltuion with Tractable Shared Fitness (Dolin et al., 2002; Eggermont and van Hemert, 2001; Hoai et al., 2002). Where possible, we compare with their best reported results and match performance metrics as closely as possible.

We compare performance based on point evaluations. The coevolution algorithm is stopped based on the number of function evaluations the compared algorithm made during each experiment. Since each compared algorithm differs in fitness calculation, we assume that each individual's fitness is measured by evaluating it on the training set each generation. Likewise, we force the coevolution algorithm to calculate fitness for every individual every generation also, even though different selection algorithms do not require it.

Many of these experiments are on simple functions but are stopped at a very low number of point evaluations. So, finding the target function quickly is the highest priority. The cosine identity and the Gaussian function experiments are noticeably more challenging to regress.

Significant improvements in Table 8-2 are shown in bold text. The coevolution algorithm has significantly higher convergence than the PSAW and GGGP algorithms. The TAG3P algorithm performs significantly higher in the polynomial functions. Coevolution makes a large improvement in convergence in the cosine double angle identity experiment however.

Table 8-2. Research Comparison Summary

Algorithm	Target Function	Metric	Results	Coevolved Models
PSAW	$F(x) = x^5 - 2x^3 + x$	*Convergence*[†]	85.9%	**93.9%**
	$f(x) = x^6 - 2x^4 + x^2$	*Convergence*[†]	81.8%	**86.9%**
GGGP	P2, P3, P4, P5*	*Convergence*[††]	92%, 64%	**100%, 86%**
	$f(x) = cos(2x)$**	*Convergence*[††]	20%	**76%**
TAG3P	P2, P3, P4, P5*	*Convergence*[††]	100%, 100%, **96%, 84%**	100%, 86% **62%, 52%**
	$f(x) = cos(2x)$**	*Convergence*[††]	36%	**76%**
Coevolved Tractable	Gaussian	*Evaluations*[†††]	3.384e7	**2.107e7**

* P2, P3, etc. refer to polynomials $(x^3 + x^2 + x, x^4 + x^3 + x^2 + x, x^5 + x^4 + x^3 + x^2 + x$, etc.

** The operator set does not include the cos function, a trigonometric identity must be found

[†]The percent of successful convergences from 100 test runs

[††]The percent of successful convergences from 50 test runs

[†††]The maximum number of evaluations before convergence for 100 test runs

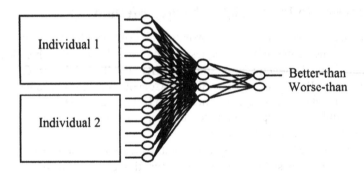

Figure 8-8. The neural network comparator fitness model.

Evolving Pen Stroke Drawings

In this experiment we evolve drawings produced by a series of closed pen strokes. Each individual encodes each coordinate drawn to on a 32 by 32 pixel image. Drawings are composed of six pen strokes. Here we evaluate the algorithm's ability to identify a preference for star-shaped drawings. We compare results with random search and local search techniques.

Random Search Comparison

We split the drawing space into six regions to approximate the number of possible star drawings. Note that a five point star is uniquely determined by three of its vertices. The probability,P_{star}, and expected time to encounter a random star shape, T_{star}, is calculated:

$$P_{star} \approx \frac{5}{3888} \approx 0.128 \qquad (8.5)$$

and

$$\therefore E(T_{star}) \approx 777.6 \qquad (8.6)$$

Perfect Local Search Comparison

In the local search algorithm, the user is given a random individual and asked to fine tune parameters individually. The variation we compare with can be thought of as a perfect local search where the user is assumed to make optimal choices to transform the drawing into a star. The optimal expected number of prompts required is lower-bounded by:

$$< steps >= \frac{1}{9} * \sum_{x=0}^{8} x + |\sqrt{8^2 - x^2}| \approx 9 \qquad (8.7)$$

Empirical Results

Figure 8-9 shows the median run out of ten to evolve an approximate star shaped drawing. The user has a consistent strategy when answering comparison prompts to prefer shapes with multiple sharp corners such as a star shape has. The user's preferred response for each comparison is shown in bold.

A well formed star is evolved as the top modeled shape after five user prompts. No prior prompts required a star shape. The next three prompts are given to show the fitness model is stable and continues to favor the consistent star-like shapes. Figure 8-10 compares the expected user prompts required by each algorithm.

Inferring the Fitness Landscape

In this experiment visualize the fitness landscape learned by the fitness models. We evolve single pen-stroke drawings appear as a clock hour hand. The user is then asked to prefer two times where the hand points to either 3:00 or 7:00. The target solution therefore has two optimal solutions.

To visualize the fitness landscape in this experiment we sum the comparisons between all possible drawings. Figure 8-11 shows four fitness landscapes of the fitness models over six user prompts. At zero prompts, the fitness landscape is flat but becomes more distinct with user responses.

The fitnesses on the xz-plan resemble an arch which peaks at approximately the target 3:00 position. The yz-plane fitnesses exhibit the same behavior for the 7:00 position. This final resulting landscape is a surprisingly friendly terrain

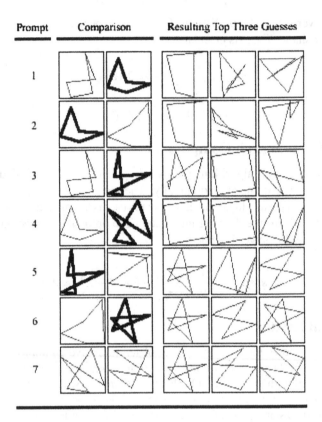

Figure 8-9. The user prompts and the resulting top three drawings evolved. User choices are shown in bold.

for the evolutionary search. Very gradual gradients exist near the target clock hand locations that should be easily descended.

6.   Conclusion

We have addressed three fundamental challenges faced when using fitness models in evolutionary algorithms: (1) the model training investment, (2) choosing a level of approximation, and (3) lack of convergence to global maxima.

We have introduced a coevolutionary approach where fitness models are evolved in parallel with original problem solutions. In this framework, the fitness models do not require prior training investment, can optimize to the current population, and can actively select the most informative solutions to evaluate in full for model training.

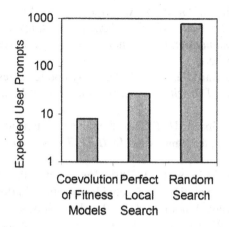

Figure 8-10. The number of user prompts expected between the compared algorithms to find the target star shape

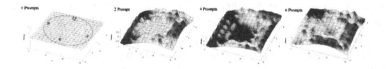

Figure 8-11. The clock time fitness landscapes learned over six user prompts.

We applied this approach in symbolic regression to measure its impact. Results show a significant improvement in both fitness and convergence rates over other fitness model and exact fitness algorithms. In the research comparison, the coevolution algorithm significantly outperforms PSAW, GGGP, and coevolved tractable fitness. The coevolution algorithm is outperformed by TAG3P on polynomial functions but makes a large improvement in the more difficult problem of deriving a trigonometric identity.

Finally, we applied the coevolution of fitness models to human interactive evolution where no fitness function is defined. Results show the fitness models are able to infer the user preference in pen-stroke drawings through very limited user feedback. Fitness models converged on trends in the user responses to identify the target drawing which was never explicitly presented to the user.

References

Albert, Laura A. and Goldberg, David E. (2002). Efficient discretization scheduling in multiple dimensions. In Langdon, W. B., Cantú-Paz, E., Mathias, K., Roy, R., Davis, D., Poli, R., Balakrishnan, K., Honavar, V., Rudolph, G.,

Wegener, J., Bull, L., Potter, M. A., Schultz, A. C., Miller, J. F., Burke, E., and Jonoska, N., editors, *GECCO 2002: Proceedings of the Genetic and Evolutionary Computation Conference*, pages 271–278, New York. Morgan Kaufmann Publishers.

Augusto, D.A. and Barbosa, H.J.C. (2000). Symbolic regression via genetic programming. In *VI Brazilian Symposium on Neural Networks (SBRN'00)*, volume 1.

Bongard, J.C. and Lipson, H. (2004). Nonlinear system identification using co-evolution of models and tests. In *IEEE Transactions on Evolutionary Computation*.

Bongard, Josh C. and Lipson, Hod (2005). 'managed challenge' alleviates disengagement in co-evolutionary system identification. In Beyer, Hans-Georg, O'Reilly, Una-May, Arnold, Dirk V., Banzhaf, Wolfgang, Blum, Christian, Bonabeau, Eric W., Cantu-Paz, Erick, Dasgupta, Dipankar, Deb, Kalyanmoy, Foster, James A., de Jong, Edwin D., Lipson, Hod, Llora, Xavier, Mancoridis, Spiros, Pelikan, Martin, Raidl, Guenther R., Soule, Terence, Tyrrell, Andy M., Watson, Jean-Paul, and Zitzler, Eckart, editors, *GECCO 2005: Proceedings of the 2005 conference on Genetic and evolutionary computation*, volume 1, pages 531–538, Washington DC, USA. ACM Press.

Chen, Jian-Hung, Goldberg, David E., Ho, Shinn-Ying, and Sastry, Kumara (2002). Fitness inheritance in multi-objective optimization. In Langdon, W. B., Cantú-Paz, E., Mathias, K., Roy, R., Davis, D., Poli, R., Balakrishnan, K., Honavar, V., Rudolph, G., Wegener, J., Bull, L., Potter, M. A., Schultz, A. C., Miller, J. F., Burke, E., and Jonoska, N., editors, *GECCO 2002: Proceedings of the Genetic and Evolutionary Computation Conference*, pages 319–326, New York. Morgan Kaufmann Publishers.

Cliff, Dave and Miller, Geoffrey F. (1995). Tracking the red queen: Measurements of adaptive progress in co-evolutionary simulations. In Morán, F., Moreno, A., Merelo, J. J., and Chacón, P., editors, *Proceedings of the Third European Conference on Artificial Life : Advances in Artificial Life*, volume 929 of *LNAI*, pages 200–218, Berlin. Springer Verlag.

Dolin, B., Bennett, F., and Rieffel, E. (2002). Co-evolving an effective fitness sample: Experiments in symbolic regression and distributed robot control. In *Proceedings of the 2002 ACM Symposium on Applied Computing*.

Duffy, J. and Engle-Warnick, J. (2002). Using symbolic regression to infer strategies from experimental data. In Chen, S.H, editor, *Evolutionary Computation in Economics and Finance*. Physica-Verlag, New York.

Eggermont, J. and van Hemert, J.I. (2001). Stepwise adaptation of weights for symbolic regression with genetic programming. In *Proceedings of EuroGP*.

Ferreira, C. (2003). Function finding and the creation of numerical constants in gene experssion programming. In *Advances in Soft Computing - Engineering Design and Manufacturing*, pages 257–266. Springer-Verlag.

Ficici, S.G. (2004). *Solution Concepts in Coevolutionary Algorithms*. PhD thesis, Computer Science Dept., Brandeis University.

Ficici, S.G. and Pollack, J.B. (2001). Pareto optimality in coevolutionary learning. In *Advances in Artificial Life, 6th European Conference (ECAL2001)*, pages 316–327.

Hillis, W. Daniel (1992). Co-evolving parasites improve simulated evolution as an optimization procedure. In Langton, Christopher G., Taylor, Charles, Farmer, J. Doyne, and Rasmussen, Steen, editors, *Artificial life II*, volume 10 of *Sante Fe Institute Studies in the Sciences of Complexity*, pages 313–324. Addison-Wesley, Redwood City, Calif.

Hoai, N. X., McKay, R. I., Essam, D., and Chau, R. (2002). Solving the symbolic regression problem with tree-adjunct grammar guided genetic programming: The comparative results. In Fogel, David B., El-Sharkawi, Mohamed A., Yao, Xin, Greenwood, Garry, Iba, Hitoshi, Marrow, Paul, and Shackleton, Mark, editors, *Proceedings of the 2002 Congress on Evolutionary Computation CEC2002*, pages 1326–1331. IEEE Press.

Jin, Y. (Jan 2005). A comprehensive survey of fitness approximation in evolutionary computation. *Soft Computing - A fusion of Foundations, Methodologies and Applications*, 9(1):3.

Jin, Yaochu, Olhofer, Markus, and Sendhoff, Bernhard (2001). Managing approximate models in evolutionary aerodynamic design optimization. In *Proceedings of the 2001 Congress on Evolutionary Computation CEC2001*, pages 592–599, COEX, World Trade Center, 159 Samseong-dong, Gangnam-gu, Seoul, Korea. IEEE Press.

Jin, Yaochu and Sendhoff, Bernhard (2004). Reducing fitness evaluations using clustering techniques and neural network ensembles. In Deb, Kalyanmoy, Poli, Riccardo, Banzhaf, Wolfgang, Beyer, Hans-Georg, Burke, Edmund, Darwen, Paul, Dasgupta, Dipankar, Floreano, Dario, Foster, James, Harman, Mark, Holland, Owen, Lanzi, Pier Luca, Spector, Lee, Tettamanzi, Andrea, Thierens, Dirk, and Tyrrell, Andy, editors, *Genetic and Evolutionary Computation – GECCO-2004, Part I*, volume 3102 of *Lecture Notes in Computer Science*, pages 688–699, Seattle, WA, USA. Springer-Verlag.

Jong, Edwin D. De and Pollack, Jordan B. (2004). Ideal Evaluation from Coevolution. *Evolutionary Computation*, 12(2):159–192.

Keijzer, M. (2003). Improving symbolic regression with interval arithmetic and linear scaling. In *Sixth European Conference on Genetic Programming*, pages 70–82, Essex, UK. Springer.

Koza, J. R. (1992). *Genetic Programming: On the programming of computers by means of natural selection*. Bradford Books, Cambridge, MA.

Luke, Sean and Wiegand, R. Paul (2002). When coevolutionary algorithms exhibit evolutionary dynamics. In Barry, Alwyn M., editor, *GECCO 2002:*

Proceedings of the Bird of a Feather Workshops, Genetic and Evolutionary Computation Conference, pages 236–241, New York. AAAI.

Ong, Y., Nair, P., and Keane, A. (2003). evolutionary optimization of computationally expensive problems via surrogate modeling. *AJAA J.*, 41(4):678–696.

Potter, Mitchell A. and De Jong, Kenneth A. (2000). Cooperative coevolution: An architecture for evolving coadapted subcomponents. *Evolutionary Computation*, 8(1):1–29.

Rosin, Christopher D. and Belew, Richard K. (1996). New methods for competitive coevolution. Technical Report CS96-491, Cognitive Computer Science Research Group, University of California, San Diego, CA. to appear in Evolutionary Computation 5:1.

Soule, Terence and Heckendorn, Robert B. (2001). Function sets in genetic programming. In Spector, Lee, Goodman, Erik D., Wu, Annie, Langdon, W. B., Voigt, Hans-Michael, Gen, Mitsuo, Sen, Sandip, Dorigo, Marco, Pezeshk, Shahram, Garzon, Max H., and Burke, Edmund, editors, *Proceedings of the Genetic and Evolutionary Computation Conference (GECCO-2001)*, page 190, San Francisco, California, USA. Morgan Kaufmann.

Stanley, K. O. and Miikkulainen, R. (2004). Competitive coevolution through evolutionary complexification. *Journal of Artificial Intelligence Research*, 21:63–100.

Watson, Richard A. and Pollack, Jordan B. (2001). Coevolutionary dynamics in a minimal substrate. In Spector, Lee, Goodman, Erik D., Wu, Annie, Langdon, W. B., Voigt, Hans-Michael, Gen, Mitsuo, Sen, Sandip, Dorigo, Marco, Pezeshk, Shahram, Garzon, Max H., and Burke, Edmund, editors, *Proceedings of the Genetic and Evolutionary Computation Conference (GECCO-2001)*, pages 702–709, San Francisco, California, USA. Morgan Kaufmann.

Yang, Dekun and Flockton, Stuart J. (1995). Evolutionary algorithms with a coarse-to-fine function smoothing.

Zykov, V., Bongard, J., and Lipson, H. (2005). Co-evolutionary variance guides physical experimentation in evolutionary system indentification. In *The 2005 NASA/DoD Conference on Evolvable Hardware*.

Chapter 9

MULTI-DOMAIN OBSERVATIONS CONCERNING THE USE OF GENETIC PROGRAMMING TO AUTOMATICALLY SYNTHESIZE HUMAN-COMPETITIVE DESIGNS FOR ANALOG CIRCUITS, OPTICAL LENS SYSTEMS, CONTROLLERS, ANTENNAS, MECHANICAL SYSTEMS, AND QUANTUM COMPUTING CIRCUITS

John R. Koza[1], Sameer H. Al-Sakran[2] and Lee W. Jones[2]
[1] *Stanford University, Stanford, California;* [2] *Genetic Programming Inc., Mountain View, California*

Abstract   This paper reviews the recent use of genetic programming to automatically synthesize human-competitive designs of complex structures in six engineering domains, namely analog electrical circuits, optical lens systems, controllers, antennas, mechanical systems, and quantum computing circuits. First, the paper identifies common features observed in the human-competitive results produced by genetic programming in the six domains and suggests possible explanations for the observed similarities. Second, the paper identifies the characteristics that make a particular domain amenable to the application of genetic programming for the automatic synthesis of designs. Third, the paper discusses certain domain-specific adjustments in technique that may increase the efficiency of the automated process in a particular domain. Fourth, the paper discusses several technique issues that have arisen in more than one domain.

Keywords: Genetic programming, automated design, analog circuits, controllers, optical lens systems, antennas, mechanical system, quantum computing circuits, developmental process, replication of previously patented invention, human-competitive result

1.   Introduction

Genetic programming has now been successfully used to automatically synthesize designs for complex structures from a high-level specification of the structure's desired behavior and characteristics in a number of engineering domains. These domains include analog electrical circuits, optical lens systems, controllers, antennas, mechanical systems, and quantum computing circuits. Many of the automatically synthesized designs produced by genetic programming are "human-competitive" as defined in Koza, Bennett, Andre, and Keane (Koza et al., 1999). Despite variation in representation and technique used by the various groups doing the above work, there are a considerable number of similarities in terms of the characteristics of the domains chosen, in terms of the methods used, and in terms of the common features observed in the results that were achieved. The observations in this paper are based on the following reported work using genetic programming:

- an X-Band Antenna for NASA's Space Technology 5 Mission (Lohn et al., 2004),

- quantum computing circuits (Spector, 2004),

- a previously patented mechanical system (Lipson, 2004),

- analog electrical circuits patented in the 20th-century (Koza et al., 1999) and 21st-century (Koza et al., 2003),

- previously patented optical lens systems (Al-Sakran et al., 2005; Jones et al., 2005; Jones et al., 005a; Koza et al., 2005a; Koza et al., 2005b),

- previously patented controllers (Koza et al., 2003), and new controller designs that have been granted patents (Keane et al., 2005).

Section 2 provides background on genetic programming and developmental genetic programming. Section 3 identifies common features observed in the human-competitive results produced by genetic programming in various engineering domains and suggests possible explanations for the observed similarities. Section 4 identifies the characteristics that make a particular domain amenable to the application of genetic programming for the automatic synthesis of designs for complex structures in that domain. Section 5 discusses certain domain-specific adjustments in technique that may increase the efficiency of the process in a particular domain. Section 6 discusses several technique issues that have arisen in more than one domain. Section 7 is the conclusion.

2.   Background on genetic programming and developmental genetic programming

Genetic programming is an extension of the genetic algorithm (Holland 1975) to the arena of computer programs. Genetic programming is a domain-independent algorithm that starts from a high-level statement of what needs to be done and automatically creates a computer program to solve the problem. Genetic programming employs the Darwinian principle of natural selection along with analogs of recombination (crossover), mutation, gene duplication, gene deletion, and mechanisms of developmental biology to breed an ever-improving population of programs. Information about genetic programming can be found in Koza 1990, 1992; Koza 1993; Koza 1994; Banzhaf, Nordin, Keller, and Francone 1998; Koza, Bennett, Andre, and Keane 1999; Langdon and Poli 2002; Koza, Keane, Streeter, Mydlowec, Yu, and Lanza 2003.

Developmental genetic programming is especially relevant to work involving the automated design of complex structures using genetic programming. Pioneering work on developmental representations for use with genetic algorithms was done by Wilson (Wilson, 1997) and Kitano (Kitano, 1990). Pioneering work on developmental genetic programming was done by Gruau (Gruau, 1992) for the automatic design of neural networks. In 1993, Koza (Koza, 1993) used developmental genetic programming to evolve developmental rewrite rules (Lindenmayer system rules) using a turtle to create shapes such as the quadratic Koch island. In 1996, Koza, Bennett, Andre, and Keane (Koza et al., 1996a) used developmental genetic programming to automatically synthesize a variety of analog electrical circuits, including several previously patented circuits and human-competitive results. This work for automated circuit synthesis entailed the integration of a complex simulator into the runs of genetic programming. Koza, Bennett, Andre, and Keane also provided for reuse of portions of circuits (by means of subroutines and iterations), parameterized reuse, and hierarchical reuse of substructures in evolving circuits (Koza et al., 1996b). In 1996, Brave (Brave, 1996) used developmental genetic programming to evolve finite automata. In 1996, Spector and Stoffel extended the notion of developmental genetic programming by pioneering the biologically motivated concept of ontogenetic (conditional) genetic programming (Spector, 2004).

3.   Cross-domain common features of human-competitive results produced by genetic programming

This section identifies the following five common features observed in the human-competitive results produced by genetic programming in various engineering domains and suggests possible explanations for the observed similarities:

- Native representations have proven to be sufficient when working with genetic programming;

- Genetic programming breeds simulatability;

- Genetic programming starts small;

- Genetic programming frequently exploits a simulator's implicit assumption of reasonableness; and

- Genetic programming creates novel designs and engineers around existing patents more frequently than it creates duplications of previous solutions or infringing solutions.

Some of the above cross-domain observations are clearly surprising and could not have been anticipated prior to the work being done.

Native representations have proven sufficient for genetic programming

The problem of synthesizing a complex structure from a high-level specification is regarded as a significant unsolved problem in each of the six engineering domains discussed in this paper. The designs reviewed in this paper are considered to be human-competitive results. Genetic programming is a domain-independent algorithm. Taking these three facts into account, one would expect that it would be necessary to bring considerable in-depth domain knowledge to bear in order to arrive at a suitable representational scheme (that is, the function set and terminal set) for a run of genetic programming. It is thus surprising that, for all six domains, human-competitive results were obtained by using native representational schemes employing only the most elementary kind of information about the domain involved.

For example, for optical lens systems (Al-Sakran et al., 2005; Jones et al., 2005; Jones et al., 005a; Koza et al., 2005a; Koza et al., 2005b), the representational scheme used to create human-competitive designs was simply the long established format for optical prescriptions (and lens files for optical analysis software) that is widely used in the domain of optical design. In particular, the function set for problems of spherical refractive optics contains one function that inserts a material (e.g., a specified type of glass, air) and a surface (with a specified radius of curvature) at a specified distance from the previous surface (or starting point). This single function encapsulates the information contained in a row of a standard tabular optical prescription. No knowledge of the mathematics for analyzing the behavior of an optical system (e.g., laws of optics, ray tracing, modulation transfer functions, spot diagrams) or engineering know-how about optical design was required to arrive at this native representational scheme. Instead, all that was used was syntactic information about the grammatical structure of a long-established and widely used way to describe a lens system.

The situation was similar for analog electrical circuits (Koza et al., 1996a; Koza et al., 1999). In the domain of analog circuits, the function set consists of functions that insert electrical components (e.g., transistors, capacitors, resistors) and create topological connections among the components in well-known and widely used ways (e.g., parallel division, series division, via connections between arbitrary points).

For wire antennas (Comisky et al., 2000), the representational scheme is based on the way a draftsman might draw an antenna (either on paper or using a two- or three-dimensional graphical interface for engineering drawings). In particular, the function set consists of a function that draws a straight line with a specified length and at a specified angle starting at a specified point, using a turtle (Koza, 1993). The work by Comisky, Yu, and Koza in 2000 on antennas added the ability of the turtle to move a specified distance at a specified angle without depositing metal as the movement takes place. The work of Lohn, Hornby, and Linden (Lohn et al., 2004) added the additional, and highly advantageous, feature of permitting a wire to bifurcate.

For controllers (Koza et al., 2003; Keane et al., 2005), the function set consists of the signal-processing functions that are commonly used in controllers (e.g., integrators, differentiators, amplifiers, adders, subtractors, leads, lags). A controller is simply a composition of these signal-processing functions (i.e., a LISP S-expression) operating on the controller's two externally supplied signals (i.e., the reference signal and the plant output) or on the signal emanating from an earlier signal-processing function.

For mechanical systems (Lipson, 2004), the function set consists of two functions that construct the mechanical device while maintaining the originally specified degrees-of-freedom of the embryonic starting structure. One function modifies a link by attaching two new linked nodes to each end of the specified link, with two numerical arguments specifying the directional orientation of the to-be-added triangle. A second function modifies a link by replacing it with two new links that pass through a newly created common node, with the two numerical arguments specifying the direction of growth (the free end of each of the new links being attached to the mechanism at the closest nodes).

For quantum computing circuits (Spector, 2004), the function set consists of quantum gates that modify the state of the evolved systems qubits. These include a function that inverts the states of a qubit, a function that inverts the state of a qubit conditional on another qubit's value, a function that rotates the qubit, a function that swaps the state of two qubits, as well as the square root of a NOT gate, the Hadamard gate, a generalized rotation function, a controlled phase function, and a function that allows the state of a qubit to be read.

Of course, the native representations chosen by the various research groups that performed the above work in the six domains are not necessarily the most efficient representations (and the human-competitive results would have been noteworthy even if a more knowledge-intensive representation had been used). Nonetheless, prior to the completion of the above work, one would not have predicted that different research groups would each generate human-competitive results, given their choices of a straight-forward native representational scheme employing only the most basic and elementary kind of information about the domain involved. This experience in six engineering domains suggests that GP may be able to yield human-competitive results in additional domains.

Genetic programming breeds simulatability

Simulators were used to evaluate the behavior and characteristics of candidate individuals during the runs of genetic programming used to synthesize designs in all six domains discussed in this paper.

Specifically, the SPICE (Simulation Program with Integrated Circuit Emphasis) simulator developed at the University of California at Berkeley was used for simulating analog circuits (Quarles et al., 1994). Optical lens systems may be simulated with commercially available software (e.g., OSLO, Code V), public-domain software (e.g., KOJAC), or custom ray-tracing software. The Numerical Electromagnetics Code (NEC) is a "method of moments" simulator for wire antennas that was developed at the Lawrence Livermore National Laboratory (Burke, 1992). Controllers may be simulated by SPICE. (Lipson, 2004) used a custom kinematic simulation program for his work with mechanical systems. (Spector, 2004) used a custom simulator (QGAME) for simulating quantum computing circuits.

Each of these simulators is remarkably robust. However, with the exception of QGAME, the above simulators generally cannot simulate every conceivable structure that may be described using the representation scheme used in the domain involved. Most simulators cannot simulate the often-pathological individuals that are randomly created for the run's initial population or the individuals that are created later in the run by the probabilistic genetic operations used by genetic programming (crossover and mutation). When simulators are employed in conjunction with genetic programming, unsimulatable individuals are typically assigned a severe penalty and unsimulatable individuals are never, or almost never, selected to be reproduced into the next generation or to participate in the genetic operations of crossover and mutation. Of course, culling out unsimulatable individuals does not itself guarantee that simulatable parents will beget simulatable offspring. Thus, at the time when work began in each of the above problem domains, it was unknown whether a run of genetic programming could produce any significant number of simulatable offspring.

For the first problem in which genetic programming successfully synthesized both the topology and sizing of an analog electrical circuit, namely the lowpass filter problem [discussed in chapter 25 of (Koza et al., 1999), 72% of the circuits were unsimulatable; however, the percentage of unsimulatable circuits drops precipitously to 31% by generation 1, 16% by generation 2, 15% by generation

3, and to single-digit percentages by generation 10. Remarkably, similar rapid declines were observed in every run of every circuit synthesis problem (including those involving transistors) reported in (Koza et al., 1999) for which such data was collected.

Turning to an illustrative control problem [section 3.7.2 of (Koza et al., 2003)], 60% of the controllers in generation 0 could not be simulated, but the percentage dropped to 14% by generation 1 and 8% by generation 10.

The same observation concerning unsimulatability applied to runs involving the automatic synthesis of antennas (Koza et al., 2003) as well as optical lens systems (Al-Sakran et al., 2005; Koza et al., 2005a; Koza et al., 2005b). We consider the fact that genetic programming breeds simulatability to be a very surprising recurring feature of the work discussed because new individuals are introduced into the population by probabilistic operations (i.e., crossover, mutation) that are not specifically structured in any way to guarantee simulatability.

Genetic programming starts small

The initial population (generation 0) for a run of genetic programming is created using a probabilistic growth process for program trees that typically fosters the creation of program trees having a wide range of sizes and shapes. One of the common features of runs of genetic programming appears to be that the best-of-generation structure of generation 0 tends to have a small number of operative parts.

For example, consider work in which GP was used to automatically synthesize complete design for the previously patented (Konig, 1940) four-lens optical system (Al-Sakran et al., 2005). The best individual of generation 0 (Figure 1a in Table 9-1) is a lens system with one positive lens of flint glass. This single lens performs the important threshold task of focusing the axial rays (Figures a, b, and c in Table 9-1) coming through the entry pupil into the neighborhood of the desired area of the image surface. This single lens does not, of course, satisfy the multiplicity of additional specifications contained in the Konig patent; however, it provides a toehold from which the evolutionary process can begin to make further progress. Figure 1b in Table 9-1 shows the best-of-run lens optical lens system– a four-lens system that infringes on the Konig patent. As can be seen, the best-of-run individual has considerably more lenses, lens surfaces, and lens groups than the best-of-generation individual from generation 0.

Figure 2a in Table 9-1 shows the best-of-generation circuit from generation 0 of a run whose goal was to synthesize the topology and sizing for a lowpass filter with requirements on passband ripple and stopband attenuation equivalent to that of a fifth-order elliptic filter [chapter 25 of (Koza et al., 1999)]. As can be seen, this circuit contains only one capacitor shunting the input signal to

Table 9-1. Best of initial populations and best of run for several design problems

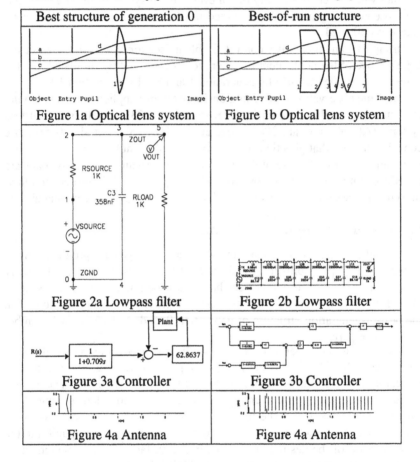

Best structure of generation 0	Best-of-run structure
Figure 1a Optical lens system	Figure 1b Optical lens system
Figure 2a Lowpass filter	Figure 2b Lowpass filter
Figure 3a Controller	Figure 3b Controller
Figure 4a Antenna	Figure 4a Antenna

ground. Figure 2b in Table 9-1 shows the best-of-run circuit– a cascade of seven rungs of a ladder, with each rung consisting of a shunt capacitor and a series inductor and that infringes the patent of George Campbell of AT&T (Campbell, 1917). As can be seen, the best-of-run individual has considerably more components and repeated substructures (ladder rungs) than the best-of-generation individual from generation 0. The best-of-generation 0 constituted a toehold for later evolution.

Figure 3a in Table 9-1 shows the best-of-generation controller from generation 0 for the two-lag plant problem [section 3.7 of (Koza et al., 2003)]. This individual is small and simple and has a threshold characteristic of the ultimate solution. Figure 3b in Table 9-1 shows the best-of-run controller, which infringes on the Jones [1942] patent. Again, the best-of-run individual has considerably more components and structural complexity than the best-of-generation individual from generation 0.

In the domain of antenna design, Figure 4a in Table 9-1 shows a best-of-node antenna from generation 0. It consists of only two elements. Figure 4b in Table 9-1 shows the best-of-run antenna that satisfies the specifications of a Yagi-Uda antenna (Comisky et al., 2000). Again, genetic programming started small in generation 0, and created a more complex, and better-performing, structure by the end of the run.

A structure with multiple operative parts can attain a reasonable level of fitness only if all the parts are appropriately connected and all the numerical parameters of each part are coordinated harmoniously with one another. We suggest that the reason that randomly created individuals in generation 0 of a run of genetic programming usually have only a small number of operative parts is that the appropriate connectivity and coordination can be achieved, at an early stage of a run, only when a small number of parts are involved.

Genetic programming frequently exploits a simulator's implicit assumptions of reasonableness

Most simulation software is written with the expectation that it will be used to analyze carefully considered designs created by human engineers as part of an iterative design-and-test process. Thus, most simulation software does not test the reasonableness of the to-be-simulated structure. For example, there is nothing in the grammar of an optical prescription to preclude choices of lens thickness and radii of curvature that correspond to two pieces of glass occupying the same space. Simulation software for optical systems usually does not test whether two pieces of glass may occupy the same physical space because such a design would never occur to a human engineer and because of the burden of writing and executing checking software. Similarly, the specifications of certain analog electrical circuits can sometimes be seemingly satisfied by circuits that draw billions of times more current than the tiny transistors from which the circuit is to be built. The component models used by simulators are often inaccurate for extreme values or idealized for the purpose of efficiency of simulation. In antenna design, the input to the simulator is typically a geometry table containing spatial dimensional coordinates of the two ends of the wires. However, when two wires are close, they must be merged in order to obtain an accurate simulation. A search conducted by genetic programming will exploit any opening created by a simulator that assumes reasonableness.

Genetic programming typically creates novel designs and engineers around existing patents

In two of the six domains discussed in this paper, genetic programming duplicated the functionality of groups of previously patented structures– six patented 21st-century analog electrical circuits (Koza et al., 2003) and seven patented optical lens systems (Al-Sakran et al., 2005; Koza et al., 2005a; Koza et al., 2005b; Jones et al., 2005; Jones et al., 005a).

In both groups of patents, genetic programming infringed only one of the patents. In the other cases in each group, genetic programming did one of two things. In some cases, it creatively "engineered" around the original patent– that is, it rediscovered the essence of the invention. In other cases, genetic programming created a novel solution (i.e., a new invention) that satisfied the high-level specifications of the original patented invention, but did not resemble the solution created by the human inventor.

We suggest that the reason for the infrequency of infringement is that there are often many ways to satisfy a set of engineering specifications. Genetic programming conducts a search for a satisfactory solution, but has no a priori knowledge about (and hence no particular preference for) the solution that a human may have thought of, or patented, in the past. In addition, while a patent is a solution for a problem, it is rarely the only solution. Moreover, a patented approach is not necessarily (or even usually) an optimal solution. GP seeks a solution that optimizes the fitness measure provided by the human user. That fitness measure does not, in general, encompass all the considerations (conscious or unconscious) motivating the original human inventor.

4.   Amenability of a domain to the application of genetic programming to automated design

Genetic programming is more likely to be useful for the automatic synthesis of designs to the extent that a particular engineering domain possesses many of the following characteristics:

- The existence of a method to evaluate the fitness of a large number of candidate individuals;

- Reasonableness of time to evaluate fitness;

- Need to automatically synthesize the size and shape of the to-be-evolved structure, not just the discovery of numerical parameters to size an existing structure.

- Design is considered to be an art, and not a science, in the domain; and

- Existence of problems in the domain that are not adequately addressed by existing methods and a need for creativity.

Existence of a method to evaluate the fitness of a large number of candidate individuals

The existence of a method to evaluate the fitness of a large number of candidate individuals is a precondition to applying searches by means of genetic and evolutionary computation in general and genetic programming in particular. First, as already mentioned, highly general and robust simulators exist in many fields of engineering. Second, rapidly reconfigurable digital circuitry (e.g., field-programmable gate arrays), rapidly reconfigurable analog circuitry (e.g., field-programmable transistor arrays), and rapidly reconfigurable antenna systems are currently available. Finally, in some domains (e.g., artificial evolution of mechanical systems embodied by nano-scale devices and artificial evolution of living biological systems), it may be efficient and economical to manufacture specified candidate individuals as part of a run of genetic programming. In that case, the behavior and characteristics of each candidate individual may simply be observed, evaluated, and recorded during the run.

Reasonableness of time to evaluate fitness

The computational effort required to solve a problem with genetic programming is the product of the average time required to evaluate the fitness of a candidate individual, the population size, the number of generations, and the number of independent runs likely to required to yield a satisfactory solution (an often-overlooked final multiplicative factor). Parallel computation can accelerate the process. The relentless exponential increase in available computational power tracked by Moore's law means that problems that cannot be considered in one year because of a lack of computational resources may be easily solved in a future year.

Need to automatically synthesize the size and shape of the to-be-evolved structure

GP is especially appropriate if there is a need to automatically synthesize the size and shape (that is, the topology) of the to-be-evolved structure– not just the discovery of numerical parameters to size an existing structure.

Design is considered to be an art, not a science

In many engineering domains, mathematical techniques and software tools enable a practicing engineer to analyze the behavior and characteristics of a particular already-designed structure. However, in most domains of engineering, there is no general mathematical solution to the inverse problem, namely that of synthesizing a structure from a high-level specification of the structure's desired behavior and characteristics. Thus, the problem of automatically synthesizing the design of complex structures in most domains of engineering is regarded as an art, rather than a science.

Existence of problems that are not adequately addressed by existing methods and a need for creativity

In a few specialized areas of design, closed-form mathematical methods (say, to design time-synchronous Boolean circuits) or heuristic approaches may be sufficient to automatically synthesize the design of satisfactory solutions to practical problems. That is, there is no need for genetic or evolutionary search and there is no need for creativity in solving the problem. Genetic or evolutionary search does not necessarily find optimal solutions, so if existing heuristic methods (e.g., the traveling salesperson problem) leave little room for improvements, there is little need for genetic or evolutionary methods. However, for the vast majority of engineering domains, there is no closed-form method or satisfactory heuristic approach for synthesizing the design of a complex structure.

5.   Genetic or evolutionary search domain-specific specializations

It is often advantageous, and sometimes necessary, to make domain-specific adjustments in order to use genetic programming most effectively in designing structures in a particular domain. For example, in almost every engineering domain, domain-specific practical considerations dictate limitations on the numeric values that parameters may assume. In optical lens systems, there are typically minimal and maximum thickness for the materials involved. As another example, when parts possess non-numerical parameters, it is necessary to introduce a symbolic mutation operation to permit a change from one non-numeric value to another. In domains where parts possess two or more non-numerical parameters, this mutation is most naturally executed as a move to a nearby neighbor in the multi-dimensional space involved. As yet another example, it is advisable (but not necessary) to use a toroidal mutation operation in the domain of optical design when perturbing a surface's radius of curvature (thereby equating a very large positive or negative radius of curvature). As another example, it may be helpful to use certain heuristics that are known to be useful in converting a good design to an even better design. Our optically neutral lens-splitting operation (Jones et al., 2005) is an example of a technique for improving designs that is widely used in optical design (Smith, 1992).

6.   Techniques issues observed in multiple domains

Several technique issues that have arisen in more than one domain.

Higher-level sub-structures

The entities that are inserted into a developing structure need not be as primitive as a single electrical component, a single lens surface, a single wire of an antenna, or a single signal-processing function in a controller. Instead, the entity-inserting functions can insert frequently occurring combinations of primitive components that are known to be useful in constructing practical systems. For example, current mirrors, voltage gain stages, Darlington emitter-follower sections, and cascodes might be inserted into developing circuits. In general, the insertion of higher-level entities corresponds to the incorporation of human domain knowledge as to what entities are useful subsystems. Graeb, Zizala, Eckmueller, and Antreich (Graeb et al., 2001) identified (for a purpose entirely unrelated to evolutionary computation) a promising set of frequently occurring combinations of transistors that are known to be useful in a broad range of analog circuits.

Absolute versus relative location of parts

Second, while working on optical lens systems, we noticed the reappearance of a representational issue that first arose during our work on the automatic synthesis of circuits, namely whether new substructures should generally be inserted at a relative location to the previously inserted substructure. In the context of optical lens systems, the question can be posed as to whether a new surface should be inserted at a specified distance relative to the previously inserted surface or at a location that is a specified relative to a fixed point (e.g., the object location or the entry pupil). In the context of circuits, this issue was partially addressed by the introduction of the NODE function and the NODE_INCREASED_SCOPE function described at the 2004 Genetic Programming Theory and Practice workshop (Koza et al., 2004). A parallel issue potentially arises in the design of antenna using developmental genetic programming.

Compliance-preserving representations

One of the recurring problems in approaching design problems with genetic and evolutionary computation is that the structures created in the initial random generation of a run and the structures produced by the probabilistic operations used to produce offspring later in the run do not satisfy the minimum requirements for suitable structures in the engineering domain involved. The problem is not that the probability of a compliant structure is typically vanishingly small.

For example, if circuits are represented by vectors of unrestricted numerical values that determine connectivity between components, most of the structures that are created in the initial random generation and by the genetic operations later in the run will not be valid circuits. Instead, there will be dangling components and isolated sub-circuits.

As another example, if the specifications for a design of an optical lens system specify a particular focal length and the population contains lens systems of variable focal length, an inordinate portion of the computational effort required to design the lens system may be expended in an ongoing attempt to assure compliance with the desired focal length. On the other hand, if all individuals in the initial random generation are created with the specified focal length and all genetic operations preserve compliance with that requirement, the search process is greatly accelerated.

It is thus advantageous to employ a representational scheme in which all structures created the initial random generation of a run and all offspring structures produced later in the run are compliant structures. A developmental process is often one way to guarantee compliance.

7.   Conclusions

This paper reviewed the recent use of genetic programming to automatically synthesize human-competitive designs in six domains, including analog electrical circuits, controllers, optical lens systems, antennas, mechanical systems, and quantum computing circuits. First, the paper identified common features observed in the human-competitive results produced by genetic programming in various engineering domains and suggests possible explanations for the observed similarities. Second, the paper identified the characteristics that make a particular domain amenable to the application of genetic programming for the automatic synthesis of designs for complex structures in that domain. Third, the paper discussed the specialization of general techniques that may increase the efficiency of the process of automatically synthesizing the design of structures in a particular domain. Fourth, the paper discussed several technique issues that have arisen in more than one domain.

References

Al-Sakran, Sameer H., Koza, John R., and Jones, Lee W. (2005). Automated reinvention of a previously patented optical lens system using genetic programming. In Keijzer, Maarten, Tettamanzi, Andrea, Collet, Pierre, van Hemert, Jano I., and Tomassini, Marco, editors, *Proceedings of the 8th European Conference on Genetic Programming*, volume 3447 of *Lecture Notes in Computer Science*, pages 25–37, Lausanne, Switzerland. Springer.

Brave, S. (1996). Evolving deterministic finite automata using cellular encoding. In Koza, J.R., Goldberg, D.E., Fogel, D.B., and Riolo, R.L., editors, *Genetic Programming 1996: Proceedings of the First Annual Conference, July 28-31, Stanford University*, pages 39–44, Cambridge, MA. MIT Press.

Burke, G.J. (1992). Numerical electromagnetics code – nec-4: Method of moments – user's manual. Technical report, Lawrence Livermore National Labratory, Livermore, CA.

Campbell, G.A. (1917). Electric wave filter. U.S. Patent 1,227113. filed july 15, 1915, issued may 22, 1917.

Comisky, William, Yu, Jessen, and Koza, John R. (2000). Automatic synthesis of a wire antenna using genetic programming. In Whitley, Darrell, editor, *Late Breaking Papers at the 2000 Genetic and Evolutionary Computation Conference*, pages 179–186, Las Vegas, Nevada, USA.

Graeb, H.E., Zizala, S., Eckmueller, J., and Antreich, K. (2001). The sizing rules method for analog circuit design. pages 343–349, Piscataway, NJ. IEEE Press.

Gruau, F. (1992). Cellular encoding of genetic neural networks. Technical report 92-21, Laboratoire de l'Informatique du Parallilisme. Ecole Normale Supirieure de Lyon, France.

Jones, Lee W., Al-Sakran, Sameer H., and Koza, John R. (2005). Automated design of a previously patented aspherical optical lens system by means of genetic programming. In Yu, Tina, Riolo, Rick L., and Worzel, Bill, editors, *Genetic Programming Theory and Practice III*, volume 9 of *Genetic Programming*, chapter 3, pages 33–48. Springer, Ann Arbor.

Jones, L.W., Al-Sakran, S.H., and Koza, J.R. (2005a). Automated synthesis of both the topology and numerical parameters for seven patented optical lens systems using genetic programming. In Mouroulis, P.Z., Smith, W.J., and Johnson, R.B., editors, *Current Developments in Lens Design and Optical Engineering VI*, volume 5874, pages 24–38, Bellingham. SPIE.

Keane, M.A., Koza, J.R., and Streeter, M.J. (2005). Apparatus for improved general-purpose pid and non-pid controllers. U.S. Patent 6,847,851. filed july 12, 2002, issued january 25, 2005.

Kitano, H. (1990). Designing neural networks using genetic algorithms with graph generation system. *Complex Systems*, 4:461–476.

Konig, A. (1940). Telescope eyepiece. U.S. Patent 2,206,195. filed in Germany December 24, 1937, filed in U.S. December 14, 1938, issued July 2, 1940.

Koza, John R. (1993). Discovery of rewrite rules in lindenmayer systems and state transition rules in cellular automata via genetic programming. In *Symposium on Pattern Formation (SPF-93), Claremont, California, USA*.

Koza, John R., Al-Sakran, Sameer H., and Jones, Lee W. (2005a). Automated re-invention of six patented optical lens systems using genetic programming. In Beyer, Hans-Georg, O'Reilly, Una-May, Arnold, Dirk V., Banzhaf, Wolfgang, Blum, Christian, Bonabeau, Eric W., Cantu-Paz, Erick, Dasgupta, Dipankar, Deb, Kalyanmoy, Foster, James A., de Jong, Edwin D., Lipson, Hod, Llora, Xavier, Mancoridis, Spiros, Pelikan, Martin, Raidl, Guenther R., Soule, Terence, Tyrrell, Andy M., Watson, Jean-Paul, and Zitzler, Eckart, editors, *GECCO 2005: Proceedings of the 2005 conference on Genetic and evolutionary computation*, volume 2, pages 1953–1960, Washington DC, USA. ACM Press.

Koza, John R., Al-Sakran, Sameer H., and Jones, Lee W. (2005b). Cross-domain features of runs of genetic programming used to evolve designs for analog circuits, optical lens systems, controllers, antennas, mechanical systems, and quantum computing circuits. In Lohn, Jason, Gwaltney, David, Hornby, Gregory, Zebulum, Ricardo, Keymeulen, Didier, and Stoica, Adrian, editors, *Proceedings of the 2005 NASA/DoD Conference on Evolvable Hardware*, pages 205–214, Washington, DC, USA. IEEE Press.

Koza, John R., Andre, David, Bennett III, Forrest H, and Keane, Martin (1999). *Genetic Programming 3: Darwinian Invention and Problem Solving.* Morgan Kaufman.

Koza, John R., Bennett III, Forrest H, Andre, David, and Keane, Martin A (1996a). Automated design of both the topology and sizing of analog electrical circuits using genetic programming. In Gero, John S. and Sudweeks, Fay, editors, *Artificial Intelligence in Design '96*, pages 151–170, Dordrecht. Kluwer Academic.

Koza, John R., Bennett III, Forrest H, Andre, David, and Keane, Martin A (1996b). Reuse, parameterized reuse, and hierarchical reuse of substructures in evolving electrical circuits using genetic programming. In Higuchi, Tetsuya, Masaya, Iwata, and Liu, Weixin, editors, *Proceedings of International Conference on Evolvable Systems: From Biology to Hardware (ICES-96)*, volume 1259 of *Lecture Notes in Computer Science*, Tsukuba, Japan. Springer-Verlag.

Koza, John R., Jones, Lee W., Keane, Martin A., and Streeter, Matthew J. (2004). Towards industrial strength automated design of analog electrical circuits by means of genetic programming. In O'Reilly, Una-May, Yu, Tina, Riolo, Rick L., and Worzel, Bill, editors, *Genetic Programming Theory and Practice II*, chapter 8, pages 120–?? Springer, Ann Arbor. pages missing?

Koza, John R., Keane, Martin A., Streeter, Matthew J., Mydlowec, William, Yu, Jessen, and Lanza, Guido (2003). *Genetic Programming IV: Routine Human-Competitive Machine Intelligence.* Kluwer Academic Publishers.

Lipson, Hod (2004). How to draw a straight line using a GP: Benchmarking evolutionary design against 19th century kinematic synthesis. In Keijzer, Maarten, editor, *Late Breaking Papers at the 2004 Genetic and Evolutionary Computation Conference*, Seattle, Washington, USA.

Lohn, Jason, Hornby, Gregory, and Linden, Derek (2004). Evolutionary antenna design for a NASA spacecraft. In O'Reilly, Una-May, Yu, Tina, Riolo, Rick L., and Worzel, Bill, editors, *Genetic Programming Theory and Practice II*, chapter 18, pages 301–315. Springer, Ann Arbor.

Quarles, T., Newton, A.R., Pederson, D.O., and Sangiovanni-Vincentelli, A. (1994). Spice 3 version 3f5 user's manual. Technical report, Department of Electrical Engineering and Computer Science, University of California, Berkeley, California.

Smith, W.J. (1992). *Modern Lens Design: A Resource Manual*. McGraw-Hill, Boston, MA.

Spector, Lee (2004). *Automatic Quantum Computer Programming: A Genetic Programming Approach*, volume 7 of *Genetic Programming*. Kluwer Academic Publishers, Boston/Dordrecht/New York/London.

Wilson, S.W. (1997). Genetic algorithms and their applications. In John, J., editor, *Proceedings of the Second International Conference on Genetic Algorithms*, pages 247–251, Hillsdale, NJ. Lawrence Erlbaum Associates.

Chapter 10

ROBUST PARETO FRONT GENETIC PROGRAMMING PARAMETER SELECTION BASED ON DESIGN OF EXPERIMENTS AND INDUSTRIAL DATA

Flor Castillo,[1] Arthur Kordon[1] and Guido Smits[2]

[1] *The Dow Chemical Company, Freeport, TX.*
[2] *Dow Benelux, Terneuzen, The Netherlands.*

Abstract   Symbolic regression based on Pareto-Front GP is a very effective approach for generating high-performance parsimonious empirical models acceptable for industrial applications. The chapter addresses the issue of finding the optimal parameter settings of Pareto-Front GP which direct the simulated evolution toward simple models with acceptable prediction error. A generic methodology based on statistical design of experiments is proposed. It includes determination of the number of replicates by half width confidence intervals, determination of the significant factors by fractional factorial design of experiments, approaching the optimum by steepest ascent/descent, and local exploration around the optimum by Box Behnken design of experiments. The results from implementing the proposed methodology to different types of industrial data sets show that the statistically significant factors are the number of cascades, the number of generations, and the population size. The optimal values for the three parameters have been defined based on second order regression models with R^2 higher than 0.97 for small, medium, and large-sized data sets. The robustness of the optimal parameters toward the types of data sets was explored and a robust setting for the three significant parameters was obtained. It reduces the calculation time by 30% to 50% without statistically significant reduction in the mean response.

Keywords: Genetic programming, symbolic regression, industrial applications, design of experiments, parameter selection

1.   Introduction

One of the issues any researcher and practitioner needs to resolve dealing with Genetic Programming (GP) is to select a proper set of parameters, such as number of generations, population size, crossover probability, mutation rate, *etc*. There are several investigations on using experimental design for determination of the key Genetic Algorithm (GA) parameters (Reeves and Wright, 1995), (Chan et al., 2003). Recently, Petrovski et al (Petrovski et al., 2005) investigated the performance of genetic algorithms and parameter tuning using experimental design and optimization techniques.

Surprisingly, there are very few investigations on this topic known in the literature for GP. In his first book, Koza (Koza, 1992) gives several rules of thumb for parameter selection based on simulation experience. Similar recommendations are given in (Banzhaf et al., 1998). The only statistically-based study by Feldt and Nordin (Feldt and Nordin, 2000) investigated the effect of 17 GP parameters on three binary classification problems using highly fractionated experimental statistical designs assuming, in some cases, that even second- and third-order interactions are not significant, *i.e.*, the combined effect of two factors and three factors has no effect on the response. However, these assumptions have not been verified.

Recently, the growing interest of industry in GP (Kordon et al., 2005) requires a more systematic approach for the GP model generation process to guarantee consistency of delivered results. An important part of this process is the appropriate parameters setting for each specific type of applications, which will improve the efficiency of model development and minimize the development cost. One of the best ways to address this issue is by using statistical Design Of Experiments (DOE) on industrial data (Box et al., 2005). Fortunately, as a result of the current successful GP applications, a set of industrial benchmark data sets has been collected. A summary for the applications in the chemical industry is given in (Kordon et al., 2005). They are with different sizes and data quality and each one is a source of a successful real world application based on GP-generated symbolic regression.

The chapter describes the statistical methodology and the results for finding the optimal parameter settings of a specific type of GP, called Pareto-Front GP , based on multi-objective optimization (Smits and Kotanchek, 2004). The results are within the scope of symbolic regression applications. The paper is organized in the following manner. First, the specific features of the Pareto-Front GP approach, its importance to industrial applications, and the selected setting parameters are discussed in Section 2. A generic DOE methodology for optimal GP parameter selection is described in Section 3 and applied for the specific case of Pareto-Front GP parameter selection. The results for finding optimal GP parameter settings for a medium-size industrial data set are given in Section 4 and the robustness issues of the optimal settings are discussed in Section 5.

2. Key Parameters of Pareto Front Genetic Programming for Symbolic Regression

One of the areas where GP has a clear competitive advantage in real world applications is fast development of nonlinear empirical models (Kordon et al., 2005). However, if the GP-generated functions are based on high accuracy only, the high-fitness models are very complex, difficult to interpret, and crash on even minor changes in operating conditions. Manual selection of models with lower complexity and acceptable accuracy requires time consuming screening through large number of models. The solution is by using multi-objective optimization to direct the simulated evolution toward simple models with sufficient accuracy. Recently, a special version of GP, called Pareto-Front GP, has significantly improved the efficiency of symbolic-regression model development. The detailed description of the algorithm is given in (Kotanchek et al., 2006). In Pareto-Front GP the simulated evolution is based on two criteria prediction error (for example, based on $1-R^2$) and complexity (for example, based on the number of nodes). The optimal models fall on the curve of the non-dominated solutions, called Pareto front, *i.e.*, no other solution is better than the solutions on the Pareto front in both complexity and performance. Of special importance to industry are the most parsimonious models with high performance, which occupy the lower left corner of the Pareto front (see Figure 10-1). From that perspective, the objective of parameter settings is to select GP parameters that push the simulated evolution toward the parsimonious models with high performance, *i.e.* to guarantee a consistent convergence to the lower left corner of the Pareto front.

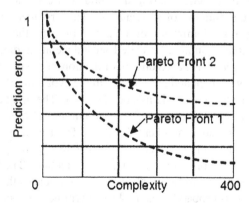

Figure 10-1. Responses for Pareto Front GP.

For the statistical DOE we need to define the target or response variable and the independent parameters or factors we would like to explore. The proposed response variable is the percentage of the area below the Pareto front (see Figure 10-1). In this case the accuracy or the prediction error is calculated as $(1-R^2)$ and the complexity is represented by the sum of the number of nodes of all sub-equations (Smits and Kotanchek, 2004). From practical consideration, an upper complexity limit of 400 is defined. The Pareto front line is obtained by interpolating through the points on the Pareto front. The area below the Pareto front is calculated within the limits of the prediction error between 0 and 1 and complexity between 0 and 400. This area is divided on the full rectangle area and the response is the calculated percentage. For example, the response of Pareto front 1 is 23% and the response of Pareto front 2 is 56% (see Figure 10-1). The objective of the DOE is to select factors that minimize the response, *i.e.*, to push the Pareto front toward the origin where the simple models with low prediction error are located.

The selected Pareto-Front GP parameters (factors) and their ranges are presented in the following table:

Table 10-1. Factors for the Pareto front GP DOE.

Factor	Low Level (-1)	High Level (+1)
x_1 - Number of cascades	10	50
x_2 - Number of generations	10	50
x_3 - Population size	100	500
x_4 - Prob. of function selection	0.4	0.65
x_5 - Size of archive	50	100

One of the key features of Pareto-Front GP is the availability of an archive to save the Pareto front models during the simulated evolution. This creates two measures for the duration of simulations. The first measure is based on starting conditions of randomization of the population and the archive and the duration of the whole simulation is called an independent run. The second measure, called a cascade, is based on randomization of the population but the content of the archive is kept and participates in the evolution, *i.e.* it is possible to have several cascades in a single independent run. The number of cascades is the first factor in the DOE and it reflects the number of runs with a freshly generated starting population and kept the Pareto front models in the archive. Factor x_2 represents the number of generations; Factor x_3 is the population size. Factor x_4 determines the probability of function selection. The probability of function selection is used during initialization and influences the initial size of the function trees. This probability is used to determine whether the next node is a function or a terminal during function generation. The higher this number is, the larger the initial trees are. Factor x_5 defines the archive size in percentage of the population size. The ranges of the factors have been selected based on the experience from various types of practical problems, related to symbolic regression. Since the objective is a consistent Pareto front close to the origin, they differ from the recommendations for the original GP algorithm.

3. A Generic Methodology for Optimal GP Parameter Selection Based On Statistical Design of Experiments

Design of Experiments is a statistical approach that allows to further enhance the knowledge of a system by quantifying the effect of a set of inputs (factors) on an output (response). This is accomplished by systematically running experiments at different combinations of the factor settings (Box et al., 2005).

A classical DOE is the 2^k design in which all factors are investigated at an upper and lower level of a range resulting in 2^k experiments where k is the number of factors. This design has the advantage that the effects of the individual factors (main effects) as well as all possible interactions (combination of factors) can be estimated. However the number of experimental runs increases rapidly as the number of factors increases. If the number of experiments is impractical, fractional factorial (FF) design can be used. In this case only a fraction of the full 2^k design is run by assuming that some interactions among factors are not significant. However in this case the main effects and interactions are confounded (cannot be estimated separately).

Depending on the type of fractional factorial, main effects may be confounded with second-, third-, or fourth-order interactions. The level of confounding is dictated by the design resolution. The higher the design resolution, the less confounding among factors. For example, a resolution III design confounds main effects with second-order interactions; a resolution IV design confounds second-order interaction with other second-order interactions; and a resolution V design confounds second-order interactions with third-order interactions.

When the objective of experimentation is to find the values of the inputs that will yield a maximum or a minimum for a specific response, the DOE strategy used is known as *response surface*. In this case fractional factorials are initially used to determine if the initial setting of the inputs are far from the desired optimum. This initial design is used to determine new levels of the inputs which approach to the optimum (this is known as the steepest ascent path). As the optimum is approached, other DOE techniques such as central composite designs (CCD) or Box Behnken are used for local explorations so that the optimum can be identified and the conditions for practical use can be determined (Box et al., 2005).

Applying DOE techniques to determine the optimal set of GP parameters needs to address also the issue of the statistically significant number of replications (independent runs). This is of key importance because the variability of the response may not be the same for the different combination of factors. To estimate the number of required replications, the half width (HW) confidence interval method (Montgomery, 1995) can be used. The half width (HW) is defined as:

$$HW = t_{n-1,\alpha/2}\frac{S}{\sqrt{n}} \qquad (10.1)$$

where $t_{n-1,\alpha/2}$ is the upper $\alpha/2$ percentage point of the t distribution with $n-1$ degrees of freedom, S is the standard deviation and n is the number of runs. A plot of the $100(1-\alpha)\%$ HW confidence interval reveals the minimum number of replications for a determined value of HW. The $100(1-\alpha)\%$ *confidence interval* is a range of values in which the true answer is believed to lie with $1-\alpha$ probability. Usually α is set at 0.05 so that a 95% confidence interval is calculated. Half width, sometimes called accuracy of the confidence interval, is the distance between the estimated mean and the upper or lower range of the confidence interval.

The response surface and sample size techniques described in this section are the key components of a generic methodology for identifying the optimal set of GP parameters for any type of applications. The methodology can be depicted in the following diagram, shown in Figure 10-2.

The objective of the first step in the proposed methodology is to give an answer to the question of the necessary number of replications (independent runs) that will guarantee statistically reproducible results. The discussed approach for HW confidence interval is used and an initial number of at least 50 replicates is recommended.

The purpose of the second step is to obtain the statistically significant inputs by fractional factorial design. The next three steps are needed to find the optimal parameters. First, the new levels of the input variables (factors) which would lead to the optimum are calculated by the steepest ascent/descent method and the experimental runs on them are performed (Step 3). Second, the area around the optimum is further explored locally by a new experimental design, usually central composite (or Box Behnken) design (Step 4). The expected result from this step is a regression model around the optimum with the key factors. The final optimal parameters, however, are obtained in Step 5 by using the desirability function approach (Derringer and Suich, 1980). It is strongly recommended that the optimal settings are validated on other similar applications.

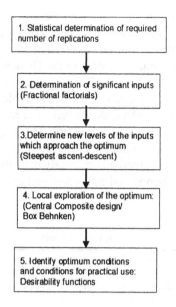

Figure 10-2. Methodology for identifying the optimal set of GP parameters.

4. Results

Experimental Setup

The full experimental study includes three types of data sets: small-sized, middle-sized, and large-sized. The small-sized data set includes up to 5 inputs and up to 50 data points. The middle-sized data set includes up to 10 inputs and up to 500 data points. The large-sized data set includes more than 10 inputs and may include thousands of data points. In this chapter, the results of applying the methodology for middle-sized data set are presented. The results for small-sized data sets are presented in (Castillo et al., 2006).

The explored medium-sized data set is described in (Kordon et al., 2003b) and it uses 8 process inputs variables and an emission variable as model output. The data set includes 251 data points of emission and process data measurements.

Optimal Pareto GP Parameters for Medium-Sized Data Set

This section describes the results of applying the proposed methodology for the medium-sized data set.

Steps 1-2. *Determination of required number of replications- Determination of significant inputs.*

In order to understand the effect of the GP inputs on the response and if the initial input settings were far removed from the optimum, a 2_V^{5-1} resolution

V fractional factorial design was used with the inputs (GP factors) shown in Table 10-1 and the percentage area under the Pareto front as the response. The 2_V^{5-1} Fractional Factorial (FF) design consisted of 16 experimental runs (not to be confused with independent runs, used in the GP algorithm) plus one center point located at (30, 30, 300, 0.53, 0.75) in x_1, x_2, x_3, x_4, x_5 respectively. The corresponding experimental design is presented in Table 10-2 and was executed with 50 initial replications (independent runs). The results for the response in Table 10-2 are based on the average value from the 50 replications.

Calculation of the required number of replications for each experimental run was done with the 95% HW method previously described. The corresponding curves for each of the experimental runs presented in Table 10-2 are shown in Figure 10-3.

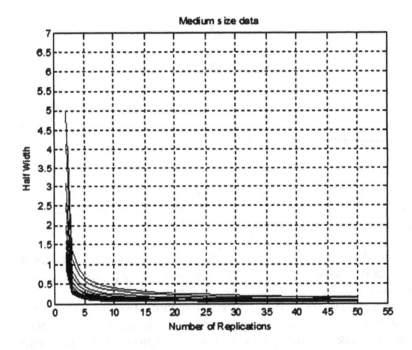

Figure 10-3. A 95% Half Width Confident interval - Determination of Required number of replications for 2_V^{5-1} FF experiments.

The HW method reveals that 50 replicates are enough to be within a half width of 0.5% area under the Pareto front. Most of the experiments (except the ones for which population size was in the lower level of 100) required less than 50 replications. The average area under Pareto front is used as the response because the variability existing between the replications for an experimental condition (the rows in Table 10-2) does not measure the variability between the experimental runs.

Table 10-2. 2_V^{5-1} Fractional Factorial Design.

Experimental run	x_1	x_2	x_3	x_4	x_5	Response
1	10	10	500	0.65	100	6.02
2	50	50	500	0.4	50	5.38
3	50	10	100	0.4	50	6.17
4	10	10	100	0.65	50	6.69
5	50	10	100	0.65	100	6.00
6	50	50	100	0.65	50	5.94
7	10	10	500	0.4	50	6.02
8	50	10	500	0.4	100	5.69
9	10	50	100	0.65	100	5.99
10	10	10	100	0.4	100	7.88
11	30	30	300	0.525	75	5.58
12	10	50	100	0.4	50	6.28
13	50	50	100	0.4	100	5.70
14	10	50	500	0.65	50	5.58
15	50	50	500	0.65	100	5.23
16	10	50	500	0.4	100	5.68
17	50	10	500	0.65	50	5.53

The results of the 2_V^{5-1} fractional factorial design with 50 replicates per experimental run are shown in Table 10-3. The analysis was completed using the statistical package JMP ©. [1]

If Prob>|t| is less than 0.05 the factor has a statistically significant effect on the response at the 95% confidence level. Based on the results, the only statistically significant factors are the number of cascades, the number of generations and the population size (highlighted in Table 10-3).

Step 3. *Determination of new levels of the inputs which approach the optimum*

To find conditions that led to a minimum response the path of steepest ascent-descent was calculated using the first order estimates (Myers and Montgomery, 1995). Using the estimates of Table 10-3, the vector of steepest ascent is calculated as (-0.28,-0.26,-0.34,-0.11, 0.29). The length of this vector is 0.6 so the unit length vector is (-0.47,-0.4,-0.57,-0.19, 0.48). Therefore of every -0.47 units in x_1 we need to move -0.4 in x_2, -0.57 in x_3, -0.19 in x_4 and 0.48 in x_5.

---

[1] JMP is a registered trademark of SAS Institute Inc. Cary, NC, USA.

Table 10-3. Statistical Results from 2_V^{5-1} Fractional Factorial Design for a Medium-Sized Data Set.

Factor	Estimate	Prob>|t|
Intercept	6.27	4.53E-05
Number of Cascades	-0.28	**0.011958**
Number of Generations	-0.25	**0.016473**
Population Size	-0.34	**0.004191**
Prob. Func. Selection	-0.11	0.229607
Size of Archive	0.29	0.686794
Number of Cascades*Number of Generations	0.12	0.200071
Number of Cascades*Population Size	0.10	0.288629
Number of Generations*Population Size	0.09	0.333296

The calculated path in which minimum and maximum response is expected is given in Table 10-4.

Given that the objective is to minimize the response, the next experiments were planned in the direction of steepest descent centered on the base line. This was decided because of the change in response around the base line (from 5.58 to 5.38) and because of practical considerations (further away from the center in the direction of steepest descent represent experiments that are unrealistic from the point of view of computation time for the required number of replications (like response 5.30), based on higher population size than the high limit of 500 in Table 10-4).

Table 10-4. Local exploration of the optimum.

Direction	x1	x2	x3	x4	x5	y
↑ Steepest ascent	13	14	95	0.48	97	6.51
	14	15	106	0.49	95	6.23
	16	17	129	0.49	93	6.11
	21	21	186	0.5	87	5.86
Base line	30	30	300	0.53	75	5.58
↓ Steepest descent	39	39	414	0.55	63	5.38
	49	47	528	0.57	51	5.30

The response surface experiment uses a Box Behnken design with the significant factors (number of cascades, number of generations and population size). Table 10-5 gives the parameter estimates for the medium data set which are represented as a regression model shown in equation 10.1.

Table 10-5. Parameter estimates from the Box Behnken Design- Medium data set.

Factor	Estimate	Prob>|t|
Intercept	5.55	1.53E-15
Number of Cascades	-0.20	3.35E-08
Number of Generations	-0.19	4.93E-08
Population Size	-0.23	1.75E-08
Number of Cascades*Number of Cascades	0.10	1.96E-05
Number of Cascades*Number of Generations	0.04	0.002823
Number of Generations*Number of Generations	0.12	6.95E-06
Number of Cascades*Population Size	0.03	0.007175
Population Size*Population Size	0.12	6.28E-06

$$y = 5.55 - 0.2X_1 - 0.19X_2 - 0.23X_3 + 0.04X_1X_2 + 0.03X_1X_3$$
$$+0.1X_1^2 + 0.12X_2^2 + 0.12X_3^2$$

where $X_1 - X_3$ are the significant factors (number of cascades, number of generations and population size) in coded form between -1 and +1 and y is the response (the percentage of the area below the Pareto front).

The model presented in equation 10.1 has an R^2 of 0.99 and includes statistically significant quadratic effects for the number of cascades, number of generations and population size.

Step 5. *Identify optimum conditions and conditions for practical use*

The desirability function approach (Derringer and Suich, 1980), has been used to find the optimal values of the parameters that minimize the response. The desirability method is commonly used with multiple responses. The method finds input conditions (x_i) that provide the "most desirable" response values. For each response $Y_i(x_i)$, a desirability function $d_i(Y_i)$ assigns numbers between 0 and 1 to the possible values of Y_i, with $d_i(Y_i) = 0$ representing a completely undesirable value of Y_i and $d_i(Y_i) = 1$ representing a completely desirable or ideal value. The individual desirabilities are then combined using the geometric mean, which gives the overall desirability D.

The prediction profiler in Figure 10-4 below shows *desirability* traces for the number of cascades, number of generations and population size. A desirability trace is the predicted response and its desirability as one variable is changed while the others are held constant at the current values. The overall desirability measure shows on a scale of zero to one at the left of the row of desirability traces.

The profile in Figure 10-4 shows the settings of the parameters *number of cascades, number of generations and population size* (vertical dotted lines) that minimize the area under the Pareto front (5.315824 or horizontal dotted line).

Of special importance are curvilinear desirability traces because they indicated a response highly sensitive to a range of input variables. As an example, in

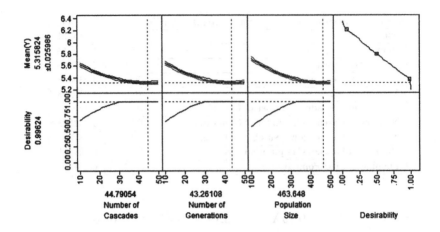

Figure 10-4. Prediction Profiler showing the setting of Pareto front GP parameters that mini-mizes the response.

the case of number of cascades there is little improvement beyond 45. Likewise there is little improvement in minimizing the response beyond 44 for number of generations and beyond 464 for population size. These optimal values are closer to the upper range of all three statistically significant factors. For example, the range of the number of cascades is between 10 and 50 and the optimal value is 45. The optimum values for each factor for the medium-sized data set are: number of cascades = 45, number of generations = 44, population size = 464, probability of function selection = 0.53, size of the archive = 75%, and number of replications = 10.

Valdation on Different Medium-Sized Data Sets

In order to verify the optimal medium-sized data set setting of Pareto-Front GP parameters, we will compare the performance with an additional industrial medium-sized data set. The data set was generated from a fundamental model of a chemical process by a 32-run Plackett-Burman experimental design with 10 factors at four levels (Kordon et al., 2003a). The output is a key process parameter that was used for intermediate product optimization between two chemical plants in The Dow Chemical Company. The training data set consisted of 320 data points.

The optimal parameters, given in the previous section were compared with the following non-optimal parameter set: number of cascades = 10, number of generations = 25, population size = 100, probability of function selection = 0.6, and size of the archive = 75% (used in model development before parameter optimization). The following figure shows the difference in the performance based on optimal and non-optimal factors, applied to the validation medium-sized data set.

In order to validate if the difference in the performance based on optimal and non-optimal factors is statistically significant, Welch ANOVA was used given that the variances of the two groups are different (Welch, 1951). The p value for this test is 0.0001 indicating that the use of Pareto-Front GP optimal parameter set results in a statistically significant lower area under the Pareto front GP (mean value of 5.35) as compared with the non-optimal parameter set (mean value of 11.78). It validates the use of suggested Pareto front parameter settings on different medium-sized data set and can be recommended for symbolic regression class of problems.

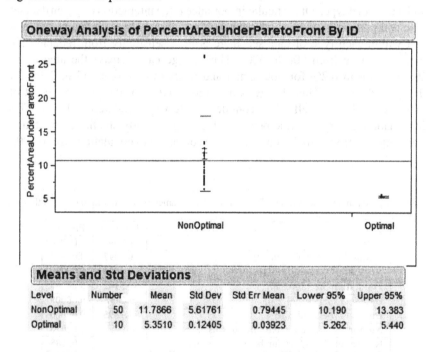

Figure 10-5. Comparison between optimal and non-optimal responses for the validation data set.

5. Robustness

For industrial applications, in addition to finding the optimal settings, it is desirable to understand whether there are GP parameters that are robust to the type of data set. In other words, are there GP parameters that are insensitive to the small, medium and large data set? The methodology previously described was applied to a large data set (17 process inputs and 1000 data points) and the optimal parameters are: number of cascades = 50, number of generations = 50, population size = 490, probability of function selection = 0.53, size of the archive = 75%. The complete analysis of the small data set results is given in (Castillo et al., 2006).

For robustness analysis, we will focus on the results from the Box Behnken design for small, medium and large-sized data sets considering the number of cascades (x1), number of generations (x2) and population size (x3). The statistical analysis of this data can be seen in Table 10-6. Statistically significant effects at the 95% confidence level are shown in bold.

This table reveals statistically significant interaction between GP parameters and the data set type. Of particular importance is the interaction between data set type and population size which is shown in Figure 10-6. This figure suggests that within each type of data set, there is little sensitivity from reducing the population size from 500 to 300. This change can increase the area under Pareto Front in 0.2% for both small and medium data sets and in 0.4% for the large data set. This change is not significant from the practical point of view (recall that the half width confidence interval considered is 0.5%). This information is very valuable because of the significantly smaller computation time required from population size of 300 compared to population size of 500.

Table 10-6. Parameter estimates for Pareto-Front GP parameters considering the size of the data sets.

Term	Estimate	Prob>|t|
Intercept	7.1546	0.00000
Number of Cascades(10,50)	**-0.4097**	**0.00000**
Number of Generations(10,50)	**-0.4006**	**0.00000**
Population Size(100,500)	**-0.5142**	**0.00000**
DataSetType[Large]	**5.6057**	**0.00000**
DataSetType[Medium]	**-1.7895**	**0.00000**
Number of Cascades*Number of Cascades	**0.1965**	**0.00078**
Number of Cascades*Number of Generations	0.0028	0.95588
Number of Generations*Number of Generations	**0.2085**	**0.00042**
Number of Cascades*Population Size	-0.0023	0.96354
Number of Generations*Population Size	-0.0023	0.96354
Population Size*Population Size	**0.2805**	**0.00001**
Number of Cascades*DataSetType[Large]	**-0.2632**	**0.00001**
Number of Cascades*DataSetType[Medium]	**0.2072**	**0.00029**
Number of Generations*DataSetType[Large]	**-0.2682**	**0.00001**
Number of Generations*DataSetType[Medium]	**0.2166**	**0.00018**
Population Size*DataSetType[Large]	**-0.2996**	**0.00000**
Population Size*DataSetType[Medium]	**0.2892**	**0.00000**

In order to check this observation, two additional runs for each data set were made. The first run is with the optimal parameters (for small-sized data set the parameters are: number of cascades = 43, number of generation = 47, population size = 429, probability of function selection = 0.53, and size of the archive = 75%; for the medium and large-sized data set the optimal parameters are given in the previous section. The second run is with the robust population size of 300 and all other parameters at the optimal values. In all cases the difference for small, medium and large data set from switching from population size of 500 to 300 is less than 0.5% which although statistically significant, it is insignificant from practical purposes.

This confirms that the population size can be set to the robust value of 300 for the three data sets instead of the optimal values of 429 for the small data set; 464 for the medium data; and 490 for the large dataset set with very little effect on the response. At the same time, the reduction of the computation time is significant: 52% for the small data set and 48% for the medium data set and 39% for the large data set.

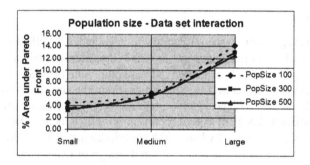

Figure 10-6. Interaction between the data set size and population size.

The interactions between data set type and number of cascades and data set type and number of generations were analyzed in a similar way as the interaction between data set type and population size previously presented. In this case it was desirable to find robust parameter setting that were slightly different from the optimal condition but that would result in a mean area under Pareto front that was < 0.5% different from the area obtained under optimal conditions. For small and medium-sized data sets the robust parameters are: number of cascades = 30, number of generation = 30, population size = 300, probability of function selection = 0.53, and size of the archive = 75%; for the large-sized data set the robust parameters are: number of cascades = 40, number of generation = 40, population size = 400, probability of function selection = 0.53, and size of the archive = 75%.

The robust settings and the corresponding savings in computation time are presented in Table 10-7. As can be seen from Table 10-7, the most significant savings in computation time for small, medium and large data sets are associated with the robust setting for population size.

Table 10-7. Optimum and robust parameter estimates and savings in computation time.

Small	Parameters	Optimum	Rob.-PopSize	Rob.-all
	#Cascades, #gen., pop. size	43,47,429	43,47,**300**	**30,30,300**
	Mean % Area Under Pareto Front	2.94	3.19	3.16
	%Saving-Computation Time		49%	48%
Medium	#Cascades, #gen., pop. size	45,44,464	45,44 **300**	**30,30,300**
	Mean % Area Under Pareto Front	5.28	5.45	5.6
	% Saving-Computation Time		48%	53%
Large	#Cascades, #gen., pop. size	50,50,490	50,50,**350**	**40,40,400**
	Mean % Area Under Pareto Front	11.47	11.85	12.05
	% Saving-Computation Time		34%	31%

6.   Summary

Symbolic regression based on Pareto-Front GP is a very effective approach for generating high-performance parsimonious empirical models acceptable for industrial applications. The chapter addresses the issue of finding the optimal parameter settings of Pareto front GP which direct the simulated evolution toward simple models with acceptable prediction error. A generic methodology based on statistical design of experiments is proposed. It includes determination of the number of replicates by half width confidence intervals, determination of the significant factors by fractional factorial design of experiments, approaching the optimum by steepest ascent/descent, and local exploration around the optimum by Box Behnken design of experiments. The results from implementing the proposed methodology to different types of industrial data sets show that the statistically significant factors are the number of cascades, the number of generations, and the population size. The optimal values for the three parameters have been defined based on second order regression models with R^2 higher than 0.97 for small, medium, and large-sized data sets. The robustness of the optimal parameters toward the types of data sets was explored and a robust setting for the three significant parameters was obtained. It reduces the calculation time by 30% to 50% without statistically significant reduction in the mean response.

References

Banzhaf, W., Nordin, P., Keller, R., and Francone, F. (1998). *Genetic Programming: An Introduction*. Morgan Kaufmann, San Francisco, CA.

Box, G., Hunter, W., and Hunter, J. (2005). *Statistics for Experiments: An Itroduction to Design, Data Analysis, and Model Building*. Wiley, New York, NY, 2 edition.

Castillo, F., Kordon, A., Smits, G., Christenson, B., and Dickerson, D. (2006). Pareto front genetic programming parameter selection based on design of experiments and industrial data. In *Proceedings of GECCO 2006*.

Chan, Kit Yan, Aydin, M. Emin, and Fogarty, Terence C. (2003). New factorial design theoretic crossover operator for parametrical problem. In Ryan, Conor, Soule, Terence, Keijzer, Maarten, Tsang, Edward, Poli, Riccardo, and Costa, Ernesto, editors, *Genetic Programming, Proceedings of EuroGP'2003*, volume 2610 of *LNCS*, pages 22–33, Essex. Springer-Verlag.

Derringer, G. and Suich, R. (1980). Simultaneous optimization of several response variables. *Journal of Quality Technology*, 28(1):61–70.

Feldt, Robert and Nordin, Peter (2000). Using factorial experiments to evaluate the effect of genetic programming parameters. In Poli, Riccardo, Banzhaf, Wolfgang, Langdon, William B., Miller, Julian F., Nordin, Peter, and Fogarty, Terence C., editors, *Genetic Programming, Proceedings of EuroGP'2000*, volume 1802 of *LNCS*, pages 271–282, Edinburgh. Springer-Verlag.

Kordon, A., Kalos, A., and Adams, B. (2003a). Empirical emulators for process monitoring and optimization. In *Proceedings of the IEEE 11th Conference on Control and Automation MED'2003*, page 111, Greece. Rhodes.

Kordon, A., Smits, G., Kalos, A., and Jordaan, E. (2003b). Robust soft sensor development using genetic programming. In Leardi, R., editor, *Nature-Inspired Methods in Chemometrics*, Amsterdam. Elsevier.

Kordon, Arthur, Castillo, Flor, Smits, Guido, and Kotanchek, Mark (2005). Application issues of genetic programming in industry. In Yu, Tina, Riolo, Rick L., and Worzel, Bill, editors, *Genetic Programming Theory and Practice III*, volume 9 of *Genetic Programming*, chapter 16, pages 241–258. Springer, Ann Arbor.

Kotanchek, M., Smits, G., and Vladislavleva, E. (2006). Pursuing the pareto paradigm. In Yu, Tina, Riolo, Rick L., and Soule, Terry, editors, *Genetic Programming Theory and Practice IV*. Kluwer, Ann Arbor.

Koza, John R. (1992). *Genetic Programming: On the Programming of Computers by Means of Natural Selection*. MIT Press, Cambridge, MA, USA.

Montgomery, D. (1995). *Design and Analysis of Experiments*. Wiley, New York, NY.

Myers, R. and Montgomery, D. (1995). *Design and Analysis of Experiments*.

Petrovski, A., Brownless, A., and McCall, J. (2005). Statistical optimization and tuning of ga factors. In *Proceedings of the Congress of Evolutionary Computation (CEC'2005)*, pages 758–764, Edinburgh, UK.

Reeves, C. and Wright, C. (1995). An experimental design prespective on genetic algorithms. In Whitley, D. and Vose, M., editors, *Foundations of Genetic Algorithms 3*, San Mateo, CA. Morgan Kaufmann.

Smits, G. and Kotanchek, M. (2004). Pareto front exploitation in symbolic regression. In Yu, Tina, Riolo, Rick L., O'Reilly, U.M., and Worzel, Bill, editors, *Genetic Programming Theory and Practice II*, pages 283–300. Springer, New York.

Welch, B.L. (1951). On the comparison of several mean values: An alternative approach. *Biometrika*, 38:330–336.

Chapter 11

PURSUING THE PARETO PARADIGM: TOURNAMENTS, ALGORITHM VARIATIONS AND ORDINAL OPTIMIZATION

Mark Kotanchek[1], Guido Smits[2] and Ekaterina Vladislavleva[2]

[1]*Evolved Analytics;* [2]*Dow Benelux B.V.;* [2]*Dow Benelux B.V. and Tilburg University.*

Abstract   The ParetoGP algorithm which adopts a multi-objective optimization approach to balancing expression complexity and accuracy has proven to have significant impact on symbolic regression of industrial data due to its improvement in speed and quality of model development as well as user model selection, (Smits and Kotanchek, 2004), (Smits et al., 2005), (Castillo et al., 2006). In this chapter, we explore a range of topics related to exploiting the Pareto paradigm. First we describe and explore the strengths and weaknesses of the ClassicGPand Pareto-Front GP variants for symbolic regression as well as touch on related algorithms. Next, we show a derivation for the selection intensity of tournament selection with multiple winners (albeit, in a single-objective case). We then extend classical tournament and elite selection strategies into a multi-objective framework which allows classical GP schemes to be readily Pareto-aware. Finally, we introduce the latest extension of the Pareto paradigm which is the melding with ordinal optimization. It appears that ordinal optimization will provide a theoretical foundation to guide algorithm design. Application of these insights has already produced at least a four-fold improvement in the ParetoGP performance for a suite of test problems.

Keywords: symbolic regression, Pareto GP, multi-objective optimization, tournament selection, ordinal optimization

1.   Introduction

The ParetoGP algorithm, (Smits and Kotanchek, 2004), was originally inspired by the need to sort through the plethora of results produced by application of genetic programming to symbolic regression of industrial datasets. Once the key insight occurred that the expressions of interest would lie along the Pareto front trading off expression accuracy and expression complexity (which was

assumed to be a metric linked to the risk of overfitting), it was a natural evolution to modify the genetic programming algorithms to accommodate our view
that the Pareto front is where the interesting models resided which should be
explored during the evolutionary process. The resulting ParetoGP algorithm
was interesting on a number of fronts. First, the orders-of-magnitude improvement in modeling efficiency opened up the size and scope of data sets which
could be handled with the natural variable selection capability proving to be an
important additional benefit for complementary nonlinear modeling techniques
such as neural networks and support vector regression. The second aspect was
that the user was presented with a natural set of models which explored the
trade-off between expression complexity and accuracy and, thereby, facilitated
post-processing model selection for subsequent model exploitation. The third
aspect was that ParetoGP required significantly smaller population sizes for
evolving good solutions (Castillo et al., 2006) than conventional GP theory
predicted. We believe that this is due to the inclusion of an archive. Finally,
the industrial impact of the resulting modeling successes inspired additional
research into the algorithm (Castillo et al., 2006), its applications, (Kordon and
Lue, 2004) and additional extensions and enhancements (Smits and Vladislavleva, 2006).

In this chapter we briefly review the ClassicGP and ParetoGP algorithms
and their characteristics and typical parameter settings. With that context established, we take a look at tournament selection within the context of multiple
objective optimization and propose a ParetoTourneySelect method which facilitates a Pareto-aware implementation of the classic GP methodology. This
method is attractive due to its simplicity and ease of tuning the selectivity focusing. Prior to introducing the ParetoTourneySelect method, however, we review
the selection intensity of single-objective tournament selection with single and
multiple winners. This is of practical importance since single-objective tournament selection is often used within the ParetoGP algorithm as its selection
method.

Finally, we introduce the notions of ordinal optimization and its application
to genetic programming algorithm design. Although still in the early stages
of the research, the insights derived from these concepts have been applied to
ParetoGP to produce significant improvements in both modeling efficiency and
consistency as measured by the shape of the resulting Pareto fronts.

2.   Pareto-Aware GP - Variations on the Pareto Theme

A number of researchers independently explored parallel optimization of
competing objectives in genetic programming. We partition their approaches
into three broad algorithmic categories: ClassicGP, ParetoGP and Hierarchal

Fair Competition (HFC). In this section, we briefly review the ClassicGP and ParetoGP classes.

When evolutionary search uses competing criteria, the optimal solution may not exist. Instead,a set of alternatives,called the Pareto-optimal set,will be an optimum. Pareto-optimal set consists of individuals for which no other individual is superior in all criteria. In the objective space (e.g.model error vs.model complexity) this set will form the Pareto front. So, each member of the Pareto-optimal set surpasses all individuals of the search space (or all considered so far) in at least one objective, and hence becomes a candidate for careful consideration and protection.

Variations on the Pareto Theme

Within the ClassicGP framework, Bleuler, et al, (Bleuler et al., 2001), assigned breeding rights based upon the SPEA2 metric of a population with members of the Pareto front persisting across generational boundaries. Saetrom and Hetland, (Saetrom and Hetland, 2003), also essentially followed this approach. De Jong & Pollack, (de Jong et al., 2001), proposed a Pareto front-centric approach wherein they synthesize new models each generation which are merged with a persistent Pareto front and used to define an updated Pareto front with propagation restricted to those models on the front (this approach did not work very well).

Recently, we have recognized that HFC, (Hu et al., 2003), should be included in the Pareto-aware algorithm category since it partitions models based upon accuracy fitness and restricted breeding and competition to models operating on similar levels of the fitness axis. Although not explicitly using the Pareto front by name, this approach is functionally Pareto-aware.

Obviously, the authors and their colleagues have pursued the ParetoGP variant (Smits and Kotanchek, 2004), (Smits et al., 2005). However, the development of the ParetoTourneySelect strategy has prompted them to include the ClassicGP framework within their research repertoire.

Strangely, the publications from the other researchers have not noted the explosive improvement in computational efficiency and robustness which has been associated with ParetoGP on real-world problems. (The exception being HFC which Erik Goodman noted had a similar improvement in efficiency in private conversation). This may be due to the nature of their test suites or the computational loads of the multi-objective selection schemes used to assign breeding rights.

ClassicGP And ParetoGP

In the ClassicGP approach, illustrated in Figure 11-1, starting from a supplied model set (if not supplied, random models will be synthesized), populations are

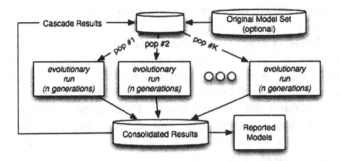

Figure 11-1. ClassicGP Modeling Flow. There is room for Pareto-aware selection strategies such as ParetoTourneySelect. Notice, the cascades are executed in sequence and runs in parallel.

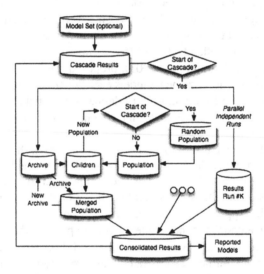

Figure 11-2. ParetoGP Modeling Flow. Because ParetoGP defines its archive using Pareto layers from the evolving populations, it is intrinsically a Pareto-aware GP algorithm even if conventional single-objective strategies are used to select from the archive and population.

supplied to each of the parallel and independent evolutionary runs. Each run consists of n generations wherein survival-of-the-fittest is applied to assign breeding rights for the next generation. We enhanced the classic GP approach by partitioning each evolution into cascades - groups of parallel and independent short evolutions (runs) of different populations to prevent inbreeding and maintain the diversity of solutions. Results consolidated at the end of a cascade may be used to seed subsequent cascades. At the end of the processing, the reported models are selected from the final cascade results.

Conversely, as illustrated in Figure 11-2, the ParetoGP approach uses archive independently from a population. The archive survives across the cascade boundaries, while the population for each parallel independent run (however, only one run is typically run in parallel) is wiped out and replaced by a new random population at the start of a new cascade. As shown in Figure 11-2, breeding is pairwise with one parent from the archive and the other from the population. At the end of a generation, after a new population is created, the archive is updated with the Pareto layers from the archive combined with the new population until the specified archive size is met. Because the archive is defined and updated using Pareto layers, ParetoGP is intrinsically a multi-objective algorithm even if more classical selection methods such as single-objective tournament selection are used to select the breeding pool from the population and archive.

Choosing model complexity as a second optimization criterion in symbolic regression involves a trade-off between exploration for good structural foundations and exploitation of those foundations to achieve models which are both parsimonious and accurate. In ClassicGP, the exploration is accomplished by the parallel independent evolutionary runs with the exploitation provided by the subsequent cascades as the foundation structures are refined and recombined to produce the desired quality models. As a result, generally the proper balance is to have many parallel independent runs feeding relatively few cascades. In contrast, for the ParetoGP approach, the exploration comes in primarily through the random populations introduced with each cascade whereas the exploitation comes from the persistence of the archive which survives across the evolution boundaries. Since new genetic material is introduced with each random population, the exploitation continues despite the maturation of the archive solution. Hence, for ParetoGP, many cascades and fewer independent parallel runs is generally required. However, despite the similarity of the resulting Pareto front results, the founder effect still applies so that apparent structures from a ParetoGP thread will generally differ across independent evolutions.

We recommend extending the ClassicGP strategy from the conventional single-objective realm (wherein accuracy is reduced by a complexity penalty) into the multi-objective by using multiple selection criteria (e.g., ParetoTourneySelect or ParetoEliteSelect). In the next sections we will show that this is a very powerful extension.

It appears that defining a methuselah function of the top 30% of the population mimics the effect of the ParetoGP archive and allows ClassicGP to be competitive with ParetoGP performance. It may be, however, that the inflicted influx of new genetic material at cascade boundaries may be advantageous in simultaneously maintaining exploration along with exploitation.

3.   Tournament Selection Intensity - Single and Multiple Winners with One Objective

In the GP realm, tournament selection appears to have dominated its competition (proportional, rank-based, elitist and random selection) due to being efficient and able to balance exploration and exploitation simply by tuning the tournament size used to select a winner. One reason for tournament selection being efficient as well as robust is that the ranking used to identify the winner is *ordinal* rather than depending on the absolute fitness values relative to the rest of the population. This helps to avoid premature convergence in selecting from a population as well as being computationally easy. We shall revisit the implications of ordinality later in the chapter.

The likelihood of being both selected for a tournament as well as emerging from the tournament as a winner is known as the selection intensity. In this section we explore the selection intensity as a function of population size, n, tournament size, t, and number of winners, w. As we shall see, allowing multiple winners to emerge from each tournament pool adds an additional ability to shape the selection intensity. There are two basic tournament selection variants depending upon whether we allow replacement or not. If we allow replacement, a model can compete against itself for breeding rights. While not physically realizable, this is often easier algorithmically than ensuring that the tournament pool competitors are unique when we are making a random draw. From a practical perspective, the selection intensities with or without replacement are comparable for reasonably large population sizes. With that as an introduction, we turn our attention first to the tournament selection with replacement.

Tournament Selection with Replacement - single winner situation

This approach is courtesy a conversation with Steffen Christensen. Basically, we make a geometric argument that if we make t draws from a population - and allow replacement - then we are really defining a location in a t-dimensional space wherein each dimension is quantized. In order to get into the game, the individual must be selected. In order to win the tournament, no better individual may be selected. To compute the likelihood of being a winner, we calculate the probability that the selected ensemble (where any given ensemble is represented by a node, i.e., quantized location in the t-dimensional space) doesn't contain any higher quality individuals, this is simply represented by the volume of the hypercube which excludes the higher-ranked models divided by the hyper-volume of the overall space which includes the entire population. This is calculated as $\frac{r^t}{n^t}$ where r is the rank of the individual in question (with larger numbers corresponding to higher rank). Excluding the likelihood of only selecting individuals from the lower ranked models corresponds to identifying

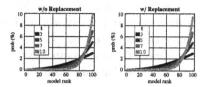

Figure 11-3. Selection Intensity Behavior for a Single Winner. Selection intensity for tournaments of different sizes with a single winner for both the tournament selection with and without replacement. t stands for the size of the tournament.

the probability that only those models are selected, i.e., $\frac{(r-1)^t}{n^t}$. Combining these results gives us the probability (a.k.a., *selection intensity*), p, of an individual with rank r winning a randomly selected tournament of size t from a population of n individuals.

$$p = \frac{r^t - (r-1)^t}{n^t} \tag{11.1}$$

In Figure 3, we show the flexibility possible simply by varying the tournament size. Note the nonlinear nature of the selection intensity as the tournament size increases. Also note that due to the possibility of replacement, that the likelihood of the top-ranked individual being selected is slightly *less* than it would be in the selection without replacement cases. For example, with a population size of 100 and a tourney size of 10, the top individual will win breeding rights 9.56% of the time whereas without replacement, it should achieve 10% of the breeding rights.

Selection Intensity without Replacement - single winner situation

Now let us turn our attention to the situation wherein each member of the tournament pool must be unique. Under the assumption of random selection, the likelihood of any given individual being selected is simply the ratio of the tournament size to the population size, i.e., $\frac{t}{n}$. To win the tournament, we have the restriction that none of the other selections can be higher ranking than the rth individual. The likelihood of this happening - conditioned on the rth individual already having been selected is the product of the successive likelihood of not selecting a better individual in any of the remaining t-1 draws to fill the tournament

$$\frac{r-1}{n-1}\frac{r-2}{n-2}\cdots\frac{r-(t-1)}{n-(t-1)} \tag{11.2}$$

Notice that the pool decreases with each selection due to our assumption of unique individuals being drawn. Also note that we need to handle the special case when we have negative numbers; this happens at the point where there is no chance that the individual will win a tournament - e.g., the bottom t-1 individuals. Pulling this together, we have the result,

$$p = \begin{cases} \frac{t}{n} \prod_{k=1}^{t-1} \frac{r-k}{n-k} & r \geq t-1 \\ 0 & r < t-1 \end{cases} \qquad (11.3)$$

This response behavior is also shown in Figure 3. As noted previously, despite the visual similarity of the two plots, there is a slight difference due to the avoidance of repeated models in a given draw.

Selection Intensity without Replacement - multiple winner situation

If we have more than one winner in a tournament, it is a fairly simple to extend the above logic. Assuming a tournament size, t, which has w winners, we need to consider w scenarios ranging from the situation wherein the given entity is the top ranked tourney contender to the situation where it is the wth ranked member of the pool (and, therefore, barely squeaking into breeding status). Under the top-ranked member scenario, we simply have the prior single winner situation, i.e.,

$$\frac{r-1}{n-1} \frac{r-2}{n-2} \cdots \frac{r-(t-1)}{n-(t-1)} \qquad (11.4)$$

Note that the above is the product of t-1 terms since we are implicitly assuming the given ranked model has entered the pool with a probability of $\frac{t}{n}$ where n is the population size. The probability of there being one higher-ranked model is:

$$\binom{t-1}{1} \left(\frac{r-1}{n-1} \frac{r-2}{n-2} \cdots \frac{r-(t-2)}{n-(t-2)} \right) \left(\frac{n-r}{n-(t-1)} \right). \qquad (11.5)$$

Here we need the binomial coefficient, $\binom{t-1}{1}$, to account for the fact that there are t-1 different ways that the better model can enter the tourney - under the conditional assumption that the rth model has been selected. If the top ranked model was being examined, then n-r would be zero so the series would naturally truncate and zero out all successive scenarios. In a similar vein, the probability of two higher ranked models is:

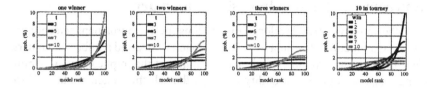

Figure 11-4. Multiple Winners in Tournaments. The selection intensity effect of changing the number of winners from a tournament for different tournament sizes for tournament selection without replacement. Views varying the tournament size as well as holding the tourney size constant and varying the number of winners are shown.

$$\binom{t-1}{2}\left(\frac{r-1}{n-1}\frac{r-2}{n-2}\cdots\frac{r-(t-3)}{n-(t-3)}\right)\left(\frac{n-r}{n-(t-1)}\cdots\frac{n-r-1}{n-(t-2)}\right).$$
(11.6)

This sequence of situations to be considered would terminate at the point wherein there are w-1 higher ranked models in the pool, i.e.,

$$\binom{t-1}{w-1}\left(\frac{r-1}{n-1}\cdots\frac{r-(t-w)}{n-(t-w)}\right)\left(\frac{n-r}{n-(t-1)}\cdots\frac{n-r-(w-2)}{n-(t-w-1)}\right).$$
(11.7)

Assembling the terms from the possible scenarios lead us to the summary expression for the probability,

$$p=\sum_{s=1}^{w-1}\left(\binom{t-1}{s}\left(\prod_{k=1}^{t-(s+1)}\frac{r-k}{n-k}\right)\left(\prod_{g=1}^{s}\frac{n-r-(g-1)}{n-(t-g)}\right)\right)\cdots$$
$$\cdots\frac{t}{n}\cdot\prod_{k=1}^{t-1}\frac{r-k}{n-k}+\frac{t}{n}\left(\prod_{k=1}^{t-1}\frac{r-k}{n-k}\right)^{2}$$
(11.8)

Note that the above expression is the probability of being selected for and winning a given tournament. Under normal circumstances where we are trying to assemble a group of breeders, we would need to execute fewer tournaments if we had multiple winners. Hence the above probability would typically be normalized by the number of winners to get the population percentage.

In Figure 11-4 we show the effect of varying the number of winners and tournament sizes. The important thing here is the ability to shape the selectivity. A perusal of the GP literature seems to show that a tournament size of between two and five is generally used with a single winner emerging from each tourney.

Tournament Selection Intensity - Summary

In the above we have developed expressions for the tournament selection intensity as a function of population size, tournament size and number of winners. This allows us to have an explicit understanding of the implications of parameter settings as well as the ability to shape the selection intensity to produce elitist-like behavior by having multiple winners.

4.   Tunable Pareto-Aware Selection Strategies

As noted previously, the tournaments have emerged as the dominant selection strategy in genetic programming because of their simplicity, robustness and effectiveness. Intuitively, we would like to incorporate this strategy in the Pareto-aware GP implementations; unfortunately, the Pareto paradigm implies multiple definitions of success so we have the problem of declaring the winner from a tournament.

There are a wide variety of selection strategies which have been used in multi-objective-optimization (MOO): NGSA, NSGA-II, SPEA, SPEA2, MOGA, NPGA, DMOEA, VLSI-GA, PDE, PAES, PESA, etc. Most of these rely upon the notion of dominance (the number of models which a given model beats), domination (the number of models which beat the given model), dominance layer or a combination with breeding rights awarded based upon the scores relative to the entire rest of the population. There are three fundamental problems with most of these selection strategies:

- **selection effort** - it is computationally intensive (Jensen, 2003) to evaluate the population for large population sizes (and the curse-of-dimensionality means that we want large population sizes in multi-objective-optimization),

- **requirement for global awareness** - the requirement for global awareness of the population and their relative fitness makes it difficult for the selection methods to scale well with population size or number of objectives,

- **tunability** - we want to be able to have an easily controlled parameter which will tweak the exploitation vs. exploration balance in selecting models from the population for development.

Our approach to implementing a multi-objective tournament selection strategy (which we call ParetoTourneySelect) is very simple: we form pools of randomly selected models and, since we cannot distinguish between them, the winners are all of the models on the Pareto front of that pool. We keep repeating this process until we achieve the desired selection size. The attraction of this strategy is that identifying the Pareto front of a population is significantly easier

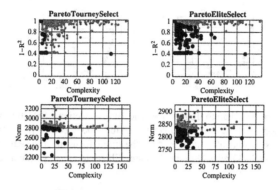

Figure 11-5. Selection behavior of the ParetoTourneySelect and ParetoEliteSelect strategies. Here we select 1000 models from a population of 1000 random models with no duplicate phenotypes with an elite size of 10% and a tourney size of 10% of the population, as appropriate. We ran evolutions with model selection in two accuracy metrics and plotted models that got selected in black. Note the strong focusing of the ParetoTourneySelect strategy favoring models from an interesting area of the objective space (here, an area of low model error and low complexity).

computationally than doing the ranking associated with conventional schemes. Additionally, working with smaller subsets of the population improves the efficiency of the Pareto front identification. Of course, there is an additional obvious selection strategy - ParetoEliteSelect - in which we assemble Pareto layers from the total population until a specified elite size is achieved.

In this section we will use a very simple response model without any additive noise, $x_1^2 (1 + x_2)$.

One hundred random evaluation points are created using four variables each distributed over a range of [-10,10] with the response function responding to the first two and the remaining two being spurious. We also synthesize 1000 random symbolic regression models with unique genomes (albeit, not necessarily unique phenotypes) and evaluate the models against the observed input-output data using a variety of accuracy metrics (2-norm and $1-R^2$) as well as a model complexity metric (total sum of the sum of the nodes of all subtrees in the genome).

In Figure 11-5, we show the results from identifying 1000 models from the population using a TournamentSize or an EliteSize of 10% of the population size, as appropriate. Note that this method has focused the selection process on the best models from a multi-objective perspective. As we can see, both selection strategies focus on models which are candidates for further development.

In Figure 11-6 we look at the distribution of the selected models and we see the focusing effect of the Pareto tournament selection approach. Cleaning the population and removing the models with duplicate phenotypes (defined as having identical fitness values) improves the diversity in model selection and

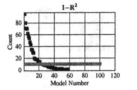
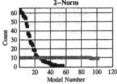

Figure 11-6. Metric vs. Pareto Tournament and Elite Selection. Selection intensity of the ParetoTourneySelect as a function of accuracy metric for 1000 selections from 1000 models with a 10% tournament size or a 10% elite size. Note the strong focusing of the ParetoTourneySelect strategy (depicted in black) relative to the flat ParetoEliteSelect strategy (depicted in gray).

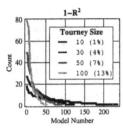
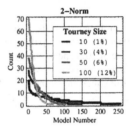

Figure 11-7. Tourney Size vs. Selection Intensity. Here we show the tuning effect for selecting 1000 models from the unique phenotype random models in the test case. Note that although the choice of fitness metric has an effect on the selectivity, the shape of the selectivity is controlled by changing the tournament size.

strengthens the focusing effect of the ParetoTourneySelect strategy. Note that less than 100 of the 1000 model population would have been selected for further evolutionary exploration and this subset is strongly skewed towards a relative handful of models. However, this focusing considers the multiple objectives. For comparison, we also show the results from the ParetoEliteSelect strategy.

One of our stated goals at the start of this section was to provide a multi-objective selection function which replicated the one-objective characteristics of tournament selection for ordinality, localized comparison and ease of selection intensity tuning. We have accomplished the first two; before we leave this topic, let us demonstrate the tunability capability in Figure 11-7.

Selection Efficiency and Discussion.   Table 11-1 and Table 11-2 show tabular looks at two scenarios. The first shows the effect of tournament size on computation time as well as model diversity resulting from applying Pareto-TourneySelect to the 1000 model population (evaluated with the norm metric). The second shows the effect of different population sizes holding the tournament size fixed as fraction of population size. Note that the selection diversity (as measured by the % of population selected) seems to be tied more to tourna-

Table 11-1. Selection Time and Diversity vs Tournament Size. Here we look at the effect of tournament size on both the model diversity and selection time. The Pareto tournaments was applied to the norm-metric set of 1000 models (processed so that there were no more than two of any given phenotype) and 1000 models were selected. As a reference point, calculating the model fitness requires 1.7 seconds for the population.

Pop Size	Tourney Size	% Selected	Time (sec)	Time/Model (ms)
1000	10	24	2.44	2.44
1000	20	18	2.31	2.31
1000	40	11	2.45	2.45
1000	80	6	2.75	2.75
1000	100	5	2.83	2.83

Table 11-2. Selection Diversity and Time vs. Population Size. Here we assume that the population size is maintained and that the tournaments consist of 10% of the population so, for example, 100 models are selected from the 100 model population using a sequence of 10 model (10% of population) tournaments. (Subsets of the model set of Table 11-2 are used). Looking at the time/model selected column shows the increasing Pareto front identification effort required with increasing tournament sizes. Also note that the model fitness evaluation time scales linearly so the time required for the 100 model population for this example is 0.17 seconds - which makes the selection effort relatively small for that size population.

Pop Size	Tourney Size	% Selected	Time (sec)	Time/Model (ms)
100	10	34	0.03	0.3
200	20	20	0.1	0.52
400	40	13	0.34	0.85
800	80	7	1.1	1.38
1000	100	4	1.68	1.68

ment size than to fraction of population used within the tournament - which is an interesting result to be investigated in the future. Also note that the time per model selected increases with increasing tournament size since a lower fraction of the tournament emerge as winners as the tournament size increases. A surprising result here is that evolutions with the ParetoTourneySelect method executed in 35% less time than those using the classical accuracy-based tournament selection scheme! The fact that it happens despite all overhead in the Pareto front calculation for ParetoTourneySelect is again explained by focusing of the multi-objective tournaments on a small fraction of 'potentially' optimal individuals and keeping the average size of expressions smaller, which makes for faster evaluations. We illustrate these results in Figure 11-8.

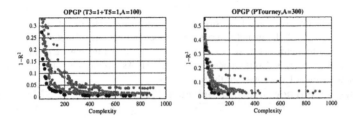

Figure 11-8. Comparison of classical tournament selection with the ParetoTourney. We plot the results of 11 independent evolutions per each method, and overall Pareto-optimal sets (depicted in bold black). Note that the Pareto tournaments (plot at the right) focus the energy on the most interesting area of the objective space. Surprisingly, while computationally demanding, evolutions with the ParetoTourneySelect method have shown 35% improvement in the execution time compared with the classical single-objective tournament selection.

5. Ordinal Optimization and Application to Symbolic Regression

The basic notion of ordinal optimization (OO) (Ho, 1996) is that for computationally hard problems, our target is generally a *good enough* solution rather than the true optimal model. Since this is a similar viewpoint to industrial application of symbolic regression, an exploration of the ordinal optimization and its application to symbolic regression is warranted. The foundation principles of OO are first, that it is easier to get a ranking of candidate solutions than it is to exactly compute the fitness values of the candidates. As a result, if we can quickly identify a subset of solutions which are worth further investigation, then we should be able to improve the efficiency of the model search. Second, goal softening helps to smooth and direct the search i.e. instead of asking for the absolute best it is better to ask for good enough with high probability.

Concepts and Tuning Parameters.

The OO mantra of "goal softening" could be expressed in the management literature as "fail forward" - in other words, identify promising solutions as quickly as possible and then pursue them. To a large extent, GP is already ordinal in nature; however, as we shall see, the OO viewpoint leads to some additional gains. First, let us review the aspects of Pareto-aware GP which we can control to allow us to fail forward:

- **fitness evaluation** - evaluating the model quality is, typically, where most of the computational effort is spent in symbolic regression. Within that broad category, there are two knobs to turn:

   1) **fitness metric** - even for symbolic regression choice of fitness metric has a computational load component. Similarly, model complexity could

be represented by a variety of schemes as simple as node count or as complex as nonlinearity estimates. This aspect is even more significant in other genetic programming applications since a first-principles model evaluation will require much more effort than needed for a first-order approximation.

2) **data subset size** - rather than evaluating the model at all data points, subsets of the data can be used with, generally, a linear shift in the computational load required. If the data subset is static, then care must be taken to properly balance the subset so that it is representative of the overall data set. If the subset varies, then care must be taken that apples-to-apples comparisons are made of quality results.

- **variable selection** - one of the best features of the Pareto-aware symbolic regression is the automatic variable selection during the evolutionary process so that ill-conditioned data sets with a plethora of nuisance variables may still be effectively analyzed. However, if the spurious variables can be rejected, the efficiency of the modeling can be increased.

- **selection method** - selection has two aspects from a computational efficiency viewpoint. The first is the effort required to identify quality solutions (which is a strength of the single-objective tournament selection). The second aspect is the focusing efficiency and controllability. For multi-objective optimization, this is a strength of the Pareto tournaments since it has a fuzzy threshold to separate good and bad models which can easily be tuned. Also note that for multiple objectives that criteria subsets may be used for model selection analogous to the data subsetting.

- **population (and archive) size** - the size of the model set, obviously, has a direct mapping into the computational load. One attraction of OO is that it may provide a theoretical foundation for identifying the proper problem-specific population size.

- **generations per run** - typically, the number of generations in a run corresponds to the exploitation effort of discovered solutions. In the spirit of OO we would want to use minimal generations in the early cascades with increased generations in the later stages as we refine and explore the foundation models.

- **runs per cascade** - the number of parallel runs within a cascade corresponds to the exploration component of the symbolic regression. Especially for a ClassicGP approach, OO would seem to guide us towards many short runs in the early cascades and shifting towards fewer longer runs in the latter stages.

- **cascades per evolution** - the number of cascades determines the extent of model exploitation. For ParetoGP the inclusion of additional cascades is generally worthwhile due to the influx of new genetic material at the cascade boundaries; for ClassicGP, additional cascades represent diminishing returns after a certain point since the exploration component is primarily associated with mutation.

- **number of independent evolutions** - the founder effect results in early fit solutions dominating the population. Therefore, consistency of the functional quality resulting from independent evolutions is an indicator that an appropriate evolutionary effort has been applied.

Initial Application of OO to ParetoGP

Smits & Vladislavleva (Smits and Vladislavleva, 2006) adopted the viewpoint that the majority of symbolic regression time is spent in the fitness evaluation and, therefore, performing an ordinal evaluation using random subsets of the data rather than the complete set was an attractive starting point for exploiting OO within GP. They looked at three cases using ParetoGP wherein they varied the characteristics of the cascades within the evolution process. The quality metric to compare the results was the area under the modeling Pareto front for a 1-R^2 accuracy metric and a genome complexity metric ranging from 1 to 400. The population and archive size of 100 models was run for ten cascades of 25 generations each (250 total generations). A single-objective (accuracy) tournament selection was used for both the archive (tourney size of 3) and population (tourney size of 5) model selection. Three types of test problems, small, medium and large were used. The small-sized problem was based on a known analytical function with two inputs and a training set of 100 records generated by random uniform sampling. The medium (8 inputs, 251 datapoints) and large-sized (18 inputs, 1000 datapoints) problems were based on real-life datasets with process noise.

Case I: constant subset and population size - keeping a constant data subset size for all of the cascades with the subset randomly selected for each generation, actually led to the surprising result of improved Pareto front quality as the data subset size decreased up to 40% of the original data set size. The exception was a problem using data from a designed experiment where each data point was unique and critical.

Case II: increasing subset and constant population size - here the approach was to linearly increase the (random) subset size from 10% to 100% of the data over a number of generations and finish the symbolic regression using the full data set. This produced improved modeling results in comparison to the first case with an interpretation that the smaller subsets in the earlier generations

Large Dataset **Medium Dataset** **Small Dataset**

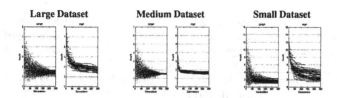

Figure 11-9. Comparison of ParetoGP with Ordinal ParetoGP. Here we show the results from the increasing subset and decreasing population size case. The initial scatter in quality metric (% area under the Pareto front) for OPGP is due to the differing random subsets used for the first 80% of the generations. Note the improved model ensemble quality (as measured by the area under the Pareto front) relative to the conventional ParetoGP as well as the improved consistency of results.

introduced more noise into the modeling process and, therefore, resulted in more exploration - analogous to simulated annealing.

Case III: increasing subset and decreasing population size - in this case the data subset size was linearly increased from 10% to 100% of the data over the first 80% of the generations with the full data set used for the remaining 20% of the generations. The computational effort was kept constant by starting with a model population of 1000 and linearly decreasing it as the data subset size was linearly increased. Effectively, this resulted in a large population for an initial coarse screen shifting to an intensive exploitation with a smaller population in the final generations. This approach was a clear winner both in terms of Pareto front quality and in consistency of modeling results as measured by the standard deviation from 30 independent evolutions. The results for this case are illustrated in Figure 11-9.

Smits & Vladislavleva also compared Ordinal ParetoGP (OPGP) running for 250 generations to conventional ParetoGP (PGP) running for 1000 generations for 30 independent evolutions. OPGP produced higher quality and more consistent results than PGP despite only having a quarter of the CPU cycles allocated to it relative to PGP.

Although ParetoGP was used in these initial studies, the computational efficiency and accuracy gains should also apply to other flavors of genetic programming. Actually, we should expect greater advantages since those approaches do not have an archive which would also have to be evaluated against the various data subsets for each generation. The previous results on tournament selection and Pareto tournament selection with single and multiple winners offers some of the ingredients to advance the OO theory from Ho *et al* to an 'iterative' OO theory.

Table 11-3. Here we compare the Ordinal ParetoGP performance against the conventional Pare-toGP for each of the data sets. Note that the OPGP running for 250 generations outperforms the PGP algorithm running for 1000 generations (40 cascades). This is the basis of the claim of at least a four-fold improvement in algorithm efficiency.

Test Problem	Method	Mean Area%	SD Area%
Small	OPGP 250 gen	1.63	0.32
	PGP 250 gen	2.83	0.90
	PGP 1000 gen	1.69	0.46
Medium	OPGP 250 gen	1.53	0.04
	PGP 250 gen	1.65	0.09
	PGP 1000 gen	1.51	0.08
Large	OPGP 250 gen	3.42	0.14
	PGP 250 gen	3.76	0.19
	PGP 1000 gen	3.49	0.20

6.   Conclusions and Summary

In this chapter we have introduced the notion of ordinal optimization and its application to genetic programming. As demonstrated by the significant performance gains of the exploratory investigations, this is a very exciting synergy with much promise for both the practitioner as well as the theoretician since improvements in algorithm efficiency is always welcome to the practitioner and ordinal optimization could provide a new theoretical foundation for genetic programming as well as guide the development of new algorithms and concepts. The introduction of the ParetoTourneySelect method is also significant in that it allows classical GP schemes to be easily migrated to being Pareto-aware. It is also an extension of the single-objective tournament selection method and, therefore, attractive because of the ease of tuning the selection focus and diversity as well as exploiting a local ordinality (the tournament pool) in the selection process - features which are useful as we migrate to an ordinal optimization perspective with an explicit goal of failing forward and initial exploration segueing into a refinement and exploitation stage.

In summary, the future is looking bright for continued advances in the theory, application and impact of GP, in general, and symbolic regression, in particular.

References

Bleuler, Stefan, Brack, Martin, Thiele, Lothar, and Zitzler, Eckart (2001). Multiobjective genetic programming: Reducing bloat using SPEA2. In *Proceedings of the 2001 Congress on Evolutionary Computation CEC2001*, pages 536–543, COEX, World Trade Center, 159 Samseong-dong, Gangnam-gu, Seoul, Korea. IEEE Press.

Castillo, Flor, Kordon, Arthur, and Smits, Guido (2006). Robust pareto front genetic programming parameter selection based on design of experiments and industrial data. In Riolo, Rick L., Soule, Terence, and Worzel, Bill, editors, *Genetic Programming Theory and Practice IV*, volume 5 of *Genetic and Evolutionary Computation*, chapter 2, pages –. Springer, Ann Arbor.

de Jong, Edwin D., Watson, Richard A., and Pollack, Jordan B. (2001). Reducing bloat and promoting diversity using multi-objective methods. In Spector, Lee, Goodman, Erik D., Wu, Annie, Langdon, W. B., Voigt, Hans-Michael, Gen, Mitsuo, Sen, Sandip, Dorigo, Marco, Pezeshk, Shahram, Garzon, Max H., and Burke, Edmund, editors, *Proceedings of the Genetic and Evolutionary Computation Conference (GECCO-2001)*, pages 11–18, San Francisco, California, USA. Morgan Kaufmann.

Ho, Y.-C. (1996). Soft optimization for hard problems" computerized lecture via private communication/distribution.

Hu, Jianjun, Goodman, Erik D., and Seo, Kisung (2003). Continuous hierarchical fair competition model for sustainable innovation in genetic programming. In Riolo, Rick L. and Worzel, Bill, editors, *Genetic Programming Theory and Practice*, chapter 6, pages 81–98. Kluwer.

Jensen, Mikkel T. (2003). Reducing the run-time complexity of multiobjective eas: The nsga-ii and other algorithms. *IEEE Trans. Evolutionary Computation*, 7(5):503–515.

Kordon, Arthur and Lue, Ching-Tai (2004). Symbolic regression modeling of blown film process effects. In *Proceedings of the 2004 IEEE Congress on Evolutionary Computation*, pages 561–568, Portland, Oregon. IEEE Press.

Saetrom, Pal and Hetland, Magnus (2003). Multiobjective evolution of temporal rules.

Smits, Guido, Kordon, Arthur, Vladislavleva, Katherine, Jordaan, Elsa, and Kotanchek, Mark (2005). Variable selection in industrial datasets using pareto genetic programming. In Yu, Tina, Riolo, Rick L., and Worzel, Bill, editors, *Genetic Programming Theory and Practice III*, volume 9 of *Genetic Programming*, chapter 6, pages 79–92. Springer, Ann Arbor.

Smits, Guido and Kotanchek, Mark (2004). Pareto-front exploitation in symbolic regression. In O'Reilly, Una-May, Yu, Tina, Riolo, Rick L., and Worzel, Bill, editors, *Genetic Programming Theory and Practice II*, chapter 17, pages 283–299. Springer, Ann Arbor.

Smits, Guido and Vladislavleva, Ekaterina (2006). Ordinal pareto genetic programming. In *Proceedings of the 2006 IEEE Congress on Evolutionary Computation*, volume 1, page to be published. IEEE Press.

Chapter 12

APPLYING GENETIC PROGRAMMING TO RESERVOIR HISTORY MATCHING PROBLEM

Tina Yu[1], Dave Wilkinson[2] and Alexandre Castellini[2]

[1]*Memorial University of Newfoundland, St. John's, NL A1B 3X5, Canada;* [2]*Chevron Energy Technology Company, San Ramon, CA 94583 USA.*

Abstract　　History matching is the process of updating a petroleum reservoir model using production data. It is a required step before a reservoir model is accepted for forecasting production. The process is normally carried out by flow simulation, which is very time-consuming. As a result, only a small number of simulation runs are conducted and the history matching results are normally unsatisfactory.

　　In this work, we introduce a methodology using genetic programming (GP) to construct a proxy for reservoir simulator. Acting as a surrogate for the computer simulator, the "cheap" GP proxy can evaluate a large number (millions) of reservoir models within a very short time frame. Collectively, the identified good-matching reservoir models provide us with comprehensive information about the reservoir. Moreover, we can use these models to forecast future production, which is closer to the reality than the forecasts derived from a small number of computer simulation runs.

　　We have applied the proposed technique to a West African oil field that has complex geology. The results show that GP is able to deliver high quality proxies. Meanwhile, important information about the reservoirs was revealed from the study. Overall, the project has successfully achieved the goal of improving the quality of history matuching results without increasing the number of reservoir simulation runs. This result suggests this novel history matching approach might be effective for other reservoirs with complex geology or a significant amount of production data.

Keywords:　　reservoir modeling, history matching, flow simulator, proxy, surrogate model, production forecast, uncertainty, response surface, meta-models, uniform design, experimental design

1.   Introduction

Petroleum reservoirs are normally large and geologically complex. In order to make management decisions that maximize oil recovery, reservoir models are constructed with as many details as possible. Two types of data that are commonly used in reservoir modeling are geophysical data and production data. Geophysical data, such as seismic and wire-line logs, describe earth properties, e.g. porosity, of the reservoir. In contrast, production data, such as water and oil saturations and pressure information, relate to the fluid flow dynamics of the reservoir. Both data types are required to be honored so that the resulting models are as close to reality as possible. Based on these models, managers make business decisions that attempt to minimize risk and maximize profits.

The integration of production data in to reservoir modeling is usually accomplished through computer simulation. Normally, multiple simulations are conducted to identify reservoir models that generate fluid dynamics matching the production data collected from the field. This process is called history matching.

History matching is a challenging task for the following reasons:

- Computer simulation is very time consuming. On average, each run takes 2 to 10 hours to complete.

- This is an inverse problem where more than one reservoir model can produce flow outputs that give acceptable match to the production data.

As a result, intensive research has been devoted to making the history matching process more efficient and to delivering quality results. In this chapter, we introduce a methodology incorporating genetic programming (GP) (Koza, 1992; Banzhaf et al., 1998) to improve the history matching process. We start by explaining the reservoir history matching problem and reviewing related works in Section 2 . The methodology is then presented in Section 3. After that, we report a case study using the developed methodology and present the results in Section 4. Finally, we conclude the chapter and outline our future work in Section 5.

2.   Reservoir History Matching Problem

When an oil field is first discovered, the reservoir model is initially constructed using geophysical data. This is a forward modeling task and can be accomplished using statistical techniques (Deutsch, 2002) or soft computing methods (Yu et al., 2003). Once the field enters into production stage, many changes take place in the reservoir. For example, the extraction of oil/gas/water from the field can cause the fluid pressures of the field to change. In order to obtain the most current state of a reservoir, these changes need to be reflected in the model. History matching is the process of updating reservoir descriptor

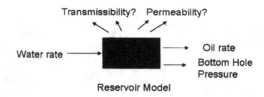

Figure 12-1. History matching is an inverse problem.

parameters to reflect such changes, based on production data collected from the field. Using the updated models, petroleum engineers can make more accurate production forecasts. The results of history matching and subsequent production forecasting strongly impact reservoir management decisions.

History matching is an inverse problem. In this problem, a reservoir model is a black box with unknown parameters values (see Figure 12-1). Given the water/oil rates and other production information collected from the field, the task is to identify these unknown parameter values such that the reservoir gives flow outputs matching production data. Since inverse problems have no unique solutions, i.e. more than one combination of reservoir parameter values give the same flow outputs, we need to obtain a large number of well-matched reservoir models in order to achieve high confidence of the history-matching results.

Figure 12-2 depicts the work flow of history matching and production forecast process. Initially, a base geological model is provided. Next, parameters which are believed to have impact on the reservoir fluid flow are selected. Based on their knowledge about the field, geologists and petroleum engineers then determine the possible value ranges of these parameters and use these value to conduct computer simulation runs.

A computer reservoir simulator is a program which consists of mathematical equations that describe fluid dynamics of a reservoir under different conditions. The simulator takes a set of reservoir parameter values as inputs and returns a set of fluid flow information as outputs. The outputs are usually a time-series over a specified period of time. That time-series is then compared with the historical production data to evaluate their match. If the match is not satisfactory, experts would modify the parameter values and make a new simulation run. This process continues until a satisfactory match between simulation flow outputs and the production data is reached.

This manual process of history matching is subjective and labor-intensive, because reservoir parameters are adjusted one-at-a-time to refine the simulations. Meanwhile, the goodness of the matching results depends largely on the experience of the team members involved in the study. Consequently, the reliability of the forecasting is often very short-lived, and the business decisions made may have a large degree of uncertainty.

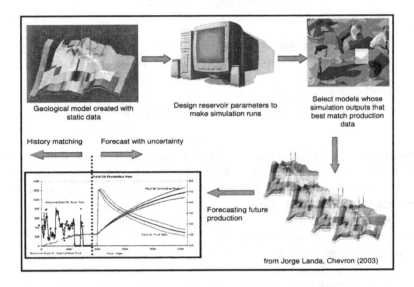

Geological model created with static data

Design reservoir parameters to make simulation runs

Select models whose simulation outputs that best match production data

History matching   Forecast with uncertainty

Forecasting future production

from Jorge Landa, Chevron (2003)

Figure 12-2. Reservoir history matching and production forecasting work flow.

To improve the quality of history matching results, several approaches have been proposed to assist the process. For example, gradient-based algorithms have been used to select sampling points sequentially for further computer simulations (Bissell et al., 1994). Although this approach can quickly find models that match production data, it may cause the search to become trapped in a local optimum and prevent models with better matches being discovered. Another shortcoming is that the method generates a single solution, despite the fact that multiple models can match the production data equally well. To overcome these issues, genetic algorithms have been proposed to replace gradient-based algorithms (Wen et al., 2004; Yu et al., 2006a). Although the results are significantly better, the computation time is not practical for large reservoir fields.

There are also several works that construct a response surface that reproduces the approximate reservoir simulation outcomes. The response surface is then used as a surrogate or proxy for the costly full simulator (Narayanan et al., 1999). In this way, a large number of reservoir models can be sampled within a short period of time.

Response surfaces are normally polynomial function. Recently, Kriging interpolation and neural networks have also been used as alternative methods (Yeten et al., 2005; Castellini et al., 2004). The response surface approach is usually carried out in conjunction with experimental design, which selects sample points for computer simulation runs (Eidi et al., 1994). Ideally, these

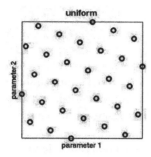

Figure 12-3. Uniform sampling gives good coverage of the parameter space.

limited number of simulation runs would obtain the most information about the reservoir. Using these simulation data to construct a proxy, it is hoped that the proxy will generate outcomes that are close to the outcomes of the full simulator. This combination of response surface estimation and experimental design is shown to give good results when the reservoir models are simple and the amount of production data is small, i.e. the oil field is relatively young (Landa and Guyaguler, 2003). However, when the field has a complex geologic deposition or is in production for many years, this approach is less likely to produce a quality proxy (Landa et al., 2005). Consequently, the generated reservoir models contain a large degree of uncertainty.

3. A Genetic Programming Solution

To improve the confidence of the uncertainty ranges of the reservoir models generated from history matching, we need to sample a dense distribution of reservoir models in the parameter space. Additionally, we need to know which of these models is a good match to the production data. With this information, we will be able to use the "good" models to forecast future production with a higher degree of confidence.

To achieve that goal, we have adopted *uniform sampling* to conduct computer simulation runs and applied *genetic programming* for proxy construction. Uniform sampling, developed by Fang (Fang, 1980), generates a sampling distribution that covers the entire parameter space for a pre-determined number of runs (see Figure 12-3). It ensures that no large regions of the parameter space are left under sampled. Such coverage is important to construct a robust proxy that is able to interpolate all intermediate points in the parameter space.

Using the simulation results, we then apply GP symbolic regression to construct a proxy. Unlike other research works where the proxy is constructed to give the same type of output as the full simulator, this GP proxy only labels a reservoir model as a good match or bad match to the production data, according

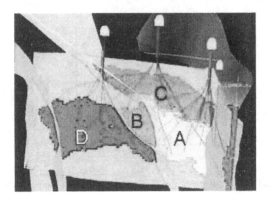

Figure 12-4. The studied oil field.

to the criterion decided by field engineers. In other words, it functions as a classifier to separate "good" models from "bad" ones in the parameter space. The actual amount of fluid produced by the sampled reservoirs is not estimated. This is a different kind of learning problem and it will be shown that GP is able to learn the task very well.

After the GP classifier is constructed, it is then used to sample a dense distribution of reservoir models in the parameter space (millions of reservoir models). Those that are labeled as "good" are then studied and analyzed to identify their associated characteristics. Additionally, we will use these "good" models to forecast future production. Since the forecast is based on a large number of good models, the results are considered more accurate and closer to reality than those based on a limited number of simulation runs.

4.   A Case Study

The oil field we studied is a complex, clastic channel, reservoir situated off-shore Africa. The primary reservoirs are sandstones deposited in a channelized system and have been in production since 1998. For history matching purposes, computer simulations on 4 blocks (A, B, C, D) of the area were conducted (see Figure 12-4). The reservoir parameters and their value ranges used to conduct the simulations are listed in Table 12-1. The 6 multiplier parameters are in log10 values, while the other 4 parameters are in normal scale. They are applied to the base values in each grid of the reservoir field during computer simulation.

Using uniform design to select parameter values, we conducted 1000 computer simulation runs. Among them, 894 were successful while the other 106 runs did not make to the end of the run due to system failures. Each successful run produces 3 types of fluid flow data: water rate (WR), oil rate (OR) and bottom hole pressure (BHP), between the years 1998 to 2004.

Table 12-1. Reservoir parameters and value ranges for computer simulation.

Parameters	Min	Max	Parameters	Min	Max
KRW_A	0.3	0.7	ZPERM_A Multiplier	0.01	1
KRW_B	0.1	0.5	ZPERM_B Multiplier	0.01	1
KRW_C	0.1	0.5	ZPERM_C Multiplier	0.01	1
KRW_D	0.1	0.5	ZPERM_D Multiplier	0.01	1
XPERM Multiplier	1	2	FAULT_A_B Multiplier	0.0001	1

The simulation outputs from each run were compared with the production data collected from the field. The "error", defined as the mismatch between the two, is the sum squared difference which is calculated as follows:

$$E = \sum_{i=1998}^{2004} (WR\_obs_i - WR\_sim_i)^2 + (OR\_obs_i - OR\_sim_i)^2 + (BHP\_obs_i - BHP\_sim_i)^2$$

Here, "obs" indicates production data while "sim" indicates computer simulation outputs. The largest E that can be accepted as good match is 2.8×10^9. Based on this criterion, 541 models were labeled as "good" models while 353 are labeled as "bad" models by a petroleum engineer.

GP Experimental Setup

To conduct the GP symbolic regression, we first divided the 894 data into three groups: 298 for training, 298 for validation and 298 for blind testing. Training data are used for GP to construct the classifier while validation data is used to select the final classifier. In this way, over-fitting is less likely to happen. The evaluation of the classifier is based on its performance on the blind testing data.

The GP system is a commercial package that makes multiple runs (Francone, 2001). Table 12-2 lists some of the GP parameters used to train the classifiers. There are other GP parameters that are not fixed but are selected by the software for each run. These parameters include population size, maximum program size, and crossover and mutation rates. In the first run, one set of values for these parameters was specified. When the run does not produce an improved solution for a certain number of generations, the run is terminated and a new set of parameter values is selected by the system to start a new run. The system maintains the best 50 solutions found throughout the multiple runs. When the GP system is terminated, the best classifier among the pool of 50 solutions is the final solution. In this work, we let the GP system continue for 120 runs and then manually terminated the system.

The fitness is based on hit rate: the percentage of the training data that are correctly classified. During tournament selection, four candidates are randomly

Table 12-2.   Some of the parameters for GP symbolic regression.

Objective	Evolve a classifier that separates good reservoir models from bad ones.
Functions	addition;subtraction;multiplication;division;abs;data transformation
Terminals	The 10 reservoir parameters listed in Table 12-1
Fitness	Hit rate then mean squared error
Hit Rate	The percentage of the training data that are correctly classified.
Selection	Tournament (4 candidates/2 winners)

selected and paired to compete for two slots. If two candidates are tied in their hit rates, the mean squared error measurement is used to select the winners. The "tied threshold" for mean squared error measurement is 0.01% in this work. If two classifiers are tied in both their hit rates and mean squared error measurements, a winner is randomly selected from the two competitors.

In this application, we made two sets of batch runs. In the first batch, parsimony pressure is turned on to promote shorter classifiers. During tournament selection, the GP system selects the shorter solution to be the winner if its fitness is not worse than 1% of its competitor. To avoid the system over protecting short solutions and sacrifice quality, we allow parsimony pressure to affect only 50% of the tournament selection. Also, we disallow parsimony pressure to have any effect during the first 3 generations when the evolution search is exploring the parameter space. In the second batch, parsimony pressure is turned off; the evolutionary search is free to explore classifiers with arbitrarily complex structures. With this setup, we can learn how much performance can be gained by trading with complexity.

Results

Table 12-3 gives the results from both batch runs. When parsimony pressure is on, the best GP classifier contains 4 parameters: KRW_C, ZPERM_D, ZPERM_A and FAULT_A_B. The classification accuracy is approximately 91%. When parsimony pressure is off, the best GP classifier contains 8 parameters and gives a slightly higher classification accuracy of 94%. Both results are very good. From the practical point of view, simpler models are easier to understand and analyze. We therefore selected the one with 4 parameters as our final solution. Figure 12-5 gives the classification results on all 894 data in the space of the 3 most important parameters (KRW_C, ZPERM_A and ZPERM_D). As shown, good models are of low ZPERM_D value while bad models are with high ZPERM_D value. Although there are a small number of misclassification, the overall trend of good reservoir models is consistent.

There are other machine learning methods which can be used to train classifiers. Among them, we tested a fuzzy classifier, a linear discriminant analysis-based classifier, a self-organized map and a support vector machine. The results

Table 12-3.   Results of GP symbolic regression runs.

	Parsimony On	Parsimony Off
Training Data Accuracy	91.61%	94.97%
Validation Data Accuracy	91.28%	93.62%
Testing Data Accuracy	90.94%	93.29%
Number of Reservoir Parameters Selected	4	8

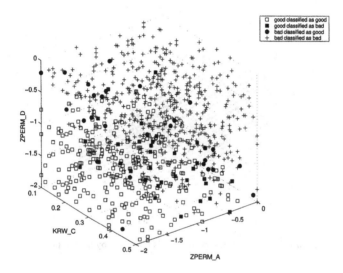

Figure 12-5.   Reservoir models classification results.

Table 12-4.   Results of other learning methods.

Method	Training Data	Validation Data	Testing Data
Fuzzy Classifier	74.232%	71.53%	69.922%
LDABased Classifier	63.5915%	58.389%	58.695%
SOM	65.3105%	59.0105%	56.0155%
SVM (radial kernel)	100%	91.2895%	92.8125%
GP	94.97%	93.62%	93.29%

are shown in Table 12-4. For this set of data, the support vector machine (SVM) gives comparable results to the GP classifier. We used a radial kernel with gamma value 0.04 for SVM learning. The SVM classifier shows a tendency of over-fitting toward training data, which is not observed in the GP classifier.

Interpolation and Interpretation

We used the simpler classifier (with 4 parameters) to evaluate new sample points in the parameter space. For each of the 4 parameters, 21 samples were selected, evenly distributed between their minimum and maximum values. The resulting total number of samples is $21^4 = 194,481$. Running the GP classifier on these samples resulted in 73,135 being identified as good models while 121,346 were classified as bad models.

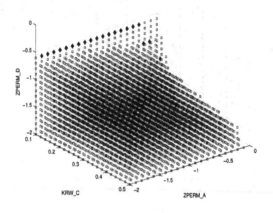

Figure 12-6. Good reservoir models identified by the GP proxy.

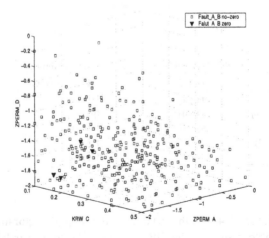

Figure 12-7. Good reservoir models identified by computer simulator.

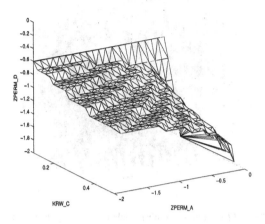

Figure 12-8. The upper bound of good models in the parameter space.

Figure 12-6 shows the 73,135 good models in the parameter space. They are located in the bottom half, where the ZPERM_D value is less than -0.6. This is consistent with the results of computer simulation (Figure 12-7). Also, good models in both Figures show a consistent trend of decreasing ZPERM_D value when both KRW_C and ZPERM_A increase. Another characteristic of good models is that very few of them have a FAULT_A_B value of zero (diamond shape in Figure 12-7 and 12-6). This indicates that the faults separating geobody A field and B field are not completely sealing. With these sampling results, we can draw an upper bound for good models in the parameter space (see Figure 12-8).

Bad models identified by the GP classifier are shown in Figure 12-9. They occupy most parts of the parameter space, except two significant areas. One is on the left lower corner where KRW_C is less than 0.18, ZPERM_A is between -2 and -0.2 and ZPERM_D is between -2 and -1.1 (see Figure 12-11). The other is on the corner where ZPERM_A is 0, KRW_C is less than 0.18 and ZPERM_D is between -0.5 and -1.9 (see Figure 12-12). The bad model area identified by GP classifier covers all the bad models resulting from computer simulation (shown in Figure 12-10). Additionally, it also identifies that FAULT_A_B zero value models are bad in the lower half of the parameter space, shown in diamond shape. Figure 12-11 and 12-12 give the lower bound of the bad models in the parameter space.

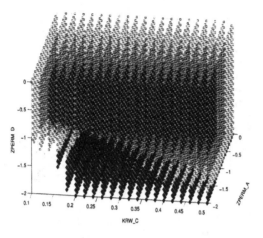

Figure 12-9. Bad reservoir models identified by the GP proxy.

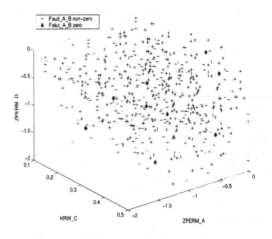

Figure 12-10. Bad reservoir models identified by computer simulator.

Project Contributions

Based on the history matching results, which were obtained using the developed framework and proposed techniques of uniform design and GP, we delivered the following information to the reservoir engineers.

- The most important 4 parameters that influence match to the production data.

- The ranges of values for these 4 parameters that give good match to production data.

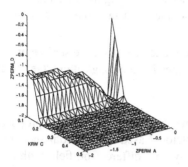 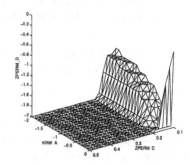

Figure 12-11. Lower bound of bad models.   *Figure 12-12.* Lower bound of bad models.

- The boundary of good and bad models in the parameter space.

- Insights in the geological compartmentalization of the reservoir.

These results are well received and verified by the field reservoir engineers. Overall, the project has successfully achieved the goal of improving the quality of the reservoir models by history matching, without increasing the number of computer simulations. This result suggests that this novel method might be effective for other reservoirs with complex geology or significant amounts of production data.

5.   Concluding Remarks

Reservoir history matching and production forecasting are of great importance to the planning and operation of oil reservoir fields. Under time pressure, it is often necessary to curtail the number of computer simulation runs and make decisions based on a limited amount of information. This work proposes using GP to construct a proxy for the full computer simulator. In this way, we can replace the simulator by the proxy in order to sample a much larger number of reservoir models and, consequently, obtain more information, which in turn, it is hoped, will lead to better reservoir decisions being made.

We have conducted a case study using the proposed approach. The results have shown that the proxy gives comparable performance to that of the full simulator in distinguishing between reservoir models that are close to the reality and those that are not. This is an improvement on what has reported in the literature (see Section 2). We believe there are two possible reasons for our success:

- The innovative idea of casting the proxy as a classifier, which changes the nature of the problem from other works using the difference between computer simulation results and production data as the response surface.

- Applying genetic programming to model this response surface, which is more suitable for this task than other learning algorithms (see Section 12-3).

As far as we know, this is the first time such a method has been proposed to construct a proxy for the reservoir simulator. Based on the initial encouraging results, we have conducted another study on a different oil field with a large amount of production data. In that study, we also forecast reservoir production using the good models sampled by the GP proxy. This work is reported separately in (Yu et al., 2006b).

Acknowledgment

We would like to thank Iba Hitoshi and Michael Korns for their comments and suggestions.

References

Banzhaf, Wolfgang, Nordin, Peter, Keller, Robert E., and Francone, Frank D. (1998). *Genetic Programming – An Introduction; On the Automatic Evolution of Computer Programs and its Applications*. Morgan Kaufmann, San Francisco, CA, USA.

Bissell, R. C., Sharma, Y., and Killough, J. E. (1994). History matching using the method of gradients: two case studies. Paper SPE 28590, presented at the SPE Annual Technical Conference and Exhibition, New Orleans, LA, September 25-28.

Castellini, Alexandre, Landa, Jorge, and Kikani, Jitendra (2004). Practical methods for uncertainty assessment of flow predictions for reservoirs with significant history – a field case study. Paper A-33, presented at the 9th European Conference on the Mathematics of Oil Recovery, Cannes, France, August 30 - September 2.

Deutsch, Clayton V. (2002). *Geostatistical Reservoir Modeling*. Oxford University Press.

Eidi, A. L., Holden, L., Reiso, E., and Aanonsen, S. I. (1994). Automatic history matching by use of response surfaces and experimental design. paper presented at the Fourth European Conference on the Mathematics of Oil Recovery, Roros, Norway, June 7-10.

Fang, Kai-Tai (1980). Uniform design: Application of number theory in test design. *ACTA Mathematicae Applicatae Sinica*.

Francone, Frank D. (2001). *Discipulus Owner's Manual.* 11757 W. Ken Caryl Avenue F, PBM 512, Littleton, Colorado, 80127-3719, USA, version 3.0 draft edition.

Koza, John R. (1992). *Genetic Programming: On the Programming of Computers by Means of Natural Selection.* MIT Press, Cambridge, MA, USA.

Landa, Jorge L. and Guyaguler, Baris (2003). A methodology for history matching and the assessment of uncertainties associated with flow prediction. paper SPE 84465, presented at the SPE Annual Technical Conference and Exhibition, Denver, CO, October 5-8.

Landa, Jorge L., Kalia, R. K., Nakano, A., Nomura, K., and Bashishta, P. (2005). History match and associated forecast uncertainty analysis – practical approaches using cluster computing. paper IPTC 10751, presented at The International Petroleum Technology Conference, Doha, Qatar, November 21-23.

Narayanan, K., White C.D., Lake, L. W., and Willis, B. J. (1999). Response methods for up-scaling heterogeneous geologic models. paper SPE 51923, presented at the SPE Reservoir Simulation Symposium, Houston, TX, February 14-17.

Wen, Xian-Huan., Yu, Tina, and Lee, Seong (2004). Coupling sequential-self calibration and genetic algorithms to integrate production data in geostatistical reservoir modeling. In *Proceedings of the Seventh Geostatistics Congress,* pages 691–702.

Yeten, Burak, Castellini, Alexandre, Guyaguler, Baris, and Chen, Wen (2005). A comparison study on experimental design and response surface methodologies. paper SPE 93347, presented at the SPE Reservoir Simulation Symposium, Houston, TX, January 31 - February 2.

Yu, Tina, Wen, Xian-Huan, and Lee, Seong (2006a). A hybrid of sequential-self calibration and genetic algorithms inverse technique for geostatistical reservoir modeling. In *Proceedings of the IEEE World Congress on Computational Intelligence.*

Yu, Tina, Wilkinson, Dave, and Castellini, Alexandre (2006b). Constructing reservoir flow simulator proxies using genetic programming for history matching and production forecast uncertainty analysis. submitted.

Yu, Tina, Wilkinson, Dave, and Xie, Deyi (2003). A hybrid GP-fuzzy approach for reservoir characterization. In Riolo, Rick L. and Worzel, Bill, editors, *Genetic Programming Theory and Practise,* chapter 17, pages 271–290. Kluwer.

Chapter 13

COMPARISON OF ROBUSTNESS OF THREE FILTER DESIGN STRATEGIES USING GENETIC PROGRAMMING AND BOND GRAPHS

Xiangdong Peng,[1] Erik D. Goodman[1] and Ronald C. Rosenberg[2]

[1] *Genetic Algorithms Research and Applications Group (GARAGe), Dept. of Electrical and Computer Engineering, Michigan State University.*
[2] *Department of Mechanical Engineering, Michigan State University.*

Abstract   A possible goal in robust design of dynamic systems is to find a system topology under which the sensitivity of performance to the values of component parameters is minimized. This can provide robust performance in the face of environmental change (e.g., resistance variation with temperature) and/or manufacturing-induced variability in parameter values. In some cases, a topology that is relatively insensitive to parameter variation may allow use of less expensive (looser tolerance) components. Cost of components, in some instances, also depends on whether "standard-sized" components may be used or custom values are required. This is true whether the components are electrical components, mechanical fasteners, or hydraulic fittings. However, using only standard-sized or preferred-value components introduces an additional design constraint. This chapter uses genetic programming to develop bond graphs specifying component topology and parameter values for an example task, designing a passive analog low-pass filter with fifth-order Bessel characteristics. It explores three alternative design approaches. The first uses "standard" GP and evolves designs in which components can take on arbitrary values (i.e., custom design). The second approach adds random noise to each parameter; then, at the end of evolution, for the best design found, it "snaps" its parameter values to a small (component-specific) set of "standard" values. The third approach uses only the small set of allowable standard values throughout the evolutionary process, evaluating each design after addition of noise to each standard parameter value. Then the best designs emerging from each of these three procedures are compared for robustness to parameter variation, evaluating each of them with random perturbations of their parameters. Results indicated that, the third method produced the most robust designs, and the second method was better than the first.

Keywords: Genetic Programming, bond graph, robust design strategy, Bessel analog filter design

1.   Introduction

GP has been effectively applied to topologically open-ended computational synthesis (Koza et al., 2003). Though system performance is an important criterion, robustness, as the ability of a system to maintain its target performance even with changes in internal structure (including variations of parameters from their specified values) or external environment (Carlson and Doyle, 2002), is also critical to engineering design decisions. If the designed system is robust with respect to parameter values, it can run a harsh environment or perhaps can be built with inexpensive components. In many areas of design, the use of a small family of "standard" components significantly reduces costs by eliminating the need for components fabricated to custom specifications. For example, tubing in diameters of one inch or one centimeter may be much less expensive than tubing of 2.43 centimeters or 0.383 inches diameter that must be custombuilt. Or, for a second example, inexpensive resistors and capacitors for use in through-hole printed circuit boards are available only for certain "standard" or "preferred" values, typically twelve per decade (i.e., 100, 120, 150, 180, 220, 270, 330, 390, 470, 560, 680, and 820 ohms or microfarads, respectively).

As there are many factors that affect system performance, it is difficult to take all system uncertainties or variability into consideration in robust engineering design. Two kinds of system robustness are often considered. One kind, widely investigated in robust engineering design (Du and Chen, 2000), is system robustness with respect to perturbation of component parameter values. Another kind is system robustness with respect to topology perturbation, such as component failure, short circuiting, etc. In this chapter, only robustness to parameter perturbation is considered.

This chapter considers evolution of a particular type of dynamic system, a passive analog low-pass filter, as a design environment in which to do preliminary examination of some hypotheses about robust evolutionary design. The synthesis tool used throughout is called GPBG, a genetic programming (GP) system that uses trees to specify operations for construction of a bond graph (BG), which is a multi-energy-domain representation for dynamic systems. This GPBG system has earlier been used by the authors for automated design of a number of types of dynamic systems (Fan et al., 2001). In this chapter, three hypotheses regarding robust design are put forward for preliminary study:

- Systems with similar "base" (unperturbed) performance can be evolved if robustness is considered during the evolutionary process, without the need for a much larger number of function evaluations than is needed for conventional (non-robust) synthesis.

- Selection for performance in the presence of noise perturbing the parameter values during evolution will improve the robustness of the systems evolved.

- Constraining parameters to take on only a small set of standard values (but still subject to perturbations) during evolution will produce more robust designs than will snapping the parameters to those values after evolution is completed.

The chapter is organized as follows. Section 2 presents a short survey of robust design and introduction of evolutionary computation in this field. Section 3 discusses the GPBG methodology, which applies Genetic Programming and Bond Graphs for automated synthesis of dynamic systems. Section 4 discusses topologically open-ended evolution and three strategies for robust design with components from a small set of "standard" values, motivated by the frequent availability of such sets of components at reduced cost. Section 5 compares experimental results of these approaches. Conclusions and future research are discussed in Section 6.

2.   Related Work

A method for robust design, called the Taguchi Method, pioneered by Dr. Genichi Taguchi, has greatly improved engineering productivity (Tay and Taguchi, 1993). After its introduction, it has been intensively studied in the community of engineering design (Zhu, 2001). In robust design, the control parameter settings are determined so the system produces the desired mean values for the performance, while at the same time minimizing the variance of the performance (Tay and Taguchi, 1993).

The most commonly applied system design methodology is the top-down procedure from system analysis, proceeding from functional design to detailed design. Within this methodology, robust design is most commonly treated during the detailed design phase. Design for robustness of system topology is normally not considered in this methodology. So the task of robust design is downgraded to parameter tuning and tolerance specification to maintain performance within acceptable limits. Topologically open-ended synthesis by genetic programming provides a way to move robust design forward to the conceptual/functional design stage and thus consider design for robustness from the very beginning, which will augment the current practice of design for robustness in practical design (Hu and Goodman, 2002).

Application of evolutionary computation to robust design has been investigated since the early 1990s and can be classified into three categories (Forouraghi, 2000). The first type applies an evolutionary algorithm to parametric design for robustness. The second type focuses on evolving robust solutions in a noisy environment (Hammel and Baeck, 1994). A very active area of evolving robust systems is called evolvable hardware (Thompson, 1998). But most of these studies still separate the topology search and parameter tuning.

Two primary approaches to evolution of robust systems have been used by others – Robustness by Multiple Simulation ("RMS") and Robustness by Perturbed Evaluation ("RPE").

A common approach for evolving robust design is to use multiple Monte Carlo samplings with different environmental or system configurations (e.g., perturbation of parameter values of the system) to calculate a worst-case or an average fitness for a given candidate solution. This GP robust-by-multiple-simulation (RMS) method is used in (Wiesmann et al., 1998), and in some of the experimental conditions reported here.

Another method is simply to add perturbations to the design variables before evaluation and evaluate a single, perturbed design. The perturbations, however, are not incorporated into the genome, making it different from a "normal" parameter mutation operator or Larmarckian-style evolutionary algorithm. This robust-by-perturbed-evaluation (RPE) method is used in (Tsutsui and Ghosh, 1997) and is suggested to be more efficient by in (Jin and Sendhoff, 2003). It is attractive because it uses only a single simulation run for evaluation of each design, relying on the fact that the design will persist and be re-evaluated in future generations if it is a good one. However, it is not used in the study reported here.

3.   Analog Filter Synthesis Using Bond Graphs and Genetic Programming

Bond Graphs

The bond graph is a modeling tool that provides a unified approach to the modeling and analysis of dynamic systems, especially hybrid multi-domain systems including mechanical, electrical, pneumatic, and hydraulic components (Karnopp et al., 2000). The explicit representation of model topology used in bond graphs makes them particularly good candidates for use in open-ended design search using genetic programming – for example, both series and parallel connections appear graphically as trees, unlike their conventional circuit-diagram representation. Complex electrical circuits and mechanical systems, or a synthesis of both, can be modeled as a tree structure using a bond graph, which is easy to evolve with one genetic programming tree. Bond graphs have four embedded strengths for evolutionary design application – namely, the wide scope of systems that can be created because of the multi- and inter-domain nature of bond graphs, the efficiency of evaluation of design alternatives, the natural combinatorial features of bond and node components for generation of design alternatives, and the ease of mapping to the engineering design process. Notation details and methods of system analysis related to the bond graph representation can be found in (Karnopp et al., 2000).

Standard components of bond graphs for design of passive systems are the inductor (I), resistor (R), capacitor (C), transformer (TF), gyrator (GY), 0-junction (J0), 1-junction (J1), source of effort (SE), and source of flow (SF). In the electrical context, a source of effort corresponds to a voltage source, and a source of flow, to a current source. In this chapter, we concentrate discussion on analog filter design, and the resulting bond graph will be composed of only I, R, C, SE, SF components.

Combining Bond Graphs and Genetic Programming

The problem of automated synthesis of bond graphs involves two basic searches: the search for a good topology and the search for good parameters for each topology, in order to be able to evaluate its performance. Building upon Koza's work on automated synthesis of electronic circuits, we created a developmental GP system for open-ended synthesis of mechatronic systems represented as bond graphs. It includes the following major components: 1) an embryo bond graph with modifiable sites at which further topological operations can be applied to grow the embryo into a functional system, 2) a GP function set, composed of a set of topology manipulation and other primitive instructions which will be assembled into a GP tree by the evolutionary process. Execution of this GP program leads to topological and parametric manipulation of the developing embryo bond graph, and 3) a fitness function to evaluate the performance of candidate solutions.

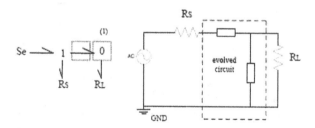

Figure 13-1. Embryo bond graph and its corresponding electric circuit

In developmental GP, an embryo is used as the root of the GP tree, and is often used to guarantee that each tree contains the minimum structure to allow evaluation of its fitness. For this example, as shown in Figure 13-1, the embryo assures that each circuit has a voltage source at which the input is applied, a source resistor, and a load resistor across which the output of the filter can be measured. In the GPBG system, the GP tree does not represent the bond graph directly, but is instead a tree-structured program for construction of a bond graph, beginning with the embryo as the root. Figure 13-2 shows a bond graph construction tree, but the details (Hu et al., 2004) are not needed to understand the experiments described here.

Choosing a good function set for bond graph synthesis is not trivial. In our earlier work, we used a very primitive "basic" function set, and later, we developed the following hybrid function set to reduce redundancy while retaining good flexibility in topological exploration:

$$F = \{Insert\_J0E, Insert\_J1E, Add\_C/I/R, EndNode, EndBond, ERC\}$$

$$(13.1)$$

This function set has produced some promising results, as discussed in (Hu et al., 2004). In order to enable choosing component values only from a small set of preferred values, we made changes to the original Add_C/I/R function. One bit determines whether the value will be snapped to the nearest preferred value. One point to be heeded is that snapping has the effect of decreasing the actual mutation rate, so when snapping is used, the ERC mutation rate must be set higher relative to the non-snapping strategies to produce comparable rates of changed designs resulting from mutation. Figure 13-2 shows a GP tree that specifies how a complete bond graph solution is constructed from the embryo bond graph.

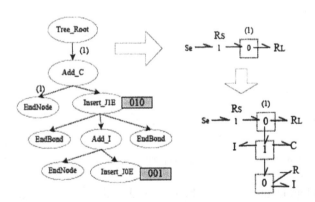

Figure 13-2. A sample GP tree (left), composed of topology operators applied to an embryo (Tree_Root and bond graph on right), generating a bond graph (lower right) after depth-first execution (numeric nodes omitted).

The Example Lowpass Filter Problem

In this study, a lowpass filter with fifth-order Bessel characteristics is to be synthesized. We say a lowpass filter of Bessel characteristics, rather than a Bessel lowpass filter, because a Bessel filter is designed with one strict mathematical equation and a well-defined synthesis procedure, while we simply used the fifth-order Bessel filter magnitude and phase frequency response as reference for design fitness evaluations.

In this GPBG-based filter design problem, a bond-graph-represented an analog filter composed of capacitors, resistors, and inductors is to be evolved such that the magnitude and phase of its frequency response approximates the Bessel filter frequency response specification. This procedure will not use the sophisticated SPICE simulation program, as is typically done in analog circuit analysis. Instead, the frequency response of the circuit modeled by the bond graph can be calculated in a faster and more convenient way: first, the state equation of the bond graph is automatically derived from the model, yielding the A, B, C, and D matrices of linear system theory. The frequency response of these state space models is then calculated on a Linux PC using C++ simulation code generated by the Matlab 3.0 compiler.

The detailed specifications of the lowpass filter problem addressed here are as follows: the frequency response performance of a candidate filter is defined as the weighted sum of deviations from ideal magnitude and phase frequency responses evaluated at 101 points:

$$F_{magnitude}(t) = \sum_{i=0}^{100} [W(d(f_i), f_i) * d(f_i)] \qquad (13.2)$$

$$F_{phase}(t) = \sum_{i=1}^{100} [W(d(f_i), f_i) * d(f_i)] \qquad (13.3)$$

The definition of the frequency response magnitude is the same as in our earlier study (Hu et al., 2004). However, in this study, we also include frequency response phase in the calculation of fitness, where f_i is the sampled frequency, $d(x)$ is the absolute deviation of candidate frequency response from target response at frequency x, and $W(x, y)$ is the weight function specifying the penalty level for a given frequency response at a specified frequency range. The sampling points range from 1Hz to 100 KHz, evenly distributed on a logarithmic scale. If the deviation from ideal phase is less than 30 degrees, the weight is 1. If the deviation is more than 30 degrees, the weight is 10, aimed at reflecting the relatively small importance of small deviations in the phase response from ideal. The pass band is [1, 1k] Hz, the stop band is [2K, 10K] Hz. A "don't care" band between 1 KHz and 2 KHz neglects any deviation from the target response there. The phase is weighted as 0.1 and magnitude is weighted 0.9

in the final fitness calculation. An alternative could be to treat magnitude and phase as separate objectives in a multi-objective search, but our design here is simple and produces an acceptable result. If we want to have stringent control of the phase, we need to consider other alternatives, but that was not seen as critical to this study.

Before introduction of any robustness considerations, the fitness function is defined as follows. First we calculate the raw fitness defined as the average absolute deviation between the frequency response magnitude and phase of the candidate solution and the target frequency response over all 101 sampling frequencies.

$$f_{raw} = \frac{1}{101}(0.9 * f_{magnitude} + 0.1 * f_{phase}) \qquad (13.4)$$

$$f_{norm} = \frac{NORM}{NORM + f_{raw}} \qquad (13.5)$$

Differences from the Usual GP System

The GPBG system includes the following "non-standard" features:

- A flag bit mutation operator is introduced to evolve the configuration of C/I/R elements attached to a junction. That is, junctions introduced into a bond graph by the Insert_J0E or Insert_J1E operators may each have zero or one C, I, and R elements, as specified by three binary flags (rectangles in Figure 13-2 are an example). A special mutation operator can manipulate those flag bits at the junctions.

- A subtree-swapping operator is used to exchange non-overlapping subtrees of the same individual (GP tree).

- A Gaussian ERC mutation operator, as is commonly used in evolution strategies, is developed to evolve the parameter values of all C/I/R components; the value generated for the ERC is arbitrary within the range specified for each component; another bit will specify whether or not it is to be snapped to the nearest "preferred" value.

Elitism of one individual is used throughout the evolution process– that is, the best individual in the population is always preserved to the next generation.

Except for the above, the GPBG system is a standard strongly-typed multi-population generational GP. The parameter values are specified in Section 5.

4.   Evolving Robust Analog Filters with Components of Preferred Values Using Bond Graphs and Evolutionary Algorithms

This section examines the design of analog filters for robustness to parameter variations, using components chosen from a set of "preferred" or "standard" values. There are many ways this might be attempted using GP as an open-ended topological search tool. Three approaches will be described:

- GP, the "plain" GP approach;

- GPRMS, which seeks robustness using multiple (Monte Carlo) simulations of each design, and

- GPPV, which uses the GPRMS approach, but allows parameters to be selected only from a small set of Preferred Values during the evolutionary process.

The distinction is made here between design evaluations (fitness calculations) and filter simulations. Evaluating the fitness of one design may require several filter (Monte Carlo) simulations. For all of these methods, a fixed number of total filter simulations is allocated to ensure fairness of comparison. The latter two approaches are described in more detail below.

GPRMS

For the GPRMS multi-simulation method, the raw fitness for a design solution, including a robustness criterion, is defined as the sum of a number NS (here, 10) of (here, 101-point-) deviation sums from the target frequency response curve, resulting from NS filter simulations of the same design:

$$f_{robustraw} = \sum_{k=1}^{NS} f_{raw}^k \qquad (13.6)$$

where NS is the number of Monte Carlo sampling evaluations (filter simulations) for each individual, and f is the raw fitness of the kth sampled evaluation with a different Monte Carlo perturbation of the parameters, as defined in Equation 13.4. With this raw robustness from Equation 13.6, we then calculate the final fitness similarly to Equation 13.5.

Although the GPRMS runs can choose parameter values arbitrarily from within the allowable range during the GP run, at the end of each GPRMS experiment, each parameter value found is "snapped" to the nearest preferred value, so that the designs are directly comparable to the GPPV results described below.

GPPV

The GP with Preferred Values method, denoted GPPV, does not allow arbitrary values for the parameters of its components, but rather restricts choice to a small, discrete set of values, the "Preferred Values." Thus, when the bond graph is constructed from the GP tree and the embryo bond graph, each component value can be only one of the limited set of discrete "preferred" values. The runs are otherwise identical to the GPRMS runs, including NS Monte Carlo simulations of values perturbed randomly from the preferred values (i.e., the actual Monte Carlo values are not restricted to the PV set).

5.   Experiments and Results

In this section, a series of experiments is conducted to verify the three hypotheses given in Section 1 about robust design of an analog filter by genetic programming. In these experiments, the perturbation of the component values during evolution is implemented by adding to each component's parameter(s) Gaussian noise $N(\mu, \sigma)$ with mean $\mu = 0$ and standard deviation σ set at 20% of the parameter value. This perturbation model has been widely used in previous research, and while it may not be an accurate model of component variation (introducing more than is typically present in the components), any excess noise may also be useful in discovery of robust solutions. One difficulty with this definition is that if the original parameter value is zero, then no perturbation will be generated. Although this is rare in evolutionary experiments, it is alleviated here by checking for any component value of zero, in which case the standard deviation for the perturbation is set to 1.0.

In the GPRMS and GPPV runs (using the robustness by multiple simulations approach), multiple simulations (in this case, NS = 10) are used to evaluate the fitness of each single design. For this filter design problem, the computation budget is 1,000,000 simulations, so up to 100,000 different designs can be evaluated in each run. In the "plain" GP runs, 1,000,000 designs are evaluated.

While only one parameter perturbation model was used during the evolutionary synthesis experiments – Gaussian noise $N(\mu, \sigma)$ with mean μ of 0 and standard deviation σ set at 20% of the parameter value, the later (post-run) robustness evaluations of the evolved filters include multiple perturbation magnitudes with extensive simulation.

To assess the statistical significance of the performance differences between these methods, 15 runs were done for each synthesis method. The size of these experiments was determined by the computing resources available. However, since the results were found to be quite stable across multiple runs, this level of replication appears to be sufficient for the purpose of this preliminary study.

All experiments described below used the same embryo bond graph shown in Figure 13-1. The component values of source resistor R_s and load resistor R_{load} are both 1 Ω for the lowpass filter with Bessel characteristics.

The following sections first describe separately the experimental configuration of each method, the best evolved bond graph model of the filter, and the magnitude and phase responses of the best solution from each method. These results provide some general ideas regarding how robustness is evolved with respect to the parameter perturbations. Then a statistical comparison of the performance of the three strategies for evolving filters is presented. The configuration of the experiments can be seen in the following table.

Table 13-1.

	No Perturbation	Perturbed During Evolution
Any parameter value	GP	GPRMS
Small set of allowable preferred values		GPPV

The following common running parameters (Table 13-1 were used throughout all GP experiments in this chapter.

Table 13-2.

Total population size: 2000	Number of levels: 5
Max Depth: 10	Crossover probability: 0.4
InitDepth: 3-5	Standard mutation probability: 0.05
Tournament size: 2	Parametric mutation probability: 0.3
Max Evaluations: 20,000,000	Flag mutation probability: 0.3

At the end of the run, the robustness of each final evolved solution was evaluated against a series of perturbation magnitudes: Gaussian noise $N(\mu, \sigma)$ with mean μ at 0 and standard deviation σ at 10% to 50% of parameter values, in steps of 10%, each tested with 5000 samplings with different configurations of the component parameter perturbations.

Below, we display the evolved filter with the highest performance from each of the three run types, to test its noise tolerance in the face of degradation or variation of the component parameters.

"Plain GP Run"

In the first experiment, 15 analog lowpass filters of Bessel characteristics are evolved using standard GP without incorporating a robustness criterion in the fitness function, Equation 13.4.

From Figure 13-3, first, one can see that the frequency response magnitude plot of the filters evolved by (1) is quite similar to the target. That means introducing a robustness requirement does not necessarily decrease the performance with nominal parameters significantly. However, the phase response deviates noticeably, particularly at high frequency. A possible explanation is that the weight of the phase term in the fitness function was only 10%, compared to 90% for the magnitude term. This weighting was used to reflect the differential importance of amplitude and phase for most applications. From the perspective of system performance, the phase delay is not usually a critical objective in the real application, often being set instead as a constraint with no effect on fitness so long as it does not fall outside a specified range.

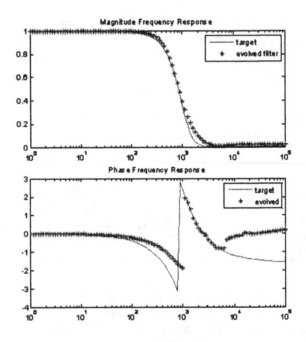

Figure 13-3.   Magnitude and Phase Frequency Responses.

Evolving Robust Analog Filters Using Genetic Programming: Open-Ended Topology Innovation for Robust Design

In the second set of runs, the GPRMS method is applied to evolve robust analog filters that have high tolerance to the variations of component values. The structure of the best bond graph produced is similar to that shown for the GPPV method (below), and is not shown for reasons of space. However, its performance is contrasted with that of GP and GPPV in the statistical comparisons below.

Evolving Robust Analog Filters with Components of Preferred Values

In the third set of runs, GPPV is used to try to evolve robust analog filters that have higher tolerance to the variations of component values but contain only components from a small set of nominal values. Figure 13-4 shows the best lowpass filter evolved using GPPV with robustness requirements. This filter uses fewer components than the "plain GP" -derived filter, while its functional performance remains similar. The robustness of this filter is compared to that of the best filter evolved using standard GP, but snapping the parameters to the small set of nominal values after evolution was completed, and to the best GPRMS filter.

In Figure 13-4, the best bond graph has a long chain of resistors. Resistor values were selected only from a small set of discrete nominal values; the evolved bond graph used combinations of resistors to get desirable fitness.

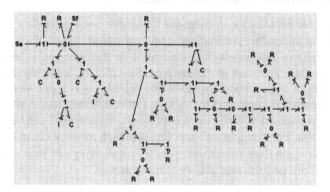

Figure 13-4.   The best bond graph evolved with GPPV

Statistical Comparisons of Three Methods

Hypothesis 1: Systems with similar "base" (unperturbed) performance can be evolved if robustness is considered during the evolutionary process, without the need for a much larger number of function evaluations than is needed for conventional (non-robust) synthesis. A t-test on the differences in performance of the filters evolved by GPRMS and by plain GP, evaluated with their nominal (unperturbed) parameter values, did not reveal any significant difference (e.g., $P > 0.20$). They were evolved using an identical number (1 million) of filter simulations.

Hypothesis 2: Introduction of noise during the process of evolution improves the robustness over the "plain GP" results: a t-test on the results of the lowpass filter problem was used to compare the robustness of the evolved solutions by GPRMS and standard GP in terms of fitness at the 0.2 (20%) perturbation level. A significance level of $P <= 0.001$ was achieved; strongly indicating that GPRMS improved the robustness over the filters evolved by plain GP, using the same number of filter evaluations.

Hypothesis 3: Introduction of nominal values during the process of evolution improves the robustness over solutions evolved by snapping evolved parameters to nominal values after the evolution is completed. A t-test was done on the results from the lowpass filter problem to compare the robustness of the evolved solutions by GPPV and GPRMS in terms of fitness at the 0.2 perturbation level. The difference is significant at $0.02 < P < 0.05$, strongly indicating that introduction of the preferred values during the process of evolution can improve the robustness of the filters evolved over that of filters evolved using arbitrary real values and snapped to the closest nominal values after the evolution.

6.   Conclusions and Future Work

This chapter exploits the open-ended topology search capability of genetic programming to conduct preliminary studies of robust design of dynamic systems. We believe that topological innovation in the conceptual design stage can improve the robustness of the systems. Specifically, we apply it to design analog filters of high robustness. Evolving robustness is a rich search theme and there are several interesting topics to be further investigated. A set of experiments was conducted to verify three hypotheses. Future work can be extended in several ways. For example, sub-topologies of high robustness can be evolved based primarily on their robustness, then a second layer can be evolved with attention to both performance and system robustness.

References

Carlson, J.M. and Doyle, J. (2002). Complexity and robustness. In *Proceedings of the National Academy of Science (PNAS)*, volume 99, pages 2538–2545.

Du, X. and Chen, W. (2000). Towards a better understanding of modeling feasibility robustness in engineering design. In *ASME*, volume 122, pages 385–394.

Fan, Zhun, Hu, Jianjun, Seo, Kisung, Goodman, Erik D., Rosenberg, Ronald C., and Zhang, Baihai (2001). Bond graph representation and GP for automated analog filter design. In Goodman, Erik D., editor, *2001 Genetic and Evolutionary Computation Conference Late Breaking Papers*, pages 81–86, San Francisco, California, USA.

Forouraghi, B. (2000). A genetic algorithm for multiobjective robust design. *Applied Intelligence*, 12:151–161.

Hammel, U. and Baeck, T. (1994). Evolution strategies on noisy functions. how to improve convergence properties. *Solving from Nature*, 3:159–168.

Hu, Jianjun, Goodman, Erik, and Rosenberg, Ronald (2004). Topological search in automated mechatronic system synthesis using bond graphs and genetic programming. In *Proceedings of American Control Conference ACC 2004*.

Hu, Jianjun and Goodman, Erik D. (2002). The hierarchical fair competition (HFC) model for parallel evolutionary algorithms. In Fogel, David B., El-Sharkawi, Mohamed A., Yao, Xin, Greenwood, Garry, Iba, Hitoshi, Marrow, Paul, and Shackleton, Mark, editors, *Proceedings of the 2002 Congress on Evolutionary Computation CEC2002*, pages 49–54. IEEE Press.

Jin, Y. and Sendhoff, B. (2003). Trade-off between optimality and robustness: An evolutionary multi-objective approach. In Fonseca, C., editor, *Second International Conference on Evolutionary Multi-Criterion Optimization*, pages 237–251. Springer.

Karnopp, D.C., Margolis, D.L., and Rosenberg, R.C. (2000). *Systems Dynamics: Modeling and Simulation of Mechatronic Systems*. John Wiley & Sons, Inc, New York.

Koza, J.R., Keane, Martin, A., Streeter, Matthew, J., Mydlowec, William, Yu, Jessen, Lanza, and Smits (2003). *Genetic Programming IV: Routine Human Competitive Machine Intelligence*. Kluwer Academic Publishers.

Tay, E. and Taguchi, W. (1993). *Taguchi on Robust Technology Development: Bringing Quality Engineering Upstream*. American Society of Mechanical Engineering Press, New York.

Thompson, A. (1998). On the automatic design of robust electronics through artificial evolution. In *International Conference on Evolvable Systems*, pages 13–24. Springer.

Tsutsui, S. and Ghosh, A. (1997). Genetic algorithms with a robust solution searching scheme. *IEEE Trans. Evolutionary Computation*, 1(3):201–208.

Wiesmann, D., Hammel, U., and Baeck, T. (1998). Robust design of multilayer optical coatings by means of evolutionary algorithms. *IEE Transactions on Evolutionary Computation*, 2(4):162–167.

Zhu, J. (2001). Performance distribution analysis and robust design. *Journal of Mechanical Design*, 123(1):11–17.

Chapter 14

DESIGN OF POSYNOMIAL MODELS
FOR MOSFETS: SYMBOLIC REGRESSION
USING GENETIC ALGORITHMS

Varun Aggarwal and Una-May O'Reilly
Computer Science and Artificial Intelligence Lab, Massachusetts Institute of Technology

Abstract   We discuss the difficulties of circuit sizing and describe manual and automatic approaches to it. These approaches make use of blackbox optimization techniques
such as evolutionary algorithms or convex optimization techniques such as geometric programming. Geometric programming requires posynomial expressions
for a circuit's performance measurements. We show how a genetic algorithm can
be exploited to evolve a posynomial expression (i.e. model) of transistor (i.e.
mosfet) behavior more accurately than statistical techniques in the literature.

Keywords: circuit sizing, genetic algorithms, symbolic regression, posynomial models, geometric programming

1.   Introduction

Analog circuit design remains an important part of electronic design even
after the advent of digital electronics. This is because some components of an
electronic system must be analog. Additionally, because research also shows
(Mead, 1990) that analog systems can be designed to consume several orders
of magnitude lesser power than digital circuits, interest in analog design remains strong. Complementarily, there is active interest in the improvement and
development of methods for computer-aided design (CAD) of analog circuits.
Design and verification of analog circuits has not yielded to automation and thus
analog design is a bottleneck in achieving short time-to-market and robustness.

A circuit topology comprises of analog components that are connected to
each other to implement a certain function. A circuit topology does not specify
the parameter values of its components. Figure 14-1 shows a topology of a

differential pair that implements the differential amplification function given in Equation 14.4. The topology is a connection of mosfets, resistors and a current source. There are constraints on the parameters of the components as expressed in Equations 14.2 and 14.3. The second constraint is popularly termed a *matching requirement* in the analog design community. While there are additional constraints on parameters to keep the mosfet in saturation, we omit these for simplicity. For the given differential pair topology, the parameters of the components must be determined according to its *gain* requirements as per Equation 14.1. In general, the step of determining the parameters of a topology is called *circuit sizing.*

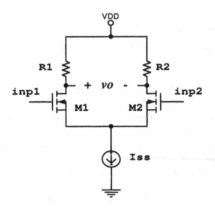

Figure 14-1. Differential pair.

$$a_v = f(R, W_i, L_i, I_{ss}, V_{DD}) \qquad (14.1)$$

Constraints

$$\frac{W_1}{L1} = \frac{W_2}{L2} \qquad (14.2)$$

$$R1 = R2 = R \qquad (14.3)$$

CircuitFunctionality

$$v_o = -a_v(v_{inp1} - v_{inp2}) \qquad (14.4)$$

where a_v is gain, v_0 is AC output and v_{inp1}, v_{inp2}: AC inputs.

Every analog circuit has an associated function and performance measurements. For instance, the function of a differential pair is that its output voltage is proportional to the difference of its input voltages. The proportionality constant, *gain* or a_v, is a performance measurement of the differential pair. Other measurements for a differential amplifier are, for example, its gain, unity gain frequency, phase margin, noise and slew rate. Given a model of the behavior of each component, its parameter values and the topology, the measurements will have specific values. The analog design problem is an inversion of this derivation: given a required function, a set of requirements for (the values of or bounds on) performance measurements and a class of components (e.g., use only mosfets), a designer must come up with the connection of components (topology) and the component parameters to meet the function and performance measurements requirements.

Circuit sizing is the process of determining the parameter values of all components to meet the required performance measurements given the circuit topology. Given the parameter values, the performance of the circuit can be determined, but as in the case above, we need to solve the inverse problem, i.e. to find the components' parameters' values given the performance measurement requirements.

The next two sections give an insight into how the parameters of circuits map to performance measurements and elucidate the methodologies to do sizing.

Circuit Sizing: Complex behavior models and Interconnection Effects

Circuit sizing is complex even though it is possible to determine circuit performance measurements given the behavior of components, their parameter values and interconnection. This is due to the complex behavior of the transistor. A transistor is an active device with non linear behavior which has multiple interactions between its three nodes as a result of fabrication. The model of this relationship depends on many facets of the specific fabrication technology.

Beyond single component behaviorial complexity, the behavior of the entire circuit is even more complex due to interaction between the complex models of the individual devices. This results in very large expressions for some performance measurements (as shown in (Pookaiyaudom and Jantarang, 1996)) and no closed-form solutions for others. These are computationally expensive to solve and non-intuitive in nature. An accurate, yet time consuming means of measuring circuit performance is to use a circuit simulator with component models acquired from the fabrication phase. SPICE(Quarles et al., 1994) is one such circuit simulator which handles all the model and inter-model complexity.

Circuit Sizing: Manual and Automatic Methodologies

There are both manual and automatic methodologies for sizing circuits.

Manual Design: Given the dismal cognition-starved, non-intuitive factors in sizing, it is hard to imagine how analog circuit sizing could be done manually. The reality is contrary to this intuition. Analog circuit sizing has been conventionally done manually and even today, is done manually by highly-paid analog design engineers!

Roughly, the design methodology is the following: The designer uses an approximate quantitative first order model for the transistor behavior (strongly informed by his prior design experience with the fabrication technology). The simplified quantitative expressions are used to model the interaction between the components to come up with simplified expressions for the performance measurements. Using these expressions, the component parameters are worked out. This is an iterative process where at one step the designer may select parameters that manage to satisfy one measurement requirement but which "fall out" on others. At the next step some adjustment is made to (hopefully) bring the measurements closer (or completely) to requirements. Intuition of the designer regarding the higher-order interactions between components and feedback from simulations (which in turn sharpens intuition) informs the readjustments to components to meet specifications. As the designer works more and more on a given topology, intuition about the higher order interaction of components improves and yields expertise in sizing circuits optimally. At each step, the design is simulated on SPICE for verification with respect to requirements.

Automated blackbox Optimization: SPICE technically performs a mapping function between parameter values and performance measurements. It is empirically known that such a direct mapping function would be misbehaved and multimodal. Also, performance measurements are coupled and in tradeoff. The problem is very high dimension in input variable space; the number of parameters varies from 10's to a few hundreds. For instance, a simple opamp has around 13 parameters that need to be set. Thus, rather than replacing SPICE with a function, it can be exploited as a blackbox. This conceptualization of SPICE lays the foundation for casting the sizing problem as a large scale multi-objective optimization problem for which a blackbox function evaluator is available. There has been a lot of work in applying different stochastic blackbox optimization algorithms (also termed non-structural) to sizing such as genetic algorithms (De Smedt and Gielen, 2003) and simulated annealing (Siarry et al., 1997). Genetic algorithms and programming has been applied to the combined topology and sizing design problem (Koza et al., 1997; Grimbleby, 2000; Shibata et al., 2002; Botelho et al., 2003).

Equation-based approaches have also been used instead of invoking SPICE in the optimization loop(Gielen et al., 1990). Here, a simplified model for the transistor is used and multiple symbolic equations are derived to express the performance measurements. These equations, though not completely accurate, take much less time than SPICE to provide the performance measurement values. The process of sizing is thus accelerated at the cost of accuracy.

Equation-driven global optimization: When the sizing problem is solved by blackbox optimization techniques that use multiple symbolic expressions which measure the circuit's performance, any exploitation of the *structure* of the performance measurement equations is ignored. This observation reveals the possibility that a structured optimization algorithm (like linear programming, quadratic programming), if it could exploit the structure of the symbolic equations, would also be able to solve sizing. In an exciting development in sizing methodology, (Hershenson et al., 1998) showed that in the case of an opamp, circuit performance measurement equations could be accurately yet approximately expressed in *posynomial* form (which we shall define in detail in Section 2) to be solved by geometric programming. The approach used less accurate transistor models and considered only simple interconnection effects. Geometric programming is a structural optimization technique which can determine the global optimum for objectives and constraints expressed in posynomial form. It uses interior-point methods (Boyd et al., 2004) and solves in a few seconds. In (Hershenson et al., 1998; Hershenson et al., 1999; Colleran et al., 2003), it was shown that geometric programming can be used to size various analog circuits such as PLLs, opamps, OTAs and inductor circuits in a few minutes.

As convenient as the geometric programming technique might initially appear, the devil is in its details. Most significantly, all circuits do not render to posynomial equations that accurately express *real* (i.e. complex) transistor models and multiple interaction effects. When these inaccuracies then are translated into problem objectives and constraints, they lead to the determination of a faulty global optimum, i.e. the optimum of an inappropriate (or wrong) problem. The extent to which simple interaction terms impose inaccuracy on the equations depends on the topology and needs to assessed on a case-by-case basis. There may be a large unacceptable impact for a certain topology, while it could be trivial for another.

This paper investigates finding accurate posynomial expressions that are high fidelity models of a real transistor. With more accurate performance measurement equations incorporated into geometric programming's objectives and constraints, there is potential for improved sizing optimization. We have used genetic algorithms to design posynomial models for mos transistors.

2. Geometric Programming

To be more explicit, geometric programming (Boyd et al., 2004) is a special type of convex optimization which exploits the posynomial or monomial form of objectives and constraints. Let $\overline{x}$ be a vector of n real positive variables. A function f is called a posynomial function of $\overline{x}$ if it has the following form:

$$f(x_1, \ldots, x_n) = \sum_{k=1}^{t} c_k x_1^{\alpha_{1,k}} x_2^{\alpha_{2,k}} \ldots x_n^{\alpha_{n,k}}, \quad c_j > 0, \quad \alpha_{i,j} \in \Re$$

When $t = 1$, the expression is called a monomial. geometric programming solves an optimization problem of the following form:

$$\begin{aligned} \text{minimize} \quad & f_0(\overline{x}) \\ \text{subject to} \quad & f_i(\overline{x}) \leq 1, \quad i = 1, \ldots, m, \\ & g_i(\overline{x}) = 1, \quad i = 1, \ldots, p, \\ & x_i > 0, \quad i = 1, \ldots, n \end{aligned}$$

Here f_i and f_0 are posynomials while g_i are monomials. A geometric program can be solved for the global optimum in a few seconds using interior point methods. In the next section, we will show how an opamp sizing can be expressed as a geometric program. Note that posynomials exclude the expression of a negative term but can express a fraction.

Circuits as a Geometric Program

Circuit performance measurements fall in two categories: small signal and large signal. The process of expressing the circuit for geometric programming involves expressing its small signal and large signal measurements as posynomials.

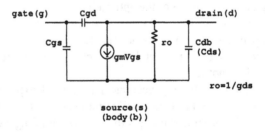

Figure 14-2. Small Signal model of mosfet.

Small Signal Measurements: The transistor despite being a non-linear device has nearly linear behavior for small changes in voltage and current. This fact is exploited (in general) by all analog circuits to implement different behaviors. The measurements of these behaviors are termed small signal performance measurements. One example is gain, the ratio of the output voltage and the input voltage when the circuit is excited by a *small* input voltage.

The circuit small signal performance is measured by expressions that interpret the interconnection of the topology and embed a *small signal model* of the mosfet. A small signal model for the mosfet is shown in Figure 14-2. Its parameters gm, gds (or r_o), Cdb, Cgs and Cgd are also shown in Figure 14-2. The symbol g stands for transconductance, r for resistance and C for capacitance. These parameters are themselves each a function of the transistor width (W), length (L) and the current (I_d) flowing through it.

Large signal Specifications: The transistor is essentially a non-linear device. The performance measures related to its non-linear characteristics are called large signal specifications and do not consider the linearity assumption of the small signal model. Slew rate and voltage swing are examples of large signal performance measures for an opamp. The value of current flowing through the transistor is also ascertained by the transistor large signal model, which is required to express the value of small signal parameters (small signal parameters are a function of W, L and I_d).

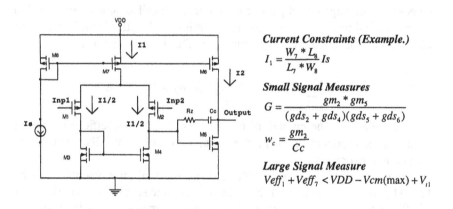

Figure 14-3. An opamp for geometric programming example.

The process of expressing the circuit as a posynomial for geometric programming is shown for an opamp in Figure 14-3. To size the given circuit, the width (W_i) and length (L_i) of all transistors, the input current (I_s), the parameter values of the resistor (R_z) and capacitor (C_c) have to be determined. The currents flowing through all mosfets are expressed using the large-signal behavior of the mosfet and topological connection information. They are a function of the input currents, W and L of transistors (example included in Figure 14-3). These are monomial constraints. Small signal performance measures, for instance, (G) and unity-gain frequency (w_c) are expressed in terms of small signal parameters. For maximization of gain or imposing a lower bound constraint on it, the inverse of the gain has to be a posynomial. This can be achieved by expressing gds and gm as posynomial and monomial respectively. Same holds true for w_c. The large signal performance measures may be expressed using the large signal model parameter Vt, $Veff$ and substitution of hand-calculated values. The figure shows the constraint on V_{eff} of transistor $M1$ and $M7$ due to a lower bound on the maximum common-mode input voltage $(Vcm(max))$. This can also be expressed as a posynomial constraint.

In this formulation, each value of the small signal parameters (for e.g., gm) and certain large-signal parameters (for example, Vt) of a mosfet must be expressed as a posynomial (or monomials in certain cases) function of the width, length and current flowing through the mosfet. This is what we dub the MOS posynomial modeling problem.

3.   The MOS Posynomial Modeling Problem

The goal of MOS posynomial modeling is to express all small signal parameters and some large signal parameters (henceforth called output variables, Y_i) as posynomial function of the transistor width (W), length (L) and the current (I_d) (henceforth called, input variables, $\overline{X}$). This is shown below.

$$Y_i = \sum_{k=1}^{t} a_k W^{\alpha_{k,1}} L^{\alpha_{k,2}} I_d^{\alpha_{k,3}}, \quad a_j > 0, \quad \alpha_{i,j} \in \Re$$

As can be seen, the number of terms, the value of the coefficients of each term and the exponent of each input variable in each term fully specifies the posynomial expression.

The values of the output variables for any value of input variables can be found by SPICE simulation of the transistor. A large set of points (in the order of 10's of thousands) enumerating the value of output variables for values of input variable is available[1]. Our GA must find a posynomial function for each output variable in terms of the input variables, which minimizes the mean square error between the actual value and calculated value (posynomial function) for each variable over the complete data set.

In earlier studies, log regression has been used to fit monomials (Boyd et al., 2004), however this approach cannot be extended for fitting posynomial models. In other works (Daems and Gielen, 2003; Li et al., 2004), posynomial models with exponents as integers between -2 and 2 have been suggested. Like a GA,

---

[1]The large number of sampling points is necessary for comprehensive representation

these approaches make no claim to finding a globally optimal solution. In our approach, the exponent can take any real value which gives the model more expressive power.

4.   Our Genetic Algorithm for MOS Modeling

We have designed a genetic algorithm (GA) to synthesize a posynomial for each of the output variables of a mosfet model. The genetic algorithm has to be executed for each output variable separately. The demonstrated method is generic for fitting a posynomial to a given input and output data.

Posynomial Representation: Genotype to phenotype mapping

The mapping of genotype to phenotype is shown in the Figure 14-4. Our phenotype is a posynomial expression. The genotype is a matrix of real numbered values as shown in Figure 14-4. Each row represents a term of the posynomial. The number of rows is fixed. A choice parameter associated with each row decides whether the row is actually used or not (1:used, 0:don't care). This allows us to have posynomials with varying number of terms in the population. The number of rows is equivalent to the maximum number of possible terms in the posynomial. Each column is associated with one of the 3 input variables. The value in a cell encodes the exponent of the variable (represented by the column) for the term (represented by the row). All cell values are in a specified range $[minVal, maxVal]$. The coefficient of each term is not a part of the genotype.

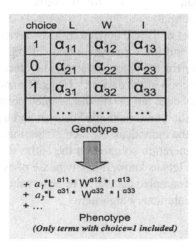

Figure 14-4. GA genotype to phenotype mapping.

This genotype might be interpreted to state that the value of the choice parameter helps exploration of posynomials with different number of terms. Because of how we determine the coefficients (that are not in the genotype), a coefficient may become zero valued. This incorporates automatic *feature selection* (term selection) in the algorithm. The determination of coefficient values and how the number of terms of the posynomial varies will be discussed in terms of fitness evaluation in Section 4.0. This representation expresses the exponents as real values (in a given bound) and our algorithm is not biased to set exponents as absolute zeros. Another option for the model would be to restrict the exponents to integers (which shall include absolute zero). Intuitively, while the current representation would evolve expressions with fewer terms (since each term has a high degree of freedom/expressibility), the latter would evolve expression with more terms. Since there is no *a priori* information about the model, our choice of the model is arbitrary.[2]

Fitness Evaluation

The GA evolves the exponents of all variables for each term. To determine the complete posynomial form of the candidate solution, the coefficient of each term must be determined. This is done deterministically, given the specific values of the exponents, with a minimization of mean square error (MSE) objective. We formulate a Quadratic Programming (QP) problem from the MSE objective function (because it is second degree) along with linear constraints that all coefficients are positive. The coefficients found by QP are the global optima for the given exponents. A QP solver within Matlab is used to solve the QP problem. The minimum value of the error (minimum MSE) is a measure of the accuracy of the posynomial.

The complete dataset of SPICE derived MOS behavior is substantially large (about 70000 points) and the formulation and solving of QP becomes computationally expensive for the whole dataset. Therefore, we only use a small randomly sampled fraction of the dataset.[3] Using this smaller fraction requires that the evolved model does not overfit the sampled points. To ensure this, we use 2-fold cross validation on the sampled data set and use the cross validation MSE as the fitness of the individual. At each generation, we fit the coefficients of only the best of generation solution on the entire dataset and calculate its MSE. This error value lets us know, if in any phase of evolution, the algorithm starts overfitting to the sampled data set. The error value is not used to provide any feedback to the evolutionary algorithm.

---

[2]The decision is not completely arbitrary since monomials with non-integer exponents yield low error results.
[3]A more principled approach to do this could be by use of Design of Experiments (Kelton, 2000)

To summarize, the candidate solution is derived by evolution of its exponents and QP optimization of its coefficients. It is evaluated on a fixed randomly sampled small fraction of the complete data set and the cross-validation error is used as the candidate's fitness.

It is worth noting here, that the problem at hand is different from a typical model building problem, where one needs to deliver a model which generalizes well to unseen data. Here a huge data-set for prediction is available but we are using only a part of it since our algorithm is computationally intractable with the complete data set. There is also a hypothesis that using more data will not help.[4] Our final adjustment of the coefficients for the exponents of the GA solution for optimal performance on the complete dataset is a flexibility that is not available in typical model building problems.

Also noteworthy is an effect arising from using QP to find the coefficients. The QP problem has the constraints that all coefficients should be more than zero. This can be visualized as an optimization problem with feasible space bounded by hyperplanes. Each hyperplane has value of one of the coefficients as zero everywhere on it. The intersection of the hyperplanes have more than one coefficient equal to zero. The solution of the QP problem in many cases lie on one of the constraining hyperplanes or their intersection. This pushes some of the coefficients to exact zero. Thus QP implicitly performs *feature selection* feature selection on the evolved terms by setting the coefficients of useless terms to zero. From the perspective of GAs, QP is identifying useful terms within the genotype. It also makes the genotype implicitly variable length though with an upper bound. It is an open question whether this QP-based selection of terms also generates useful building blocks across the population that could be exploited by a GA combination operator.

Variation Operators

Since the evolved expression is a sum-of-products, we consider the product terms as building blocks, which combine through the addition operator to form the solution. The GA employs a coarse grained term-wise uniform crossover operator that exchanges terms. The order of terms (rows in the genotype matrix) has no significance since all terms are additive so each row is chosen from one of the two parents. Two individuals are chosen from the selected population and the new individual is created by choosing each row from one of the two parents. This operator is used to do *inter building block* recombination.

The mutation operator is used to perturb the real-numbered values in the cells of the matrix. A normal distribution centered at zero with a given variance

---

[4]This is akin to bioinformatics experiments, where in motif predicting algorithms, no improvement in accuracy is observed after the data-set becomes larger than a given number.

(λ) is added to the real numbered value. The variance is adaptively decreased according to the genetic algorithm generation to make the algorithm explorative initially and exploitative in later stages. We investigated two strategies:

Strategy 1: Mutation is carried out in two phases. In the first phase, a term (equivalent to a row) is chosen for mutation by a given probability (p_{term}). In the second phase, each cell in the chosen row is mutated by a given probability (p_{cell}). This scheme chooses a building-block to mutate in the first phase. The term-wise mutation rate is set to conserve a given number of building blocks in the population depending on the selection pressure. In the second phase the intention is to direct appropriately step-sized, local search within each identified building block. The cell-wise mutation rate is set to encourage incremental search in the product-term space.

Strategy 2: Strategy 2 exploits the fact that the coefficients indicate whether a given term is a useful (i.e. contributing to fitness) component to a particular genotype's solution. We could hypothesize that a useful term in one solution might be useful in another solution and thus is an evolutionary building block. A zero coefficient term would not be a useful building block. Thus, in this strategy, terms with zero coefficients and non-zero coefficients are treated differently. A term with a zero coefficient is mutated by a probability (p_{zero_term}), the operation being reinitialization of the term randomly. A term with a non-zero coefficient is mutated by a different probability ($p_{non\_zero\_term}$) and is mutated cell-wise in the same way as Strategy 1. Here, the coefficients of the terms are considered in tandem with the genotype for the purposes of mutation only. This strategy exploits the hypothesis that a term with a non-zero coefficient is a building block. If this is true, the strategy will generate useful explorative variation only in circumstances where it seems advantageous (i.e. when a zero coefficient term has evolved).

5.   Experiments

We used the proposed genetic algorithm to evolve posynomial models for 9 mos model output variables in terms of its W, I and L for an NMOS transistor. The specific model output variables are shown in the top row of Tables 14-2 and 14-3. The silicon technology for the mosfet model is TSMC $0.18u$. Approximately 70,000 points were extracted from SPICE simulation which swept the complete operating range (in saturation) of the transistor. We sampled 2000 points uniformly from the complete set for fitness evaluation and used 2-fold cross-validation for fitness evaluation.

The GA is standard. Each genotype of generation 0 is initialized using a uniform random distribution bounded by $[minVal, maxVal]$ for each cell element. The number of rows in the genome is 5. The choice parameter is randomly initialized to 1 or 0 such that the average number of terms per individual in the initial generation is 3. We use a generation based GA with tournament selection. Each tournament produces one new member of the next generation. The genetic algorithm parameters are given in Table 14-1. The probability of term mutation for both Strategy 1 and Strategy 2 were roughly hand calculated for learning a linkage of 3 terms given the tournament size.

Table 14-1. GA Parameters.

Parameter	Value
Population Size	50
Tournament Size	6
[minVal, maxVal]	[-3, 3]
Initial λ	1
λ rate	Halved every 20 generations
$p_{crossover}$	0.5
Mixing Ratio	0.7
p_{term}	0.45
p_{cell}	0.5
p_{zero_term}	0.7
$p_{non\_zero\_term}$	0.3
Maximum number of terms	5

Experiment 1

Here we evolved posynomial models for output variable V_{eff} using Strategy 1 and Strategy 2. The average best-fitness over all runs is misleading due to outlier runs. Thus, we use quantile plots which show the fitness value range for a percent of individuals. Figure 14-5 shows the quantile plot for best-fitness individuals from 10 runs for both strategies. One can observe that 8 out of 10 solutions for Strategy 2 have lower error value than those of Strategy 1. However, one solution from Strategy 2 does much worse than Strategy 1 and maybe considered an outlier. The fitness of the posynomial expressions which gave the least error for complete data over all runs and generations was $1.030e^{-4}$ for Strategy 1 and $1.022e^{-4}$ for Strategy 2. These results are just indicative in favor of Strategy 2 and no strong claim can be made on their basis. The primary aim of this investigation is to find out whether our GA can find a better posynomial than log-trained monomials. This is addressed in Experiment 2.

Experiment 2

We evolved posynomials for all 9 mos output variables using the proposed genetic algorithm. We ran 2 runs for each output variable with the same settings as above for 1000 generations. In each generation, the coefficients of the best

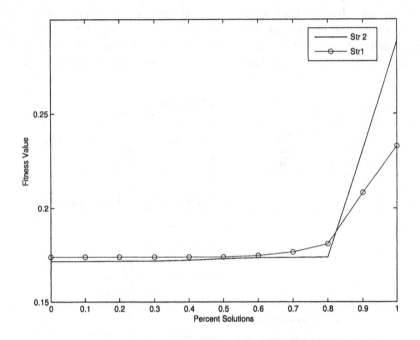

Figure 14-5. Quantile plot for best solutions of Strategy 1 and Strategy 2 over 10 runs.

	gm	gds	$Veff$	Vt	$V_{d(sat)}$
Monomial	$1.36e^{-8}$	$1.57e^{-11}$	$5.08e^{-4}$	$3.46e^{-5}$	$2.87e^{-4}$
Posynomial	$4.75e^{-9}$	$5.62e^{-13}$	$1.04e^{-4}$	$8.53e^{-6}$	$7.61e^{-5}$
Improvement (%)	65.1	96.4	79.5	75.3	73.4

Table 14-2. Results of Experiment 2 for 5 output variables. The bottom row (Imp) shows the percentage improvement of the GA evolved posynomial over over the monomial derived by a three step process (see text for details). Improvement measures decreased error.

	C_{gd}	C_{gs}	C_{db}	r_o
Monomial	6.28^{-34}	$3.94e^{-29}$	$3.48e^{-32}$	$3.35e^{13}$
Posynomial	1.99^{-35}	$3.55e^{-29}$	$1.28e^{-34}$	$1.25e^{12}$
Improvement (%)	96.8	9.7	99.63	96.2

Table 14-3. Results of Experiment 2 for 4 remaining output variables. The bottom row (Imp) shows the percentage improvement of the GA evolved posynomial over over the monomial derived by a three step process (see text for details). Improvement measures decreased error.

individual and its error were re-determined according to the complete set. The posynomial expressions which gave the least error for complete data over all runs and generations are reported in Table 14-4 for three mos parameters. For each parameter the coefficient of each term and the respective exponents are reported.

For comparison, monomials for output variables were created by a three step process. First, log regression (Boyd et al., 2004) was done to find a set of coefficients and exponents. The exponents and coefficients were re-tuned to minimize MSE using a gradient-descent method in the second step. In the third step, the coefficients for the given exponents were optimized globally by a QP formulation. A comparison of error of these monomials and GA evolved posynomial are shown in Tables 14-2 and 14-3 .

Table 14-4. Results for 3 mos parameters in Experiment 2. These are GA evolved posynomial mosfet parameter models.

Coefficient	L exponent	W exponent	I_d exponent
C_{db}			
$4.333407e^{-10}$	0.0092217	0.9867695	0.0018283
$5.303325e^{-10}$	0.0013345	1.014629	-0.0012439
V_{eff}			
$1.010186e^{+02}$	0.5113741	-0.5138530	0.5071154
$6.589195e^{-01}$	0.5540773	-1.458791	1.621552
C_{gs}			
$7.175508e^{-03}$	1.080458	0.9303338	0.05072020
$2.179441e^{-03}$	0.9974063	0.9505211	0.04358394
$4.078940e^{-07}$	0.2597072	1.171186	0.05483664

6. Summary

We have broadly described the process and methods of analog circuit design in terms of topology selection and sizing. A description of sizing as an optimization problem along with brief descriptions of hand methodologies and automatic methodologies such as black-box optimization and geometric programming was given. Geometric programming can solve an optimization problem in seconds provided the problem objectives are expressed as posynomials and the constraints are expressed as monomials. This prompted us to design a GA to evolve posynomial mos models that are embedded within posynomial equations that express the circuit's small signal measurements. We designed a GA with a fixed length genotype that implicitly has variable encoding of number of posynomial terms via its accompanying use of QP for coefficient optimization. For this particular mos technology the GA provides **much better** models than statistically fitted models. The given approach is a general posynomial model building approach and not specific to only mos parameters. However, care has to be taken when building models for higher dimensional input space because sparseness of expressions will be required. In this case a modified GA or genetic programming approach might be useful.

7.   Future Work

While we have only focused on posynomial models in this submission, a broader goal is to evaluate the value of GA evolved posynomial models in terms of how much they improve the quality of circuit sizing. Comparisons can be made to hand-sized circuits and circuits sized with posynomial models derived by other means (e.g statistically derived models and hand written circuit level posynomials). While the GA provides better accuracy, the extent to which this improved accuracy helps with sizing is unquantified as yet. The cost of the accuracy of the GA derived mos models is the computational expense and time to evolve them. High cost is unimportant because the model is very reusable. In other words, the cost is amortized over many uses of the model.

But are posynomials' inherent errors worse than using polynomials and more computationally intensive techniques? There could be potential advantages to using any kind of EA to derive less restricted models and then using another EA (i.e. in place of geometric programming) that exploits the model. This sounds easy but it is not straight forward in the circuit sizing domain because of the complexity of large signal models and the ability to express a models parameterized for a technology.

Acknowledgements

We would like to thank Joel Dawson, Tania Khanna, Ranko Sredojevic, Vladimir Stojanovic and Trent McConaghy for their assistance with test data and helpful discussions

References

Botelho, J., Leonardo, B., Vieira, P., and Mesquita, A. (2003). An experiment on nonlinear synthesis using evolutionary techniques based only on CMOS transistors. In Lohn, J., Zebulum, R., Steincamp, J., Keymeulen, D., Stoica, A., and Ferguson, M.I., editors, *2003 NASA/DoD Conference on Evolvable Hardware*, pages 50–58. IEEE Computer Society.

Boyd, S., Kim, S.-J., Vaudenberghe, L., and Hassibi, A. (2004). A tutorial on geometric programming. In *Technical report, EE Department, Stanford University*.

Colleran, D.M., Portmann, C., Hassibi, A., Crusius, C., Mohan, S.S., Boyd, S.P., Lee, T. H., and Hershenson, M. (2003). Optimization of phase-locked loop circuits via geometric programming. In *IEEE Custom Integrated Circuits Conference*, pages 377–380.

Daems, W. and Gielen, G.C.E. (2003). Simulation-based generation of posynomial performance models for the sizing of analog integrated circuits. *Computer-Aided Design of Integrated Circuits and Systems, IEEE Transactions*, 22(5):517–534.

De Smedt, B. and Gielen, G.C.E. (2003). WATSON: Design space boundary exploration and model generation for analog and rf ic design. *IEEE Transactions on Computer-Aided Design of Integrated Circuits and Systems*, 22(2):213–224.

Gielen, G.C.E., Swings, K., and Sansen, W. (1990). An intelligent design system for analogue integrated circuits. In *EURO-DAC '90: Proceedings of the conference on European design automation*, pages 169–173, Los Alamitos, CA, USA. IEEE Computer Society Press.

Grimbleby, J.B. (2000). Automatic analogue circuit synthesis using genetic algorithms. *IEE Proceedings Circuits, Devices and Systems*, 147(6):319–323.

Hershenson, M., Boyd, S. P., and Lee, T. (November 1998). GPCAD: A tool for CMOS op-amp synthesis. In *Proc. International Conference on Computer Aided Design*, pages 296–303. IEEE/ACM.

Hershenson, M., Mohan, S. S., Boyd, S. P., and Lee, T. H. (1999). Optimization of inductor circuits via geometric programming. In *DAC '99: Proceedings of the 36th ACM/IEEE conference on Design automation*, pages 994–998, New York, NY, USA. ACM Press.

Kelton, W..D. (2000). Design of experiments: experimental design for simulation. In *WSC '00: Proceedings of the 32nd conference on Winter simulation*, pages 32–38, San Diego, CA, USA. Society for Computer Simulation International.

Koza, John R., Bennett III, Forrest H, Andre, David, Keane, Martin A., and Dunlap, Frank (1997). Automated synthesis of analog electrical circuits by means of genetic programming. *IEEE Transactions on Evolutionary Computation*, 1(2):109–128.

Li, X., Gopalakrishnan, P., Xu, Y., and Pileggi, T. (2004). Robust analog/RF circuit design with projection-based posynomial modeling. In *ICCAD '04: Proceedings of the 2004 IEEE/ACM International conference on Computer-aided design*, pages 855–862, Washington, DC, USA. IEEE Computer Society.

Mead, C. (1990). Neuromorphic electronic systems. 78(10):1629–1636.

Pookaiyaudom, S. and Jantarang, S. (1996). Automatic circuit simplification for meaningful symbolic analysis using the genetic algorithm. In *1996 IEEE International Symposium on Circuits and Systems*, volume 1, pages 109–112.

Quarles, T., Newton, A.R., Pederson, D.O., and Sangiovanni-Vincentelli, A. (1994). SPICE 3, version sf5 user's manual.

Shibata, H., Mori, S., and Fujii, N. (2002). Automated design of analog circuits using cell-based structure . In *Evolvable Hardware*, pages 85–92. IEEE Computer Society.

Siarry, P., Berthiau, G., Durdin, F., and Haussy, J. (1997). Enhanced simulated annealing for globally minimizing functions of many-continuous variables. *ACM Trans. Math. Softw.*, 23(2):209–228.

Chapter 15

PHASE TRANSITIONS IN GENETIC PROGRAMMING SEARCH

Jason M. Daida,[1] Ricky Tang,[1] Michael E. Samples[1] and Matthew J. Byom[1]

[1] *The University of Michigan, Center for the Study of Complex Systems and Space Physics Research Laboratory.*

Abstract   Phase transitions occur in computational, as well as thermodynamic systems. Of particular interest is the possibility that phase transitions occur as a consequence of GP search. If this were so, it would allow for a statistical mechanics approach and quantitative comparisons of GP with a broad variety of rigorously described systems. This chapter summarizes our research group's work in this area and describes a case study that illustrates what is involved in establishing the existence of phase transitions in GP search.

1.   Introduction

A phase transition typically refers to a transformation of a thermodynamic system from one state to another (e.g., solid to liquid). This transformation is typically marked by a sudden and marked physical change, even though such a change was brought about by only a small change in system input (e.g., temperature). Many thermodynamic systems – water, hydrogen, and silica, to name a few – exhibit this behavior.

Sustained interest in phase transitions occurs in many scientific and engineering disciplines because the physics that describes phase transitions encompasses many different types of systems (and not just thermodynamic). Such systems would include ferromagnetic, paramagnetic, and superfluidic systems and their associated mathematical models, e.g., Ising models, Heisenberg models, and XY models (Chan, 2001). Such systems also include purely mathematical and computational systems, such as random graphs and constraint satisfaction problems, e.g., (Cheeseman et al., 1991). The particular physics that is associated with phase transitions is statistical mechanics.

Our particular interest in phase transitions stems from the possibility that phase transitions may come about as a natural consequence of search in GP. If this were true, it would mean that analytical methods and tools developed in statistical mechanics could also apply to GP. It would also mean that GP belongs to a broad class of phenomena and systems, which exist largely outside the field of genetic and evolutionary computation. Applying statistical mechanics to GP is appealing, if only because of the potential in offering a new insight into GP for understanding its dynamics or improving its performance.

That sudden and marked transitions occur in GP search is not a new finding. Our previous work has identified and quantified such transitions in GP search through theoretical modeling and experiment, e.g, (Daida et al., 1999a; Daida et al., 2001; Daida and Hilss, 2003; Daida et al., 1999b; Daida et al., 2005). However, to characterize these identified phenomena as phase transitions (to which statistical mechanics applies) has required the development of new tools, statistical measures, and methods. Consequently, the purpose of this chapter is to highlight our progress in this area at the University of Michigan.

Section 2 gives a background to phase transitions and our investigations. Section 3 provides an overview of some of the tools and methods that we've developed to enable such investigations. Section 4 highlights a case study that is an excerpt from our research group's larger, ongoing investigation. Section 5 discusses the implications of the case study in the broader context of using GP to solve real-world problems. Section 6 concludes.

2.   Transitions in GP Search

Background

In physics, a phase transition refers to a transformation of a thermodynamic system from one state to another. This transformation is typically marked by a sudden change in some physical property that is the result of some small change in what is called an order parameter (e.g., temperature). Phase transitions generally occur in systems that consist of many interacting particles (Sellmyer and Jaswal, 2002; Stanley, 1971).

Of particular note is that the laws of statistical mechanics can describe *critical phenomena* (the behaviors of substances in the transition between states) with only a handful of variables. Among the distinguishing characteristics of these laws are the existence of an order parameter, power-law behavior, and the applicability of scaling laws. Critical systems (those that display critical phenomena) are described as universal, in part because many seemingly dissimilar systems share a common physics. See (Chan, 2001; Stanley, 1971).

Our field has studied phase transitions and critical phenomena in three different settings. The first setting involves solving computational problems that have phase transitional behaviors. Certain well-known problem classes (like constraint satisfaction problems) have phase behaviors that result in exceptionally difficult problems with only minor changes in problem specification. Investigators have subsequently used these tunably difficult problems as a way to validate either existing or new computational search methods, e.g., (Beottcher and Percus, 2000; Beottcher and Percus, 2001; Clearwater and Hogg, 1996; Zhang and Dozier, 2004). Not surprisingly, such problem classes have also attracted those in the broader fields of artificial intelligence and optimization (Huberman et al., 1997)

The second setting involves working towards a fundamental understanding about why computational problems would exhibit phase transitions in the first place. This includes fairly specific problems in genetic and evolutionary computation, e.g., (Izumi and Ueda, 2001; Mohamed et al., 2000; Oda et al., 2000). This also includes general problems that are rooted in computational complexity and information theory, e.g., (Adamic et al., 2001; Correale et al., 2006; Gao and Culberson, 2002; Mitchell et al., 1992; Shimazaki and Niebur, 2005; van Hemert and Urquhart, 2004). In the broader context of theoretical computer science, phase transitions are not just a topic of interest, they themselves and the statistical mechanics needed to study them have been central to understanding why easy problems can suddenly turn difficult, e.g., (Achlioptas et al., 2005; Cheeseman et al., 1991; Hartmann and Weight, 2005; Hogg et al., 1996).

The third setting involves investigating whether the search methods themselves are subject to phase transitions. This effort includes genetic programming (McPhee and Poli, 2000), genetic algorithms, e.g., (Naudts and Schoofs, 2002; Yamamoto and Naito, 2002), and evolutionary methods in general, e.g., (Crutchfield and Mitchell, 1995; Mitchell et al., 1993; Oates et al., 2000). Furthermore, the application of statistical mechanics to phase transitions in evolutionary search methods does suggest the possibility of cardinal principles that underlie broad classes of search methods, e.g., (Huberman and Hogg, 1987; Toulouse et al., 2004), as well as unifying principles that might span physics, biology, and computational complexity (Crutchfield and Schuster, 2003).

Our investigation focuses on the third setting, and considers the possibility of phase transitions that may come about as a natural consequence of search in GP. GP search involves both random graphs (e.g., trees) and networks (e.g., populations), both of which have been studied for phase transitions. For example, some of the earliest work on phase transitions in random graphs was done by Erdos and Rényi (Erdos and Rényi, 1960; Janson et al., 1999). Many complex networks (such as those found in the real world) also have phase transitions and are also amenable to statistical mechanics, e.g., (Barabási, 2003; Bianconi and Barabási, 2001).

As mentioned in the introduction to this chapter, GP search is marked by transitions, some of which are possible candidates for further consideration as

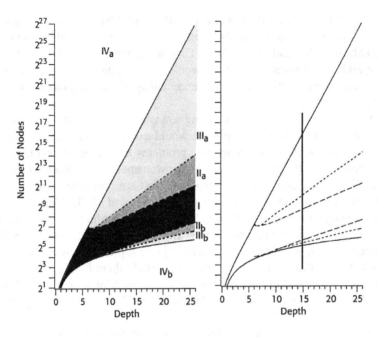

Figure 15-1. (Left) Several regions are predicted that describe transitions associated with trees. Region I represents the most easily attainable structures by GP; Region III, the most difficult. Region II represents a transition region. (Right) Measurements that are discussed in this chapter are sampled along a traversal (indicated by the dark line at depth 15).

phase transitions. The next two subsections subsequently review works that have examined these transitions.

Predictions of Transition in GP

The dynamics of GP search are complex and nuanced, even when just considering how structure evolves over the course of a GP run (Daida et al., 2003). However, we have shown in our previous work that the evolution of tree structures can be modeled as an iterative aggregate of small, sparse subtrees (Daida and Hilss, 2003). The model suggests that more common tree structures are mixed aggregations of several different types of small, sparse subtrees. Transition regions are marked by decreasing numbers of types of these subtrees. The model predicts for not only the transition regions but also for regions of improbable tree structures, if only because iterative aggregation produces a limited number of tree shapes. Figure 15-1 shows the various regions that the model predicts.

A Test for Empirical Validation

Empirical evidence with several well-known test problems do support the predictions made by the model (Daida, 2003). Furthermore, the nature of the model does suggest that the regions should persist, even if 100% of computational effort was dedicated to finding a particular tree shape. Consequently, we devised a "probe" – a GP test problem – that would allow us to focus computational effort in selected, targeted regions that are predicted by the model. The Lid problem, as this probe is called (Daida et al., 1999b), has a function set consisting of the single primitive function JOIN {J}, which is of arity-2, and a terminal set consisting of the single primitive {X}.

The *Lid* problem requires the specification of both a target tree depth (i.e., d_{target}) and a target number of tree terminals (i.e., t_{target}). We assume that Lid trees are rooted, and that the convention for measuring depth presumes that the node at the root lies at the null (0) depth.

How an arbitrary Lid tree measures against its target specifications is given by the following metrics for depth and terminals – Equations 15.1 and 15.2, respectively.

$$metric_{depth} = W_{depth}(1 - (\frac{|d_{target} - d_{actual}|}{d_{target}}))$$ (15.1)

$$metric_{terminal} = \begin{cases} W_{depth}(1 - (\frac{|d_{target} - d_{actual}|}{d_{target}})), & \text{if } metric_{terminals} = W_{terminals} \\ 0, & \text{otherwise} \end{cases}$$

(15.2)

where d_{actual} and t_{actual} correspond to the depth and number of terminals for the measured Lid tree, respectively. (Note: $metric_{depth} = 0$ if $d_{actual} > 2$ d_{target}). Weights W_{depth} and $W_{terminals}$ are chosen arbitrarily such that:

$$W_{depth} + W_{terminals} = 100.$$ (15.3)

Raw fitness is defined as:

$$fitness_{raw} = metric_{depth} + metric_{terminals}.$$ (15.4)

To compare a tree that meets a *Lid* specification with other published results, it is sometimes useful to describe a tree by its total number of nodes (and not by its number of terminals). The relationship between the total number of nodes and the total number of terminals in a Lid tree is given as:

$$Size_{target} = 2t_{target} - 1.$$ (15.5)

The idea behind the Lid problem is simple. If we treat either specification for depth (i.e., d_{target}) or the number of terminals (i.e., t_{target}) as a tuning parameter, we should be able to traverse regions that have been identified by the model. Furthermore, if GP does have phase transitions, one should be able to detect fairly significant changes in outcome with only small changes in tuning parameter (i.e., either t_{target} or d_{target}).

In (Daida et al., 1999b), we chose as an outcome the relatively crude measure of success rate. In particular, for every sample taken in a region, we ran N number of trials. The ratio of the number of successful trials to the total number of trials is a crude measure of computational effort – higher success rates roughly correspond to lower amounts of computational effort. While not a perfect measure of computational effort, (Hogg et al., 1996) has indicated that phase transitions in search methods would be identified by changes in computational effort.

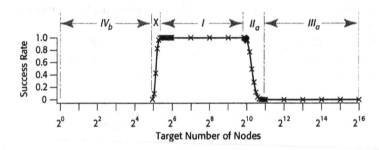

Figure 15-2. Empirical results, where each cross represents the fraction of successful trials out of 1000 trials.

Figures 15-1 and 15-2 summarize some of the results published in (Daida et al., 1999b). In particular, Figure 15-1 indicates where the traversal took place relative to the predicted regions (i.e., constant depth at 15, with a varying number of tree sizes). Figure 15-2 shows the measured success rates as a function of the number of nodes in a tree. The annotation in Figure 15-2 highlights where the measured outcomes coincide with predicted regions, except for the region indicated by an "X."

Although the results in (Daida et al., 1999b) (and repeated in Figure 15-2) do show reasonable qualitative agreement with the predicted regions in (Daida and Hilss, 2003), they do raise questions. For example, are the empirical measurements sensitive to the way the Lid problem is specified? This latter question is of interest not only because of experimental robustness, but also because phase transitions are considered to be an outcome of only a few variables (and to remain relatively insensitive to problem variations).

There are two other major variations to the Lid problem that have not been tested (but should be to see whether phase transitions apply). The original Lid is a depth-first / terminals-second problem, meaning that the depth specification needs to be met before the terminal specification is active. Consequently, one major variant is a terminals-first / depth-second variant, i.e.:

$$metric_{depth} = \begin{cases} W_{depth}(1 - (\frac{|d_{target} - d_{actual}|}{d_{target}})), & \text{if } metric_{terminals} = W_{terminals} \\ 0, & \text{otherwise} \end{cases}$$

(15.6)

$$metric_{terminals} = W_{terminals}(1 - (\frac{|t_{target} - t_{actual}|}{t_{target}})).$$

(15.7)

The other is an unbiased version (depth or terminal specifications can be met at any time during a run). (Note: For Equations 15.7 and 15.9, $metric_{terminals}$ = 0 if $t_{actual} > 2\ t_{target}$. For Equation 15.8, $metric_{depth} = 0$ if $d_{actual} > 2\ d_{target}$).

$$metric_{depth} = W_{depth}(1 - (\frac{|d_{target} - d_{actual}|}{d_{target}})).$$

(15.8)

$$metric_{terminals} = W_{terminals}(1 - (\frac{|t_{target} - t_{actual}|}{t_{target}})).$$

(15.9)

Each major variation in the *Lid* problem implicitly has several minor variations, where more (or less) weight is given to the depth specification (or alternately, the terminal specification).

We know that the existence of transitions in the Lid problem for just one configuration is not sufficient to claim the existence of phase transitions in the search method itself. If phase transitions exist in the search method (and not just the problem examined by the search), the observed transitions should remain robust over a wide variety of problems and problem variations. At the very least, one should examine GP behavior for each of the major Lid variations. One should also allow for a systematic evaluation of the minor variations.

The amount of testing represented by such an empirical investigation of phase transitions is subsequently nontrivial. Instead of several hundred GP runs, which would satisfy many published analyses, what is suggested is an investigation on the order of several hundred thousand GP runs. To accommodate investigations of this magnitude, we needed to develop a systematic method and associated tools to work with computational experiments of this size. Consequently, Section 3 describes our efforts in making such investigations possible.

3. Methods and Tools

The scaling of computational experiments – from hundreds of runs to several hundreds of thousands of runs – could be done with technologies as basic as

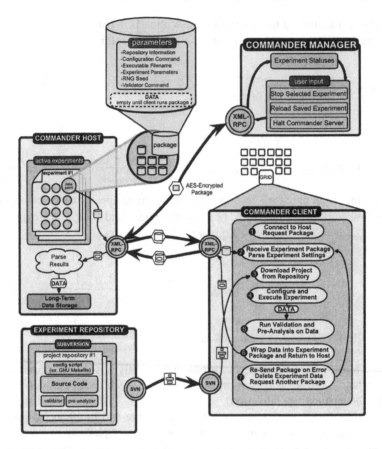

Figure 15-3. Diagram of system that automates experiments that look for phase transitions in GP search.

shell scripts. However, even if a script were to manage a thousand trials on one machine, there would remain the matter of several hundred scripts left to manage. The process becomes untenable. For example, for resource-intensive problems (like the Lid), an hour of CPU time is not unusual. A computational experiment of a half-million trials could take close to six years to finish, even with 100 machines running 1000 trials at a time. That estimate worsens, as networks break, machines fail, and lost runs need to be redone.

For these and other reasons, our research group has spent a significant amount of effort in developing an automated system to manage large-scale computational experiments in a distributed computing environment. Figure 15-3 shows the current architecture of this system (called *Commander*) that manages our computational experiments. It can automatically farm out a computational

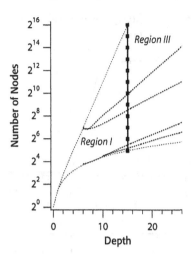

Figure 15-4. Traversal taken for case study. Each dot respresents a sample location.

experiment with varying parameters to a grid with as little as one trial per machine – all the while managing parameters, source code, and input data for that trial. Furthermore, the system automatically retrieves the resulting data from a finished run, archives it, and then collates the data for subsequent analysis. Finally, the system has some basic error-correction built-in, so that it re-runs failed trials (e.g., because a machine runs out of disk space). This Python-based system is described in detail in (Samples et al., 2006) and is downloadable at http://sitemaker.umich.edu/umacers.

The large volume of data that is collected has led to the development of new metrics and multivariate visualization techniques. These are described elsewhere (Daida et al., 2004; Daida, 2005; Daida et al., 2005).

4.   Case Study

This chapter details a case study that considers phase transitions in GP search. One way to go about this is to determine the sensitivity of GP behaviors to variations in a presented problem. If transitions are intrinsic to the search method (and not just to the problem), such behavior should be robust over a wide range of problem variations. Of course, the identification of robust behavior does not by itself mean that phase transitions have been found. It would, however, strengthen the possibility that phase transitions do exist in GP search. This section subsequently describes an ongoing sensitivity study on the Lid function, which uses an earlier variant of the Commander system. In particular, the Sampling Strategy subsection describes the specific strategy used in this investigation. The Case Study Method subsection summarizes the method used, while the Case Study Results subsection shows and describes preliminary results from this study.

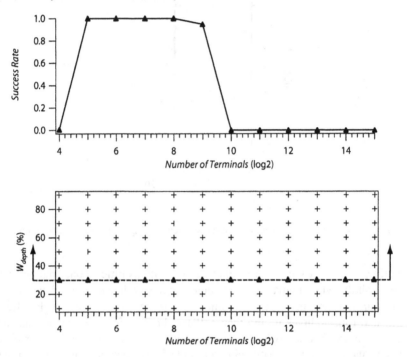

Figure 15-5. (Top) A resampled version of the data shown in Figure 15-2. Although the resolution is coarse, it does allow for repeating the traversal for varying values of W_{depth}. (Bottom) Location of samples for varying W_{depth}. Each cross shows the location where N = 1000 trials were run.

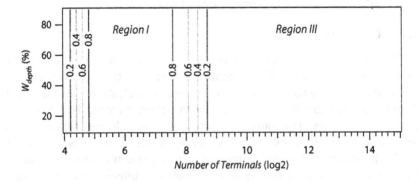

Figure 15-6. Predicted contours (coarse estimation). Contours presume a mapping of region to success rate contours by making major simplifying assumptions.

Sampling Strategy

One key question that needs to be addressed in the identification of possible phase transitions in GP search is whether observed behaviors are the result of GP search, the problem itself, or a combination of both. A sensitivity study should, at the very least, examine the behaviors of a problem over its parameters and variants. For the Lid problem, there are three major variants (depth-first, terminal-first, and unbiased), two tuning parameters (i.e., d_{target} and t_{target}), and two weights (i.e., W_{depth} and $W_{terminals}$) that can shift the emphasis of a search between terminals and depth. While an exhaustive study can be done over varying each and every parameter, it is somewhat impractical to do with the current state of technology (a rough estimate is on the order of a few CPU-centuries using Pentium-IV technologies).

For that reason, we used traversals in both (Daida et al., 1999b) and this study to examine for GP behaviors along slices of the 2-tuple (d_{target}, t_{target}). Since (Daida et al., 1999b) gave results for two orthogonal slices that are consistent with the predicted regions, we picked one of those slices to examine for the effects of problem variants and weights. We specifically chose the fixed-depth slice (i.e., $d_{target} = 15$).

In (Daida et al., 1999b), it was practical to adaptively sample within a traversal to capture detailed GP behavior in the transition regions. For the fixed-depth slice, that meant 60 samples of 1000 trials apiece. Not only would this be prohibitively expensive to repeat this effort for a sensitivity study that examines Lid variants and varying weights (roughly on the order of a CPU-decade), but it is also beyond the current capability of Commander to adaptively sample a search space. A tradeoff was made to coarsely sample the traversal at regular intervals, as shown in Figure 15-4.

To study GP behaviors as a function of weights, we varied one weight since the other weight can be expressed as a dependent variable. We specifically varied W_{depth} in coarse increments of 10%. Lower values of W_{depth} mean less emphasis is placed on the depth-part of the Lid score; $W_{depth} = 0$ basically means that a score for the Lid is driven entirely by the terminal specification. The fixed-depth traversal was repeated for each specified value of W_{depth}. Figure 15-5 shows this sampling strategy with respect to the single vertical slice that was given in (Daida et al., 1999b). The results in that figure have been re-sampled to show the degradation of how the results shown in Figure 15-5 would look like in this study. In Figure 15-5, that slice is indicated as a dotted line in a two-dimensional grid of W_{depth} and t_{target}. The process was repeated again for each of the major Lid variants.

Figure 15-6 shows what we might expect in terms of plotting the contours for success rates. It presumes that Region I yields a 100% success rate and that Region III yields a 0% success rate. It further presumes only a simple log-linear interpolation between Region I and Region III. If the transitions between Region I and Region III represent phase transitions, at the very least the transitions themselves would not change in shape (although the location of those transitions may change). Figure 15-6 shows what one would expect if the transitions found were to be invariant with respect to the non-tuning parameter W_{depth}.

Case Study Method

We used a modified version of lilgp as was described in (Daida et al., 1999b). Most of the GP parameters were identical to those mentioned in Chapter 7 of (Koza, 1992). Unless otherwise noted: population size = 500; crossover rate = 0.9; replication rate = 0.1; population initialization with ramped half-and-half; and initialization depth of 2 − 6 levels. As in (Daida et al., 1999b), fitness-proportionate selection was used. Other parameter values were maximum generations = 200 and the maximum depth = 512 (defining root node to be at depth = 0). Note that as in stock lilgp, crossover is biased towards the internal nodes of an individual (i.e. 90% internal, 10% terminals). The parameters for the Lid problem were as follows: the target depth d_{target} was fixed at 15, while the target numbers of terminals t_{target} were chosen to be powers of two (i.e., 2^x with the integer x varying from 4 − 15 for a total of twelve settings for t_{target}, which spans the full range of allowable depth-15 binary trees). W_{depth} was varied using the following sequence: 10, 20, 30, 40, 50, 60, 70, 80, 90. $W_{terminals}$ was selected for each setting of W_{depth} such that these weights add up to 100.

For each parameter setting, a total of 1000 trials were run on an AMD 32-bit cluster that consists of 67 dual-processor Athlon XP nodes. (Note: only a fraction of the available nodes were used at any one time.) Runs were managed by an AMD XP server running an early version of *Commander* .

The process was repeated for each of the three Lid variants described in the Test for Empirical Validation subsection in Section 2. Consequently, there were 324 data sets collected of 1,000 trials apiece, for a total of 324,000 trials.

Case Study Results

Figure 15-7 shows the results of this case study, from which several observations can be made about fitness-proportionate GP behavior with respect to variations in Lid parameters:

- The existence of a transition region between Regions I and IIIa remains, regardless of Lid variant or changes in W_{depth}. In other words, the existence of what amounts to a "barrier" in the middle of the search space – transition Region II – is a robust feature that separates regions of easy and hard problems. It supports the existence of a phase transition.

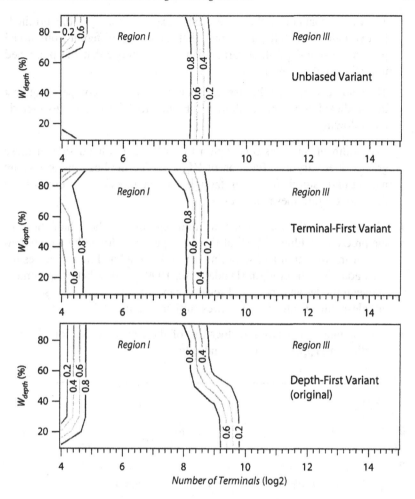

Figure 15-7. Results from the sensitivity study.

- The width of the transition between Regions I and IIIa remains relatively constant, even though the transition itself may shift in absolute location. It indicates, then, that the mechanisms that determine this particular transition do not change (although there are factors that influence where the transition appears). This, too, supports the existence of a phase transition.

- The absolute location of the edge of the transition region that is between Regions I and IIIa and that is closest to Region IIIa does agree well with the model predictions, at least for the unbiased and the terminal-first variants of the Lid problem.

- The variant that comes the closest to the expected theory is the terminal-first variant. (Ironically, the variant that is the most different from model predictions–the depth-first variant–is the original one that was published in (Daida et al., 1999b).

  The study also raises other issues when the results are compared against the predicted contours, as shown in Figure 15-6. These issues include the following:

- The width of the transition region towards the left-hand side of these graphs does vary as a function of W_{depth}. The implications of this are not yet understood. It is clear, though, that the model in its current form does not capture these nuances.

- The widths of the measured transition regions are about half those of the predicted widths. Much of the discrepancy is driven by a combination of interpolation and sampling for both model and measured results (i.e., adaptive sampling in (Daida et al., 1999b) shows better agreement between model and measured results than this case study shows). Nevertheless, this discrepency requires further scrutiny.

- The change in the absolute location of the transition Region IIa as a function of W_{depth} is not well understood.

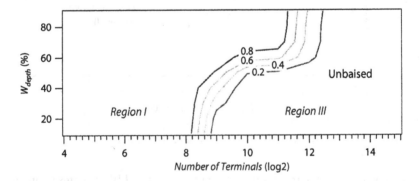

Figure 15-8. Excerpt of results for the unbiased Lid variant, except for tournament selection. Compare with Figure 15-7.

5. Discussion

Rather than go through an analysis of whether the transitions shown in Section 4 are phase transitions that are amenable to statistical mechanical methods (which is left for another paper), in this section we discuss the broader implications of this work and what it could mean to a practitioner.

- The existence of phase transitions in GP search has not been proven, although it has been alluded to in works like (McPhee and Poli, 2000). The results from this chapter's case study would also suggest that phase transitions do exist in GP search. However, we stop short of calling this case study's phenomena a phase transition because it still needs to be shown that key laws in statistical mechanics do apply.

- The existence of a phase transition in GP search would mean that the search method in and of itself would be a determinant of whether a problem is difficult for GP to solve. While there is ample evidence of this happening anyway (Daida, 2004), a determination of phase transitions in GP search could offer further insight into the class of search methods that exhibit phase transitions (Hogg et al., 1996).

- The existence of phase transitions would offer insight into what causes the constraints that limit the complexity of solutions that can be attained with standard GP. Understanding these causes is a step towards controlling GP to attain even more complex structures, if only to understand the limitations of what can or cannot be assembled by standard GP.

Our investigation into what is arguably a simple question about the kinds of tree structures that GP can evolve has raised other concerns, as well. Regardless of whether a GP behavior is classifiable as a phase transition, we have found nuances in GP behaviors that can profoundly affect outcomes. For example, the transitions described in this chapter are not just sudden, but with just minor changes in parameter values, turn an easy problem into one that is at least three orders of magnitude harder to solve. See also (Daida et al., 1999b; Daida, 2004). Where easy and hard problems lie can depend on the nuances of what is being asked of GP search.

We also find it necessary to exercise caution in extrapolating these behaviors to other GP settings, in spite of the size of this case study (i.e., 324,000 trials). For example, while fitness-proportionate selection has useful properties for doing theoretical work, tournament selection is the selection method used by most practitioners. Figure 15-8 shows an additional excerpt from our larger investigation that repeats the case study's procedure, except using tournament selection (m = 7). In comparison to Figure 15-7, the phenomena where the transition region varies as a function of W_{depth} happened under a different variant of the Lid (i.e., unbiased instead of depth-first). Furthermore, the behavior mirrors that given in this chapter's case study. Mechanisms that can explain both kinds of behavior require further investigation.

6.   Conclusions

This chapter has considered the possibility of phase transitions in GP search. Phase transitions and critical phenomena describe the behaviors that are exhibited by a broad class of thermodynamic and nonphysical systems. Although transitions in GP behaviors have been documented in previous work, establishing these transitions as critical phenomena would offer the potential of placing GP in a broader theoretical context. Furthermore, this context would apply not just to search but also to other physical systems, as well.

We have described our research group's efforts in determining phase transitions in GP search, which has led to the development of new tools and methods that assist in the empirical side of our investigations. These tools allow for orders of magnitude improvement in exploring for GP behaviors, while identifying key variables that likely influence these behaviors.

We have highlighted excerpts from an extended investigation on the structural transitions that occur as a consequence of GP search. The investigation features the Lid problem, which has previously been used to validate a model's predications of regions and transitions in the kinds of trees GP can assemble. Even though only a portion of this empirical investigation was shown, the results argue for the robustness of transitions in spite of how the Lid problem was changed. This in turn strengthened a case for classifying at least one GP transition region as a critical phenomenon.

Finally, we have discussed how phase transitions in GP search might have relevance for practitioners. The short-term benefits suggest that it might be worthwhile to adjust the parameters of a GP problem to see if one is on the "wrong" side of a transition. The long-term benefits suggest that if indeed GP search exhibits critical phenomena, insights could be gleaned to the causes that influence what solutions can or cannot be assembled by GP. Knowledge of these causes may point to additional GP processes that would permit the assembly of suitably complex solutions.

7.   Acknowledgements

We thank the following individuals from our research group: A. Hilss, H. Li, D. Ward, S. Long, M. Pizzimenti, P. Chuisano, R. O' Grady, C. Kurecka, M. Hodges, J. Kriesel, F. Tsa, M. Rio, B. McNally, T. Weltzer, K. McNamara, J. Thomas, E. Chen, and K. Jham. Financial support of some of the UMACERS was given and administered through S. Gregerman. Supercomputer usage and support was given and administered through both CAEN and the Center for Advanced Computing. The Center for the Study of Complex System and the U-M / Santa Fe Institute Fall Workshops have played significant roles in the formative development of this work. The first author thanks S. Daida and I.

Kristo. Finally, we thank the workshop organizers R. Riolo, T. Soule and W. Worzel.

References

Achlioptas, D., Naor, A., and Peres, Y. (2005). Rigorous location of phase transitions in hard optimization problems. *Nature*, 435(7043):759–754.

Adamic, L.A., Lukose, R.M., Puniyani, A.R., and Huberman, B.A. (2001). Search in power-law networks. *Phys Rev E*, 64(4):046135/1 – 8.

Barabási, A.L. (2003). Emergence of scaling in complex networks. In Bornholdt, S. and Schuster, P., editors, *Handbook of Graphs and Networks*, pages 69–84. Wiley-VCH, Weinheim.

Beottcher, S. and Percus, A.G. (2000). Combining local search with co-evolution in a remarkably simple way. In *CEC*, pages 1578–1584, La Jolla, CA, USA. IEEE.

Beottcher, S. and Percus, A.G. (2001). External optimization for graph partioning. *Phys Rev E*, 64(2 II):26114/1–13.

Bianconi, G. and Barabási, A.L. (2001). Bose-einstein condensation in complex networks. *Physical Review Letters*, 86(24):5632–5635.

Chan, M.H.W. (2001). *Critical Phenomena*. McGraw-Hill.

Cheeseman, P., Kanefsky, B., and Taylor, W. (1991). Where the really hard problems are. In *Proc Int Joint Conf on AI*, pages 331–337. Morgan Kaufmann.

Clearwater, S.H. and Hogg, T. (1996). Problem structure heuristics and scaling behavior for genetic algorithms. *AI*, 81(1-2):327.

Correale, L., Leone, M., Pagnani, A., Weight, M., and Zecchina, R (2006). Core percolation and onset of complexity in boolean networks. *Phys Rev Letters*, 96(1):018101/1 – 4.

Crutchfield, J.P. and Mitchell, M. (1995). The evolution of emergent computation. *Proceedings of the National Academy of Sciences of the United States of America*, 92(23):10742–10746.

Crutchfield, J.P. and Schuster, P. (2003). *Evolutionary Dynamics: Exploring the Interplay of Selection, Accident, Neutrality, and function*. Oxford University Press, New York.

Daida, Jason (2004). Considering the roles of structure in problem solving by a computer. In O'Reilly, Una-May, Yu, Tina, Riolo, Rick L., and Worzel, Bill, editors, *Genetic Programming Theory and Practice II*, chapter 5, pages 67–86. Springer, Ann Arbor.

Daida, Jason, Ward, David, Hilss, Adam, Long, Stephen, and Hodges, Mark (2004). Visualizing the loss of diversity in genetic programming. In *Proceedings of the 2004 IEEE Congress on Evolutionary Computation*, pages 1225–1232, Portland, Oregon. IEEE Press.

Daida, Jason M. (2003). What makes a problem GP-hard? A look at how structure affects content. In Riolo, Rick L. and Worzel, Bill, editors, *Genetic Programming Theory and Practice*, chapter 7, pages 99–118. Kluwer.

Daida, Jason M. (2005). Towards identifying populations that increase the likelihood of success in genetic programming. In Beyer, Hans-Georg, O'Reilly, Una-May, Arnold, Dirk V., Banzhaf, Wolfgang, Blum, Christian, Bonabeau, Eric W., Cantu-Paz, Erick, Dasgupta, Dipankar, Deb, Kalyanmoy, Foster, James A., de Jong, Edwin D., Lipson, Hod, Llora, Xavier, Mancoridis, Spiros, Pelikan, Martin, Raidl, Guenther R., Soule, Terence, Tyrrell, Andy M., Watson, Jean-Paul, and Zitzler, Eckart, editors, *GECCO 2005: Proceedings of the 2005 conference on Genetic and evolutionary computation*, volume 2, pages 1627–1634, Washington DC, USA. ACM Press.

Daida, Jason M., Bertram, Robert R., Polito 2, John A., and Stanhope, Stephen A. (1999a). Analysis of single-node (building) blocks in genetic programming. In Spector, Lee, Langdon, William B., O'Reilly, Una-May, and Angeline, Peter J., editors, *Advances in Genetic Programming 3*, chapter 10, pages 217–241. MIT Press, Cambridge, MA, USA.

Daida, Jason M. and Hilss, Adam M. (2003). Identifying structural mechanisms in standard genetic programming. In Cantú-Paz, E., Foster, J. A., Deb, K., Davis, D., Roy, R., O'Reilly, U.-M., Beyer, H.-G., Standish, R., Kendall, G., Wilson, S., Harman, M., Wegener, J., Dasgupta, D., Potter, M. A., Schultz, A. C., Dowsland, K., Jonoska, N., and Miller, J., editors, *Genetic and Evolutionary Computation – GECCO-2003*, volume 2724 of *LNCS*, pages 1639–1651, Chicago. Springer-Verlag.

Daida, Jason M., Hilss, Adam M., Ward, David J., and Long, Stephen L. (2003). Visualizing tree structures in genetic programming. In Cantú-Paz, E., Foster, J. A., Deb, K., Davis, D., Roy, R., O'Reilly, U.-M., Beyer, H.-G., Standish, R., Kendall, G., Wilson, S., Harman, M., Wegener, J., Dasgupta, D., Potter, M. A., Schultz, A. C., Dowsland, K., Jonoska, N., and Miller, J., editors, *Genetic and Evolutionary Computation – GECCO-2003*, volume 2724 of *LNCS*, pages 1652–1664, Chicago. Springer-Verlag.

Daida, Jason M., Polito, John A., Stanhope, Steven A., Bertram, Robert R., Khoo, Jonathan C., and Chaudhary, Shahbaz A. (1999b). What makes a problem GP-hard? analysis of a tunably difficult problem in genetic programming. In Banzhaf, Wolfgang, Daida, Jason, Eiben, Agoston E., Garzon, Max H., Honavar, Vasant, Jakiela, Mark, and Smith, Robert E., editors, *Proceedings of the Genetic and Evolutionary Computation Conference*, volume 2, pages 982–989, Orlando, Florida, USA. Morgan Kaufmann.

Daida, Jason M., Samples, Michael E., and Byom, Matthew J. (2005). Probing for limits to building block mixing with a tunably-difficult problem for genetic programming. In Beyer, Hans-Georg, O'Reilly, Una-May, Arnold, Dirk V., Banzhaf, Wolfgang, Blum, Christian, Bonabeau, Eric W., Cantu-Paz,

Erick, Dasgupta, Dipankar, Deb, Kalyanmoy, Foster, James A., de Jong, Edwin D., Lipson, Hod, Llora, Xavier, Mancoridis, Spiros, Pelikan, Martin, Raidl, Guenther R., Soule, Terence, Tyrrell, Andy M., Watson, Jean-Paul, and Zitzler, Eckart, editors, *GECCO 2005: Proceedings of the 2005 conference on Genetic and evolutionary computation*, volume 2, pages 1713–1720, Washington DC, USA. ACM Press.

Daida, J.M., Bertram, R.R., Stanhope, S.A., Khoo, J.C., Chaudhary, S.A., Chaudhri, O.A., and II, J.A. Polito (2001). What makes a problem gp-hard? analysis of a tunably difficult problem in genetic programming. *GPEM*, 2(2):165–191.

Erdos, P. and Rényi, A. (1960). On the evolution of random graphs. *Publications of the Mathematical Institute of the Hungarian Academy of Sciences*, 5:17–61.

Gao, Y. and Culberson, J. (2002). An analysis of phase transitions in nk landscapes. *JAIR*, 17:309–332.

Hartmann, A. and Weight, M. (2005). *Phase transitions in combinatory optimization problems*. Wiley-VCH, Berlin.

Hogg, T., Huberman, B.A., and Williams, C.P. (1996). Phase transitions and the search problem. *AI*, 81(1-2):1–15.

Huberman, B.A. and Hogg, T. (1987). Phase transitions and ai systems. *AI*, 33(2):155–177.

Huberman, B.A., Lukose, R.M., and Hogg, T. (1997). An economics approach to hard computational problems. *Science*, 275(5296):51–54.

Izumi, K. and Ueda, K. (2001). Phase transition in a foreign exchange market-analysis based on an artificial market approach. *IEE TEC*, 5(5):456.

Janson, S., Luczak, T., and Rucinski, A. (1999). *Random Graphs*. John Wiley, New York.

Koza, John R. (1992). *Genetic Programming: On the Programming of Computers by Means of Natural Selection*. MIT Press, Cambridge, MA, USA.

McPhee, Nicholas Freitag and Poli, Riccardo (2000). A schema theory analysis of the evolution of size in genetic programming with linear representations. Technical Report CSRP-00-22, University of Birmingham, School of Computer Science.

Mitchell, D., Selman, B., and Levesque, H. (1992). Hard and easy distributions of sat problems. In Rosenbloom, P. and Szolovits, P., editors, *Tenth National Conference on AI*, pages 459–465, Menlo Park. AAAI.

Mitchell, M., Hraber, P.T., and Crutchfield, J.P. (1993). Revisiting the edge of chaos: evolving cellular automata to perform computations. *Complex Systems*, 7(2):89–130.

Mohamed, H.M., Munzir, S., Abdulmuin, M.Z., and Hameida, S. (2000). Fuzzy modeling and control of a spark ignition engine idle mode. In *TENCON*, pages II–586–II–591, Kuala Lumpur. IEEE.

Naudts, B. and Schoofs, L. (2002). Ga performance distributions and randomly generated binary constraint satisfaction problems. *Theoretical COmputer Science*, 287(1):167–185.

Oates, M.J., Corne, D.W., and Loader, R.J. (2000). Tri-phase performance profile of evolutionary search on uni- and multi-modal search spaces. In *CEC*, pages 357–364, La Jolla. IEEE.

Oda, A., Nagao, H., Kitagawa, Y., Shigeta, Y., and Yamaguchi, K. (2000). Theoretical studies on magnetic behavior in clusters by the genetic algorithms. *International Journal of Quantum Chemistry*, 80(4-5):646–656.

Samples, M.E., Byom, M.J., and Daida, J.M. (2006). Parameter sweeps for exploring parameter spaces of evolutionary algorithms. In Lobo, F.G., Lima, C.F., and Michalewicz, Z., editors, *Parameter Settings in Evolutionary Algorithms*, New York. Springer.

Sellmyer, D.J. and Jaswal, S.S. (2002). *Phase transitions*. McGraw-Hill, New York.

Shimazaki, H. and Niebur, E. (2005). Phase transitions in multiplicative competitive processes. *Physical Review E*, 72(1):1–4.

Stanley, H.E. (1971). *Introduction to Phase Transitions and Critical Phenomena*. Oxford University Press, New York.

Toulouse, M., Crainic, T., and Sansó, B. (2004). Systemic behavior of cooperative search algorithms. *Parallel Computing*, 30(1):57–79.

van Hemert, J.I. and Urquhart, N.B. (2004). Phase transition properties of clustered traveling salesman problem instances generated with ec. In *PPSN*, pages 151–160, Birmingham. Springer-Verlag.

Yamamoto, K. and Naito, S. (2002). A study on schema preservation by crossover. *Systems and Computers in Japan*, 33(2):64–76.

Zhang, F. and Dozier, G. (2004). A comparison of distributed restricted recombination operators for gec societies of hill-climbers: a disacsp perspective. In *CEC*, pages 1988–1995, Portland. IEEE.

Chapter 16

EFFICIENT MARKOV CHAIN MODEL
OF MACHINE CODE PROGRAM EXECUTION
AND HALTING

Riccardo Poli[1] and William B. Langdon[1]

[1]*Department of Computer Science, University of Essex, UK.*

Abstract   We focus on the halting probability and the number of instructions executed by programs that halt for Turing-complete register based machines. The former represents the fraction of programs which provide useful results in a machine code genetic programming system. The latter determines run time and whether or not the distribution of program functionality has reached a fixed-point. We describe a Markov chain model of program execution and halting which accurately fits empirical data allowing us to efficiently estimate the halting probability and the numbers of instructions executed for programs including millions of instructions. We also discuss how this model can be applied to improve GP practice.

Keywords: Turing-complete GP, Machine code GP, Halting probability T7 computer, Markov chains

1.   Introduction

Recent work on strengthening the theoretical underpinnings of genetic programming (GP) has considered how GP searches its fitness landscape (Langdon and Poli, 2002; McPhee and Poli, 2002; Rosca, 2003; Sastry et al., 2003; Mitavskiy and Rowe, 2005; Daida et al., 2005). Results gained on the space of all possible programs are applicable to both GP and other search based automatic programming techniques. We have *proved* convergence results for the two most important forms of GP, i.e. trees (without side effects) and linear GP (Langdon and Poli, 2002; Langdon, 2002a; Langdon, 2002b; Langdon, 2003b; Langdon, 2003a). As remarked more than ten years ago (Teller, 1994), it is still true that few researchers allow their GP's to include iteration or recursion. Without looping and memory there are algorithms which cannot be represented and so GP stands no chance of evolving them. For these reasons, we are interested in extending the analysis of program search spaces to the case of Turing-complete languages.

In a recent paper (Langdon and Poli, 2006), we started extending our results to Turing complete linear GP machine code programs. We analysed the formation of the first loop in the programs and whether programs ever leave that loop. The investigation started by using simulations on a demonstration computer. In particular we studied how the frequency of different types of loops varies with program size. In addition, we performed a mathematical analysis of the halting process based on the fragmentation of the code into jump-free segments. Under the assumption that all code fragments had the same length we were then able to derive a scaling law indicating that the halting probability for programs of length L was of the order $1/\sqrt{L}$, while the expected number of instructions executed by halting programs was of the order $\sqrt{L}$. Experimental results confirmed theory and showed that, the fraction of programs that halt is vanishingly small. Finally, to further corroborate our results we developed a first Markov chain model of program execution and halting. Given its complexity and the limitations of space available, however, in (Langdon and Poli, 2006) we only provided a one-page summary of its structure and results. The results confirmed both the simulations and the "$\sqrt{L}$" scaling laws.

Since (Langdon and Poli, 2006), we further developed, validated and refined our Markov chain model, developing ways of iterating its transition matrix efficiently. In this paper we present the new model in detail and we discuss its implications for genetic programming research. As with (Langdon and Poli, 2006) we will corroborate our theoretical investigation using a particularly simple computer, the T7.

Section 2 describes the T7 computer. Sections 3 and 4 describe the states of our Markov chain model and the calculation required to compute the chain's transition probabilities. Section 5 shows how the model can be used to compute important quantities, such as the halting probability. Section 6 describes ways to speed up the iteration of the Markov chain for the purpose of evaluating halting probabilities and the expected number of instructions executed by halting programs. In Section 6 we also compare the model's predictions with empirical data. We discuss the implications of the model for GP practice and further possible improvements in Section 7. In particular, in Section 7, we explain how this research provides a characterisation of the search space explored by Turing-complete GP systems operating at the level of machine code. In addition, we indicate that our theoretical model allows us to predict the initial effective population size (i.e., the number of programs which are expected to terminate, and, therefore, to return results) and how this can be tuned in an informed way. Furthermore, we explain how the model can be used to identify and artificially abort non-terminating programs in GP runs. Finally, Section 8 summarises our findings.

2. The T7 computer

To test our results we used a simple Turing complete system, T7. This is based on the Kowalczy F-4 minimal instruction set computer, cf. (Langdon and Poli, 2005). Our CPU T7 has 7 instruction (Table 16-1) including: directly accessed bit addressable memory, a single arithmetic operator (ADD), an unconditional JUMP, a conditional Branch if oVerflow flag is Set (BVS) jump and four copy instructions. COPY_PC allows a programmer to save the current program address for use as the return address in subroutine calls, whilst the direct and indirect addressing modes allow access to stacks and arrays.

Table 16-1. Turing Complete Instruction Set. Every ADD operation either sets or clears the overflow bit v. LDi and STi treat one of their arguments as the address of the data. They allow array manipulation without the need for self modifying code. (LDi and STi data addresses are 8 bits). JUMP addresses are reduced modulo the program length.

Instruction	#operands	operation
ADD	3	$A + B \rightarrow C$
BVS	1	$\#addr \rightarrow pc$ if v=1
COPY	2	$A \rightarrow B$
LDi	2	$A \rightarrow B$
STi	2	$A \rightarrow B$
COPY_PC	1	$pc \rightarrow A$
JUMP	1	$addr \rightarrow pc$

Eight bit data words are used. The number of bits in address words is just big enough to be able to address every instruction in the program. E.g., if the program is 300 instructions, then BVS, JUMP and COPY_PC instructions use 9 bits. The experiments reported in (Langdon and Poli, 2006) used 12 bytes (96 bits) of memory.

The T7 instruction set has been designed to have as little bias as possible. In particular, given a random starting point a random sequence of ADD and copy instructions will create another random pattern in memory. The contents of the memory is essentially uniformly random. I.e. the overflow v bit is equally likely to be set as to be clear, and each address in memory is equally likely. So, until correlations are introduced (e.g., by re-executing instructions), we can treat JUMP instructions as being to random locations in the program. Similarly we can treat half BVS as jumping to a random address. The other half do nothing.

3.   Markov chain model: States

We model the process of executing instructions in a program as a Markov chain. The states of the chain represent how many instructions have been visited so far (i.e., how many different values the program counter register has taken) and whether or not the program has looped or halted. The state transition matrix represents the probability of moving from one state to another.

The process starts with the system being in state 0, which represents the situation where no instruction has been visited. From that state, we can only go to state 1, where one instruction has been visited. (Note that this instruction is not necessarily the first in the program. For example, in in (Langdon and Poli, 2006) we started execution at a random location within the program.) From this new state, however, the system can do three different things: 1) it can halt (this can happen if the current instruction is the last in the program), 2) it can perform a jump and revisit the single instruction we have just executed, or 3) it can proceed visiting a new instruction (thereby reaching state 2). Naturally, if the system halts there is no successor possible other than the halt state again. If instead the system reaches a new instruction, the process repeats: from there we can halt, revisit an old instruction or visit a new instruction.

Note that if the system revisits an instruction, this does not automatically imply that the system is trapped in a loop. However, determining the probability that a program will still be able to halt if it revisits instructions is very difficult, and, so, we will assume that all programs that revisit an instruction will not halt. For this reason, our model will provide an underestimate of the true halting probability. Note, however, that in the experiments reported in (Langdon and Poli, 2006) we found that the proportion of programs that really halt also follows a $1/\sqrt{L}$ law, the only difference w.r.t. the proportion of programs that never loop being a constant multiplicative factor. So, we expect the results of the model to be qualitatively applicable to the true halting probability.

In the following we will call "sink" the state where the system has revisited one or more instructions. If the system is in the sink state at one time step it will remain in the sink state in future time steps. This is similar to what happens in the halt state.

Note also that with our representation it is impossible to go from a state i to a state j where $j < i$ (we cannot "unvisit" visited instructions) or $j > i+1$ (we cannot visit more than one instruction per time step). This property will greatly simplify the calculations involved in iterating the Markov chain. So, every time step the state number must increment unless the system halts or revisits. Of course, however, there is a limit to how many times this can happen. Indeed, in programs of length L, even the luckiest sequence of events cannot result in more than L new instructions being visited. So, the states following state

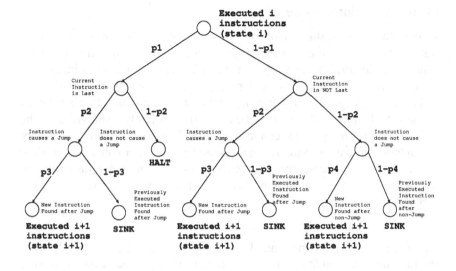

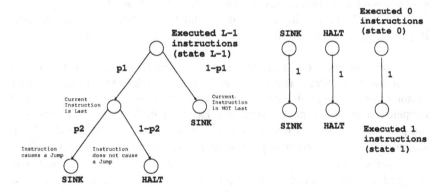

Figure 16-1. Event diagram used to construct our Markov chain model of the program execution and halting process.

$i = L - 1$ can really only result in revisiting or halting. We will discuss this in more detail in Section 4.0.

4. Markov chain model: transition probabilities

In order to determine the probability of moving from one state to visit a new instruction, halt or reach the sink, we need to make a number of assumptions, represented diagrammatically with the probability tree in Figure 16-1.

State transitions: general case

Probability of being the last instruction.   Assuming that we are in a generic state $0 < i < L$, where L is the program length, our first question when we consider the instruction currently being visited is whether or not that instruction is the last in the program. This is important because it is only by first visiting, and then going beyond the last instruction, that a program can halt. So, we want to estimate the probability, p_1 that the instruction currently being visited is the last. If we start program execution from a random position and the memory is randomly initialised and, so, any jumps land at (approximately) random locations, we can assume that the probability of being at the last instruction in a program is independent of how may (new) instructions have been executed so far. So, we set

$$p_1 = \frac{1}{L}.$$

If program execution was not started at a random position, but, for example, from the first instruction in the program, it would be easy to modify the expression above to reduce the probability of being the last instruction for small values of i (i.e., when the probability of having encountered a jump instruction is low). In particular, in this situation, it must be the case that $p_1 = 0$ for $i = 1$.

Probability of instruction causing a jump.   Irrespective of whether or not the current instruction is the last in the program, we then need to ask whether or not the instruction will cause a jump to be performed. Naturally, jumps will happen as a result of a jump instruction. However, certain types of conditional jump instructions may or may not cause a jump, depending on the state of flag registers (e.g., the overflow flag). For simplicity, we will assume that we have two types of jumps: 1) unconditional jumps, where the program counter is assigned a value retrieved from memory or from a register, and 2) conditional jumps. We will assume that unconditional jumps are present in the stream of instructions with probability p_{uj}, while conditional jumps are present with probability p_{cj}.[1] We further assume that the flag bit which causes a conditional jump instruction to perform a jump is set with probability p_f. Therefore, the total probability that the current instruction will cause a jump is

$$p_2 = p_{uj} + p_{cj} \times p_f.$$

For the CPU T7, we set $p_{uj} = \frac{1}{7}$, $p_{cj} = \frac{1}{7}$, and $p_f = \frac{1}{2}$, whereby $p_2 = \frac{3}{14}$.

Probability of next instruction not having been unvisited before.   In order to determine other state transitions we need to ask one additional question.

---

[1]Note: p_{uj} and p_{cj} do not typically add up to 1. This is because other (non-jump) instructions must be present is any useful program.

Whether or not this instruction will cause a jump, is the next instruction one that has not previously been visited? To calculate the probability of this event with the necessary accuracy, we need to distinguish between the case where we jump and the case where we simply increment the program counter. These are represented by the probabilities p_3 and p_4 in Figure 16-1.

Probability of new instruction after jump. Let us start from the case where instruction i is about to cause a jump, and let us estimate the probability of finding a new instruction, thereby reaching state $i+1$, after the jump. Because we assume that the program counter after a jump is effectively a random number between 1 and L, the probability of finding a new instruction is therefore the ratio between the number of instructions still not visited and the total number of instructions in the program. That is

$$p_3 = \frac{L - i}{L}.$$

This probability clearly decreases linearly with the number of instructions executed. This is one of the reasons why it is really difficult for a program to execute many instructions without looping. Naturally, if we don't find a new instruction we must be revisiting, and so we are in the sink state, that is, we assume that the program is a non-terminating one.

Probability of new instruction after non-jump. Let us now consider the case where instruction i is *not* going to cause a jump, and let us estimate the probability of finding a new instruction, thereby reaching state $i + 1$ after the increment in program counter. Here the situation is much more complex than the previous one. Let us first consider a simple case in which we have executed a certain number of instructions, i, but we have not found any jump instructions so far. Since there have been no jumps, the visited instructions form a contiguous block within the program. Clearly, if the current instruction is not going to cause a jump and we have not reached the end of the program, then we can be certain that the next instruction has not been previously visited, irrespectively of the number of instructions executed. Similarly, if we have executed one or more jumps, but the blocks of previously visited instructions precede the current instruction, then again with probability 1 we will find another new instruction. In general, however, the more jumps we have executed the more fragmented the map of visited instructions will look. In the presence of such fragmentation, we should expect the probability of finding a new instruction after a non-jump to decrease as a function of the number of jumps/fragments. Our estimate for p_4 is motivated by these considerations.

To construct this estimate we start by computing the expected number of fragments (jumps) in a program having reached state i (i.e., after the execution of i new instructions). This is given by

$$E[J] = i \times p_2 = i \times (p_{uj} + p_{cj} \times p_f)$$

In the case of T7 this gives us $E[J] = \frac{3i}{14}$.

$[E[J]]$ gives us an upper bound for the expected number of contiguous blocks of instructions that have previously been visited. Let us, for the moment, neglect the possibility that a block began at the first instruction of a program or that two blocks are contiguous. In these conditions, each block will be preceeded by at least one unvisited instruction. If the system has executed J jumps and i instructions so far, then there is a probability $\frac{J}{L-i-1}$ that the current instruction (the i-th) is one of the J unvisited instructions immediately preceeding a block of previously visited instructions. So the next instruction will be a previously visited one and the state of the system will be the sink. Naturally, we don't know J but, as we have see above, we can estimate and use $E[J]$ instead. So, we could estimate

$$p_4 \approx 1 - \frac{J}{L-i-1} = \frac{L - E[J] - i - 1}{L - i - 1}.$$

This gives us a reasonably good model of program behaviour. However, as the number of jumps grows the probability that blocks of previously visited instructions will be contiguous becomes important. In fact, beyond a certain i, we are virtually certain that some blocks of instructions will be contiguous. So, our estimate for p_4 is expected to become inaccurate as $E[J]$ grows. To improve it we have used the following combinatorial approximation for the *actual* number of blocks of contiguous instructions:

$$E[B] \approx \max\left(E[J] - \frac{E[J](1 + E[J])}{2(L - i)}, 0 \right)$$

$$= \max\left(i \cdot (p_{uj} + p_{cj} \cdot p_f) \left(1 - \frac{1 + i \cdot (p_{uj} + p_{cj} \cdot p_f)}{2(L - i)} \right), 0 \right)$$

where the max operation is to ensure the number of blocks never becomes negative. The quality of the approximation is very good, at least for T7, as shown in Figure 16-2, where we compared it with fragmentation statistics obtained by simulating the execution process. Thus, we can confidently take

$$p_4 = \frac{L - E[B] - i - 1}{L - i - 1}.$$

State transition probabilities

We can now calculate the total transition probabilities from state i to states "halt", $i + 1$ and "sink". These are simply the sums of the products of the probabilities on the paths connecting the root node to each leaf in Figure 16-1.

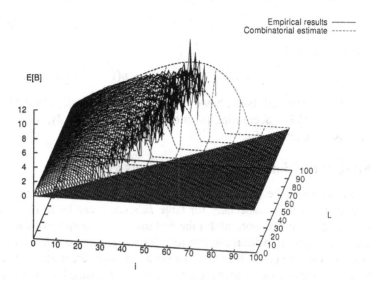

Empirical results ——————
Combinatorial estimate ------

Figure 16-2. Actual number of contiguous blocks of visited code as a function of the number of instructions executed, i, and program length, L, together with the predictions of our combinatorial model for T7. Empirical data were obtained by simulating the process of program execution 5,000 times for each program length L and instruction count i. All runs that did not terminate at exactly instruction i were discarded. For the remaining runs the blocks of code executed were analysed and statistics on executed-code fragmentation were collected. These were then used to estimate $E[B]$ for each pair of L and i. The noise affecting the data is due to the limited number of runs that met the necessary conditions when L is large and i is close to L.

The simplest case is the transition from i to the halt state, since in this case there is only one path from the root to the leaf "halt". If the current instruction is the last (probability p_1) and it did not cause a jump to occur (probability $1 - p_2$) then the program will halt (see Figure 16-1). That is, the probability of going from a generic state i to the halt state (in one step) is

$$p(i \rightarrow halt) = p_1(1 - p_2) = \frac{1 - p_{uj} + p_{cj} \cdot p_f}{L}.$$

For T7, $p(i \rightarrow halt) = \frac{11}{14L}$. Note that this probability does not depend on i, the number of instructions visited (executed) so far, but is inversely proportional to the program length.

In the case of the "sink" state there are three paths from the root to leafs labelled as "sink", leading to the following equation

$$p(i \rightarrow sink) = p_1 p_2 (1 - p_3) + (1 - p_1) p_2 (1 - p_3) + (1 - p_1)(1 - p_2)(1 - p_4).$$

There are three paths also in the case of state $i + 1$, which gives

$$p(i{\rightarrow}i + 1) = p_1p_2p_3 + (1 - p_1)p_2p_3 + (1 - p_1)(1 - p_2)p_4.$$

It is easy to verify that

$$p(i{\rightarrow}halt) + p(i{\rightarrow}i + 1) + p(i{\rightarrow}sink) = 1$$

for all i, as expected. Note, however, that while $p(i{\rightarrow}halt)$ is not a function of i, $p(i{\rightarrow}i + 1)$ is a decreasing function of i while, obviously, $p(i{\rightarrow}sink)$ is an increasing function of i.

State transitions: $L - 1$ instructions visited

To complete the picture we need to turn to the case where $i = L - 1$. This is a rare state, especially for large L, since it can be reached only if we execute $L - 1$ instructions all for the first time. So, any approximation errors in evaluating state transition probabilities for this state would have little impact. Nonetheless, we can still model this situation fairly precisely. Again, we use an event diagram (see bottom left of Figure 16-1). Like before, we start from the question of whether or not this is the last instruction in the program. If it is and does not cause a jump, then again we halt. This happens with probability

$$p(L - 1{\rightarrow}halt) = p_1(1 - p_2)$$

which is exactly the same as before.

If this is the last instruction but it causes a jump, the program will loop. This is because even assuming that the jump landed on the unique new instruction remaining, but that instruction was itself a jump and that such jump returned to the last instruction, that instruction would have been visited before. So, the state would be the sink. This is why in the event diagram at the bottom left of Figure 16-1 we label the leftmost leaf with "sink".

Similarly, if the current instruction is not the last in the program, then most likely the program will loop. However there are two ways in which the program could still terminate: 1) the current instruction is the penultimate, it does not cause a jump, the final instruction has not been visited before and it does not cause a jump, or 2) the current instruction is not the penultimate, it causes a jump, the jump lands on the last instruction, the final instruction has not been visited before and it does not cause a jump. Both chains of events are so unlikely that we can safely label the rightmost branch of the event diagram at the bottom left of Figure 16-1 as "sink" as well. To summarise

$$p(L - 1{\rightarrow}sink) = p_1p_2 + (1 - p_1).$$

As we mentioned above, all other state transitions are impossible and so they have an associated probability of 0.

Transition matrix

We can now write down the state transition matrix. In doing so, we will represent the sink as state L and the halt state as state $L + 1$, while states 0 through to $L - 1$ represent the number of instructions executed so far, as already mentioned above.

For example, for T7 and $L = 7$ we obtain

$$M = \begin{pmatrix}
0 & 0 & 0 & 0 & 0 & 0 & 0 & 0 & 0 \\
1 & 0 & 0 & 0 & 0 & 0 & 0 & 0 & 0 \\
0 & 0.8312 & 0 & 0 & 0 & 0 & 0 & 0 & 0 \\
0 & 0 & 0.7647 & 0 & 0 & 0 & 0 & 0 & 0 \\
0 & 0 & 0 & 0.6812 & 0 & 0 & 0 & 0 & 0 \\
0 & 0 & 0 & 0 & 0.566 & 0 & 0 & 0 & 0 \\
0 & 0 & 0 & 0 & 0 & 0.3868 & 0 & 0 & 0 \\
0 & 0.05655 & 0.1231 & 0.2065 & 0.3217 & 0.501 & 0.8878 & 1 & 0 \\
0 & 0.1122 & 0.1122 & 0.1122 & 0.1122 & 0.1122 & 0.1122 & 0 & 1
\end{pmatrix}.$$

5. Halting probability

With the M matrix in hand, we can compute the probability of more complex events, such as the probability of reaching the sink state after a certain number of instructions or the total halting probability. To do this, it is sufficient to compute the appropriate power of M and multiply this by the unit vector $x = (1, 0, 0, \cdots, 0)^T$, which represents the normal initial condition for the system where no instructions have been marked as visited before program execution begins. Doing so provides the vector

$$p_{states} = M^i x$$

which represents the probability distribution over states after i instructions have been executed. For example, using the M matrix shown above, for $i = 3$ we obtain

$$p_{states} = \begin{pmatrix}
0 \\
0 \\
0 \\
0.6356 \\
0 \\
0 \\
0 \\
0.1589 \\
0.2055
\end{pmatrix}.$$

The last element of p_{states} represents the probability of halting by instruction i, which is 20.55% in the example. The penultimate element of p_{states} represents the probability of having revisited at least one instruction (sink). Clearly, the only other non-zero element in p_{states} can be the one representing state i.

In order to compute the total halting probability for random programs of length L one needs to set $i = L$. In our example, that produces

$$p_{states} = \begin{pmatrix} 0 \\ 0 \\ 0 \\ 0 \\ 0 \\ 0 \\ 0 \\ 0.6364 \\ 0.3636 \end{pmatrix},$$

indicating that the halting probability for programs of length $L = 7$ is approximately 36.36%. Note that, given the particular lower triangular structure of M, $M^i \equiv M^L$ for $i > L$.

This technique is simple and gives us a full picture of how the probability over states changes. However, as L increases, the size of the the Markov transition matrix increases and the values of i of interest increase too. So, for example, if we are interested in the halting probability we have a potentially exponentially explosive computation to perform (M^L).

In Section 6 we look at the structure of the problem in more detail and reorder the computations in such a way to make it possible to compute halting probabilities for very large programs. This will allows us to easily compute other quantities, such as the expected number of instructions executed by halting programs or the expected number of instructions executed by a looping program before it revisits a previously executed instruction.

6.   Efficient formulations of the model

As we have already mentioned, it is impossible for the system to go from a higher state to a lower state (we cannot "unvisit" visited instructions) or from a state to a higher state more than one instruction away. This property is reflected in the structure of the transition matrix M and can be exploited to speed up calculations.

In Figure 16-1 we presented our event decomposition for the program execution process. If, as we want to do here, we focus only on the possible outcomes of the process – loop, halt or move to next state – then we could condense the generic event diagram into a simple tree including just a root node with three children (labelled as sink, halt and $i + 1$) and the penultimate-instruction event diagram as an even simpler tree including just a root node and two children (labelled as sink and halt). The edges of these trees would be weighted with the

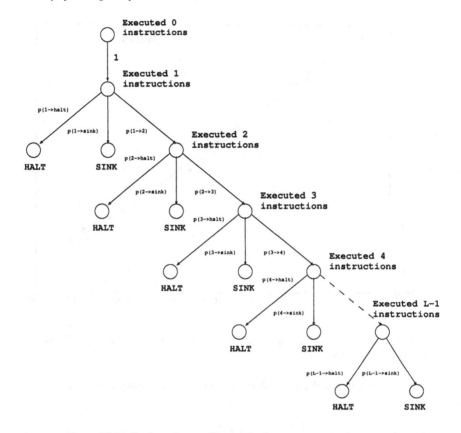

Figure 16-3. Condensed event diagram for the program execution process.

transition probabilities $p(i{\rightarrow}i+1)$, $p(i{\rightarrow}halt)$, $p(i{\rightarrow}sink)$, $p(L-1{\rightarrow}halt)$ and $p(L-1{\rightarrow}sink)$, which we previously calculated. We could then assemble the events for each execution stage into the tree shown in Figure 16-3.

The structure of the tree makes it clear that the system can halt or loop after the first instruction, or it can be faced with the same opportunity after two instructions, three instructions and so on. That is

$$p(\text{halt}) = \sum_{i=1}^{L-1} p(0{\rightarrow}i)p(i{\rightarrow}halt)$$

and

$$p(\text{sink}) = \sum_{i=1}^{L-1} p(0{\rightarrow}i)p(i{\rightarrow}sink).$$

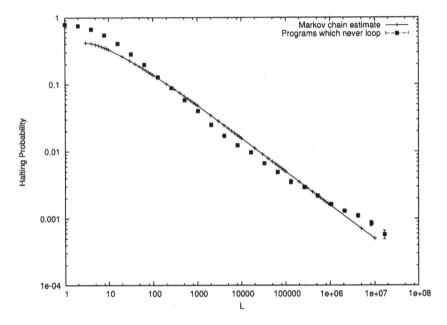

Figure 16-4. Estimate of the halting probability computed using our Markov chain model vs. real execution data for T7.

Given the structure of the event diagram, however, it is easy to see that

$$p(0 \rightarrow i) = \prod_{j=0}^{i-1} p(j \rightarrow j+1),$$

and so, for example,

$$p(\text{halt}) = \sum_{i=1}^{L-1} p(i \rightarrow halt) \prod_{j=0}^{i-1} p(j \rightarrow j+1).$$

The computation required with this decomposition is much less than that required for the calculation of the powers of M. Indeed, as shown in Figure 16-4 we were easily able to compute halting probabilities for programs of 10,000,000 instructions. (This was achieved in a few minutes with a naive C implementation on a single PC.)

With this decomposition of the halting probability we can also easily compute the expected number of instructions executed by halting programs:

$$E[\text{instructions}] = \sum_{i=1}^{L-1} i \cdot p(i \rightarrow halt) \prod_{j=0}^{i-1} p(j \rightarrow j+1).$$

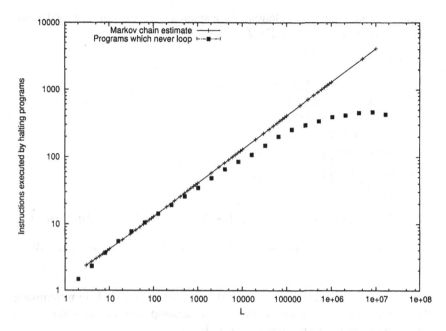

Figure 16-5. Estimate of the expected number of instructions executed by halting programs computed using our Markov chain model vs. real execution data for T7. See also Figure 16-7.

This is plotted for programs of up to $10,000,000$ instructions in Figure 16-5.

For T7 the model predicts very accurately the halting probability for random programs over around 5 orders of magnitude of program lengths (from about 10 instructions to about 1,000,000 instructions). The model also predicts accurately the average number of instructions performed by halting programs over at least 4 orders of magnitude. These results are remarkable considering the complexity program execution in a real machine code.[2]

---

[2]The calculation of the expected number of instructions is a sum of products between the number of executed instructions before halting and the corresponding halting probability. So, approximation errors in the estimation of the halting probability, albeit small, propagate and reduce the accuracy of the calculation.

Let us expand these calculations for a small L to show how the model can be run even more efficiently. For $L = 4$, we have

$p(\text{halt})$

$$
\begin{aligned}
&= \sum_{i=1}^{3} p(i \to halt) \prod_{j=0}^{i-1} p(j \to j+1) \\
&= p(1 \to halt)p(0 \to 1) \\
&+ p(2 \to halt)p(0 \to 1)p(1 \to 2) \\
&+ p(3 \to halt)p(0 \to 1)p(1 \to 2)p(2 \to 3) \\
&= p(0 \to 1) \\
&\times \Big(p(1 \to halt) + p(2 \to halt)p(1 \to 2) + p(3 \to halt)p(1 \to 2)p(2 \to 3) \Big) \\
&= p(0 \to 1) \Big(p(1 \to halt) + p(1 \to 2)\big(p(2 \to halt) + p(3 \to halt)p(2 \to 3)\big)\Big)
\end{aligned}
$$

This illustrates the recursive nature of the calculation and leads to minimising the number of multiplications required. The decomposition applies in general. So, algorithmically we can compute $p(\text{halt})$ as

$$
p(\text{halt}) = p^0(\text{halt})
$$

where, for a particular L, $p^k(\text{halt})$ is given by the following recursion:

$$
p^k(\text{halt}) = p(k \to \text{halt}) + p^{k+1}(\text{halt})p(k \to k+1)
$$

which is terminated with

$$
p^{L-1}(\text{halt}) = p(L-1 \to \text{halt}).
$$

Note $p(0 \to \text{halt}) = 0$.

Another, equivalent, alternative is to perform the computation iteratively. To do that we go back to the formulation

$$
p(\text{halt}) = \sum_{i=1}^{L-1} p(0 \to i)p(i \to halt)
$$

but note that we can compute the quantities $p(0 \to i)$ efficiently by exploiting the relation

$$
p(0 \to i) = p(0 \to i-1)p(i-1 \to i).
$$

Following exactly the same principles we can compute $E[\text{instructions}]$ either recursively or iteratively in a very efficient way.

7.   Discussion

Implications for Genetic Programming Research

One might wonder what is the relevance of the previous model and its results to GP research. Firstly, these results contribute to characterising the search space explored by GP systems operating at the level of machine code. From earlier research we know that for those programs that terminate, as the number of instructions executed grows, their functionality approaches a limiting distribution. In this respect, actual program length is an insufficient indicator of how close the distribution is to the limit. It is only by computing the expected number of instructions actually executed by halting programs that we can assess this. For T7, for example, one can see that very long programs have a tiny subset of their instructions executed (e.g., of the order of 1,000 instructions in programs of $L = 1,000,000$). We can, therefore, think of $E[\text{instructions}]$ as the *effective size* of programs of a particular length.

The introduction of Turing completeness into GP raises the problem of how to assign fitness to a program which may loop indefinitely (Maxwell III, 1994). Often, from a GP point of view, those programs that do not terminate are wasted fitness evaluations and they are given zero fitness. So, if the halting probability is very low, the fraction of the population that is really contributing to the search can be very small, thereby reducing GP ability to solve problems. Our theoretical model allows us to predict the effective population size for the initial generation. I.e. the number of non-zero fitness individuals within it. Since the initial population is composed of random programs only a fraction $p(\text{halt})$ are expected to halt and so have fitness greater than zero. We can use this to improve the size of the population or to put in place measures which ensure that a larger fraction of the programs in the population do terminate. This is particularly important because if not enough programs in the initial generation terminate, evolution may not even start.

A simple way to control how many programs terminate in the initial generation is to modify the probability of using instructions that may cause a jump. For example, instead of using unconditional and conditional jumps in their natural proportions of $\frac{1}{7}$ in T7, one might choose to reduce these to a much smaller fraction (correspondingly increasing the probability of using non-jump instructions). But what fraction should one use? For any specific assembly language and program length we can answer this question by just looking at the plot of $p(\text{halt})$ as a function of p_{uj} and p_{cj}. For example, in Figure 16-6 we plot $p(\text{halt})$ of T7 programs for $L = 10$, $L = 100$, $L = 1,000$ and $L = 10,000$ and for values of $p_{uj} = p_{cj} \in [\frac{0.01}{7}, \frac{1}{7}]$. If then one wanted to be certain that, on average, at least, say, 10% of the programs in the population terminate, one could avoid initialising the population with programs that are too long (e.g., for the standard $p_{uj} = p_{cj} = \frac{1}{7}$, any $L \leq 100$ guarantees that). If it is not

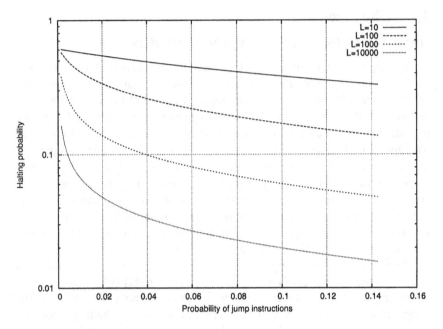

Figure 16-6. Halting probability for different values of the jump instruction probabilities $p_{uj} = p_{cj}$ and program length.

appropriate or possible to freely choose the value for L, one could alternatively decrease p_{uj}, p_{cj} or both appropriately. For example, for T7 programs of length $L = 1,000$, we could guarantee that 10% of programs in the initial generation terminate by setting $p_{uj} = p_{cj} < 0.04$.

An alternative approach would be to just keep generating and running random programs until we reach the desired number of random, halting programs. Naturally, this would be totally impractical if the halting probability is very low. It would also require setting some threshold beyond which we declare a program as non-terminating. However, these problems could be solved using our model. That is we could use our estimate for $p(\text{halt})$ to determine whether the method is practical, and, when it isn't, we could switch to altering jump probabilities as explained above. In addition, we could use the method described below to determine what threshold to use.

The model can also be used to decide after how many instructions to abort the evaluation of a program with confidence that the program would never terminate. In particular, we could fix the threshold to be some (small) multiple m of the expected number of instructions executed by terminating programs, $E[\text{instructions}]$. With this measure in place, we would then be in a position to evaluate the expected run time of a genetic programming system, at least for the first few generations of a run. As we mentioned above, the initial population is composed of random programs and so, on average, only a fraction $p(\text{halt})$ will halt. So, the expected program runtime would just be

$$
\begin{aligned}
E[\text{runtime}] &= mE[\text{instructions}](1 - p(\text{halt})) + E[\text{instructions}]p(\text{halt}) \\
&= (m(1 - p(\text{halt})) + p(\text{halt})) \cdot E[\text{instructions}].
\end{aligned}
$$

Naturally, formally, this calculation would be applicable only at the initial generation. However, we should expect the estimate to remain reasonable for at least some generations after the first.

Improving the Model's Accuracy

As we have shown in the previous section, for the T7 the model predicts accurately the halting probability and the average number of instructions performed by halting programs over many orders of magnitude. There are, however, unavoidable approximations and inaccuracies of the model. We discussed some of these when we presented our event decomposition in the previous sections.

One important assumption is that the memory is random and, so, jump landing-addresses are uniformly distributed over the length of a program. This assumption becomes progressively less and less applicable as the number of instructions executed grows. In programs of large size several hundred instructions are executed. Some of these write to memory. As a result, the memory available in the machine will eventually become correlated. This means that when a jump is executed some addresses are more likely than others. As a result, the probability of finding a new instruction after a jump decreases faster than what is predicted by our estimate $p_3 = \frac{L-i}{L}$. This is the main reason for the saturation shown in Figure 16-5 by the empirical data for T7, starting in the region $L = 1,000,000$.

Naturally, one could construct a more refined model for p_3. Nothing in our calculations in relation to the Markov chain would be affected by this change except, of course, the numerical results. For example, the approximation

$$
p_3 = \frac{(L - i)}{L} \cdot \frac{2}{1 + \exp\left(\frac{i}{40,000}\right)}
$$

where the number of new instructions after a jump, $L - i$, is modulated by a squashing function, produces the saturation effect mentioned above (Figure 16-7).

Also, one could consider better models of the probability p_f that the flag be set. For example, p_f might not be not constant, but it might increase with i. This effect might cause an increase of the effective jumping probability, thereby leading to fewer programs halting and fewer instructions being executed in those

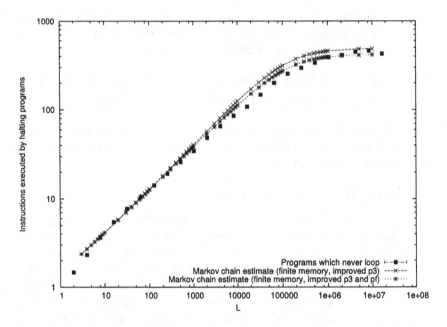

Figure 16-7. Estimate of the expected number of instructions executed by halting programs computed using two variants of our Markov chain model where memory correlation is considered.

that do halt. Again, we could model this effect by applying an appropriate squashing function to our $p_f = \frac{1}{2}$ original model. For example,

$$p_f = \frac{1}{1 + \exp\left(-\frac{i}{100}\right)}$$

in conjunction with our improved estimate for p_3 produces the reduction in the slope of the plot in Figure 16-7 leading to an even better fit with the empirical data. Similarly, one could improve the accuracy of the model for small L.

Note that the values 100 and 40,000 used in the two squashing functions above have been empirically determined. While the relative order of magnitude of the two makes entirely sense, at this stage we have no empirical evidence to justify these values, nor, indeed, our particular choice of squashing functions. We have used these values and functions simply to illustrate the ample possibilities for improvement that our Markov chain model offers.

8. Conclusions

We provide a detailed Markov chain model for the execution process and halting for programs written in Turing-complete assembly-like languages. Unusually, this model scales well with the size of structures under investigation (programs). So, we are able to accurately estimate the halting probability and the number of instructions executed by programs that halt for programs including millions of instructions in just a few minutes. We tested this model for T7, but the model is general and can be applied to other machines.

Although these results are of a theoretical nature and aim at understanding the structure of the search space of computer programs, we feel this is a fundamental step for understanding and predicting the behaviour of systems that explore such a search space, such as a genetic programming system. Indeed, we were able to show that there are very clear implications of this research from the point of view of GP practice. For example, Section 7 provides recipes to ensure that enough programs in GP system actually terminate, recipes for halting non-terminating programs and recipes for assessing the run-time requirements of GP runs with Turing-complete assembly languages.

References

Daida, Jason M., Hilss, Adam M., Ward, David J., and Long, Stephen L. (2005). Visualizing tree structures in genetic programming. *Genetic Programming and Evolvable Machines*, 6(1):79–110.

Langdon, W. B. (2002a). Convergence rates for the distribution of program outputs. In Langdon, W. B., Cantú-Paz, E., Mathias, K., Roy, R., Davis, D., Poli, R., Balakrishnan, K., Honavar, V., Rudolph, G., Wegener, J., Bull, L., Potter, M. A., Schultz, A. C., Miller, J. F., Burke, E., and Jonoska, N., editors, *GECCO 2002: Proceedings of the Genetic and Evolutionary Computation Conference*, pages 812–819, New York. Morgan Kaufmann Publishers.

Langdon, W. B. (2002b). How many good programs are there? How long are they? In De Jong, Kenneth A., Poli, Riccardo, and Rowe, Jonathan E., editors, *Foundations of Genetic Algorithms VII*, pages 183–202, Torremolinos, Spain. Morgan Kaufmann. Published 2003.

Langdon, W. B. (2003a). Convergence of program fitness landscapes. In Cantú-Paz, E., Foster, J. A., Deb, K., Davis, D., Roy, R., O'Reilly, U.-M., Beyer, H.-G., Standish, R., Kendall, G., Wilson, S., Harman, M., Wegener, J., Dasgupta, D., Potter, M. A., Schultz, A. C., Dowsland, K., Jonoska, N., and Miller, J., editors, *Genetic and Evolutionary Computation – GECCO-2003*, volume 2724 of *LNCS*, pages 1702–1714, Chicago. Springer-Verlag.

Langdon, W. B. (2003b). The distribution of reversible functions is Normal. In Riolo, Rick L. and Worzel, Bill, editors, *Genetic Programming Theory and Practise*, chapter 11, pages 173–188. Kluwer.

Langdon, W. B. and Poli, R. (2005). On Turing complete T7 and MISC F-4 program fitness landscapes. Technical Report CSM-445, Computer Science, University of Essex, UK.

Langdon, W. B. and Poli, R. (2006). The halting probability in von Neumann architectures. In Collet, Pierre, Tomassini, Marco, Ebner, Marc, Gustafson, Steven, and Ekárt, Anikó, editors, *Proceedings of the 9th European Conference on Genetic Programming*, volume 3905 of *Lecture Notes in Computer Science*, pages 225–237, Budapest, Hungary. Springer.

Langdon, W. B. and Poli, Riccardo (2002). *Foundations of Genetic Programming*. Springer-Verlag.

Maxwell III, Sidney R. (1994). Experiments with a coroutine model for genetic programming. In *Proceedings of the 1994 IEEE World Congress on Computational Intelligence*, volume 1, pages 413–417a, Orlando, Florida, USA. IEEE Press.

McPhee, Nicholas Freitag and Poli, Riccardo (2002). Using schema theory to explore interactions of multiple operators. In Langdon, W. B., Cantú-Paz, E., Mathias, K., Roy, R., Davis, D., Poli, R., Balakrishnan, K., Honavar, V., Rudolph, G., Wegener, J., Bull, L., Potter, M. A., Schultz, A. C., Miller, J. F., Burke, E., and Jonoska, N., editors, *GECCO 2002: Proceedings of the Genetic and Evolutionary Computation Conference*, pages 853–860, New York. Morgan Kaufmann Publishers.

Mitavskiy, Boris and Rowe, Jonathan E. (2005). A schema-based version of Geiringer's theorem for nonlinear genetic programming with homologous crossover. In Wright, Alden H., Vose, Michael D., De Jong, Kenneth A., and Schmitt, Lothar M., editors, *Foundations of Genetic Algorithms 8*, volume 3469 of *Lecture Notes in Computer Science*, pages 156–175. Springer-Verlag, Berlin Heidelberg.

Rosca, Justinian (2003). A probabilistic model of size drift. In Riolo, Rick L. and Worzel, Bill, editors, *Genetic Programming Theory and Practice*, chapter 8, pages 119–136. Kluwer.

Sastry, Kumara, O'Reilly, Una-May, Goldberg, David E., and Hill, David (2003). Building block supply in genetic programming. In Riolo, Rick L. and Worzel, Bill, editors, *Genetic Programming Theory and Practice*, chapter 9, pages 137–154. Kluwer.

Teller, Astro (1994). Turing completeness in the language of genetic programming with indexed memory. In *Proceedings of the 1994 IEEE World Congress on Computational Intelligence*, volume 1, pages 136–141, Orlando, Florida, USA. IEEE Press.

Chapter 17

A RE-EXAMINATION OF A REAL WORLD BLOOD FLOW MODELING PROBLEM USING CONTEXT-AWARE CROSSOVER

Hammad Majeed[1] and Conor Ryan[1]

[1]*Department of Computer Science and Information Systems, University of Limerick, Ireland.*

Abstract   This chapter describes *context-aware* crossover. This is an improved crossover technique for GP which always swaps subtrees into their best possible context in a parent. We show that this style of crossover is considerably more constructive than the standard method, and present several experiments to demonstrate how it operates, and how well it performs, before applying the technique to a real world application, the Blood Flow Modeling Problem.

1.   Introduction

The standard crossover in GP, subtree exchange (or one point crossover) is generally considered to be one of the main explorative operators in the system, but much research (Ito et al., 1998b; Yuen, 2004; Ito et al., 1998a; Poli and Langdon, 1998a) has shown that it can act in a mostly destructive way, which in turn leads to code bloat as evolution strives to protect useful subtrees.

The placement of a subtree in a good context in the generated children is an important factor for the success of a crossover operation (Majeed and Ryan, 2006b; Majeed and Ryan, 2006a). However, one point crossover has an inherent property of ignoring the context of a subtree-to-be-exchanged which makes it destructive. To combat this issue, Majeed and Ryan(Majeed and Ryan, 2006b) introduced a new *context-aware* crossover operator and demonstrated its performance on different benchmark problems.

On the tested problems, it was reported not only to perform better than standard GP crossover but do so inexpensively, with the generation of relatively small individuals. It works by placing a subtree-to-be-exchanged in the best possible context in the generated children. The search for the best context of a subtree is an expensive operation, but, as was shown in (Majeed and Ryan,

2006b; Majeed and Ryan, 2006a), the resulting improvement in GP generally results in far fewer total evaluations.

This chapter describes context-aware crossover, and some experiments that shed light into how it operates. It then goes on to apply it to a real world blood flow modeling problem. The chapter is organised as follows. The following section discusses the preceding crossover techniques and their shortfalls. Section 3 discusses context-aware crossover in detail and ways to improve its performance and reduce its expensiveness. Its performance on different benchmark problems is also briefly discussed. This is followed by an introduction to the the blood flow modeling problem, experimental setup and our findings. Section 5 concludes the chapter by presenting our future plans.

2.   Background

One point crossover is the simplest and most commonly used recombination operator in standard GP. Its reliance on random selection and placement is widely accepted as the factor limiting its performance (Ito et al., 1998b; Yuen, 2004; Ito et al., 1998a; Poli and Langdon, 1998a). This realization shifted the focus of the research in GP's standard crossover operator to define *less destructive* crossover operators, and resulted in the introduction of different crossover operators. Various approaches were adopted by researchers, the most commonly used of which was the *preservation of the context* of a subtree, which works by preserving the context of a selected subtree in the produced children. Different researchers define the context of a subtree differently. Some believe in the strict preservation of all the parent nodes of a subtree in the produced children while, others are satisfied with only the preservation of the immediate parent node of the selected subtree.

D'haeseleer used the former approach while defining *strong context preserving crossover* (SCPC) and *weak context preserving crossover* (WCPC) (D'haeseleer, 1994). He proposed a node co-ordinate system to identify the context of a subtree within a tree. It uniquely identifies the context of the subtree of a tree by traversing and recording all the nodes from the root node of the tree to the subtree node. In SCPC, he only allowed crossover between the subtrees with the exactly same node coordinates. This is a very strict and restrictive approach as the depth of the swapped subtree cannot change between the parent and the newly generated child. In WCPC, this problem was addressed by relaxing the restrictions. In this, two subtrees T1 and T2 with the same node coordinates are selected for crossover, and then for T1, T2 or any subset of T2 is a valid crossover point.

Some researchers focused on the importance of selection of the good crossover points, and defined different techniques to identify them. Hengraprohm and Chongstitvatna (Hengproprohm and Chongstitvatana, 2001) introduced *selective crossover* for GP which identifies a good subtree by measuring its impact on the fitness of the container tree by removing it and replacing it with a randomly selected terminal from the terminal set. This way they were able to preserve the best subtrees in an individual. Ito *et. al* (Ito et al., 1998b), proposed the selection of shallower subtrees in an effort to preserve building blocks, as well as only allowing individuals better than their parents in the next generation.

Tackett (Tackett, 1994) introduced a *brood recombination* operator. This works by generating n children from the selected parents by using standard crossover and then introducing the best two to the next generation.

Poli and Langdon (Poli and Langdon, 1998b) inspired by the uniform crossover for GA, introduced a *uniform crossover* for GP and found it a more global search operator than one point crossover. To minimize the destructive effect of the crossover, they aligned the root nodes of the selected parent trees and then swapped the corresponding nodes of the trees. This preserves the structure of the trees to the maximum extent.

Chi Chung refined this idea by using *gene dominance* in his *Selective crossover using gene dominance* (Yuen, 2004). Gene dominance is a numerical value attached to each node of a tree and is updated throughout a run. The magnitude of the change in its value is directly proportional to its impact on the fitness of the generated children. Furthermore, he calculated the dominance of a subtree by adding the gene dominance of each node of the subtree and then dividing the result by the number of nodes in the subtree. He used this idea to detect subtrees which have a good impact on the population during crossover and called them *dominant subtrees*.

This crossover works by first selecting the dominant subtrees of the selected parents and then swapping them. The impact of the swapped subtrees on the fitness of the generated children is calculated by subtracting the fitness of the parents and the generated children. Finally the impact on the fitness is used to updated the gene dominance of the swapped nodes. Effectively, this crossover preserves the dominant subtrees by keeping them with the individuals with higher fitness.

Most of these methods work by preserving the context of the selected subtree in the generated children. However, we believe that preserving the context of the selected subtree is not the best approach to improve the performance of a crossover as better context of the selected subtree can exist in the children. To ensure the use of the selected subtree in the best possible context in the children, a new crossover operator, named context-aware crossover, is devised and presented in this chapter.

3.   Context-aware crossover for GP

Keeping in mind the issues of standard crossover operators, a new approach named *context-aware crossover* was introduced by Majeed and Ryan (Majeed and Ryan, 2006a). It works by placing the randomly selected subtree from one parent in the best possible context in the second parent. The best possible context is found by placing the randomly selected subtree into every possible position in the second parent and evaluating each resulting child and finally selecting the best child from the pool of the children.

Although, this may sound expensive, it was observed that the resulting increase in performance permits the use of dramatically smaller populations, so that the total number of individuals evaluated decreased. Furthermore, this crossover has a tendency to remove the unused nodes from the individuals hence generating much smaller individuals.

Figure 17-1 shows the operation of this crossover. To make the figure more readable we have set tree-depth to five for this example. Two parents are selected for crossover as normal[1], and crossover cannot take place at the root node.

In this example, node 2 of parent 2 is selected *randomly* as a crossover point (the subtree is shown shaded in parent 2). Next, all possible valid offspring are generated, that is, all those individuals that are within depth limits, etc. Each of these individuals is then evaluated, and the best one introduced to the next generation. Only *one* individual per crossover is entered into the following generation.

The selection of the crossover points is followed by generation of a pool of offspring and their evaluation. The best individual among them is introduced into the next generation.

In the initial implementation of the crossover, the probability of using standard crossover and context-aware crossover was varied as follows:

$$standard\_xover\_prob = 1 - (curr\_gen/max\_gen) \qquad (17.1)$$

$$context\_aware\_prob = 1 - standard\_xover\_prob \qquad (17.2)$$

The motivation behind the selection of these equations was the work of Banzhaf (Banzhaf et al., 1998), who showed that in standard implementation of GP, standard crossover operator is most effective in the early part of the runs. In the initial paper, no attention was given to optimise these varying rates, rather focus was on the introduction of a less destructive crossover operator than standard crossover.

In this chapter we will improve the implementation of context-aware crossover by discussing different techniques. We will examine performance

---

[1]The operator works independently of the selection scheme.

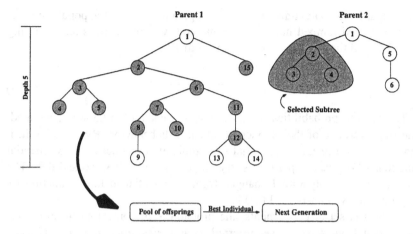

Figure 17-1. Context-aware crossover. The shaded nodes in parent-1 are possible crossover points where selected-subtree from parent-2 can go in. All generated children are evaluated and the best selected.

in terms of fitness attained, the total number of individuals evaluated, and the size of these individuals.

Optimising GP's Performance

To test the efficacy of the parameter settings used in (Majeed and Ryan, 2006a), a few tests were conducted. In the first set of tests, the probabilities of standard and context-aware crossovers were varied over time and the effect on the performance was noted. The tests suggested that the order of application of these crossover operators might have significant effect on the outcome of runs. To further explore this, another set of tests was conducted by changing the order of application of the crossovers. We hypothesize that standard GP crossover acts destructively when used with context-aware crossover.

For the tests, we selected the same set of experiments used in the introductory paper of context-aware crossover (Majeed and Ryan, 2006a).

Varying order and rates of crossovers

In the first test, the probabilities of standard and context-aware crossovers were varied over time in an effort to find an optimized setting for the probabilities of the crossovers. A number of different problems were used for the experiment, but only the standard Koza's quartic symbolic regression problem will be discussed here for the sake of brevity.

For these experiments, a population size of 200 was allowed to evolve for 50 generations. No mutation was used, and the only variation operators were the standard and context-aware crossover operators. The initial population was generated used ramped half and half method with initial trees sizes varying from 2-6, and the maximum tree depth set to 17.

$$exp^{\frac{curr\_gen^{slope}}{curr\_gen-max\_gen}} \qquad (17.3)$$

To vary the probabilities of the crossovers equation 17.3 was generated. The *slope* variable of the exponential dictates its behavior. By adjusting it, it can behave as a linear, exponential or combination of linear and exponential functions. For these experiments, the slope was set to 0.3, 0.6 and 0.9. The behavior of the polynomial changes from exponential to linear function by varying slope value from 0.3 to 0.9.

In the first set of experiments, the probability of context-aware crossover was varied from zero to one, referred to as *conext_aware_prob*, while the probability of standard crossover varied from one to zero using equation $1 - context\_aware\_prob$. In the second set of experiments, the probability

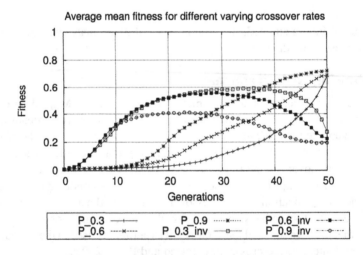

Figure 17-2. Mean average fitness of the quartic polynomial symbolic regression problem with varying crossover rates of context-aware and standard crossover operators. $P\_0.3$, $P\_0.6$ and $P\_0.9$ are obtained by setting slope variable to 0.3, 0.6 and 0.9 respectively in equation 17.3. $P\_0.3\_inv$, $P\_0.6\_inv$ and $P\_0.9\_inv$ are the inverse of each of these.

of standard crossover varied from one to zero, referred to as *standard_prob*, using equation 17.3 and the probability of context-aware crossover varied using equation $1 - standard\_prob$.

Apart from varying the crossover rates, these experiments show the importance of the order of application of the crossovers. In the first setup, context-aware crossover was applied before standard crossover, while in the second setup it is applied after standard crossover.

Results are averaged over 50 runs and plotted in Figure 17-2. Clearly, the activation of context-aware crossover ($P\_0.3$, $P\_0.6$ and $P\_0.9$)has a significant positive effect on the mean fitness of the population . Additionally, the use of standard crossover with high probability after context-aware crossover ($P\_0.3\_inv$, $P\_0.6\_inv$ and $P\_0.9\_inv$) has resulted in a significant drop in the mean fitness of the population.

Clearly these experiments suggest us to use standard crossover (if any) before the application of context-aware crossover to get better performance.

Effect of standard crossover on performance

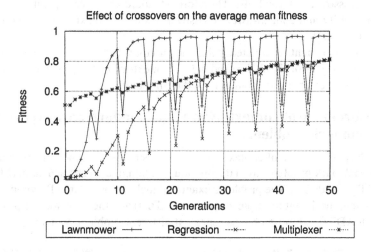

Figure 17-3. Destructive effects of standard crossover on GP performance when applied at regular intervals.

The combined effect of standard and context-aware crossovers is studied in the previous section. It is shown that the application of standard crossover after the use of context-aware crossover has an adverse effect on the performance. To quantify the effect of standard crossover, another set of experiments was conducted. For these experiments, only context-aware and standard crossover operators were used. Standard crossover operator was applied periodically (every five generations), and the rest of the time context-aware crossover was used. Note that only one of the two crossover operators was active a time. This is to calculate the effect of the active crossover on the overall performance of the system. The standard Koza's Quartic Symbolic Regression, the 11-bit multiplexer (without ADFs) and the Lawnmower problems were used for these experiments. Population sizes of 500, 50 and 100 were used for the problems respectively. For all the experiments, the maximum number of generation was set to 50, the initial population was generated using ramped half and half method with initial tree depths varying from 2-6 and the maximum tree depth was set to 17. Results are averaged over 50 runs and the mean population fitness is plotted in Figure 17-3.

The results suggest that standard crossover operator is consistently destructive on all the problems. The destructive effect on the multiplexer problem is comparatively less obvious than the other two. This is due to the inherent property of the problem to generate relatively fitter initial random population and the unlikelihood of finding individuals inferior than the initial random population during a run. The spikes in the graphs are clear indication that context-aware crossover regained the initial mean fitness value as soon the destructive standard crossover is turned off. Therefore, standard crossover operator is acting as a liability and context-aware crossover has to put in extra effort to undo its destructive effects.

The experiments conducted in this and previous sections suggest that standard crossover operator should be used *before* context-aware crossover, and that only one crossover operator should be used during a run.

Performance of context-aware and standard crossovers on benchmark problems

The performance of context-aware crossover was examined on the same set of benchmark problems as in the previous section,mand is presented in (Majeed and Ryan, 2006b). The problems examined include the Quartic Polynomial Regression, the 11-bit multiplexer (without ADFs) and the Lawnmower problems (with ADFs). These problems represent different problem domains.

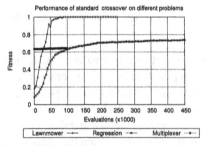 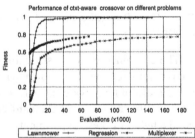

Figure 17-4. Mean best fitness of different benchmark problems with standard context-aware and standard GP crossovers.

In an effort to find the best settings for the use of context-aware crossover, it was turned on at different stages of a run and its impact on the performance was noted. For the most part, the use of context-aware crossover throughout the run resulted in the best results, although with certain set ups, delaying the use of context aware crossover until after the first few generations gave slightly better performance. In general, the results showed that the use of context-aware crossover resulted in an improvement in performance using substantially fewer individuals, and generated smaller individuals. Figure 17-4 shows the average mean fitness comparison of standard context-aware and standard GP crossovers on the aforementioned benchmark problems.

The Quartic Polynomial regression problem was the exception. For this problem, the use of context-aware crossover from 20% of a run onwards resulted in the best performance. We believe that it is due to the presence of unhelpful genetic material in the initial generations and the greed of context-aware crossover to improve the fitness.

The Multiplexer problem (without ADFs) is very difficult problem, which can't be solved by standard GP unless ADFs are added, and typically, no evolution happens. Using context-aware crossover, however, we were not only able to improve the overall fitness of GP but able to solve this problem.

The Lawnmower problem with the use of ADF turned out to be an easy problem and the performance of standard and context-aware crossovers was comparable, although context-aware crossover managed to attain this performance computationally cheaply and by generating comparatively smaller individuals.

Introduction of multiple children in a generation

In the standard implementation of context-aware crossover only the best child is introduced in the next generation, and we wished to see if increasing the number of children introduced for each crossover would improve the performance further.

Another set of experiments was conducted, using the Quartic Polynomial Symbolic Regression problem. The population size was set to 200 and fitness proportionate selection was used. The initial generation was generated with the ramped half and half method. 50 independent runs were allowed to complete 250 generations. The results are averaged and presented in Figure 17-5.

In the first setup, context-aware crossover was used throughout the run and the two best children who were more fit than at least one of the parents were introduced to the next population (labeled *multi_2* in Figure 17-5). The second setup was the same, except that up to four children could enter the population (labeled *multi_4* in Figure 17-5). In the third setup, *any* child better than one of the parents was allowed to enter the next generation (labeled *multi_either* in Figure 17-5), while the fourth setup allowed only the children better than *both* the parents into the next generation (labeled *multi_both* in Figure 17-5).

One of our concerns with these setups was the possibility of premature convergence of the population. To combat this issue, mutation was introduced in
the fifth setup. This is similar to *multi_either* setup with a difference of the
introduction of mutation operator with a probability of 0.2 once the population
was 95% converged (labeled *multi_mutation* in Figure 17-5). Notice that the
introduction of multiple children in the earlier stages of a run increases the
chance of the premature convergence of the population to a local optima. For
this reason, the first five percent of each run was completed by using the standard form of context-aware crossover, i.e. introduction of only the best child in
the next generation.

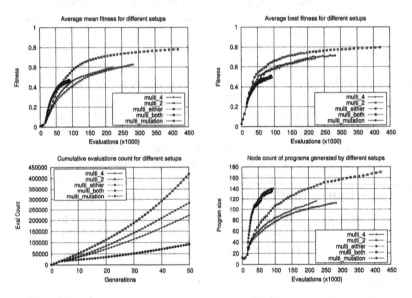

Figure 17-5. Different performance measures for context-aware with the introduction of multiple children in the generations.**Top Left:** Comparison of the average mean fitness.**Top Right:**
Comparison of the average best fitness. **Bottom Left:** Comparison of the running evaluations
count and **Bottom Right:** is the comparison of the tree size generated by different setups.

Of all the setups, *multi_both* performs the best due to a very high *replacement
pressure*. It is difficult to produce fitter children than their parents in the final
generations and requires a lot of exploration of the search space. It is evident
from the highest evaluations count and largest tree size generated by *multi_both*
in Figure 17-5 (Bottom Left) and Figure 17-5 (Bottom Right) respectively.
Although the performance of *multi_both* and standard context-aware (Figure
17-4 Right) "Regression") is the same in terms of fitness, *multi_both* requires
20% more evaluations, and, on average, produces trees that are twice as larger.
multi_either and *multi_mutation* show the very same performance and mutation

is almost ineffective in the run. One possible reason is the production of the inferior mutated children not playing any role in the production of the next generation. *multi_2* shows a slightly better performance in the final generations over *multi_4*, due to a slightly higher replacement pressure. *multi_4* turns out to be relatively cheaper than *multi_2* due to the introduction of more children than *multi_2* in the next generation.

4. Blood Flow Modeling problem

The blood flow problem was first introduced and successfully solved by Azad *et al.* in (Azad et al., 2004). It is effectively a regression problem and concerned with the lower limb arteries setnoses (reduction of internal crosssection area) and occlusions (blockages). When the femoral artery becomes blocked (stenosed) it is often necessary to use a graft to bypass the area, as in Figure 17-6. The start and the end junctions of the graft are labeled as "Proximal Anastomosis" and "Distal Anastomosis" respectively.

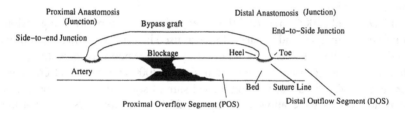

Figure 17-6. A visual demonstration of a bypass graft.

The flow of blood from the graft to the main artery exerts pressure on the bed of the graft/artery junction. This stress is the function of the velocity and the viscosity of the fluid flowing through the graft.

The complete details of the problem are discussed in (Ethier et al., 1998) and (Ohja et al., 1994). In that work, experiments were conducted to model the behavior of blood flowing through an artery, and the point velocity of blood (u) was recorded at various distances from the graft/artery function point (r). This generated a data set of fifteen points which was used in the GP experiments. The GP experiments in this paper use the same data.

Experimental Setup

We tried two different setups for context-aware and standard crossovers to solve this problem. The results obtained are compared with the results reported by Azad *et. al* in (Azad et al., 2004). For the sake of comparison, we tried to keep our experimental setup similar to the one used in (Azad et al., 2004). The function and terminal sets used were $\{+, -, \div, \times, \sin, \cos, \log, \exp, pow\}$ and

$\{x, \Re\}$ respectively. *pow* function is an arity two function and calculates the power of a real number. $\Re$ is the commonly used ephemeral random constant. The sum of squared errors and fitness propionate selection were used to calculate the fitness and selection of the individuals respectively. The initial population was generated using ramped half and half and initial tree depths varied from 2-6. The maximum tree depth was set to 17. For the context-aware crossover setup a population size of 200 and for the standard crossover setup it was set to 16000. The high population size for the standard crossover setup was to make comparison fair between the two setups. Additionally, it is commonly accepted that GP performs better with big populations.

The original experiments used *linear scaling* (Keijzer, 2003), a well known, simple to use and computationally inexpensive technique to adjust the intercept and the slope of an evolved expression. In general, the use of this technique results in better performance and smaller individuals.

We report results with and without linear scaling. For each experiment, 50 independent runs were conducted and the averaged results are presented in the following sections.

In (Azad et al., 2004), a set of different experimental setups involving various initializing techniques and linear scaling was used in an effort to find the optimal solution. The best results were reported by using randomly generated population and linear scaling. A population size of 2000 and one point crossover were used, and fitness was the normalised sum of squared error was noted. 30 independent runs were allowed to run for 250 generations. Notice that one point crossover for Chorus works by randomly selecting crossover points in the parent genomes and then swapping the tails of the parents. This crossover has been reported to be ineffective with bloated individuals (Azad, 2003)(Azad and Ryan, 2005). This is due to the selection of the crossover points in the bloated tails which do not take part in the mapping process.

Without Linear Scaling .   In the first set of experiments, we tried to solve the blood flow problem without using linear scaling. This was to check the performance of the systems without using any additional help. Results are shown in Figure 17-7.

In Figure 17-7 (Top Left) the average mean fitness of context-aware and standard crossover is compared. Both the crossovers have shown exponential growth in the initial generations, and context-aware crossover keeps on improving its performance and reaches the fitness as high as 0.99, while standard crossover becomes flat after 500,000 evaluations and shows no significant improvement in its performance.

Figure 17-7 (Top Right) shows the mean best fitness of the two crossovers. All experiments start with highly fit initial populations, and context-aware crossover keeps on improving the population and reaches the maximum pos-

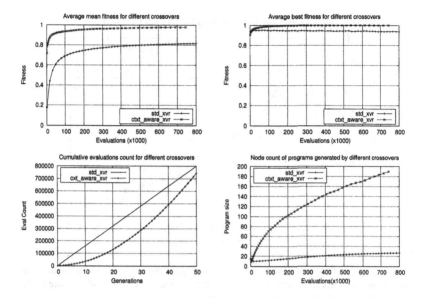

Figure 17-7. Different performance measures for context-aware and standard crossovers. **Top Left:** Comparison of the average mean fitness. **Top Right:** Comparison of the average best fitness. **Bottom Left:** Comparison of the running evaluations count and **Bottom Right:** is the comparison of the tree size generated by the two crossovers.

sible fitness, while standard crossover fails to discover better individuals and maintains its initial performance. It is worth noting that for standard crossover, the improvement in the average mean fitness of the population is not due to the discovery of new and better individuals, rather it is the result of the influence of the fit individuals on the rest of the population. The results suggest that this is not that difficult for GP to do quite well on this problem, although it is very difficult to improve on the initial generations. Typically, the initial generation mostly contains simple trees due to initial tree depth limit, and any further performance gain over the initial generation needs complex and larger trees as evidenced by Figure 17-7 (Bottom Right).

Figure 17-7 (Bottom Left) shows the average running evaluations count for both the crossovers. We can see that context-aware crossover evaluates considerably fewer individuals, even though the numbers evaluated increase towards the end of the run as individuals get larger.

Figure 17-7 (Bottom Right) compares the size of the trees generated by context-aware and standard crossovers. Clearly, context-aware crossover generates larger trees than its counterpart. It looks like any improvement in the fitness beyond 0.95 requires larger trees. After couple of thousand evaluations, the performance of both the crossovers is comparable and so is the tree sizes

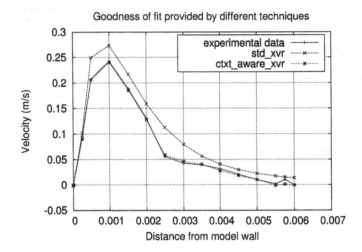

Figure 17-8. Plot of r^2 values for the best individuals generated by standard and context-aware crossovers in 50 independent runs without using linear scaling. It is a good measure to check the the goodness of the fit to the experimental data.

generated by them. Beyond this point, context-aware crossover has to generate large trees to fine tune the fitness of the population. In other words, the use of the higher evaluations count and the large trees in the final generations is evidence of the need of more exploration of the search space in the final generations to generate better individuals.

To check the goodness of the fit of the evolved expressions, we plotted the best-of-run individual for both the crossover operators against the experimental data. The best individuals is show in Figure 17-8.

Although the adjusted fitness values of both the best individuals generated by context-aware and standard crossovers are quite close (0.9998 and 0.9900 respectively) but clearly, as evident from Figure 17-8, the individual generated by context-aware crossover has a far better fit.

With Linear Scaling .   In the second set of experiments, we employed linear scaling, the results of which are shown in Figure 17-9. Note, the setup used for these experiments resembles the one used in the original implementation of the problem (Azad, 2003). Therefore, we will also compare our results with the Chorus system along with the results obtained by standard crossover.

Figure 17-9 (Top Left) compares the average mean fitness of different techniques used. As expected, the use of linear scaling improves the fitness of both set ups considerably, however, as in the previous experiment, GP using standard crossover doesn't improve on the initial best fitness

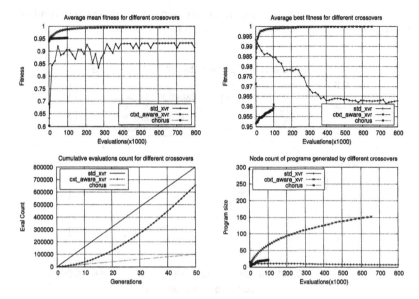

Figure 17-9. Performance comparison of standard crossover, context-aware crossover and the Chorus system. **Top Left:** Comparison of the average mean fitness. **Top Right:** Comparison of the average best fitness. **Bottom Left:** Comparison of the running evaluations count and **Bottom Right:** is the comparison of the tree size generated by each setup.

One possible reason is the small margin of improvement and difficulty in the generation of better children at this stage of the run. The use of one point crossover in Chorus is another possible reason for the slow improvement in its performance over time. Recall, one point crossover for Chorus is mostly ineffective with long bloated individuals. Context-aware crossover on the other hand, starts with a very fit initial population and manages to improve it to the best possible value. Clearly, context-aware crossover is acting as a refinement operator as it manages to improve the population even with the small margin of improvement.

Figure 17-9 (Top Right) shows the average best fitness of the techniques used. Interestingly, standard crossover has shown a deterioration in the performance with time. This is due the high selection pressure and the use of generational replacement technique. The Chorus system has effectively maintained its high fitness and shown a very small improvement throughout the run, while context-aware crossover has again improved its performance to the best possible fitness value.

Figure 17-9 (Bottom Left) compares the evaluations count of each setup. At a first glance, the Chorus system looks like the cheapest of all. However, the figures are somewhat deceptive, as, although Chorus evaluate fewer individuals, GP using context aware crossover achieved a higher fitness.fff

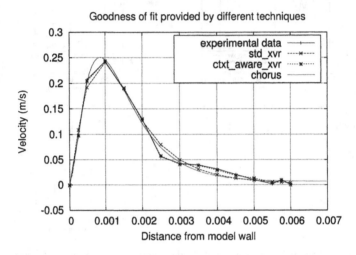

Figure 17-10. Plot of r^2 values for the best individuals generated by the different setups in 50 independent runs with linear scaling.

As is evidenced by Figure 17-9 (Bottom Right), clearly context-aware crossover has generated considerably larger trees than the other two. Standard crossover and the Chorus system not only produced the smaller individuals, but was able to simplify them further over time, a consequence of the use of the linear scaling. However, although, in this case, linear scaling gives a performance boost in the short term, those populations find it difficult to make jumps in fitness. GP using context aware crossover, however, is able to make these jumps, due to the better use it makes of the genetic material available.

Notice that the size of the individuals generated and the performance of context-aware crossover after 2000 evaluations are comparable to the other two setups. Beyond this point context-aware crossover generates larger trees as it improves the fitness of the population, which is consistent with the behavior of in the experiments without linear scaling, shown in Figure 17-7.

To check the goodness of the fit of the three setups, the best-of-run evolved epxression is plotted in Figure 17-10. All the setups fit the experimental data quite well, with context-aware crossover is showing a slightly better fit than the rest two.

To have a detailed insight into the functioning of context-aware and standard crossovers the r^2 values for the best-of-generation individuals were recorded for each crossover and are plotted in Figure 17-11. Standard crossover has mostly shown flat curves without any evidence of the discovery of better individuals

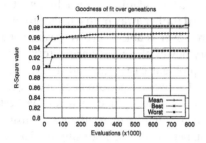
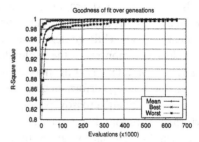

Figure 17-11. **Left:** Plots of r^2 values for the best, the mean and the worst fit found in a generation for standard crossover. **Right:** Plots of r^2 values for the best, the mean and the worst fit found in a generation for context-aware crossover.

through the run. On the other hand, context-aware crossover started slower due to the use of smaller population size but has shown consistent improvement with time and reached the maximum possible r^2 value, i.e. 1.

Discussion. We have tested the performance of context-aware crossover on a real world problem, that of modeling blood flow, and compared our work to the original results reported in (Azad et al., 2004). The initial fit generations tell us that it isn't difficult to produce good individuals, although it is very difficult to get any performance gain over these initial generations.

Any further improvement in the fitness requires the generation of fitter individuals and a refinement operator with a high exploratory capability. Context-aware crossover, on the other hand, performs equally well in the initial generations and manages to fine tune the performance to the best possible value in the later generations. Clearly, in the initial generation it acts as a *global search* operator and later its role switches to a *local search*(refinement) operator.

Context-aware and standard crossovers show relatively slow fitness gain in the initial stages of the experiments not using linear scaling. The use of linear scaling translates a curve close to the target curve and hence improves its fitness value. In the absence of linear scaling, a system has to first evolve an expression following the trend of the target curve and then translate it closer to the target curve (evolution of the constants of the expression). The evolution of the constants of an expression is a difficult job for evolutionary techniques and often holds back performance increases. (Keijzer, 2003).

The initial fit population leaves the two crossovers with little room for improvement. Using its local search capability, context-aware crossover is able to improve its performance at the expense of generating larger program trees. The generation of the larger trees seems like a good approach to improve the fitness of the population under the given conditions.

The fit for the best program generated by standard crossover follows the overall trend of the target curve but is located further away from it in the absence of linear scaling, while context-aware crossover is able to evolve a very good fit. It clearly demonstrates the exploratory power of context-aware crossover.

The use of linear scaling makes the problem easier, and all the systems using linear scaling performed quite well. The average performance of context-aware and standard crossovers improves dramatically and matches the best performance reported in (Azad et al., 2004). Furthermore, the setups using linear scaling generate program trees smaller than those not using it. This is due to the removal of the subtrees generating the constants for the expression, because linear scaling translates the evolved curve closer to the target curve by evolving the constants required by the evolved curve to do so.

As expected, the use of linear scaling has improved the goodness of fit of the best individuals generated by each setup. Context-aware crossover with linear scaling start with a comparatively low r^2 value due to the small population size and reaches the maximum possible r^2 value at the end. Again this is the evidence of the exploratory power of context-aware crossover. Standard crossover on the other hand, shows a minimal sign of evolution throughout the run. The comparison of the r^2 values for different setups is presented in Table 17-1.

Table 17-1. Comparison of the mean and best r^2 values for different techniques.

Technique	Best r^2	Mean r^2
Chorus - with scaling	0.9890	0.9004
Sensible Crossover - without scaling	0.9985	0.9919
Sensible Crossover - with scaling	0.9994	0.9982
Standard Crossover - without scaling	0.9775	0.8023
Standard Crossover - with scaling	0.9853	0.9689

5.   Conclusion & Future Work

Context-aware crossover is a much more powerful crossover operator than standard GP, driven by its use of the best possible context for the placement of subtrees. While GP crossover is often destructive in the early to middle stages of a run, and emasculated by the bloat that so often occurs later in a run, context-aware crossover continues to discover useful new combinations long into runs. Furthermore, code bloat to protect individuals from crossover does not occur in context-aware crossover, as there is no selective advantage, due to the the manner in which every possible crossover point is examined.

Although context-aware crossover may intuitively seem like an expensive approach, the empirical results show that it evaluates substantially fewer individuals than the standard one. Similarly, although context-aware crossover may appear to be greedy, it isn't too much so, and consistently keeps improving even late in the run. Experiments increasing the number of children per crossover introduced to the population suggest that it is on the limit, though, as once more than one child was introduced, performance suffered.

We applied context-aware crossover to a real world problem, and discovered a better solution than that which has previously been published. We demonstrate that while GP with standard crossover was unable to make small improvements to the best fitness discovered once close to the solution, GP using context-aware crossover didn't suffer from this issue.

Currently, we select subtrees randomly from the parent trees for crossover, in the future we are planning to use some heuristic for their selection. The method used for the selection of dominant subtrees by Chi Chung in (Yuen, 2004) is one of the possibilities.

References

Azad, R. Muhammad Atif, Ansari, Ali R., Ryan, Conor, Walsh, Michael, and McGloughlin, Tim (2004). An evolutionary approach to wall sheer stress prediction in a grafted artery. *Applied Soft Computing*, 4(2):139–148.

Azad, R. Muhammad Atif and Ryan, Conor (2005). An examination of simultaneous evolution of grammars and solutions. In Yu, Tina, Riolo, Rick L., and Worzel, Bill, editors, *Genetic Programming Theory and Practice III*, volume 9 of *Genetic Programming*, chapter 10, pages 141–158. Kluwer, Ann Arbor.

Azad, Raja Muhammad Atif (2003). *A Position Independent Representation for Evolutionary Automatic Programming Algorithms - The Chorus System*. PhD thesis, University of Limerick, Ireland.

Banzhaf, Wolfgang, Nordin, Peter, Keller, Robert E., and Francone, Frank D. (1998). *Genetic Programming – An Introduction; On the Automatic Evolution of Computer Programs and its Applications*. Morgan Kaufmann, San Francisco, CA, USA.

D'haeseleer, Patrik (1994). Context preserving crossover in genetic programming. In *Proceedings of the 1994 IEEE World Congress on Computational Intelligence*, volume 1, pages 256–261, Orlando, Florida, USA. IEEE Press.

Ethier, C.R., Steinman, D.A., Zhang, X., Karpik, S.R., and Ohja, M. (1998). Flow waveform effects on end-to-side anastomotic flow patterns. *Journal of BioMechanics*, 31(7):609–617.

Hengproprohm, S. and Chongstitvatana, P. (2001). Selective crossover in genetic programming. In *ISCIT International Symposium on Communications and Information Technologies*, ChiangMai Orchid, ChiangMai Thailand.

Ito, Takuya, Iba, Hitoshi, and Sato, Satoshi (1998a). Depth-dependent crossover for genetic programming. In *Proceedings of the 1998 IEEE World Congress on Computational Intelligence*, pages 775–780, Anchorage, Alaska, USA. IEEE Press.

Ito, Takuya, Iba, Hitoshi, and Sato, Satoshi (1998b). Non-destructive depth-dependent crossover for genetic programming. In Banzhaf, Wolfgang, Poli, Riccardo, Schoenauer, Marc, and Fogarty, Terence C., editors, *Proceedings of the First European Workshop on Genetic Programming*, volume 1391 of *LNCS*, pages 71–82, Paris. Springer-Verlag.

Keijzer, Maarten (2003). Improving symbolic regression with interval arithmetic and linear scaling. In Ryan, Conor, Soule, Terence, Keijzer, Maarten, Tsang, Edward, Poli, Riccardo, and Costa, Ernesto, editors, *Genetic Programming, Proceedings of EuroGP'2003*, volume 2610 of *LNCS*, pages 70–82, Essex. Springer-Verlag.

Majeed, Hammad and Ryan, Conor (2006a). A less destructive, context-aware crossover for gp. In *Genetic Programming 9th European Conference, EuroGP 2006, Proceedings*. Springer-Verlag.

Majeed, Hammad and Ryan, Conor (2006b). Using context-aware crossover to improve the performance and lower the cost of gp. In *Sumitted to GECCO 2006: Proceedings of the 2006 conference on Genetic and evolutionary computation*.

Ohja, M., Cobbold, R.S., and Johnston, K.W. (1994). Influence of angle on wall shear stress distribution for an end-to-side anastomosis. *Journal of Vascular Surgery*, 19:1067–1073.

Poli, Riccardo and Langdon, William B. (1998a). On the ability to search the space of programs of standard, one-point and uniform crossover in genetic programming. Technical Report CSRP-98-7, University of Birmingham, School of Computer Science. Presented at GP-98.

Poli, Riccardo and Langdon, William B. (1998b). On the search properties of different crossover operators in genetic programming. In Koza, John R., Banzhaf, Wolfgang, Chellapilla, Kumar, Deb, Kalyanmoy, Dorigo, Marco, Fogel, David B., Garzon, Max H., Goldberg, David E., Iba, Hitoshi, and Riolo, Rick, editors, *Genetic Programming 1998: Proceedings of the Third Annual Conference*, pages 293–301, University of Wisconsin, Madison, Wisconsin, USA. Morgan Kaufmann.

Tackett, Walter Alden (1994). *Recombination, Selection, and the Genetic Construction of Computer Programs*. PhD thesis, University of Southern California, Department of Electrical Engineering Systems, USA.

Yuen, Chi Chung (2004). Selective crossover using gene dominance as an adaptive strategy for genetic programming. Msc intelligent systems, University College, London, UK.

Chapter 18

LARGE-SCALE, TIME-CONSTRAINED SYMBOLIC REGRESSION

Michael F. Korns

Investment Science Corporation, Investment Finance Research, Henderson, Nevada.

Abstract   This chapter gives a narrative of the problems we encountered using genetic programming to build a symbolic regression tool for large-scale, time-constrained
regression problems. It describes in detail the problems encountered, the commonly held beliefs challenged, and the techniques required to achieve reasonable
performance with large-scale, time-constrained regression. We discuss in some
detail the selection of the compilation tools, the construction of the fitness function, the chosen system grammar (including internal functions and operators),
and the chosen system architecture (including multiple island populations). Furthermore in order to achieve the level of performance reported here, of necessity,
we borrowed a number of ideas from disparate schools of genetic programming
and recombined them in ways not normally seen in the published literature.

Keywords: artificial intelligence, genetic programming, stock selection, data mining, fitness
functions, grammars, quantitative portfolio management

1.   Introduction

This is the story of the problems encountered by Investment Science Corporation in using genetic programming techniques to construct a large-scale,
time-constrained symbolic regression tool.

Since any in-depth discussion of our financial methods is strictly forbidden
by our corporate policy, we introduce our financial motivations very briefly
and from these motivations quickly construct the requirements of a generic
symbolic regression tool which could be used for our application and for many
other large-scale, time-constrained data mining applications.

In the main, the published genetic programming literature addresses problems which are small-scale, without serious time constraints, and often complex.

In this historical context, a number of commonly held beliefs and a number of disparate schools of thought have developed in the GP community. In our pursuit of industrial scale performance with large-scale, time-constrained data mining problems, time and again we were required to reexamine many commonly held beliefs and, of necessity, to borrow a number of ideas from disparate schools of genetic programming and recombine them in ways not normally seen in the published literature.

These commonly held beliefs were challenged and these disparate schools of genetic programming were combined into unusual hybrids:

- *Challenged:* "That standard GP parameters (such as population size, crossover rate, etc.) will work for large-scale, time-constrained problems"

- *Combined:* "Hybrid combination of grammar and tree-based GP"

- *Combined:* "Hybrid fitness measure combining value prediction with order prediction in GP symbolic regression"

- *Combined:* "Hybrid combination of multiple island populations and greedy search with tree-based GP"

This narrative follows the pattern of typical applied research projects at Investment Science involving man years of engineering effort and hundreds of experiments. Each of the challenges we faced are explained in detail, and the hybrid solutions required to overcome the challenges are also described in detail. The narrative is punctuated with descriptions of the seminal experiments leading up to the final experiment which produced a generic symbolic regression tool capable of processing one million row by twenty column data mining tables in less than fifty hours on a single workstation computer (specifically an Intel XPS 3.4Ghz Extreme Edition with 800Mhz front side bus and 2GB of 533MHz RAM, running our Analytic Information Server software generating Lisp agents that maximize the on-board Intel registers and on-chip vector processing capabilities).

Financial Motivation

We introduce our financial motivations only very briefly. From these motivations we construct the requirements for a generic symbolic regression tool which can be used not only for our financial application but for many other large-scale, time-constrained data mining applications.

Consider a quantitative (quant) trading system for the top 800 exchange-traded common stocks with the largest dollar-volume traded in the prior week (Yu et al., 2004; Caplan and Y.Becker, 2005). These securities are so active that we will be able to move millions of dollars in and out of these investments without appreciably perturbing their prices. We will retrain the system weekly using a sliding training window of five years or 1,250 training days of historical data (Yu et al., 2004). This allows relatively frequent system retraining (weekly) while providing a relatively long retraining period of fifty hours (the weekend).

Our first issue is selecting a basket of 20 sample column data points from the over 500 available data points such as Open, High, Low, Close, Volume, EPS, Analyst Rating, etc. We solve this issue by implementing multiple independent trading systems. For instance one might have a value trading system with one set of 20 training points, a growth trading system with another set of training points, and a chartist trading system with yet another set of training points. If one has a farm of 100 workstations, each workstation could retrain each of 100 independent trading systems once per week.

Our second issue is the large volume of data which is fed to the system on every retraining period (1,250 historical daily samples for each of 800 common stocks is 1,000,000 rows of training data by 20 columns). The solution to this second issue is the subject of this paper as we pursue the construction of a generic regression tool which can perform a single 1,000,000 row by 20 column symbolic regression in less than 50 hours on a single workstation computer. Clearly such a tool would prove useful not only in our own financial application but in many other large-scale, time-constrained applications.

Experimental Setup

All our experiments are scored on testing data sets different from the data sets they were trained on. We have crafted nine separate test cases (formulas), from simple to complex. All of our test cases are trained on one million row by M column randomly generated training matrices (where M is either 1, 5, or 20). Then a separate randomly generated one million row by M column testing matrix is used for scoring. All of our nine test case formulas are shown below (generated with five columns).

Test Case Formulas

linear
$$y = 1.57 + (1.57*x0) - (39.34*x1) + (2.13*x2) + (46.59*x3) + (11.54*x4);$$

hidden
$$y = 1.57 + (2.13*\sin(x2));$$

cubic
$$y = 1.57 + (1.57*x0*x0*x0) - (39.34*x1*x1*x1) + (2.13*x2*x2*x2) +$$

(46.59*x3*x3*x3) + (11.54*x4*x4*x4);

elipse
y = 0.0 + (1.0*x0*x0) + (2.0*x1*x1) + (3.0*x2*x2) +
    (4.0*x3*x3) + (5.0*x4*x4);

hyper
y = 1.57 + (1.57*tanh(x0*x0*x0)) -
    (39.34*tanh(x1*x1*x1)) + (2.13*tanh(x2*x2*x2)) +
    (46.59*tanh(x3*x3*x3)) + (11.54*tanh(x4*x4*x4));

cyclic
y = 14.65 + (14.65*x0*sin(x0)) -
    (6.73*x1*cos(x0)) - (18.35*x2*tan(x0)) -
    (40.32*x3*sin(x0)) - (4.43*x4*cos(x0));

cross
y = -9.16 - (9.16*x0*x0*x0) -
    (19.56*x0*x1*x1) + (21.87*x0*x1*x2) -
    (17.48*x1*x2*x3) + (38.81*x2*x3*x4);

mixed
if ((mod(x0,4) == 0)
    {
    y = (1.57*log(.000001+abs(x0))) -
        (39.34*log(.000001+abs(x1))) +
        (2.13*log(.000001+abs(x2))) +
        (46.59*log(.000001+abs(x3))) +
        (11.54*log(.000001+abs(x4)));
    }
else
if ((mod(x0,4) == 1)
    {
    y = (1.57*x0*x0) - (39.34*x1*x1) +
        (2.13*x2*x2) + (46.59*x3*x3) +
        (11.54*x4*x4);
    }
else
if ((mod(x0,4) == 2)
    {
    y = (1.57*sin(x0)) - (39.34*sin(x1)) +
        (2.13*sin(x2)) + (46.59*sin(x3)) +
        (11.54*sin(x4));

```
     }
else
if ((mod(x0,4) == 3)
     {
     y = (1.57*x0) - (39.34*x1) +
         (2.13*x2) + (46.59*x3) +
         (11.54*x4);
     }
```

ratio
```
if ((mod(x0,4) == 0)
     {
     y = ((1.57*x0)/(39.34*x1)) +
         ((39.34*x1)/(2.13*x2)) +
         ((2.13*x2)/(46.59*x3)) +
         ((46.59*x3)/(11.54*x4));
     }
else
if ((mod(x0,4) == 1)
     {
     y = ((1.57*x0)
         ((39.34*x1)
         ((2.13*x2)
         ((46.59*x3)
     }
else
if ((mod(x0,4) == 2)
     y = ((1.57*sin(x0))/(39.34*tan(x1))) +
         ((39.34*sin(x1))/(2.13*tan(x2))) +
         ((2.13*sin(x2))/(46.59*tan(x3))) +
         ((46.59*sin(x3))/(11.54*tan(x4)));
     }
else
if ((mod(x0,4) == 3)
     y = 0.0 - (39.34* log(.000001+abs(x1))) +
         (2.13* log(.000001+abs(x2))) +
         (46.59*log(.000001+abs(x3))) +
         (11.54* log(.000001+abs(x4)));
     }
```

Our nine test cases vary from simple (linear) to complex (formulas with embedded if-then-else expressions). To add difficulty, we sometimes train and test our test cases with random noise added using the following formula:

y = (y * .80) + (y * random(.40)); ;; Plus a similar expression for ty

The addition of random noise makes each test case inexact and theoretically undiscoverable. Nevertheless, given our application, we need to test our symbolic regression tool against inexact data.

Fitness Measure

- *Combined:* "Hybrid fitness measure combining value prediction with order prediction in GP symbolic regression compiler"

Standard regression techniques utilize least squares error as a fitness measure; however, we desire a high correlation between the order of our estimates, EY, and our actual values, Y. Let us define a new term *sequence* as follows: If our estimates, EY, *sequence* our actual values, Y, perfectly, then it is true that, if EY[1] <= EY[2] then Y[1] <= Y[2] for all ey in EY and all y in Y. If we produce a perfect regression, with a percent error of zero, then EY will always *sequence* Y perfectly. Unfortunately, if the regression percent error is less than perfect, EY may not sequence Y very well at all. Furthermore, two regression formulas, with equal percent error, may sequence Y differently. Clearly, considering our end application, we are interested in regression solutions which sequence Y as well as possible. In fact, even if the regression percent error is poor but the sequencing is good, we can still have an advantage, in the financial markets, with our symbolic regression tool.

We combined a normalized average percent error score with an order preservation score to produce an optimal fitness measure for our financial application.

```
(loop for n from 0 until N do
    (setq avgDifY (+ avgDifY (/ (abs (- Y[n] avgY)) N))))
```

```
(loop for n from 0 until N do
    (setq errPct (+ errPct (/ (abs (- EY[n] Y[n])) N avgDifY))))
```

We measure the sequencing of Y by EY by counting how many Y pairs are out of order when sorted by EY.

```
(setq sortedEY (sort EY < true))
(loop for n from 0 until N do
    (setq k1 sortedEY[n]) (setq k2 sortedEY[(+ n 1)])
    (if (> Y[k1] Y[k2]) then (setq seqErr (+ seqErr (/ 1 N)))))
```

We now have a sequencing measure (seqErr) which varies from 0% (perfect) to 100% (terrible) and a normalized average percent error (errPct). We construct our final fitness measure using both as follows:

```
(setq fitness (+ errPct (* .001 seqErr)))
```

Multiple Grammars

- *Combined:* "Hybrid combination of grammar and tree-based GP"

Recently, informal and formal grammars have been used in genetic programming (O'Neill, 2001) to enhance the representation and the efficiency of a number of applications including symbolic regression. Much of the published literature on grammar-based GP focuses on alternative genome representations and evolutionary operators. After extensive experimentation, in our application domain, we discovered that alternative genome representations and evolutionary operators provided less added value than the use of multiple grammars themselves.

Therefore we settled on a hybrid combination of tree-based GP and formal grammars where the head of each sublist is a grammar rule agent with polymorphic methods for mutation, crossover, etc. Different grammar rules communicate with each other by message passing (a staple of object-oriented and agent-oriented software engineering), described in more detail as follows.

Formal grammars are a staple of computer science and are widely used in industry (Aho et al., 1986). We decided, from an engineering perspective, to allow our symbolic regression tool to use multiple grammars and even to mix grammars during the symbolic regression process.

There are two sides to every formal grammar: recognition and production. For grammar recognition we used a feature-based compiler compiler which reads a set of feature-based grammar rules. We constructed our symbolic regression tool as a large agent complex, and embedded in the symbolic regression tool a formal grammar definition file (readable by the feature-based compiler-compiler agent). When the feature-based compiler-compiler agent is pointed at the embedded formal grammar definition rules, a child agent compiler for the specified grammars is automatically generated inside the symbolic regression tool. For the production side of each formal grammar, we generated grammar production agents embedded in the symbolic regression tool.

There are three important grammars in the system. These are: a basic JavaScript-like numeric expression grammar for generating fast register and pointer integer and floating point computations (EXP); a standard regression grammar with a single s-expression genome (REG); and a multiple variable regression grammar with a multiple s-expression genome (MVL). The embedded feature-based grammar rules support recognition of each of these grammars even when mixed in the same well-formed formula (WFF). Grammar production is accomplished with embedded agent grammar complexes (one for each grammar), with matching polymorphic methods allowing each grammar to communicate with the other grammars for operations such as crossover.

We use standard Tree based genetic programming techniques with the exception that the head of every Lisp s-expression is a grammar production rule; also, the tail of each s-expression contains the arguments required by the grammar production rule. We use standard mutation and crossover operations (Koza, 1992) in our numeric expression EXP grammar. The REG grammar has only one s-expression in its chromosome so REG operates identically to the EXP grammar (using standard tree-based mutation and crossover). The multiple s-expression grammar (MVL) selects a random numeric s-expression chromosome, and performs standard tree-based mutation on the selected s-expression.

Details of each of the grammars are quite straight forward and can best be conveyed from the recognition side.

- *REG Grammar:* regress EXP ;

- *MVL Grammar:* mvlregress(EXP,EXP,...,EXP);

The weight-vectors, used as arguments to the ENN grammar rule, are standard numeric vectors whose length is determined by the number of columns in the regression problem. The numeric s-expressions, of the EXP grammar, are standard JavaScript-like numeric expressions with the variables *x0* through *xm* (where m is the number of columns in the regression problem), and with the following binary and unary operators + - / % * < <= == ! = >= > *expt max min abs cos cosh cube exp log sin sinh sqroot square tan tanh*. To these we add the ternary conditional expression operator { (...)? ... : ... ;} .

Overview of Symbolic Regression Tool

At Investment Science Corporation we have constructed a large agent complex for high volume symbolic regression applications consisting of one million rows and from five to twenty columns. Due to the heavy resources required to evaluate a candidate well-formed-formula (WFF) across one millions rows, we cannot afford to evaluate the same candidate twice. Therefore, every WFF which we have ever evaluated is saved during the course of a single training cycle. All WFF candidates are saved in a collection sorted by their fitness scores. A user option setting restricts the survivor WFF population to the "F" most fit WFF candidates. User option settings support single or multiple island populations and other potentially usefully clustering of candidate WFFs. Parenthetically, all the tool's user option settings are available at run time; therefore, it might be possible for the tool to evolve itself, although we have not attempted anything of that nature.

Within the survivor population, mutation and crossover occur in the same fashion as with standard genetic programming. Each WFF survivor is visited once per each evolution. A user-option determines the probability of mutation and another determines the probability of crossover. If warranted, Crossover occurs between the visited individual and a randomly selected individual, from the survivor population, with less fitness than the visited individual. The tool supports multiple grammars in the same training cycle as described previously.

Standard genetic programming practice encourages the use of multiple independent training *runs*. Each run incorporates one initialization step and "G" generational steps during which evolutionary operators are applied. It is standard practice for the experimenter to perform multiple independent training runs of G generations each and then report the results of the fittest individual evolved across all runs (the champion individual).

Since our symbolic regression tool is to be used in a fully automated setting, their can be no human intervention to decide how many independent training runs to perform; therefore, the concept of automatic multiple independent training runs has been incorporated into the tool. A user-option determines the number of evolutions "without fitness improvement" which trigger the system to start a new independent training run. After each independent training run, the best-of-breed champions from the previous run are saved and the training cycle restarts from scratch. Thus a training cycle of "G" generations may involve more or fewer separate independent training runs depending on the occurrence of long gaps without fitness improvement.

In every experimental report, the following standard table of results will be provided for each of the nine test cases.

- *Test:* The name of the test case

- *Gens:* The number of generations used for training

- *Minutes:* The number of minutes required for training

- *Train-Error:* The average percent error score for the training data

- *Test-Error:* The average percent error score for the testing data

- *Sorting:* The sequencing score for the testing data

Standard GP using the REG Grammar

- *Challenged:* "That standard GP parameters (e.g. population size, crossover rate) will work for large-scale, time-constrained problems"

Our first experiment was to use the REG grammar, with its very fast training time, for a straight forward approach to large scale symbolic regression. Our basic algorithmic components are WFFs, a memo cache of WFFs, the survivor population of the fittest WFFs, and a list of champion WFFs. We used the *GPSR* option settings which are almost directly in line with (Koza, 1992) and are as follows. At the initialization step of every training "run", 5000 randomly generated WFFs, in the REG grammar, are evaluated. All evaluated WFFs are memoized (saved in a memo cache) and also saved in sorted order by fitness score (in the survivor population). The top twenty-five WFFs participate in the genetic operations of mutation and crossover during each generation. The probabilities of mutation and crossover are 10% and 100%, respectively. When a WFF is chosen for crossover, its mate is chosen at random from the WFFs of lower fitness within the top twenty-five fittest individuals (in the survivor population). Crossover is always performed twice with the same parents and always produces two children which are evaluated, memoized, and saved in sorted order by fitness score (in the survivor population). The maximum number of generations before training halts is provided at the start of training time. If ten generations pass with no change in the fittest WFF, then system saves the fittest WFF in its list of champions, clears all WFFs in the survivor population (but not the memo cache) and evaluates 5000 randomly generated WFFs, starting a new "run". Any new "run" does not reset the generation count. Training always proceeds until the maximum number of generations have been reached. If G represents the maximum number of generations allowed for a fully automated training cycle, then the maximum number of independent "runs" is (G/10). Depending upon the progress in training, there may only be a single "run" during the entire training process. At the completion of training, the fittest champion WFF (the fittest WFF ever seen) is chosen as the result of the training process. The results of training on the nine test cases, using the GPSR option settings over 1 million rows and from one to five columns, returned near perfect results. The test results, with no random noise, demonstrated that more or less standard GP parameters are a great choice for one million row by one column problems even given the meager training time allowed.

Unfortunately when we increase the number of columns from one to twenty, the test results do not show the same level of excellence. We are doing very well on the simpler problems; but, the more complicated test cases are exceeding the allocated fifty hour maximum training time in only 100 generations. Clearly the hope that more or less standard GP settings will work for all large-scale, time-constrained problems has been challenged.

Thinking about our next step, we wonder could the problem be that we need more generations to train on the more complicated test cases? We decide that our next step will be to find some method of increasing the speed of the training process to allow 100 generations for training within the allocated maximum of fifty hours.

Vertical Slicing

Let us define a new procedure *Vertical slicing* as follows. First, the rows in the training matrix X are sorted in ascending order by the dependent values, Y. Then the rows in X are subdivided into S *vertical slices* by simply selecting every Sth row to be in each vertical slice. Thus the first vertical slice is the set of training rows as follows X[0], X[S], X[2*S], ... Each vertical slice makes no assumptions about the underlying probability distribution and each vertical slice contains evenly distributed training examples, in X, across the entire range of *ascending* dependent values, in Y.

After several months of study and experimentation, including using support vector machines to select training example subsets, we selected vertical slicing as the most expedient method of decreasing training time. Vertical slicing works well because it is extremely simple, makes no assumptions about the underlying probability distribution function, and is extremely fast.

Vertical slicing reduces training time by subdividing the training data into "vertical slices" each of which is representative of the whole training data set over ascending values of Y. We may subdivide the training data into as many vertical slices as practicable. The larger the number of slices, the fewer training examples are in each slice.

Next we randomly select one of the vertical training data slices as our "sample" training slice; furthermore, we modify each WFF and the memo cache to record the sample-fitness. There are now two different fitness scores for each WFF: sample-fitness and fitness. During evaluation, each WFF is first scored on the "sample" training slice and its sample-fitness is recorded. Next the sample-fitness of the WFF is compared to the sample-fitness of the least-fit WFF in the survivor population. If the sample-fitness of the WFF is greater than or equal to the sample-fitness of the least-fit WFF, the WFF is then scored against the entire training data and its true fitness is recorded. This approach will produce false negatives but no false positives.

Our next experiment was to use the REG grammar, with the *RGPSR* option settings which are exactly like the *GPSR* option settings (discussed in the previous experiment) except that the vertical slicing option is turned on. The number of vertical slices is set to 100. The results of training on the nine test cases, using the RGPSR option settings over 1 million rows and 20 columns show that the vertical slicing improves the training speed of standard GP but does not improve the regression accuracy. Now that we have the training time within our maximum limit, how can we improve accuracy?

Using the MVL Grammar

After several additional months of experimentation we decided to replace the REG grammar with the MVL grammar, and to modify the standard crossover operator to include some non-standard hill-climbing. The REG grammar, being a single expression regression, can be computed and optimized in the single pass required to compute the average percentage error. Unfortunately, the MVL grammar requires significant additional computational effort. Given an MVL grammar candidate, *mvlregress(exp1,exp2,...,expM)*, a multivariate regression must be performed in order to both provide optimized coefficients and to compute the average percentage error. In preparation for the multivariate regression we create an intermediate N row by M column transform matrix, 'X, where each expression, exp1 thru expM, is the transform creating the 'x0 thru 'xm transform variables. The transform matrix, 'X, and the dependent variable vector, Y, are then used to represent a system of linear equations, $C*'X = Y$, which we use the *Gaussian elimination* algorithm (Sedgewick, 1988) to compute the optimized coefficients and the error.

We experimented with both the standard s-expression crossover operator in (Koza, 1992) as well as the linear string-based codon style crossover operator of (O'Neill, 2001). It is possible algorithmically to linearize any tree-based grammar rule s-expression into a linear string-based codon style genome and vice-versa. Primarily because we are employing grammar based s-expressions, with a distinct separation between genotype and phenotype, we found each style of crossover operator to be different, yet to be relatively equivalent, with respect to performance in our high speed, high volume application. However, we found that adding a small amount of *hill-climbing mutation* to our crossover operator improved our regression performance. Given two parent grammar rule s-expression WFFs,

'(ruleAdd (ruleSub x0 34.5) **(ruleCos x4)**),

and

'(ruleMul **(ruleDiv x0 x5)** (ruleAdd x4 x1)),

the standard crossover operator would use substitution to swap the selected subexpressions as follows:

'(ruleAdd (ruleSub x0 34.5) **(ruleDiv x0 x5)**)

We found that we could improve our performance by, with a probability of 20%, averaging the two selected subexpressions as follows:

'(ruleAdd (ruleSub x0 34.5) **(ruleAvg (ruleCos x4) (ruleDiv x0 x5)))**

In addition to the *ruleAvg* grammar operator, we also used, with equal probability, the following grammar rules to combine the two selected subexpressions: *ruleMax, ruleMin, ruleAdd, ruleSub, ruleMul,* and *ruleDiv*. Once again, our hill-climbing crossover operates as a standard crossover operator with the exception that in 20% of the cases we average the two selected subexpression as shown above.

Our next experiment was to use the MVL grammar, with the *RMVL* option settings which are exactly like the *RGPSR* option settings (discussed in the previous experiment) except that the MVL grammar is substituted for the REG grammar and our enhanced hill-climbing crossover operator is substituted for the standard crossover operator. The results of training on the nine test cases, using the RMVL option settings over 1 million rows and 20 columns, showed an increase in performance in both average percent error and data sequencing. Unfortunately, we suffer an over all increase in computation time to the point that many of our test cases exceed the maximum allocated 3000 minutes (50 hours). Clearly we need to make additional enhancements to reduce computation time in cases with twenty columns.

Island GP using Multiple Grammars

- *Combined:* "Hybrid combination of multiple island populations and greedy search with tree-based GP"

After several additional months of experimentation we decided to make the following enhancements to increase performance and reduce computation time in cases with twenty columns. We introduced "Double Vertical Slicing" and multiple island populations using the REG and MVL Grammars.

Our first alteration induces genetic diversity via multiple independent island populations. There is a correlation between the fittest individuals in a training run and genetic diversity in the population (Almal et al., 2005). Furthermore the fittest individuals in a training run tend to cluster around a set of common root expressions (Daida, 2004; Hall and Soule, 2004). Capitalizing on these observations, we set our symbolic regression tool's options to create additional independent island populations, one for each column in the problem.

During the initialization step in every training run we generate the first 5000 possible root expressions sequentially in every independent island population. We sequentially examine every possible root expression with relevance to each column. A root expression has relevance to a column if and only if the column name appears, at least once, in the root expression. For example, the WFF "$x0$" has relevance to column zero (hence independent island population zero), while the WFF "$x4*sin(x8)$" has relevance to column four and column eight.

In each independent island population using the REG grammar, we generate 5000 root expressions (ignoring real constants and the trinary conditional expression), such that in each island population each root expression is guaranteed to have at least one reference to the name for that column $x0$ thru xm. This forces some genetic diversity and focuses each island population around the island's designated column.

Since the sequentially generated root WFFs are sorted in each island population by fitness, we have performed a defacto greedy search and made some guesses, by column, as to which grammar root expressions will be the most indicative of future evolutionary fitness. The above initialization step we call "root initialization" and it places 5000 sequentially generated REG grammar WFFs in each of M independent island populations sorted by fitness (the same number of islands as columns). It is performed once during the initialization step of every training run.

Our second alteration induces genetic diversity in the main population by borrowing information from each multiple independent island population. In the initialization step of every training "run", after the root initialization, exactly 5000 randomly generated WFFs, using the MVL grammar, are evaluated in the main population. Each of the M numeric expressions in the MVL grammar *mvlregress(exp0,...,expM)* are taken at random from the 25 fittest individuals in the respective independent island populations. These are the fittest root expressions generated in each island population during "root initialization". This modified initialization process induces genetic diversity in the main population and guarantees that each of the MVL grammar's M numeric expressions will have at least one reference to the designated terminal for that column x0 thru xm. All evaluated WFFs are memoized and saved in sorted order by fitness score. The top twenty-five WFFs, in the main population, participate in the genetic operations of mutation and crossover (Koza, 1992) during each incremental generation. The probabilities of mutation and crossover are 10% and 100%, respectively. The hill-climbing modifications to the crossover operator, introduced in the RMVL option settings, are also employed here.

Our third alteration decreases training time by enhancing the vertical slicing algorithm used to measure the fitness of each WFF. In the RMVL option settings, we selected a vertical sample data set for sampling and then trained on the full data set. Here we introduce "double vertical slicing" by selecting a vertical slice for sampling and another vertical slice for training. By not training against the full training data set we further reduce training time. The number of vertical slices is set to 100 for the sample set and is set to 10 for the training set. Scoring each individual WFF's fitness is always done on the entire training data set (defacto out-of-sample scoring). This approach will produce false negatives but no false positives.

Our fourth alteration introduces a "tournament of champions." In the RMVL option settings, any time there are 10 generations with no fitness improvement a new training run is started. In the "tournament of champions" enhancement, every 5 training runs, migration occurs between the pool of champions (from all previous training runs) and the main population after all initialization. This allows previous champions to compete in the normal evolutionary process but only once in every few training runs. This approach will produce greater accuracy but without sacrificing the independence of most of the training runs.

Our final experiment was to use the REG and MVL grammars, with the RGMVL option settings but we introduce random noise of 40%. The results of training on the nine test cases, using the RGMVL option settings over 1 million rows and twenty columns with 40% random noise, are shown in the Table 18-1.

Table 18-1. RGMVL Options 1M rows by 20 columns Random Noise. The columns are: *Test:* The name of the test case; *Gens:* The number of generations used for training; *Minutes:* The number of minutes required for training; *Train-Error:* The average percent error score for the training data; *Test-Error:* The average percent error score for the testing data; *Sorting:* The sequencing score for the testing data.

Test	Gens	Minutes	Train-Error	Test-Error	Sorting
cross	100	1950	0.831	0.901	0.396
cubic	100	702	0.399	0.392	0.005
hyper	100	2077	0.852	0.896	0.111
elipse	100	910	0.705	0.662	0.156
hidden	100	828	0.110	0.015	0.112
linear	100	708	0.102	0.016	0.001
mixed	100	896	0.676	1.210	0.037
ratio	100	758	0.309	0.942	0.145
cyclic	100	738	0.433	0.511	0.884

Fortunately training time is well within our 3000 minute (50 hour) limit. In general average percent error performance is poor with the *linear* and *hidden* problems showing the best performance. Extreme differences between training error and testing error in the *mixed* and *ratio* problems suggest over fitting. Surprisingly, order prediction is fairly robust in most cases with the exception of the *cyclic* and *cross* test cases. Furthermore order prediction is fairly robust even on many test cases where average percent error is poor.

Summary

Genetic Programming, from a rigorous corporate perspective, is not yet ready for industrial use on large scale, time constrained symbolic regression problems. However, adapting the latest research results, has created a symbolic regression tool whose promise is exciting. Academic interest in the field is growing while pure research continues at an aggressive pace. Further applied research in this field is absolutely warranted.

We favor the following research areas for further study: Using standard statistical analysis to increase genetic diversity and information flow between independent island populations and the main population; Automating Pareto front analysis to improve selection of promising WFF root grammar candidates; Additional experimentation with grammar expressions to increase the speed of evolutionary training and to develop a better understanding of hill-climbing operators from a root grammar viewpoint.

Acknowledgments

This work was completed with the support of Timothy May who pioneered the Strategy Central Project.

References

Aho, A.V., Sethi, R., and Ullman, J.D. (1986). *Compiler Principles, Techniques, Tools*. Addison-Wesley Publishing.

Almal, A., Worzel, W. P., Wollesen, E. A., and MacLean, C. D. (2005). Content diversity in genetic programming and its correlation with fitness. In Yu, Tina, Riolo, Rick L., and Worzel, Bill, editors, *Genetic Programming Theory and Practice III*, volume 9 of *Genetic Programming*, chapter 12, pages 177–190. Springer, Ann Arbor.

Caplan, M. and Y.Becker (2005). Lessons learned using genetic programming in a stock picking context. In *Genetic Programming Theory and Practice II*. Springer, New York.

Daida, Jason (2004). Considering the roles of structure in problem solving by a computer. In O'Reilly, Una-May, Yu, Tina, Riolo, Rick L., and Worzel, Bill, editors, *Genetic Programming Theory and Practice II*, chapter 5, pages 67–86. Springer, Ann Arbor.

Hall, John M. and Soule, Terence (2004). Does genetic programming inherently adopt structured design techniques? In O'Reilly, Una-May, Yu, Tina, Riolo, Rick L., and Worzel, Bill, editors, *Genetic Programming Theory and Practice II*, chapter 10, pages 159–174. Springer, Ann Arbor.

Koza, John R. (1992). *Genetic Programming: On the Programming of Computers by Means of Natural Selection*. MIT Press, Cambridge, MA, USA.

O'Neill, Michael (2001). *Automatic Programming in an Arbitrary Language: Evolving Programs with Grammatical Evolution*. PhD thesis, University Of Limerick, Ireland.

Sedgewick, R. (1988). *Algorithms*. Addison-Wesley Publishing Company.

Yu, Tina, Chen, Shu-Heng, and Kuo, Tzu-Wen (2004). Discovering financial technical trading rules using genetic programming with lambda abstraction. In O'Reilly, Una-May, Yu, Tina, Riolo, Rick L., and Worzel, Bill, editors, *Genetic Programming Theory and Practice II*, chapter 2, pages 11–30. Springer, Ann Arbor.

Chapter 19

STOCK SELECTION: AN INNOVATIVE APPLICATION OF GENETIC PROGRAMMING METHODOLOGY

Ying L. Becker[1], Peng Fei[1] and Anna M. Lester[1]

[1] *State Street Global Advisors, Boston, MA 02111.*

Abstract   One of the major challenges in an information-rich financial market is how effectively to derive an optimum investment solution among vast amounts of available information. The most efficacious combination of factors or information signals can be found by evaluating millions of possibilities, which is a task well beyond the scope of manual efforts. Given the limitations of the manual approach, factor combinations are typically linear. However, the linear combination of factors might be too simple to reflect market complexities and thus fully capture the predictive power of the factors. A genetic programming process can easily explore both linear and non-linear formulae. In addition, the ease of evaluation facilitates the consideration of broader factor candidates for a stock selection model. Based upon State Street Global Advisors (SSgA)'s previous research on using genetic programming techniques to develop quantitative investment strategies, we extend our application to develop stock selection models in a large investable stock universe, the S&P 500 index. Two different fitness functions are designed to derive GP models that accommodate different investment objectives. First, we demonstrate that the GP process can generate a stock selection model for a low active risk investment style. Compared to a traditional model, the GP model has significantly enhanced future stock return ranking capability. Second, to suit an active investment style, we also use the GP process to generate a model that identifies the stocks with future returns lying in the fat tails of the return distribution. A portfolio constructed based on this model aims to aggressively generate the highest returns possible compared to an index following portfolio. Our tests show that the stock selection power of the GP models is statistically significant. Historical simulation results indicate that portfolios based on GP models outperform the benchmark and the portfolio based on the traditional model. Further, we demonstrate that GP models are more robust in accommodating various market regimes and have more consistent performance than the traditional model.

Keywords: Genetic programming, equity market, stock selection, quantitative asset management

1.   Introduction

Quantitative asset management is the process of researching ideas, forecasting exceptional returns, constructing and implementing portfolios, and observing and refining their performance. The core part of the process, forecasting, is achieved by applying rigorous analysis and quantitative methods to search raw signals of asset returns and turn them into refined forecasts, which are so-called model scores.

For a highly information-rich equity/stock market, such as the S&P 500, there is a huge amount of information available to evaluate a firm's value. The key is to determine if the stock is fairly priced, and then make a profit by buying under-priced stocks and selling over-priced ones. In an efficient market, information spreads quickly and gets incorporated into stock prices virtually instantaneously, thereby increasing the difficulty of effectively deriving an optimum investment strategy with the vast amount of information available.

Many scholars and practitioners have done tremendous work in developing quantitative models. William Sharpe (Sharpe, 1964) first published the Capital Asset Pricing Model (CAPM). This is a theoretical linear model claiming that a stock's excess expected return depends on its systematic risk and not its total risk. Steven Ross' Arbitrage Pricing Theory (Ross, 1976), also known as APT, improves the CAPM by introducing the multi-factor linear model which states that the expected risk premium on a stock should depend on the expected risk premium associated with each factor and the stock's sensitivity to each of the factors. Furthermore, Fama and French's three factor model (Fama and French, 1992) added two additional factors to CAPM.

All these traditional models have one thing in common, linearity, which is convenient and sometimes intuitive, but may not fully capture the complexity of the market. The prior concern of searching beyond the linear pattern is computationally time consuming and labor intensive. Advancements in computing technology such as genetic programming (GP) enable us to find highly nonlinear and non-obvious relationships using only moderate computing resources. Evolved from the genetic algorithm developed by Holland (Holland, 1975) and later extended and advocated by Koza (Koza, 1992), genetic programming has been applied to a number of scientific areas such as computer science, biology, medicine and finance.

GP is still on the cutting-edge in the financial industry but its use is growing steadily. One application of GP is searching for optimal trading rules. Allen and Kajalainen (Allen and Kajalainen, 1999) use a genetic algorithm to learn technical trading rules for the S&P 500 index. Neely, Weller and Dittmar (Neely et al., 1997) use GP to construct technical trading rules in the foreign exchange markets. Wang (Wang, 2000) applies GP to enhance trading and hedging in equity spot and futures markets. Li and Tsang (Li and Tsangr, 1999) propose a GP approach capable to combine individual technical rules and adapt the thresholds based on past data. Recently, Lawrenz and Westerhoff (Lawrenz and Westerhoff, 2003) used GP to develop a simple exchange-rate model to understand the drivers of foreign exchange markets.

Based on the appealing progress in enhancing trading rules, people have started applying this technique to other investment fields. Kaboudan (Kaboudan, 2001) applies GP to evolve regression models to produce reasonable one-day-ahead forecasts of stock prices.

Another application by Wagman (Wagman, 2003) and Karunamurthy (Karunamurthy, 2003) analyzes different fitness functions to shed light on the dynamics of portfolio rebalancing by taking into account significant transaction costs and uncertain values.

The researchers at State Street Global Advisors (SSgA) have been pioneers in applying GP to explore optimal stock selection models. Zhou (Zhou, 2004) develops an effective emerging markets stock selection model by combining traditional techniques with genetic programming. Caplan and Becker (Caplan and Becker, 2004) use GP to develop a stock-picking model for the high technology manufacturing industry in the US. They concluded that the use of genetic programming techniques is important but not necessarily central to the success of the project. The use of additional analytics, algebraic simplification programs, and human judgment drove the project to a successful completion.

The purpose of this research is to continue exploring the combining of traditional techniques with genetic programming methods to develop quantitative stock selection models that are intuitive, powerful, robust, and accommodate specific investment objectives. While knowing the details of our financial models is necessary for this discussion, proprietary model details are purposefully vague. We hope that this study will help those trying to use genetic programming as a tool in quantitative asset management where information is very complex and data is extremely intensive.

The rest of this paper is organized as follows. Section 2 shows the financial data, investable universe and historical time series. In Section 3, we discuss the GP methodology and the construction of different fitness functions. Section 4 discusses the stock selection models, including traditional models and GP generated models (enhanced and aggressive). Section 5 presents the historical simulation results for each individual model, which demonstrates a successful application of GP to generate models that suit various investment objectives. Section 6 concludes the paper.

2. Financial Data

Globally, there are thousands of stocks available to investors and each of these stocks has many characteristics such as accounting, economic, financial and pricing information. Quantitative asset management firms exert much energy to collect and process this information to create a database of cleaned historical stock level data that does not suffer from survivorship or look-ahead bias. Even with such a cleaned database, it is often difficult to determine which data is relevant in predicting stock price returns because price information is noisy and influenced by human behavioral biases.

Our research universe, over which we developed statistically significant stock selection models, is the S&P 500 index. Not only is it one of the most regularly discussed stock universes but it is widely used as a benchmark by US portfolio managers against which they measure portfolio performance. We exclude the financials and utilities sectors, which have unique business models, from our study universe in order to maintain the homogeneity of the underlying assets. The monthly financial data and stock return time series used for the research are downloaded from the Compustat database for the period January 1990 to December 2005. In order to construct the potentially effective stock selection factors, we downloaded sixty-five financial variables from a variety of classes, such as fundamentals from balance sheets and income statements, earnings estimates, price returns and market perspectives on a monthly basis (192 months in total). For each given date, there are around 350 investable stocks, each of which is described by the sixty-five variables. Over the entire testing period, there are about 350*65*192 independent variables available for analysis. Compared to the research reported by Caplan and Becker (Caplan and Becker, 2004), the solution search domain in this study is much larger.

3. Genetic Programming Methodology

Overview

Genetic Programming is an evolutionary optimization algorithm that is based on Darwin's Natural Selection Theory. This method is essentially an evolutionary search process which arrives at an optimized solution by imitating the forces of natural selection via crossover and mutation procedures. The fundamental philosophy underlying the method is to replicate the stochastic process by which the fittest survive and pass their genetic material and strengths to the next generation. A population of candidate solutions is evaluated and modified based on user defined criteria in such a way that the less fit solutions are removed and replaced by variants of the fittest. The fitted solutions are used to create new individuals for subsequent generations until the best solution are found. The technique is capable of distinguishing complex patterns and searching the next set of sequences to evolve the optimized solution quickly and reliably in large search spaces. However, care must be taken with its application to avoid data over-fitting and to ensure that results are robust and intuitive.

Creating a population of randomly generated candidate solutions, formulae in our case, is the first step of imitating the evolution process. Each of the solutions in the population can be described in the form of a genome tree, which could be a program or a formula comprised of mathematical operators and variables linked together. In our study, genome trees are the candidate stock selection factor models. The leaf node contains model inputs such as macroeconomic data, financial scores or technical signals for equity models. The function nodes contain mathematical operators, which can be anything from simple addition and subtraction to more complex if-then-else statements. Considering the explainability of financial models to clients in an intuitive way, we choose to use only four basic arithmetic operators: addition, subtraction, multiplication and division, along with variables and constants, to construct our candidate models. Also, we constrained the tree depth to be up to eight and non-terminal nodes to have up to two child nodes.

The structure we used basically follows the structure applied by Neely, Weller and Dittmar (Neely et al., 1997) in identifying technical trading rules in the foreign exchange markets. The GP process is designed in three steps: training, selection and validation. The financial time series data are randomly split into three sets to be used in the three steps. The random selection of the dates will help us to avoid time-period specific issues such as dramatic market regime switching or calendar effects. The training step, using 50 percent of the randomly selected data, generates the initial population of candidate formulae. Each candidate formula is evaluated according to its ability to solve the problem and is assigned a fitness value based on this evaluation. The selection step, using 25 percent of the data sample, takes the most fitted solutions from the training step and compares them against newly generated populations. As the program progresses from generation to generation to search the desired optimal patterns, it "learns" the data. The objective value of the best fit genome continues to improve, but only because the data are over fitted. Therefore, the results become unreliable. The inclusion of a selection period allows one candidate genome to be defined as more fit than another only if its objective value is higher in both the training and selection periods. Thus, this process is designed to promote the robustness of the results, preferring more parsimonious solutions with generalized knowledge of the data rather than complex solutions based on the memorization of the previous training step. And the validation step, using another 25 percent fresh data, serves as an out-of-sample test. The program's output can be one or more of the most fit genome trees, each of which can be re-interpreted as an equation.

Fitness Function Construction

Designing a feasible fitness function is the key to successfully using the GP method in searching for an optimized solution for a problem in tack. The primary goal of an asset manager is to construct and maintain a portfolio that would outperform the market. Due to the nature of the investment portfolio construction process and risk-return tradeoff constraints, asset managers could use a variety of tools to estimate factors' or models' (a combination of factors) predictive power for future stock returns. In previous research, Zhou (Zhou, 2004) and Caplan and Becker (Caplan and Becker, 2004) have demonstrated success in setting the objective function to find a model that yields the best information ratio (IR), which is a risk-adjusted relative return against a benchmark.

Many investors in the financial markets are index followers. These investors are more risk averse and have investment objectives that result in portfolios with characteristics similar to market indices in terms of risk and return. For this reason, a good stock selection model should rank stocks pretty monotonically across the entire investment universe to ensure all stocks are available in portfolio construction. For each stock at time t, the rank is alpha, the return is R, and the number of securities in the universe is n. In this study, we construct an alternative fitness function that can generate a stock selection model providing the highest information coefficients (IC), which is the Spearman correlation between factor-ranked stocks and ranked stock returns.

$$Max \left\{ \sum_{t=1}^{T} IC_t/T \right\} \qquad (19.1)$$

where,

$$IC_t = \cfrac{\sum_{i=1}^{n_t} alpha_{i,t} * R_{i,t} - \cfrac{\left(\sum_{i=1}^{n_t} alpha_{i,t} \right) \left(\sum_{i=1}^{n_t} R_{i,t} \right)}{n_t}}{\sqrt{\left(\sum_{i=1}^{n_t} alpha^{2i,t} - \cfrac{\left(\sum_{i=1}^{n_t} alpha_{i,t} \right)^2}{n_t} \right) \left(\sum_{i=1}^{n_t} R^{2i,t} - \cfrac{\left(\sum i = 1^{n_t} R_{i,t} \right)^2}{n_t} \right)}}$$

$$t = 1, 2, \ldots\ldots T$$

While many active asset management strategies are focused on getting the best risk-adjusted returns, there are many asset mangers in the market place whose objective is to get the highest return possible even if that involves more risk. Thus, a stock selection model based on a fitness objective function aiming to find stocks in the "fat tails" of the return distribution would be more suitable. For this purpose, we construct a fitne ss function that will generate an "aggressive" formula that results in the highest top minus bottom fractiled return spreads. In this method, all the stocks in the investment universe will be ranked from high to low based upon their scores generated by an individual model. If the model does have forecasting power particularly focused on identifying the very good and very bad stocks, those stocks ranked in the top group would have highest returns and those ranked in the bottom group would have the lowest. A portfolio strategy of buying the top-ranked and selling the bottom-ranked stocks will result in a profit. A model thus developed aggressively searches the largest top to bottom spreads without taking into consideration the risks associated with large returns.

$$Max \left\{ \sum_{t=1}^{T} Spread_t / T \right\} \tag{19.2}$$

where,

$$Spread_t = \frac{\sum_{i=1}^{n_{top,t}} R_{top,i,t}}{n_{top,t}} - \frac{\sum_{i=1}^{n_{bottom,t}} R_{bottom,i,t}}{n_{bottom,t}} \quad t = 1, 2, ...T \tag{19.3}$$

Our Implementation

Flexibility is paramount. The form of the genetic programming is specific to the problem, but the details are designed by the user. Based on the complexity of the resulting genetic programs and a meaningful improvement in fitness, we choose 10 populations of size 5000 and ran 200 to 500 generations. The other GP operation parameter set-ups include the probability of cross over operation at 95% and mutation operation at 5%; 75% of leaf nodes are factor variables and 25% are constant; 50% are replacement. The GP process terminates either when a user-specified number of generations has been reached or the population converges, i.e. there is little variation between the optimized formulae.

Developing and implementing a quantitative stock selection model is a multi-step process. Genetic programming is only one of the steps, although it is no doubt an important one. As with any other quantitative stock selection model development process, care must be taken to ensure that input data is as complete and accurate as possible, and the intended application makes intuitive sense. It is possible for the application to recognize a pattern where no cause-and-effect relationship exits. In order to develop a model that makes investment sense, we used investment intuition throughout the process and chose the initial

factors carefully. In addition, models created by the GP process must be further
evaluated with other statistical tests and portfolio historical simulations.

4.   Stock Selection Models

Variables and Factors

As we have mentioned, there is much information available which can be used
to describe the market's opinion of a firm's future prospects. In this study, we
choose sixty-five variables using our knowledge of the markets. Those variables
are grouped into four categories: valuation, quality, analyst sentiment and price
sentiment. A valuation variable, such as the price-to-earnings ratio, compares
the firm's prospects to its price and favors cheap companies to buy, and vice
versa. A quality variable, such as return on assets, measures a firm's profitability
or efficiency and favors well-managed firms to buy. Both the analyst variables,
such as analyst earnings forecasts, and the price momentum variables, such
as historical stock returns, relate to sentiment, which prefers stocks favored
by the market. All these variables are inputs for the GP process. Based on
the specified objective functions, the optimized composite factors with best
variable selection and combination are constructed, as shown in Table 19-1.
For proprietary reasons, we left the factor details purposely vague.

Table 19-1. Sample of Factor for Inclusion in Stock Selection Models.

Factor	Description
Valuation	
V_1	Cash flow generation adjusted for growth
V_2	Cash flow generation
Quality	
Q_1	Asset Utilization
Q_2	Profitability
Q_3	Efficiency
Analyst	
E_1	Changes in analyst earnings forecasts adjsted for momentum
E_2	Changes in analyst earnings forecasts
Price	
P_1	Long term price momentum
P_2	Medium term price momentum
P_3	Short term price momentum

Traditional Model

A linear regression method is a traditional way to build a stock selection model, such as the single factor CAPM model and the Fama-French three-factor model.

The traditional way of using both CAPM and Fama-French requires the portfolio manager to determine the factor values in the model and the sensitivity of each stock to those factors. In order to evaluate the models generated by genetic programming, we constructed a traditional stock selection model as a comparison base. This model is a linear combination of four composite factors: valuation (V), quality (Q), analyst (E) and price (P). Each factor includes variables showing statistical significance in predicting stock returns.

Based on our investment philosophy and model development experience, we applied the regression methodology to three-month forward returns and the four factors to create the traditional model:

$$ModelT = 0.47 * V + 0.09 * Q + 0.13 * E + .31 * P \qquad (19.4)$$

The traditional model tends to favor buying cheap stocks with good management and market sentiment. According to the nature of linearity, the model only responds to each factor independently. Equation 19.4 indicates that the most important factor is valuation, thus a change in valuation would have the largest effect on stock selection.

Enhanced Model by GP

Using the GP methodology, we developed a stock selection model which maximizes the IC. The model has the following format:

$$ModelE = 2V_2 + Q_1 + Q_2 + 2P_1 - P_3 \qquad (19.5)$$

It shows that this enhanced model has a balanced factor combination by including valuation factors, quality factors and price sentiment factors. Similar to the traditional model, this model tends to favor buying cheap stocks with good management and market sentiment. Interestingly this GP model has a linear pattern yet is able to differentiate two specific measures of quality as well as price momentum. By specifying the quality factors of asset utilization and profitability as the most relevant amongst many quality factors, the model can further differentiate stocks. Further, the combination of long-term and short-term price momentum reversal reflects a well recognized investor behavior in the financial markets.

Aggressive Model by GP

Another genetic programming model is generated based on the fitness function that aggressively searches for the highest top minus bottom fractiled returns. The model has the following format:

$$Model A = V_1 * P_1 * Q_1 + V_1 * V_2 * E_1 \qquad (19.6)$$

By focusing on the fractiled return spread, this model targets the fat tails of the return distribution. The genetic programming methodology is able to form a non-linear formula that better captures these fat tail values than a linear formula. A genome tree for this formula is shown in Figure 19-1.

This non-linear model has intuitive appeal because it balances valuation, quality, earnings forecast and price sentiment. The model also better differentiates among selectable stocks because it specifies which measures of each category of factors are the most relevant. Further, the nonlinearity of the terms indicates interactions between the factors, which better reflects the complexity of the markets.

For example, the $V_1 * P_1 * Q_1$ portion of the aggressive model favors stocks that are undervalued but have good quality and sentiment. The second component indicates an interaction between valuation and analyst forecasts that aids in timing trades. Purchasing stocks that are cheap with improving analyst sentiment or selling stocks that are expensive with declining sentiment is emphasized in the tails.

In contrast to the linear models, the sensitivity of this model towards each factor is no longer constant. For example, the first partial derivative of model A to the quality factor Q_1 is a function of valuation factor V_1 and price momentum P_1, as shown in Equation 19.6. Figure 19-1 shows graphically the implication of a non-constant sensitivity by showing the relationship between Q_1 and model score A. Consider three firms, A, B and C with firm B scored by a linear model and the others by the aggressive model. For firms A and C, their model scores depend upon the value of the P_1. If firm A's P_1 value is higher than firm C's and V_1 is held constant, then firm A gets a higher model score. Because firm B was scored by a linear model, its score is independent of P_1.

$$\frac{\delta A}{\delta Q_1} = V_1 * P_1 \qquad (19.7)$$

Intuitively, a price decrease leads to a higher valuation score. That change provides either an opportunity to buy on weakness or to sell on a deterioration of a firm's prospects. The $\delta A/\delta V_1$ term shows that for companies with good sentiment, quality and valuation, it is a buying opportunity. However, when those factors are poor it is time to sell the stock. The traditional model with its constant sensitivity always suggests that such a situation is a buying opportunity.

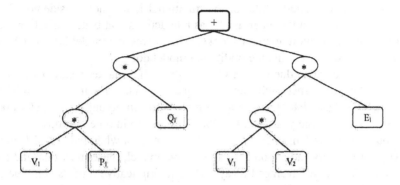

Figure 19-1. A genome tree of the aggresive model.

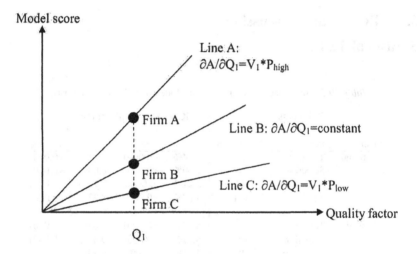

Figure 19-2. Schematic view of the linear model versus the aggressive model.

Linear versus Nonlinear

The strength of the linear approach is the simplicity of determining relevant factors and their weights but this ease comes at a price.

First, mulitcollinearity is present because many factors measure similar information and are highly correlated, such as earnings yield and cash flow yield. One solution is creating new composite factors that are the average of highly correlated ones, such as our four categories.

Second, the assumption of a linear relationship ignores the effect of factor interactions. Both the traditional and enhanced models are linear but the enhanced solution is more robust because the possibility of nonlinearity was considered and rejected while for the traditional it was not considered. The aggressive model, on the other hand, has interactions that better reflect market complexity in the more extreme stocks. The aggressive model does not have constant sensitivities while the traditional model does.

Third, biases arise due to overwhelmingly strong market behaviors during periods like the internet bubble and subsequent reversal. The traditional model, for example, has 47% of the weight on valuation implying the model works extremely well in the years 2000 to 2005, but less so in other periods.

Fourth, the problem of factor disagreement occurs when individual factors have contradictory indications. In an additive model, these individual indications are diluted or "averaged away" while multiplicative models continue to reflect all the factors. Hence, a stronger signal is created for stocks with more uniform factor values and outliers are less likely to drive results.

5.   Results and Discussion

Statistical Test

Table 19-2. Information Coefficients of Models with Forward Returns.

| | GP Process | | IC with Forward Returns | | | |
| | | | 1m | | 3m | |
Model	Period	# of month	mean	P-value	mean	P-value
Traditional	Training	95	4.34%	<0.0001	6.85%	<0.0001
	Selection	48	7.60%	<0.0001	8.09%	<0.0001
	Validation	48	3.21%	0.0008	7.15%	<0.0001
	Total	191	4.87%	<0.0001	7.23%	<0.0001
Enhanced	Training	95	5.87%	<0.0001	8.63%	<0.0001
	Selection	48	8.27%	<0.0001	9.45%	<0.0001
	Validation	48	3.12%	0.0001	5.74%	<0.0001
	Total	191	5.78%	<0.0001	8.10%	<0.0001
Aggressive	Training	95	4.81%	<0.0001	6.71%	<0.0001
	Selection	48	7.39%	<0.0001	7.94%	<0.0001
	Validation	48	2.66%	<0.0001	6.91%	<0.0001
	Total	191	4.92%	0.0082	7.07%	<0.0001

Table 19-2 shows the Information Coefficients between each model and 1-month and 3-month forward returns. The results are summarized for each GP process period, and in average. For each individual and total test period, the correlation between the models and the future returns are positive and statistically significant. This indicates that the models have predictive power in ranking stocks' future returns. It also appears that the models' predictive power increases with the longer time horizon. As we purposely designed in the fitness function, the enhanced model has the highest IC's. Notice that the aggressive model does not lose efficacy across all the stocks even though it aims to best describe the tails of the return distribution.

Historical Portfolio Evaluation

The model's stock selection power is also estimated by return spreads generated by buying the top fractile and selling the bottom fractile stocks. The results summarized in Table 5.0 show that there are positive 1-month and three-month return spreads between the top-ranked and bottom-ranked stocks on average over each GP process, as well as the total period for all three models. Taking into consideration the higher model spread returns and thus better predictive power, the aggressive model has the best capability in selecting stocks. This result is consistent with our fitness function design of maximizing the return spreads. Notice that the enhanced model has better selection capability than the traditional model, even though it is not as powerful as the aggressive model.

The selection power of genetic programming models is further demonstrated by information ratios, which are risk-adjusted returns generated by each model. On this measurement, the aggressive model is the clear winner and the traditional model falls far behind the GP developed models. This implies that not only does GP produce models with higher spreads but also reduces the risk of achieving those spreads. This combination is very appealing for active portfolio managers because it defies the generally accepted assumption that a higher return can only be achieved through higher risk.

Table 19-3. Total 1-month and 3-month forward returns from portfolios buying top quintile stocks and selling bottom quintile stocks.

	GP Process		1m forward returns			3m forward returns		
Model	Period	Num of month	Mean [%]	StdDev [%]	1R	Mean [%]	StdDev [%]	1R
Traditional	Training	95	1.28	3.66	1.21	2.88	5.69	1.01
	Selection	48	1.47	4.99	1.02	3.95	8.19	0.96
	Validation	48	0.77	3.48	0.76	3.03	6.20	0.98
	Total	191	1.20	3.98	1.04	3.18	6.51	0.98
Enhanced	Training	95	1.49	3.19	1.62	3.74	5.30	1.41
	Selection	48	1.71	4.56	1.30	4.07	8.82	0.92
	Validation	48	0.67	3.56	0.65	2.44	6.54	0.75
	Total	191	1.34	3.67	1.27	3.50	6.64	1.05
Aggressive	Training	95	1.69	2.66	2.20	4.12	4.93	1.67
	Selection	48	1.67	2.99	1.94	4.08	6.37	1.28
	Validation	48	0.91	2.53	1.24	3.83	5.22	1.47
	Total	191	1.49	2.72	1.89	4.03	5.37	1.50

Figure 19-3 illustrates annualized total returns for simulated portfolios that include the stocks selected by various models. The out-performance of the aggressive model is spread across the entire testing period rather than concentrated in a particular period. A portfolio manager would prefer such a model where predictive power is not arbitraged away as time passes.

Figure 19-3 compares the year by year performance of the three models measured by information ratio. The results show that in most years the GP models outperform the traditional model.

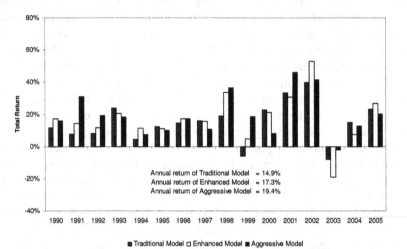

Figure 19-3. Annualized total returns from portfolios **buying** top quintile stocks and **selling** bottom quintile stocks.

In practice, we simulated the actual returns investors would achieve using each of the three strategies (Figure 19-5-Figure 19-7). The benchmark is the market cap weighted S&P 500 index excluding financials and utilities. In each figure, three portfolios are created: one for the top decile stocks, a second for the bottom decile stocks, and third for the benchmark. These portfolios are rebalanced quarterly. Over the 16 year simulation period, the top fractile outperforms the bottom fractile and the benchmark. Meanwhile the bottom fractile underperforms the top and benchmark. Amongst these three models, the aggressive model has the highest cumulative return.

Robustness Evaluation

To evaluate model stability through time, we measure 1-month and 3-month auto-correlations of the three models. Table 19-4 shows the pace at which the scores change through time and should coincide with the turnover of the portfolio. For example, if scores change rapidly, the portfolio manager must

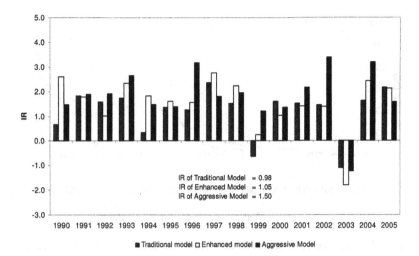

Figure 19-4. Information Ratio of portfolios **buying** top quintile stocks and **selling** bottom quintile stocks.

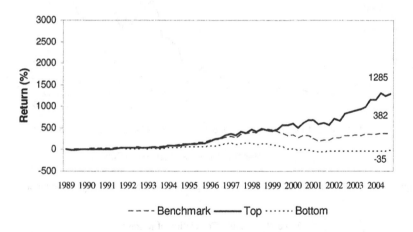

Figure 19-5. Total cumulative returns of fractile portfolios based on the traditional model.

trade often to ensure he owns the best securities and sells the worst. However, trading is not free and the portfolio manager must therefore balance the need to update his portfolio through trading with his desire to have the portfolio best reflect the model. The enhanced model has a higher auto-correlation than the traditional model. While the aggressive model auto-correlation is slightly lower than the traditional model, it is still realistic.

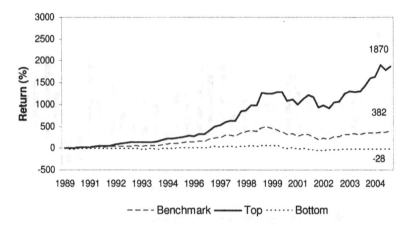

Figure 19-6. Total cumulative returns of fractile portfolios based on the enhanced model.

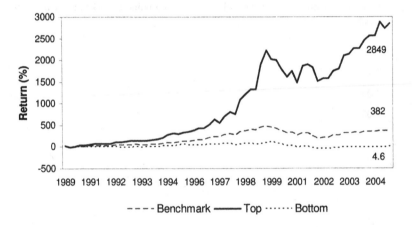

Figure 19-7. Total cumulative returns of fractile portfolios based on the aggressive model.

Table 19-4. Auto Correlation of Models.

| Model | Correlation with 1 month Lag | | | Correlation with 3 month Lag | | |
	Mean	StdDev	P-value	Mean	StdDev	P-value
Traditional	75.9%	6.0%	<0.0001	64.7%	5.9%	<0.0001
Enhanced	89.6%	3.5%	<0.0001	73.4%	6.0%	<0.0001
Aggressive	73.4%	4.6%	<0.0001	58.8%	5.5%	<0.0001

Table 19-5 shows the statistical consistency of the model performance. The hit ratio is the percentage of periods that the portfolio return is positive. The results show that the GP developed models have more winning periods than the traditional one. For a portfolio manager who is evaluated frequently, more months of outperformance are better. While on paper one can ignore periods of underperformance because the long-term performance is good, in real life periods of underperformance can shake a manager's or client's faith in the process. The hit ratio can be viewed as the percentage of months the manager or investor gets a good night's sleep.

Table 19-5. Statistical consistency of forward returns from portfolios buying top quintile stocks and selling bottom quintile stocks.

Model	Mean[%]	StdDev[%]	Min[%]	Max[%]	Hit Ratio
	1m Forward Return				
Traditional	1.20	3.98	-14.78	22.00	67.0%
Enhanced	1.34	3.67	-12.85	13.52	69.1%
Aggressive	1.49	2.72	-8.24	13.81	74.9%
	3m Forward Return				
Traditional	3.18	6.51	-13.78	28.40	69.6%
Enhanced	3.50	6.64	-21.57	2526	72.8%
Aggressive	4.03	5.37	-12.02	22.21	81.2%

We also tested model performance robustness in various investment market regimes including whether the market favors growth or value stocks. The result is striking in Table 19-6. The traditional model is clearly biased toward value periods. A portfolio manager who wants to have consistent good performance, will likely fail by following such a strategy. On the contrary, both genetic programming models work well in both value and growth market regimes.

Table 19-6. Model robustness evaluation in Growth and Value market regimes.

Market Regime	Num of month	Traditional Model			Enhanced Model			Aggressive Model		
		Mean [%]	SD [%]	IR	Mean [%]	SD [%]	IR	Mean [%]	SD [%]	IR
1m Forward Return Spreads										
Growth	85	-0.31	3.10	-0.35	0.56	3.21	0.60	1.01	2.64	1.33
Value	106	2.40	4.21	1.98	1.97	3.90	1.75	1.87	2.74	2.36
Total	191	1.20	3.98	1.04	1.34	3.67	1.27	1.49	2.72	1.89
3m Foward Return Spreads										
Growth	85	1.38	5.76	0.48	2.46	6.34	0.78	3.91	5.41	1.45
Value	106	4.63	6.73	1.38	4.33	6.80	1.27	4.13	5.36	1.54
Total	191	3.18	6.51	0.98	3.50	6.64	1.05	4.03	5.37	1.50

6. Conclusion

One of the major challenges in a highly informative financial market is how to effectively use vast amounts of available information and derive an optimum investment solution that will outperform. Traditional stock selection model development relies more on linear combinations of a limited number of factors. In this study, we have applied the genetic programming method in developing quantitative stock selection models for the S&P 500 stock universe. We have demonstrated that genetic programming greatly enhances the factor selection process by effectively searching amongst a number of variables. Most importantly, genetic programming can further combine the factors into a complex model that best predicts the stocks' future returns.

As an extension of SSgA's previous research, we designed two fitness functions that would create models for different investment objectives. The fitness function that maximizes information coefficient results in a model that improves the stock ranking capability significantly. Using this stock selection model to form a portfolio that follows an index investment style would result in out-performance compared to a portfolio constructed based on the traditional model.

Another genetic programming derived model is based on a fitness function of maximizing top to bottom fractile return spreads to aggressively search for stocks in the fat tails of the return distribution curve. The model is not only intuitively appealing but also outperforms both the benchmark and the traditional model significantly.

Genetic programming has demonstrated tremendous power in developing stock selection models. The statistical tests show that the stock selection power of GP models is statistically significant. The portfolio historical simulations demonstrate that the portfolios constructed based on GP models outperform both the benchmark and the portfolio constructed by the traditional model. Further performance diagnostic analysis shows that the GP models are more robust in various market regimes and thus more consistent over time than the traditional model.

Genetic programming also provides the opportunity for the portfolio manager to tailor his model to his investment philosophy through the selection of the fitness function. The difference between the traditional and aggressive models shows that non-linearity is present in the tails of the return distribution. While neither the enhanced nor aggressive models are completely different from the traditional model, the returns and opportunities to beat the benchmark lie in the subtle differences. With the availability of data and regression software, many competitors can develop linear models. To succeed in asset management, it is necessary to exploit the more complex relationships between factors and returns discovered by genetic programming.

As with any other quantitative stock selection model development process, care must be taken to ensure that input data is complete and accurate, and the intended application makes intuitive sense. It is possible for the application to recognize a pattern where no cause-and-effect relationship exits. Thus, by never losing sight of investment intuition and choosing the initial factors carefully, we are able to apply the process effectively. In addition, models created by the GP process must be further evaluated. What we have learned is that the application of genetic programming in a stock selection context is as much an art as a science.

7. Acknowledgements

We are grateful and appreciative of the US active equity team at SSgA for providing their investment insights. We would also like to thank Mark Hooker, Managing Director of the Advanced Research Center at SSgA, for his support and constructive feedback.

Notes

This material is for your private information. The views expressed are subject to change based on market and other conditions. The information provided does not constitute investment advice and it should not be relied on as such. It should not be considered a solicitation to buy or offer to sell a security. All material has been obtained from sources believed to be reliable, but its accuracy is not guaranteed. There is neither representation nor warranty as to the current accuracy of, nor liability for, decisions based on such information. Past performace is no guarantee of future results.

References

Allen, F. and Kajalainen, R. (1999). Using genetic algorithms to find technical trading rules. *Journal of Financial Economics*, 51:245–271.

Caplan, Michael and Becker, Ying (2004). Lessons learned using genetic programming in a stock picking context. In O'Reilly, Una-May, Yu, Tina, Riolo, Rick L., and Worzel, Bill, editors, *Genetic Programming Theory and Practice II*, chapter 6, pages 87–102. Springer, Ann Arbor.

Fama, E.F. and French, K.R. (1992). The cross-section of expected stock returns. *Journal of Finance*, 47:427–465.

Holland, J.H. (1975). The University of Michigan Press, Ann Arbor.

Kaboudan, M. A. (2001). Genetically evolved models and normality of their fitted residuals. *Journal of Economic Dynamics and Control*, 25(11):1719–1749.

Karunamurthy, Vijay (2003). A genetic programming approach to the dynamic portfolio rebalancing problem. In Koza, John R., editor, *Genetic Algorithms and Genetic Programming at Stanford 2003*, pages 100–108. Stanford Bookstore, Stanford, California, 94305-3079 USA.

Koza, John R. (1992). *Genetic Programming: On the Programming of Computers by Means of Natural Selection*. MIT Press, Cambridge, MA, USA.

Lawrenz, C. and Westerhoff, F. (2003). Modeling exchange rate behavior with a genetic algorithm. *Computational Economics*, 21:209–229.

Li, J. and Tsangr, E.P.K (1999). Improving technical analysis predictions: an application of genetic programming. In *Proceedings of Florida artificial intelligence research symposium.*

Neely, Christopher J., Weller, Paul A., and Dittmar, Rob (1997). Is technical analysis in the foreign exchange market profitable? A genetic programming approach. *The Journal of Financial and Quantitative Analysis*, 32(4):405–426.

Ross, S. (1976). The arbitrage theory of capital asset pricing. *Journal of Economic Theory*, 13:341–360.

Sharpe, W.F. (1964). Capital asset prices: A theory of market equilibrium under conditions of risk. *Journal of Finance*, 19(3):425–442.

Wagman, Liad (2003). Stock portfolio evaluation: An application of genetic-programming-based technical analysis. In Koza, John R., editor, *Genetic Algorithms and Genetic Programming at Stanford 2003*, pages 213–220. Stanford Bookstore, Stanford, California, 94305-3079 USA.

Wang, J. (2000). Trading and hedging in s&p 500 spot and futures markets using genetic programming. *Journal of Futures Markets*, 20(10):911–942.

Zhou, A. (2004). Enhanced emerging market stock selection. In *Genetic Programming Theory and Practice I.*

Index